Anonymous

A harmony of the four Gospels in English

According to the authorized version

Anonymous

A harmony of the four Gospels in English
According to the authorized version

ISBN/EAN: 9783337282530

Printed in Europe, USA, Canada, Australia, Japan

Cover: Foto ©Thomas Meinert / pixelio.de

More available books at **www.hansebooks.com**

A

HARMONY OF THE FOUR GOSPELS

IN ENGLISH,

ACCORDING TO THE AUTHORIZED VERSION,

CORRECTED BY THE BEST

CRITICAL EDITIONS OF THE ORIGINAL.

BY

FREDERIC GARDINER, D.D.,

PROFESSOR IN THE BERKELEY DIVINITY SCHOOL.
AUTHOR OF "A HARMONY OF THE GOSPELS IN GREEK," ETC.

EDINBURGH:
T. & T. CLARK, 38 GEORGE STREET.
LONDON: HAMILTON, ADAMS, & CO. DUBLIN: JOHN ROBERTSON & CO.
M DCCC LXXI.

PREFACE.

This Harmony is a reproduction in English of the author's "Harmony of the Four Gospels" in Greek. Being intended for English readers, so much of the Introduction and of the notes as require a knowledge of Greek, is omitted. Other notes have been abridged in many cases.

The text is throughout that of the Authorized or common Version, except where critical labors upon the original text, since that version was made, have established a change in the Greek; and also in a very few instances in which the translation admits of correction by common consent. In such passages the required change is made, and the words of the Authorized Version are given at the foot of the page.

The arrangement of the paragraphs, as far as the nature of the work allows, is that of the Rev. Dr. Coit, in his admirable "Paragraph Bible."

Quotations from the Old Testament, whenever the language varies at all from that given in the Gospels, are printed at the foot of the page. In the same place also a very few parallel references are given, chiefly to point out similar language or incidents in other parts of the Gospels, or passages in the Old Testament on which the language of the Gospels may be founded, or sometimes quotations in the Epistles or references to language of the Gospels.

Brief notes, relating only to matters of harmony, and not intended to serve in any sense as a commentary, have been placed at the bottom of the page. In a few instances, in which these were unavoidably of inconvenient length, the subject-matter is treated in an introduction to the part to which it pertains, and a simple reference thereto given in the foot-note.

The synoptical table of the arrangement of several Harmonists, given at the close of the Introduction is taken from the author's Greek Harmony, and it is hoped, may prove useful. It shows at a glance how general is the agreement on the main points of chronology; and also, when differences exist, with which of these Harmonists the present arrangement accords. In this table the order of each Harmonist is of course preserved without change.

That what has been done may be to the furtherance of the glory of God, and may be blessed by Him to the increase of the knowledge of His word, is the earnest prayer of the Author,

FREDERIC GARDINER.

MIDDLETOWN, CONN., Feb. 1871.

SYNOPSIS OF THE HARMONY.

Section.	Page.	Matth.	Mark.	Luke.	John.
Preface,	iii				
Table for finding any passage in the Harmony,	xv				
Introduction,	xxi				
Tabular View of several Harmonies,	xxviii				

PART I.

THE INCARNATION, BIRTH, AND CHILDHOOD OF OUR LORD.

Section.	Page.	Matth.	Mark.	Luke.	John.
Introductory Note,	1				
1. Preface to St. John's Gospel,	5				1:1-18
2. Preface to St. Luke's Gospel,	5			1:1-4	
3. Gabriel announces to Zacharias the Birth of John,	6			1:5-25	
4. Gabriel announces to the Virgin Mary the Conception and Birth of Jesus,	7			1:26-38	
5. Mary visits Elizabeth,	7			1:39-56	
6. The Birth of John the Baptist,	8			1:57-80	
7. An Angel appears to Joseph in a Dream,	9	1:18-25ᵃ			
8. Jesus is born,	10	1:25ᵇ		2:1-7	
9. The Genealogies,	11	1:1-17		3:23-38	
10. An Angel announces the Birth to the Shepherds,	12			2:8-20	
11. The Circumcision and Presentation in the Temple,	13			2:21-38	
12. Visit of the Magi,	14	2:1-12			
13. The Flight into Egypt. Herod's Cruelty,	15	2:13-18			
14. The Return, and Settlement at Nazareth,	15	2:19-23		2:39, 40	
15. Jesus in the Temple when twelve years old,	16			2.41-52	

PART II.

FROM THE BEGINNING OF JOHN THE BAPTIST'S MINISTRY TO OUR LORD'S FIRST PASSOVER.

Section.	Page.	Matth.	Mark.	Luke.	John.
16. The Ministry of John,	17	3:1-12	1:1-8	3:1-18	
17. The Baptism of our Lord,	20	3:13-17	1:9-11	3:21-23	
18. The Temptation,	22	4:1-11	1:12, 13	4:1-13	
19. Testimony of John the Baptist,	23				1:19-34

Section.	Page.	Matth.	Mark.	Luke.	John.
20. Interview of John's Disciples with our Lord,	24				1:35-43
21. Jesus, going into Galilee, takes with him Philip: Interview with Nathanael,	25				1:44-52
22. The Marriage at Cana, and departure to Capernaum,	25				2:1-12

PART III.
OUR LORD'S FIRST PASSOVER, AND THE EVENTS UNTIL HIS SECOND.

Section.	Page.	Matth.	Mark.	Luke.	John.
23. At the Passover, Jesus purifies the Temple,	27				2:13-25
24. Interview with Nicodemus,	28				3:1-21
25. Jesus baptizes in the Country of Judea: Further Testimony of John while still baptizing,	29				3:22-36
26. (A) John the Baptist is seized,	29	14:3-5	6:17-20	3:19,20	
(B) Our Lord afterwards goes into Galilee,	30	4:12	1:14	4:14	4:1-3
27. Discourse with the Woman of Samaria: Many Samaritans believe on him,	30				4:4-12
28. Jesus teaches publicly in Galilee,	32	4:17	1:14,15	4:14,15	4:43-45
29. At Cana Jesus heals the Son of a Nobleman of Capernaum,	33				4:46-54
30. Jesus teaches at Nazareth, and is rejected,	33			1:16-30	
31. Leaving Nazareth, He fixes his abode at Capernaum,	34	4:13-16		4:31	
32. The Call of Peter and Andrew, of James and John, with the miraculous Draught of Fishes,	35	4:18-22	1:16-20	5:1-11	
33. The healing of a Demoniac in the Synagogue,	37		1:21-28	4:31-37	
34. The healing of Peter's Wife's Mother, and of many others,	38	8:14-17	1:29-31	4:38-41	
35. Our Lord preaches and heals throughout Galilee: particularly He heals a Leper,	39	4:23,8:2-4	1:35-45	4:42-44, 5:12-16	
36. The healing of a Paralytic,	41	9:1-8	2:1-12	5:17-26	
37. The Call of Levi (Matthew) and his Feast,	43	9:9-13	2:13-17	5:27-32	
38. Answer to Questions about Fasting,	44	9:14-17	2:18-22	5:33-39	

PART IV.
OUR LORD'S SECOND PASSOVER, AND THE EVENTS UNTIL THE THIRD.

Section.	Page.	Matth.	Mark.	Luke.	John.
39. Jesus comes to Jerusalem at the Feast; heals an infirm Man at the Pool of Bethesda; and teaches,	46				5:1-47

Section.	Page.	Matth.	Mark.	Luke.	John.
40. The Disciples pluck Ears of Grain on the Sabbath,	48	12:1-8	2:23-28	6:1-5	
41. On another Sabbath the withered Hand is healed,	49	12:9-14	3:1-6	6:6-11	
42. The Fame of Jesus is spread abroad: He performs many Cures,	51	12:15-21, 4:24,25	3:7-12	6:17-19	
43. He withdraws to the Mountain, and chooses the Twelve,	52	10:2-4	3:13-19	6:12-17	
44. The Sermon on the Mount,	54	5:1-24.27- 6:21.7:1- 6,12-8:1		6:20-49. 16:17	
45. The Healing of the Centurion's Servant,	63	8:5-13		7:1-10	
46. Our Lord raises the only Son of a Widow,	65			7:11-17	
47. John the Baptist in Prison sends to Jesus; His Testimony concerning John,	65	11:2-19		7:18-35, 16:16	
48. Our Lord, at meat with Simon a Pharisee, is anointed by a Woman that was a Sinner,	67			7:36-50	
49. Our Lord makes another circuit of Galilee with the Twelve,	68			8:1-3	
50. A Demoniac being healed, the Scribes and Pharisees blaspheme, and seek a Sign. Our Lord's Replies,	69	12:22-45 6:22,23	3:19-30	11:14-36. 12:10	
51. Our Lord describes His Disciples as His true Kinsmen,	74	12:46-50	3:31-35	8:19-21	
52. The Parable of the Sower, and its Interpretation,	75	13:1-15; 18-23	4:1-25	8:4-18	
53. The Parable of the Tares, and other Parables,	79	13:24-53	4:26-34	13:18-21	
54. Our Lord stills the Tempest on the Lake of Galilee,	84	8:18, 23-27	4:35-41	8:22-25	
55. The Demoniacs of Gadara,	85	8:28-9:1	5:1-21	8:26-40	
56. The Woman with a bloody Flux is healed, and Jairus' Daughter is raised,	88	9:18-26	5:21-43	8:40-56	
57. Two blind Men healed, and a Spirit cast out of one Dumb,	91	9:27-34			
58. Our Lord, teaching at Nazareth, is again rejected,	92	13:54-58	6:1-6		
59. A third Circuit in Galilee. The Twelve instructed and sent forth,	93	9:35-10:1, 5-16,11:1	6:6-13	9:1-6	
60. Herod believes Jesus to be John the Baptist, whom he had beheaded,	95	14:1,2,6-12	6:14-16, 21-29	9:7-9	
61. The Twelve having returned, Jesus crosses the Lake with them, and there feeds the Five Thousand,	97	14:13-21	6:30-44	9:10-17	6:1-14
62. Our Lord walks upon the Water, and performs Cures,	101	14:22-36	6:45-56		6:15-21

Section.	Page.	Matth.	Mark.	Luke.	John.
63. Our Lord's Discourse concerning the Bread of Life,	104				6:22-7:1

PART V.
FROM OUR LORD'S THIRD PASSOVER TO HIS FINAL DEPARTURE FROM GALILEE, JUST BEFORE THE FEAST OF TABERNACLES.

Section.	Page.	Matth.	Mark.	Luke.	John.
64. The Pharisees, accusing the Disciples for eating with unwashen hands, are confuted,	107	15:1-20	7:1-23		
65. The Daughter of a Syrophenician Woman is healed,	109	15:21-28	7:24-30		
66. A Deaf and Dumb Man is healed, and many others; the Four Thousand fed,	110	15:29-38	7:31-8:9		
67. The Pharisees and Sadducees again demand a Sign,	112	15:39-16:4	8:10-12		
68. Warnings against the Leaven of the Pharisees,	113	16:4-12	8:13-21		
69. A Blind Man healed,	114	.	8:22-26		
70. The Confession of Peter: Christ foretells His own Passion and the Sufferings of His Followers,	114	16:13-28	8:27-9:1	9:18-27	
71. The Transfiguration and subsequent Discourse,	117	17:1-13	9:2-13	9:28-36	
72. The Healing of the Demoniac whom the Disciples could not heal,	119	17:14-21	9:14-29	9:37-43	
73. Our Lord again foretells His Death and Resurrection,	122	17:22,23	9:30-32	9:43-45	
74. The Tribute-money miraculously provided,	122	17:24-27	9:33ª		
75. Several Discourses with the Disciples, (A) Our Lord reproves their Ambition by the Example of a Child,	123	18:1-5	9:33ᵇ-37	9:46-48	
(B) He directs concerning Another healing in His name,	124	10:42	9:38-41	9:49,50	
(C) He teaches to avoid Offences,	124	18:6-9	9:42-50	17:1,2	
(D) Parable of the Sheep gone astray; Forgiveness taught; Parable of the King reckoning with his Servants,	126	18:10-35		17:3,4	
76. Our Lord's final Departure from Galilee at His going up to the Feast of Tabernacles,	128	19:1	10:1	9:51-56	7:2-10
77. On the Way the Devotion of new Disciples is tested,	130	8:19-22		9:57-62	
78. The Seventy sent forth,	131			10:1-11	
79. The Doom of the impenitent Cities,	131	11:20-24		10:12-16	
80. The Ten Lepers healed,	132			17:11-19	

SYNOPSIS OF THE HARMONY.

Section.		Page.	Mattb.	Mark.	Luke.	John.
	PART VI.					
	THE FESTIVAL OF TABERNACLES, AND THENCEFORWARD UNTIL OUR LORD'S FINAL ARRIVAL AT BETHANY.					
81.	Our Lord at the Feast of Tabernacles,	133				7:11-52
82.	The Woman taken in Adultery,	135				7:53-8:11
83.	Further Teaching in the Temple; the Jews attempt to stone Jesus, and He escapes,	135				8:12-59
84.	Our Lord heals one born blind; the Good Shepherd,	137				9:1-10:21
85.	The Return of the Seventy,	140	11:25-30 13:16,17		10:17-21	
86.	Parable of the Good Samaritan,	141			10:25-37	
87.	The Visit to Martha and Mary,	142			10:38-42	
88.	The Disciples again taught how to pray,	142	7:7-11		11:1-13	
89.	At meat in the House of a Pharisee, Jesus reproves the Pharisees,	143	23:4-39		11:37-51. 13:31,35	
90.	Christ teaches to avoid Hypocrisy and Timidity,	147	10:26-33,10, 41,17-20		12:1-9,11,12	
91.	He refuses to divide an Inheritance. The Parable of the Rich Man,	149			12:13-21	
92.	Further Instructions and Parables,	149	6:25-34, 24:43-51, 10:34-36, 5:25,26		12:22-59	
93.	Of the Slaughter of the Galileans; the Parable of the Fig-tree; a Woman healed on the Sabbath,	153			13:1-17	
94.	The Festival of Dedication; Jesus retires beyond the Jordan,	154				10:22-42
95.	(A) Our Lord journeys towards Jerusalem,	155	19:1,2	10:1	13:22	
	(B) He teaches on the way, and is warned against Herod,	155			13:23-33	
96.	At table with a chief Pharisee on the Sabbath, He heals the Dropsy and teaches,	156			14:1-24	
97.	What is required of Disciples,	157	10:37-39		14:25-35	
98.	Parables of the Lost Sheep, the Lost Drachma, and the Prodigal Son,	158			15:1-32	
99.	(A) The Parable of the Unjust Steward,	160			16:1-8	
	(B) The right use of Riches. The Covetous Pharisees reproved,	160	6:24		16:9-15	
	(C) The Parable of Dives and Lazarus,	161			16:19-31	
100.	The Power of Faith, and the Duty of Humility,	162			17:5-10	

[Eng. Har.]   *b*

Section.	Page.	Matth.	Mark.	Luke.	John.
101. The Resurrection of Lazarus and consequent Action of the Jews,	162				11:1-54
102. Concerning the Coming of the Kingdom of God,	164	24:26-28, 37-41		17:20-30, 32-37	
103. The Parables of the Importunate Widow and of the Pharisee and Publican,	166			18:1-14	
104. Instructions concerning Divorce,	167	19:3-12	10:2-12	16:18	
105. Our Lord receives and blesses little Children,	168	19:13-15	10:13-16	18:15-17	
106. (A) The Rich Young Man,	169	19:16-30	10:17-31	18:18-30	
(B) The Parable of the Laborers,	172	20:1-16			
107. On the Journey, our Lord again foretells His Death and Resurrection,	173	20:17-19	10:32-34	18:31-34	
108. The Ambition of the Sons of Zebedee reproved,	173	20:20-28	10:35-45		
109. Two Blind Men healed near Jericho,	175	20:29-34	10:46-52	18:35-43	
110. The Visit to Zaccheus,	176			19:1-10	
111. The Parable of the Ten Minae,	177			19:11-28	
112. Our Lord arrives at Bethany six Days before the Passover, and is there entertained in the House of Simon the Leper,	179	26:6-13	14:3-9		11:55-12:11

PART VII.

CHRIST'S TRIUMPHAL ENTRY INTO JERUSALEM, AND THE EVENTS UNTIL THE LAST SUPPER.

Schedule of the Events of each Day of the Holy Week,	183				
First Day of the Week. — Sunday.					
113. Our Lord's Triumphal Entry into Jerusalem,	184	21:1-11	11:1-11	19:29-44	12:12-19
Second Day of the Week. — Monday.					
114. The Fig-tree cursed; the Temple cleansed,	188	21:12-19	11:12-19	19:45-48, 21:37,38	
Third Day of the Week. — Tuesday.					
115. The Fig-tree found withered away,	191	21:20-22	11:20-25		
116. The Authority of Christ questioned,	192	21:23-27	11:27-33	20:1-8	
117. The Parable of the Two Sons,	193	21:28-32			
118. The Parable of the Wicked Husbandmen,	193	21:33-46	12:1-12	20:9-29	
119. The Parable of the Marriage of the King's Son,	196	22:1-14			
120. Insidious Questionings,					
(A) of Pharisees, concerning Tribute to Caesar,	196	22:15-22	12:13-17	20:20-26	

SYNOPSIS OF THE HARMONY.

Section.		Page.	Matth.	Mark.	Luke.	John.
120.	Insidious Questionings, (B) of Saducees, concerning the Resurrection,	197	22:23-33	12:18-27	20:27-39	
	(C) of a Lawyer, concerning the greatest Commandment,	199	22:34-40	12:28-34	20:40	
121.	Our Lord's Question in return: How is Christ David's Son?	201	22:41-46	12:35-37	20:41-44	
122.	Warning against the Scribes and Pharisees,	201	23:1-3	12:38-40	20:45-47	
123.	The Widow's Mite,	202		12:41-44	21:1-4	
124.	Our Lord speaks to certain Greeks, who desired to see Him, of His approaching Death. The Voice from Heaven,	203				12:20-36
	Fourth Day of the Week. — Wednesday.					
125.	The Jew's Unbelief, notwithstanding the Words and Works of Christ,	204				12:37-50
126.	Our Lord's Prophecy of the Destruction of Jerusalem, and of the Future,	204	24:1-25, 29-36, 42, 10:21-25	13:1-37	21:5-36, 17:31	
127.	The Parable of the Ten Virgins,	212	25:1-13			
128.	The Judgment foretold,	212	25:31-46			
129.	The Rulers conspire to kill Jesus. Judas agrees to betray him,	213	26:1-5,14-16	14:1,2,10,11	22:1-6	
	Fifth Day of the Week. — Thursday (ending at Sunset).					
130.	The Preparation for the Passover,	214	26:17-19	14:12-16	22:7-13	

PART VIII.
THE LAST SUPPER; OUR LORD'S PASSION; THE SABBATH.

	Introductory Note,	217				
	Sixth Day of the Week. — Friday (beginning at Sunset Thursday).					
131.	At table with the Twelve, our Lord reproves their Ambition,	222	26:20	14:17	22:14-18, 24-30	
132.	He washes the Feet of the Disciples,	223				13:1-20
133.	He points out the Traitor; Judas withdraws,	224	26:21-25	14:18-21	22:21-23	13:21-35
134.	The Institution of the Lord's Supper,	227	26:26-29	14:22-25	22:19,20	(1 Cor. 11: 23-25)
135.	The Dispersion of the Twelve, and the Denials of Peter foretold,	228	26:31-35	14:27-31	22:31-38	13:36-38
136.	Our Lord's last Discourse with his Disciples before his Passion,	231				14:1-16:33
137.	Our Lord's Sacerdotal Prayer,	235				17:1-26
138.	Our Lord goes out with the Disciples to the Mount of Olives,	236	26:30	14:26	22:39	18:1

Section.		Page.	Matth.	Mark.	Luke.	John.
139.	The Agony in Gethsemane,	236	26:36-46	14:32-42	22:40-46	
140.	Our Lord is made Prisoner,	238	26:47-56	14:43-52	22:47-53	18:2-12
141.	He is taken before Annas and Caiaphas,	242	26:57,58	14:53,54	22:54,55	18:13-16, 18
142.	While the Sanhedrim assemble, He is examined by Caiaphas. Peter denies Him thrice,	244	26:69-75	14:66-72	22:56-62	18:17, 19-27
143.	After further Examination, the Sanhedrim adjudge Jesus guilty of Blasphemy. He is mocked by the Servants,	248	26:59-68	14:55-65	22:63-65, 67-71	
144.	The Sanhedrim lead Jesus to Pilate,	249	27:1-2	15:1	22:66,23:1	18:28
145.	Judas repents and hangs himself,	250	27:3-10			(Acts 1:18, 19)
146.	Our Lord before Pilate. He seeks to release Him,	251	27:11-14	15:2-5	23:2-5	18:29-38
147.	Our Lord before Herod. He is sent back to Pilate, who again seeks to release Him,	254			23:6-16	
148.	Pilate still further seeks to release Jesus; then, after scourging Him, delivers Him to be crucified,	254	27:15-26	15:6-15	23:17-25	18:39-40, 19:1
149.	The Soldiers mock Him,	257	27:27-30	15:16-19		19:2,3
150.	Pilate makes a final Effort for His release,	258				19:4-16a
151.	Our Lord is led forth to be crucified,	259	27:31-34	15:20-23	23:26-33a	19:16b, 17
152.	The Crucifixion,	261	27:35-38	15:24-28	23:33b, 34, 38	19:18-24
153.	He is mocked upon the Cross. The penitent Thief,	263	27:39-44	15:29-32	23:35-37, 39-43	
154.	He commends His Mother to St. John,	264				19:25-27
155.	The Noon-day Darkness. The Death,	265	27:45-50	15:33-37	23:44-46	19:28-30
156.	Various Portents. The Centurion. The Women at the Cross,	266	27:51-56	15:38-41	23:45b, 47-49	
157.	The piercing of our Lord's Side,	267				19:31-37
158.	The Descent from the Cross, and Burial,	268	27:57-61	15:42-47	23:50-56	19:38-42
	The Sabbath, the Seventh Day of the Week					
159.	The Watch at the Sepulchre,	270	27:62-66			

PART IX.

THE RESURRECTION, AND THE FORTY DAYS UNTIL THE ASCENSION.

	Introductory Note,	271				
	First Day of the Week.—Sunday (beginning at Sunset Saturday).					
160.	The Resurrection. Visit of the Women to the Sepulchre,	273	28:1-1	16:1-4	24:1, 2	20:1
161.	Mary Magdalene runs to tell Peter and John,	274				20:2

Section.		Page.	Matth.	Mark.	Luke.	John.
162.	Two Angels appear to the Women; some of them are speechless with fear and amazement, others run to tell the Disciples,	274	28:5-8	16:5-8	24:3-8	
163.	Peter and John visit the Sepulchre and go away,	276			24:12	20:3-10
164.	The Angels first, and then our Lord, appear to Mary Magdalene,	276		16:9-11		20:11-18
165.	Some of the Women tell the Disciples of the Angels; to the others, Jesus Himself appears,	277	28:9-10		24:9-11	
166.	The Report of the Watch,	278	28:11-15			
167.	Our Lord joins Himself to two Disciples going to Emmaus,	278		16:12,13	24:13-35	
168.	He appears in the midst of the Apostles, Thomas being absent,	280		16:14	24:36-43	20:19-25
169.	He again appears to them, Thomas being with them,	282				20:26-29
170.	He appears to seven of them as they fish in the Sea of Galilee,	282	28:16ᵃ			21:1-24
171.	He appears to the Apostles on a Mountain of Galilee,	284	28:16ᵇ-20	16:15-18		
172.	He gives His parting Instructions, and ascends into Heaven,	285		16:19,20	24 44-53	(Acts 1:3-12)
173.	The Conclusion of St. John's Gospel,	287				20:30,31, 21:25

A TABLE
FOR
FINDING ANY PASSAGE IN THE HARMONY.

ST. MATTHEW.

Chap.	Verses.	Sect.	Page.	Chap.	Verses.	Sect.	Page.	Chap.	Verses.	Sect.	Page
i	1–17	9	11	x	42	75 B	124	xxii	1–14	119	196
	18–25ᵃ	7	9	xi	1	59	95		15–22	120 A	196
	25ᵇ	8	10		2–19	47	65		23–33	120 B	197
ii	1–12	12	14		20–24	79	131		34–40	120 C	199
	13–18	13	15		25–30	85	140		41–46	121	201
	19–23	14	15	xii	1–8	40	48	xxiii	1–3	122	201
iii	1–12	16	17		9–14	41	49		4–39	89	144
	13–17	17	20		15–21	42	51	xxiv	1–25	126	204
iv	1–11	18	22		22–45	50	69		26–28	102	165
	12	26 B	30		46–50	51	74		29–36	126	209
	13–16	31	34	xiii	1–15	52	75		37–41	102	165
	17	28	32		16, 17	85	141		42	126	211
	18–22	32	36		18–23	52	77		43–51	92	151
	23	35	39		24–53	53	79	xxv	1–13	127	212
	24, 25	42	51		54–58	58	92		14–30	111	177
v	1–24	44	54	xiv	1, 2	60	95		31–46	128	212
	25, 26	92	153		3–5	26 A	29	xxvi	1–5	129	213
	27–48	44	57		6–12	60	96		6–13	112	181
vi	1–21	44	59		13–21	61	98		14–16	129	213
	22, 23	50	73		22–36	62	101		17–19	130	214
	24	99 B	160	xv	1–20	64	107		20	131	222
	25–34	92	149		21–28	65	109		21–25	133	224
vii	1–6	44	61		29–38	66	110		26–29	134	227
	7–11	88	143		39	67	112		30	138	236
	12–29	44	62	xvi	1–4ᵃ	67	112		31–35	135	228
viii	1	44	63		4ᵇ–12	68	113		36–46	139	236
	2–4	35	40		13–28	70	114		47–56	140	238
	5–13	45	63	xvii	1–13	71	117		57, 58	141	243
	14–17	34	38		14–21	72	119		59–68	143	248
	18	54	84		22, 23	73	122		69–75	142	244
	19–22	77	130		24–27	74	122	xxvii	1, 2	144	249
	23–27	54	84	xviii	1–5	75 A	123		3–10	145	250
	28–34	55	85		6–9	75 C	124		11–14	146	252
ix	1ᵃ	55	88		10–35	75 D	126		15–26	148	254
	1ᵇ–8	36	41	xix	1ᵃ	76	129		27–30	149	257
	9–13	37	43		1ᵇ, 2	95 A	155		31–34	151	259
	14–17	38	44		3–12	104	167		35–38	152	261
	18–26	56	88		13–15	105	168		39–44	153	263
	27–34	57	91		16–30	106 A	169		45–50	155	265
	35–38	59	93	xx	1–16	106 B	172		51–56	156	266
x	1	63	94		17–19	107	173		57–61	158	268
	2–4	43	53		20–28	108	173		62–66	159	270
	5–16	59	94		29–34	109	175	xxviii	1–4	160	273
	17–20	90	148	xxi	1–11	113	184		5–8	162	275
	21–25	126	207		12–19	114	189		9, 10	165	277
	26–33	90	147		20–22	115	191		11–15	166	278
	34–36	92	152		23–27	116	192		16ᵃ	170	282
	37–39	97	157		28–32	117	193		16ᵇ–20	171	284
	40, 41	90	148		33–46	118	193				

xvi TABLE FOR FINDING ANY PASSAGE IN THE HARMONY.

ST. MARK.

Chap.	Verses	Sect.	Page.	Chap.	Verses.	Sect.	Page.	Chap.	Verses.	Sect.	Page
i	1–8	16	17	viii	1–9	66	111	xiii	1–37	126	204
	9–11	17	20		10–12	67	112	xiv	1, 2	129	213
	12, 13	18	22		13–21	68	113		3–9	112	181
	14^a	26 B	30		22–26	69	114		10–11	129	214
	14^b, 15	28	32		27–38	70	114		12–16	130	214
	16–20	32	36	ix	1	70	117		17	131	222
	21–28	33	37		2–13	71	117		18–21	133	224
	29–34	34	38		14–29	72	119		22–25	134	227
	35–45	35	39		30–32	73	122		26	138	230
ii	1–12	36	41		33^a	74	122		27–31	135	228
	13–17	37	43		33^b–37	75 A	123		32–42	139	230
	18–22	38	44		38–41	75 B	124		43–52	140	238
	23–28	40	48		42–50	75 C	124		53, 54	141	243
iii	1–6	41	49	x	1^a	76	129		55–65	143	248
	7–12	42	51		1^b	95 A	155		66–72	142	244
	13–19^a	43	52		2–12	104	167	xv	1	144	249
	19^b–30	50	69		13–16	105	168		2–5	146	252
	31–35	51	74		17–31	106 A	169		6–15	148	254
iv	1–25	52	75		32–34	107	173		16–19	149	257
	26–34	53	80		35–45	108	173		20–23	151	259
	35–41	54	84		46–52	109	175		24–28	152	261
v	1–21^a	55	85	xi	1–11	113	184		29–32	153	263
	21^b–43	56	88		12–19	114	189		33–37	155	265
vi	1–6^a	58	92		20–26	115	191		38–41	156	266
	6^b–13	59	93		27–33	116	192		42–47	158	268
	14–16	60	95	xii	1–12	118	193	xvi	1–4	160	273
	17–20	26 A	29		13–17	120 A	196		5–8	162	274
	21–29	60	96		18–27	120 B	197		9–11	164	277
	30–44	61	97		28–34	120 C	199		12, 13	167	278
	45–56	62	101		35–37	121	201		14	168	280
vii	1–23	64	107		38–40	122	201		15–18	171	284
	24–30	65	109		41–44	123	202		19, 20	172	286
	31–37	66	110								

ST. LUKE.

Chap.	Verses	Sect.	Page	Chap.	Verses	Sect.	Page	Chap.	Verses	Sect.	Page
i	1–4	2	5	v	17–26	36	41		43^b–45	73	122
	5–25	3	6		27–32	37	43		46–48	75 A	123
	26–38	4	7		33–39	38	44		49, 50	75 B	124
	39–56	5	7	vi	1–5	40	48		51–56	76	129
	57–80	6	8		6–11	41	49		57–62	77	120
ii	1–7	8	10		12–17^a	43	52	x	1–11	78	131
	8–20	10	12		17^b–19	42	51		12–16	79	131
	21–38	11	13		20–49	44	54		17–24	85	140
	39, 40	14	15	vii	1–10	45	63		25–37	86	141
	41–52	15	16		11–17	46	65		38–42	87	142
iii	1–18	16	17		18–35	47	65	xi	1–13	88	142
	19, 20	26 A	29		36–50	48	67		14–36	50	69
	21–22	17	20	viii	1–3	49	68		37–54	89	143
	23–38	9	11		4–18	52	75	xii	1–9	90	147
iv	1–13	18	22		19–21	51	74		10	50	71
	14^a	26 B	30		22–25	54	84		11, 12	90	149
	14^b, 15	28	32		26–40^a	55	85		13–21	91	149
	16–30	30	33		40^b–56	56	88		22–59	92	149
	31^a	31	34	ix	1–6	59	94	xiii	1–17	93	153
	31^b–37	33	37		7–9	60	95		18–21	53	81
	38–41	34	38		10–17	61	97		22	95 A	155
	42–44	35	39		18–27	70	114		23–33	95 B	155
v	1–11	32	35		28–36	71	117		34, 35	89	147
	12–16	35	40		37–43^a	72	119	xiv	1–24	96	156

ST. LUKE—continued.

Chap.	Verses.	Sect.	Page.	Chap.	Verses.	Sect.	Page.	Chap.	Verses.	Sect.	Page.
xiv	25–35	97	157	xix	45–48	114	190	xxii	63–65	143	249
xv	1–32	98	158	xx	1–8	116	192		66	144	249
xvi	1–8	99 A	160		9–19	118	193		67–71	143	248
	9–15	99 B	160		20–26	120 A	196	xxiii	1	144	250
	16	47	67		27–39	120 B	197		2–5	146	252
	17	44	56		40	120 C	200		6–16	147	254
	18	104	168		41–44	121	201		17–25	148	255
	19–31	99 C	161		45–47	122	201		26–33ª	151	259
xvii	1, 2	75 C	124	xxi	1–4	123	202		33ᵇ, 34	152	261
	3, 4	75 D	126		5–36	126	204		35–37	153	263
	5–10	100	162		37, 38	114	191		38	152	261
	11–19	80	132	xxii	1–6	129	213		39–43	153	264
	20–30	102	164		7–13	130	214		44, 46	155	265
	31	126	208		14–18	131	222		45ᵇ	156	266
	32–37	102	165		19, 20	134	227		47–49	156	267
xviii	1–14	103	166		21–23	133	224		50–56	158	268
	15–17	105	168		24–30	131	222	xxiv	1, 2	160	274
	18–30	106 A	169		31–38	135	229		3–8	162	274
	31–34	107	173		39	138	236		9–11	165	277
	35–43	109	175		40–46	139	236		12	164	276
xix	1–10	110	176		47–53	140	238		13–35	167	278
	11–28	111	177		54, 55	141	243		36–43	168	280
	29–44	113	184		56–62	142	244		44–53	172	285

ST. JOHN.

Chap.	Verses.	Sect.	Page.	Chap.	Verses.	Sect.	Page.	Chap.	Verses.	Sect.	Page.
i	1–18	1	5	ix	1–41	84	137	xviii	28	144	249
	19–34	19	23	x	1–21	84	139		29–38	146	251
	35–42	20	24		22–42	94	154		39, 40	148	254
	43–52	21	25	xi	1–54	101	162	xix	1	148	257
ii	1–12	22	25		55–57	112	179		2–3	149	257
	13–25	23	27	xii	1–11	112	181		4–16ª	150	258
iii	1–21	24	28		12–19	113	184		16ᵇ, 17	151	259
	22–36	25	29		20–36	124	203		18–24	152	261
iv	1–3	26 B	30		37–50	125	204		25–27	154	264
	4–42	27	30	xiii	1–20	132	223		28–30	155	265
	43–45	28	32		21–35	133	224		31–37	157	267
	46–54	29	33		36–38	135	229		38–42	158	268
v	1–47	39	46	xiv	1–31	136	231	xx	1	160	274
vi	1–14	61	98	xv	1–27	136	232		2	161	274
	15–21	62	101	xvi	1–33	136	233		3–10	163	276
	22–71	63	104	xvii	1–26	137	235		11–18	164	276
vii	1	63	106	xviii	1	138	236		19–25	168	280
	2–10	76	128		2–12	140	238		26–29	169	282
	11–52	81	133		13–16	141	242		30, 31	173	287
	53	82	135		17	142	244	xxi	1–24	170	282
viii	1–11	82	135		18	141	244		25	173	287
	12–59	83	135		19–27	142	245				

ACTS.

Chap. i. verses 3–12, § 172, page 285.   Chap. i. verses 18–19, § 145, page 250.
(Chap. xx. verse 35, § 172, note, page 285.)

1 CORINTHIANS.

Chap. xi. verses 23–25, § 134, page 227.
(Chap. xv. verses 4–8, §§ 167–172, in the notes, pages 279–285.)

INTRODUCTION.

The three first Gospels are commonly called *Synoptical*, because they each give to some extent a synopsis of our Lord's life, or rather of the part of it subsequent to his baptism; while the Gospel of St. John has always been considered as supplementary in its character. It has comparatively little in common with the others, and contains far less of narrative; yet it has generally been thought to preserve the true chronological order of the events mentioned in it, and thus to form the proper basis for the chronological arrangement of a Harmony. For the reasons for this the reader is referred to the General Introduction to the Author's Greek Harmony. The general opinion is here followed, and the events recorded by St. John are assumed to have occurred in the order in which they are written.

Having, then, adopted the order of St. John, as far as it goes, it will be found that St. Mark fully accords with this, and thus another step can be taken. The intermediate events having been arranged according to what seems the most probable sequence, it will be found, either that there are no deviations from the order of St. Mark, or, at most, that they are few and unimportant. This is shown at a glance by the synoptical table of the arrangement of various harmonists, and the evidence would be increased were there room to include a larger number. St. Mark does not especially say that he follows a chronological order; but as he accords with St. John in all the points common to the two, and as the probable order, as determined by many independent writers, is found generally to be that given by St. Mark, it seems safe — especially in the absence of all evidence to the contrary — to take his Gospel for a further basis of the chronological arrangement. The order of St. John, therefore, as more fully carried out by St. Mark, has been adopted in the following pages. It is believed also, that this is the only possible scheme by which any two of the Gospels can be both presented in the same order in which they were written.

There will still remain, on this or any other basis, a portion of the Gospel of St. Luke which is without sufficient notes of time or points of contact with the other Gospels to be positively determined in its chronological relations to them. The difficulty is not one of any inconsistency, but simply a want of sufficient data. Happily, however, the points which are thus difficult to fix, it is of little importance, except as a matter of interest and curiosity, to have fixed. They are, therefore simply placed in what seems their most probable position, with full liberty to transpose them within certain limits.

In connection with any plan of arrangement it is necessary to determine the entire length of our Lord's ministry. Any difference in regard to this will involve corresponding differences of arrangement throughout. Three several theories have been proposed at different times, called the *Bipaschal*, the *Tripaschal*, and the *Quadripaschal* schemes, from the number of Passovers subsequent to our Lord's baptism severally admitted by them.

The earliest Christian writers, before the time of Eusebius (A. D. 300), appear not to have examined the question, and in so far as they have said anything on the subject, have expressed themselves variously. A careful consideration of the matter was at last undertaken by Eusebius, and resulted in the adoption of the Quadripaschal scheme, or that which makes the duration of our Lord's ministry to have been something more than three years. In this decision, for many centuries, there was a general aquiescence; other theories, however, having been proposed, it may be well briefly to examine them.

The Bipaschal theory allows but one Passover between our Lord's baptism and that at which he was crucified. It gives little time therefore for our Saviour's teaching to have sunk into the minds of the people, and for their rulers to have wrought themselves up to their infuriated madness against him. Especially does it allow very short opportunity for the disciples to have been with him in the enjoyment of his instructions, since it was some time subsequent to his baptism that they were called. On these general grounds the presumption against it must be considered too strong to be overthrown without clear evidence.

The chief arguments in its support are these: 1st. That on this hypothesis we have the record of our Lord's attendance on all the great festivals which occurred during his ministry, and which every Israelite was by the Mosaic law required to attend at Jerusalem. 2d. From the three earlier Gospels there is no positive evidence of the occurrence of a greater number of Passovers, and "the fourth Gospel being capable of being reduced to the same number, this should be adopted as in fact the concurrent testimony of all." Such further support as this theory is thought to derive from the opinions of early writers has already been sufficiently considered.

In regard to the first of these arguments, it could only be considered of weight if our Gospels had far more the air of complete narratives and less that of *memorabilia* than they actually present. Such festivals as our Lord may have attended in a more private way it would hardly have fallen within their scope to record; and for a considerable period the determination and effort of the Jews to put him to death was a sufficient reason for his non-attendance. Moreover, unless we are prepared to make a great inversion in the order of St. John, we have the certain record of one of the greatest festivals — the approaching Passover of Jno. vi. 4 — which he certainly did not attend. The argument at best, must be looked upon rather as an inference from a supposed fitness of our Lord's conduct and the Evangelists' record thereof, than as sustained by any evidence properly so called.

Much the same things may be said of the second argument also. The inference from the silence of the three first Evangelists in regard to other Passovers is of a purely negative character, and whatever weight it might be entitled to if alone, cannot stand for a moment against any positive evidence to the contrary. In regard to the Gospel of St. John, this theory certainly derives no support therefrom, and only by a serious exegetical strain can the Passover mentioned as near, in vi. 4, be supposed to be the last Passover; while the necessity of disturbing the order of this Gospel should not be admitted without urgent reason. The method of avoiding this by a conjectural emendation of that text is still more objectionable.

On the other hand, if the feast mentioned in Jno. v. 1 is to be understood of a Passover, it is then no longer possible to maintain this theory at all. For so understanding it, as will presently appear, there is strong reason. The Bipaschal theory, then, must be left as one which lacks the support of any direct evidence, is open to serious objections on general grounds, and grave difficulties in the arrangement of St. John; while it may be, and probably is, absolutely excluded by the mention of the Feast in Jno. v. 1.

The Tripaschal theory leaves the order of St. John undisturbed, and allows the natural sense of vi. 4, as referring to a Passover close at hand, to stand. The question between this and the Quadripaschal turns upon the interpretation of Jno. v. 1; aside from this, the difficulties commonly alleged against the one are much the same as against the other. It is therefore only necessary to discuss the sense of that passage. It will indeed still remain possible that a Passover may be there understood, and yet the Passover of vi. 4 be taken to be the same as that at which our Lord was crucified; but as there is no one now to advocate this, it cannot be necessary to refute it.

The chief argument against the reference of Jno. v. 1 to the Passover has been drawn from the supposed absence of the definite article before the word *feast*. At the time the English version was made, the weight of authority was in favor of its omission; later researches, however, show that it ought probably to be inserted. Yet neither the presence nor the absence of the article can be considered as entirely decisive; "*a* feast of the Jews" undoubtedly *may* refer to the Passover; and "*the* feast of the Jews" may possibly be understood of any of the three great festivals, although there is, of course, a strong presumption that such an expression, put absolutely, means the greatest of them all, that which was emphatically "THE Feast of the Jews."

This could not have been either the Pentecost or the feast of Tabernacles following the first Passover, since they were already both past before our Lord's return from that feast into Galilee (see Jno. iv. 35 and note). This supposition, although formerly advocated, has now no defenders.

The only other interpretation (except that of the Passover) now advocated, is that which understands the expression of the feast of Purim. This festival occurred on the fourteenth and fifteenth of Adar, just one month before the Passover. The strongest argument for this view is also the chief objection, both to referring the expression to the Passover, and in general to the Quadripaschal scheme, viz. that in that case our Lord would have absented himself from Jerusalem for eighteen months, inasmuch as he did not attend the Passover of Jno. vi. 4 (on the supposition that this was not the final one), but only the subsequent feast of Tabernacles (viii. 2–10), and thus, moreover, a whole year would have intervened between Jno. v. 1 and vi. 4. A sufficient reason for our Lord's absence, may be found in the statement in vii. 1 (cf. v. 18), that the Jews sought to kill him. In regard to the abruptness of the transition in point of time, and the interval passed over in silence, it has been well remarked that such transitions are not uncommon with St. John. Thus chap. vi. is concerned with a Passover, chap. vii. with the feast of Tabernacles, six months later; so in x. 22 there is another sudden transition from the latter feast to that of the Dedication.

On the other hand, the following considerations are well urged by Robinson against the supposition that the feast of Purim is here intended: (a) That feast, so far from requiring the presence of the Jews at Jerusalem, was kept as a home festival, by reading the Book of Esther in the synagogues and "sending portions one to another and gifts to the poor" (Esth. ix. 22; Jos. Ant. ii. 6, 13). (b) It is unlikely that Jesus would have gone to Jerusalem at the feast of Purim — which was not required, nor even usual — and not have gone to the Passover. The reference in support of such a supposition to his presence at the Dedication (Jno. x. 22) is not to the point, since he seems to have gone up in that instance to attend the feast of Tabernacles (Jno. vii. 2–10), and remaining some time in or near Jerusalem, to have been at the Dedication because it happened to occur during his stay. (c) "The infirm man was healed on the Sabbath (v. 9); which Sabbath belonged to the festival, as the whole context shows, v. 1, 2, 10–13. But the Purim was never celebrated on a Sabbath; and when it happened to fall on that day was regularly deferred." Andrews well says (Life of our Lord, p. 176): "It was not one of their divinely appointed feasts, nor was there any legal obligation to keep it. It was not a feast specifically religious, but patriotic; a day, making due allowance for difference in customs and institutions, not unlike the day that commemorates our own national independence. There were no special rites that made it necessary to go up to Jerusalem, and even those residing in villages where there was no synagogue were not obliged to go to a village where one was to be found. Why, then, should Jesus go up from Galilee to be present at this feast?" If the Purim be rejected, the only other tenable interpretation is the Passover. Besides the probability of this from the presence of the article (already mentioned), it seems confirmed by the account in the other three Evangelists of the plucking of the "ears of corn" on the Sabbath (Matt. xii. 1; Mar. ii. 23; Lk. vi. 1). This must have occurred soon after some Passover, when the first-fruits had been already offered, but the harvest not yet gathered; and it seems, to say the least, most natural to refer the occurrence to a time just subsequent to the feast in question. It may be added that the phrase in Jno. v. 1, "*and Jesus went up to Jerusalem,*" implies that he went up in consequence of the feast, which must therefore have been one of the three of universal obligation; also, that the Passover having been spoken of just before as *the feast* (iv. 45, twice), if any other feast had been here intended, it would have been specified; and further, that only the Passover is spoken of in the Gospels as *the feast* (Matt. xxvi. 5; xxvii. 15; Mar. xv. 6; Lk. ii. 42; xxiii. 17). Too much stress, however, ought not to be laid upon the last point, as in every instance the context sufficiently shows what feast is meant. See an excellent note in Pusey on Daniel, Lect. iv. note 7, p. 175.

On the whole, therefore, it seems reasonable to follow the opinion of Irenæus (adv. Hær. 2, 39), — expressly bringing this text to bear on the question of the length of our Lord's ministry, — of Eusebius, Theodoret, and others among the ancients, and of Luther, Scaliger, Grotius, Lightfoot. Le Clerc, Hengstenberg, Robinson, and many more, that the feast here intended is the Passover, the second which had occurred since our Lord entered upon his public ministry.

A third Passover is expressly named in Jno. vi. 4. This renders the Bipaschal theory untenable, and it is therefore no longer of consequence to discuss whether it may not be possible to make this identical with the final Passover. Such an hypothesis is, at best, strained; and there is no longer any sufficient reason for it when a third Passover has once been admitted. It follows, therefore, that the Passover of the crucifixion was the fourth, and thus that our Saviour's ministry covered a period of something more than three years.

With this outline of the argument, it seems unnecessary to enlarge upon the many minor reasons which might be urged in favor of this view, or to spend time in answering all the unimportant difficulties that have been suggested by the ingenuity of interpreters.

But although this point be satisfactorily settled, and with it the general outline of the harmony be determined; yet it is not to be supposed that a perfect chronological arrangement in all details is attainable with the data in our possession. Everything which bears any note of time may be put in its proper place; but there will yet remain passages which, being without such note, cannot be assigned with certainity to their true chronological place. Such passages are placed in the following pages where they seem most probably to belong, but yet no disturbance would be occasioned could evidence be presented that they ought to be transposed. Indeed, the true object of a harmony is not so much the attainment of an absolutely correct chronology in every minute point, as the exhibition of the several narratives side by side for the purpose of examination and comparison.

One incidental effect of a harmony must be to present to the eye certain slight discrepancies between the several Evangelists, without the existence of which — according to the ordinary laws of human writing — it would be impossible to consider them as really independent witnesses to the truth of the evangelic story. It will be one aim of the brief notes at the foot of the page to show, as far as their limits allow, that these discrepancies are superficial only, and are consistent with entire truthfulness and accuracy on the part of each narrator. They are enough to show the independence of each, that they looked upon the events from somewhat different points of view, and wrote with different classes of readers immediately in their minds; but on the other hand, they show a substantial unity, and that each single Gospel, in a truly wonderful way, supplements all the others. It often happens that one expresses distinctly some fact or teaching which, when expressed, may be seen to have been present to the thoughts, although passed over in the explicit narrative, of the others; and each often furnishes the clew by which to understand what might otherwise have been obscure in the expression of another.

The uses of a Harmony in connection with the evidences of Christianity are thus apparent; but still greater is its value in bringing together, for examination and comparison, all the accounts of the words and acts of Him on whom alone depend our peace with God on earth and our hope of eternal salvation in heaven.

As an Appendix to this General Introduction the following extract is given from a manuscript of the late Rt. Rev. Geo. Burgess, D.D., which unfortunately remains still unpublished.

"It is affirmed by several writers of the fourth century that certain Christians actually laid the first three Gospels before St. John, and desired him to add whatever might make them more complete; and that he did thereupon attest their truth, sanction their authority, and undertake his own Gospel. External testimony to such a fact seems unimportant; since he could not but confirm those other books if he did not denounce them, and since the very character of his own Gospel is so decisive. It is essentially and evidently a sequel to the others: and had they never existed, it could never have been written in its present form and with its present contents. For it contains very little of the information which would be expected in an original and independent account of the life of Jesus. It relates nothing of His birth, His childhood, His temptation; only six of His miracles; contains not one of His narrative parables; no list of His Apostles, and no record of His sacramental supper, or of His ascension. It does contain, almost throughout, exactly that which the other Evangelists omitted. Matthew and Mark have substantially one and the same succession of facts and discourses, except as the more rapid narration of Mark studies abridgement. The materials from which the Gospel of St. Luke is constructed embrace almost all which were introduced by Matthew and Mark, but with manifold additions, which enhance its completeness; but the Gospel of St. John, except in the history of the baptism of our Lord, of the miracles of the five thousand, of the walking upon the sea, of the anointing at Bethany, of the final entry into Jerusalem, and of some of the events belonging to the betrayal, crucifixion, and resurrection, studiously avoids whatever had been told before. Even when it relates something in common with the other three, it introduces some sayings preserved by him alone. His account of the crucifixion and resurrection, with the appearances which followed, is the personal narration of an eye-witness, who singles out from his own recollections what was before passed by. Everywhere the reader is supposed to be acquainted with the previous Gospels. Jesus of Nazareth is named without any mention of his abode at Nazareth; and Andrew is introduced as calling Him "Jesus of Nazareth, the son of Joseph," as if the whole of the first two chapters of Matthew or of Luke were in fresh remembrance. When St. Luke leaves behind the childhood of our Saviour, we see His mother keeping His sayings in her heart. When St. John opens the next page of the history, after the lapse of eighteen unrecorded years, she appears with the very same consciousness, anticipating a miracle at the marriage-feast at Cana. Of John the Baptist he writes, "for John was not yet cast into prison"; and yet he alone among the Evangelists does not relate the imprisonment itself, or the death of the Baptist. He mentions the objection of some of the Jews that Christ should come out of Bethlehem, without pausing to say that Bethlehem was really His birthplace, as all readers knew from Luke and Matthew. When he mentions Bethany, it is as "the town of Mary and her sister Martha"; but he has not before told us who they were. The Gospel of St. Luke had told us; and in a few words had sketched the same striking difference in their beautiful characters which is soon expanded in the larger narration of the resurrection of Lazarus. In St. Luke, Martha is encumbered about much serving, while Mary sits at the feet of Jesus, and listens to his words. In St. John, Martha still serves at the supper; and Mary anoints the feet of Jesus, and wipes them with her hair. It seems as if John had taken up, while the ink was still fresh, the pen which Luke had dropped. When our Saviour was betrayed, one of those who were with Him in the garden, having a sword, smote with it a servant of the high-priest and cut off his ear. So much is related by Matthew, who subjoins also the command of Jesus to the disciple to put up his weapon; the warning that those who took the sword should perish with the sword; the intimation that legions of angels waited but for his summons; and the question how, if he called them to his aid, the Scriptures could be fulfilled. The account of Matthew is abbreviated, as usual, by Mark, who simply states the infliction of the wound on a servant of the high-priest by one of them that stood by; and adds no more. Luke, while he repeats as little as was possible of the account of his predecessors, introduces the facts that two swords had been produced in mistaken reply to an expression of our Lord; that, under the same mistake, they who were about him now said, "Lord shall we smite with the sword?" that it was the right ear which was wounded; and that Jesus, with the words "Suffer ye thus far," touched and healed the wound. The names of the assailant and the assailed were till now suppressed; a circumstance not in itself wonderful, when it is considered how few names are inserted at all in the Gospels; but somewhat surprising when these are given at last by the fourth Evangelist. Whatever the reason was for the omission, it had ceased when the aged John reviewed the history, after all the other actors and witnesses were in the grave. He recorded that the name of the servant was Malchus, and that Peter struck the blow. St. Matthew proceeds to relate that those who had seized Jesus led Him away to the house of Caiaphas the high-priest; and St. Mark and St. Luke add nothing beside. St. John interposes the fact that He was first brought before Annas, the father-in-law of Caiaphas; thus the order of the transactions is rearranged and completed. Immediately after, he illustrates, from his personal recollections, the thrice repeated and now thrice told denial of Peter. It was John who had opened the way for his entrance through his own acquaintance with the high-priest; for, having thus entered with Jesus, he went back and desired the portress to admit his companion. It was this very portress, he says, who first questioned Peter, and called out his first denial. The second is attributed also by Matthew and Mark to the suggestions of a maid, who drew the eyes of the bystanders upon him; while Luke, not an eye-witness, takes no notice of this maid, but only of the first, a figure prominent in all the four narratives, but identified by John only as the damsel who kept the door. At the second denial, John, like Luke, disregards the second maid, but only, as Mark had done before, shows us the picture of Peter warming himself by the fire, while his soul trembles before the suspicious questions and looks of men or women. At the third denial, the other Evangelists all represent the bystanders as insisting that Peter was a Galilean, betrayed by his very accent. But John, leaving this aside, singles out the kinsman of Malchus, who had noted the face of Peter in the garden, but perhaps in the confusion and darkness had failed to observe that it was he who drew the sword, else his arraignment of Peter might have been more decisive. The narrative of John still supplies what the others had left untold, and gleans where they have reaped; but the grain is not the less golden. The first two of the Evangelists record one cry of our Lord upon the cross; the "Eli, Eli, lama sabacthani"! The third, omitting this, relates three others: the prayer, "Father, forgive them, for they know not what they do"; the promise to the penitent thief, "Verily I say unto thee, to-day shalt thou be with me in Paradise"; and the surrender of life, "Father, into thy hands I commend my spirit." St. John had stood at the foot of the cross, and there supported the mother of the Lord in her anguish. He repeats the words which made him from that day a son unto her, and she to him a mother. He brings to our ears the accent of utmost distress, "I thirst," and the cry of solemn triumph, "It is finished." But how could he have omitted the still more affecting and still weightier words recorded by St. Luke, unless because he knew that they had been thus recorded already? So too, after the resurrection, he relates only events or circumstances which the three had left untold, and to which he gives all the freshness of his glowing memory. He is there once more at the dawn of day, outrunning the eager but older Peter, and yet pausing at the entrance of the sepulchre; and in this narrative we have the expansion of the merest mention by St. Luke of a visit of Peter. From such a mere mention by the other three Evangelists of Mary Magdalene as one of the women, and indeed the first, who saw the Lord, is developed by St. John the full story of that rapturous interview. So the account given by St. Luke of the appearance of our Lord to the eleven in the evening of that day, is filled out by St.

John through the introduction of the renewal of their commission, while the Saviour breathed upon them and bade them receive the Holy Ghost; and by the details of the absence and incredulity of Thomas, and of the appearance on the succeeding Sunday, when that incredulity ended. Throughout he perfects the story; and in more places than one, adds the full force of his personal asseveration, "He that saw it bear record." If his Gospel be, as it certainly is, a sequel which presupposes and completes the other three, it must also reaffirm them with all the weight which belonged to the last of the Apostles. "There were many other things which Jesus did, which, if every one of them should be written, the world itself could not contain the books that should be written." It seems like an attestation of the books which had been written already, and to which his own was immediately appended.

"But certainly the Gospel of St. John would never have been what it is, had not the Gospel of St. Luke existed before. The later yields to the earlier the support of its own authority and of its author. At the end of the first century, when St. John died, the Gospel of St. Luke had all the sanction and the certainty which could attend a record universally received as sacred. It was read by the Christian churches in their assemblies; it bore the name of an associate of St. Paul, who had possessed every opportunity for gathering up the facts, and every needful gift of the Spirit for judging, discriminating, and recording them as the counsel of God; and it has the seal of the patriarchal John, the only one who remained of those whom the Lord had chosen to be his companions, heralds, and witnesses."

On the following pages is presented a synoptical view of the various arrangements adopted by several harmonists. The order of each author is strictly preserved, but no attention is paid to their divisions into sections. A concurrence of them all is marked by underlining the type. The Harmonists selected are: GRESWELL, as the most common authority at present in England; STROUD (a London physician who spent thirty years in working out his scheme), as the independent and conscientious work of a layman little influenced by the labors of others, and free from any theological bias; ROBINSON, hitherto the almost universal authority in America; Archbishop THOMSON, in the article *Gospels* in Smith's Dictionary of the Bible, as giving the latest results of study in England; TISCHENDORF the latest, and best, authority in Germany; while in the last column the arrangement of the present Harmony is given for the purpose of comparison.

The eye will at once catch the points upon which all are agreed: and such points, may be considered as well settled. At the same time it will readily be seen what is the balance of opinion in regard to other passages; while in regard to a very few — after making allowance for differences occasioned by different theories in relation to the length of our Lord's ministry — it will be observed that the variations are so great as to show that the data are insufficient for a positive conclusion.

A TABULAR VIEW OF THE ARRANGEMENTS ADOPTED

THE LAST COLUMN CONTAINS THE ARRANGE-

GRESWELL.				STROUD.				ROBINSON.			
Matth.	Mark.	Luke.	John.	Matth.	Mark.	Luke.	John.	Matth.	Mark.	Luke.	John.
		1:1-4				(omit)				1:1-4	
		1:5-55				1:5-55				1:5-55	
1:18-25		1:56									
		1:57-80				1:56-80				1:56-80	
		2:1-20		1:18-25		2:1-7		1:18-25		2:1-7	
1:25		2:21									
1:1-17		3:23-38									
		2:22-38				2:8-21				2:8-21	
						2:22-39				2:22-38	
2:1-18				2:1-18				2:1-18			
2:19-23		2:39		2:19-23				2:19-23		2:39, 40	
		2:40-52				2:40-52				2:41-52	
								1:1-17		3:23-38	
			1:1-18								
3:1-12	1:1-8	3:1-18		3:1-12	1:1-8	3:1-18		3:1-12	1:1-8	3:1-18	
		3:19, 20				3:19, 20					
3:13-17	1:9-11	3:21-23		3:13-17	1:9-11	3:21, 22		3:13-17	1:9-11	3:21-23	
4:1-11	1:12, 13	4:1-13		4:1-11	1:12, 13	4:1-13		4:1-11	1:12, 13	4:1-13	
						1:1-17					
						3:23-38					
							1:1-18				1:1-18
			1:19-31				1:19-34				1:19-31
			1:35-				1:35-				1:35-
			3:36				3:36				3:36
				4:12	1:14	4:14		4:1-3			
				14:3-5				6:17-20	3:19, 20		
			4:4-42			4:4-42					4:4-42
				4:17	1:14, 15	4:14, 15					1:43-45
			4:43-45			4:43-45					
			4:46-54			4:46-54					1:46-54
			5:1-17			5:1-47					
				4:12	1:14	4:14					
		4:14, 15		4:17	1:14, 15	4:14, 15					
		4:16-30				4:16-30				4:16-30	
1:12-16	1:14	4:31		1:13-16		4:31		4:13-16		4:31	
4:17	1:14, 15										

xxviii

BY SEVERAL OF THE MORE RECENT HARMONISTS.

MENT ADOPTED IN THE FOLLOWING PAGES.

THOMSON.				TISCHENDORF.							
Matth.	Mark.	Luke.	John.	Matth.	Mark.	Luke.	John	Matth.	Mark.	Luke.	John.
			1:1-14				1:1-18				1:1-18
	1:1-4					1:1-4			1:1-4		
				1:1-17		3:23-38					
		1:5-55				1:5-55				1:5-55	
		1:56-80				1:56-80				1:56-80	
1:18-25		2:1-7		1:18-25				1:18-24			
						2:1-7		1:25		2:1-7	
1:1-17		3:23-38						1:1-17		3:23-38	
		2:8-21				2:8-21				2:8-21	
		2:22-38				2:22-38				2:22-38	
2:1-18				2:1-18				2:1-18			
2:19-23		2:39		2:19-23		2:39,40		2:19-23		2:39,40	
		2:40-52				2:41-52				2:41-52	
3:1-12	1:1-8	3:1-18	1:15-31	3:1-12	1:1-8	3:1-18		3:1-12	1:1-8	3:1-18	
3:13-17	1:9-11	3:21,22	1:32-34	3:13-17	1:9-11	3:21,22		3:13-17	1:9-11	3:21-23	
4:1-11	1:12,13	4:1-13		4:1-11	1:12,13	4:1-13		4:1-11	1:12,13	4:1-13	
							1:19-34				1:19-34
							1:35-				1:35-
		1:35-					3:36				3:36
		3:36									
		4:1-42									
14:3	6:17	3:19,20	3:21	14:3-5	6:17-20	3:19,20		14:3-5	6:17-20	3:19,20	
				4:12	1:14	4:14	4:1-3	4:12	1:14	4:14	1:1-3
							4:4-42				4:4-42
1:12	1:14,15	1:14,15	4:43-45				4:17	1:14-15	1:14,15	4:43-45	
		4:16-30									
						1:43-45					
		4:46-54				4:46-54				4:46-54	
						5:1-47					
				4:(12)17	1:14,15	4:(14)15				1:16-30	
						1:16-30				4:31	
				4:13-16		1:31		4:13-16			

xxx   TABULAR VIEW OF THE ARRANGEMENT ADOPTED

GRESWELL				STROUD				ROBINSON			
Matth.	Mark.	Luke.	John.	Matth.	Mark.	Luke.	John.	Matth.	Mark.	Luke.	John.
1:18-22	1:16-20			4:18-22	1:16-20			4:18-22	1:16-20	5:1-11	
	1:21-28	4:31-37			1:21-28	4:31-37			1:21-28	4:31-37	
8:14-17	1:29-34	4:38-41		8:14-17	1:29-34	4:38-41		8:14-17	1:29-34	4:38-41	
4:23	1:35-39	4:42-44		4:23	1:35-39	4:42-44		4:23	1:35-39	4:42-44	
4:24,25								4:24-25			
5-8:1											
		5:1-11				5:1-11					
8:2-4	1:40-45	5:12-16		8:2-4	1:40-45	5:12-16		8:2-4	1:40-45	5:12-16	
9:2-8	2:1-12	5:17-26		9:2-8	2:1-12	5:17-26		9:2-8	2:1-12	5:17-26	
9:9	2:13,14	5:27,28		9:9	2:13,14	5:27,28		9:9	2:13,14	5:27,28	
	2:15-22	5:29-39		9:10-17	2:15-22	5:29-39					
			5:1-47								5:1-47
12:1-14	2:23-3:6	6:1-11		12:1-14	2:23-3:6	6:1-11		12:1-11	2:23-3:6	6:1-11	
12:15-21	3:7-12			12:15-21	3:7-12			12:15-21	3:7-12		
				4:24,25							
10:2-4	3:13-19	6:12-16		5:1	3:13-19	6:12-16		10:2-4	3:13-19	6:12-16	
		6:17-19				6:17-19				6:17-19	
		6:20-49		5:1-7:29 *		6:20-49		5:1-7:29 *		6:20-49	
				8:1				8:1			
8:5-13		7:1-10		8:5-13		7:1-10		8:5-13		7:1-10	
					3:19-21						
				12:22-37	3:22-30	11:14-23					
				12:43-50	3:31-35	11:24-28					
				12:38-42		11:29-51					
		7:11-17				7:11-17				7:11-17	
11:2-19		7:18-35		11:2-19		7:18-35		11:2-19		7:18-35	
11:20-30				11:20-30				11:20-30			
		7:36-50				7:36-50				7:36-50	
	3:19	8:1-3				8:1-3				8:1-3	
12:22-37	3:20-30							12:22-37	3:20-30	11:14,15, 17-23	
12:38-45								12:38-45		11:16,24-26, 29-36	
12:46-50	3:31-35							12:46-50	3:31-35	11:27,28, 8:19-21	
										11:37-13:9	

* For the sake of brevity the whole of the Sermon on the Mount is here indicated; in this Harmony a

BY SEVERAL OF THE MORE RECENT HARMONISTS.

THOMSON.				TISCHENDORF.							
Matth.	Mark.	Luke.	John.	Matth.	Mark.	Luke.	John.	Matth.	Mark.	Luke.	John.
4: 13-22	1: 16-20	5: 1-11		4: 18-22	1: 16-20	5: 1-11		4: 18-22	1: 16-20	5: 1-11	
	1: 21-28	4: 31-37			1: 21-28	4: 31-37			1: 21-28	4: 31-37	
8: 14-17	1: 29-34	4: 38-41		8: 14-17	1: 29-34	4: 38-41		8: 14-17	1: 29-34	4: 38-41	
4: 23	1: 35-39	4: 42-44		4: 23	1: 35-39	4: 42-44		4: 23	1: 35-39	4: 42-44	
4: 24-25											
8: 1				8: 1							
8: 2-4	1: 40-45	5: 12-16		8: 2-4	1: 40-45	5: 12-16		8: 2-4	1: 40-45	5: 12-16	
8: 18-34	4: 35– 5: 20	8: 22-39									
9: 1				9: 1				9: 1			
9: 2-8	2: 1-12	5: 17-26		9: 2-8	2: 1-12	5: 17-26		9: 2-8	2: 1-12	5: 17-26	
9: 9	2: 13-14	5: 27-28		9: 9	2: 13, 14	5: 27, 28		9: 9	2: 13, 14	5: 27, 28	
9: 10-17	2: 15-22	5: 29-39		9: 10-17	2: 15-22	5: 29-39		9: 10-17	2: 15-22	5: 29-39	
			5: 1-47								5: 1-17
12: 1-14	2: 23-3: 6	6: 1-11		12: 1-14	2: 23-3: 6	6: 1-11		12: 1-14	2: 23-3: 6	6: 1-11	
				12: 15-21							
12: 15-21	3: 7-12							12: 15-21 4: 24-25	3: 7-12	6: 17-19	
10: 2-4	3: 13-19	6: 12-16		10: 2-4	3: 13-19	6: 12-16		10: 2-4	3: 13-19	6: 12-16	
		6: 17-19		4: 24, 25	3: 7-12	6: 17-19					
5: 1-7: 29	*	6: 20-49		5: 1-7: 29	(4: 24)	6: 20-49, (11: 2-4, 9-13, 34-36, 22-31, 33, 34, 58, 59, 13: 24-27, 14: 34, 35, 16: 13, 17, 18)		5: 1-7: 29	*	6: 20-49	
										16: 17	
				(8: 1)				8: 1			
8: 5-13		7: 1-10		8: 5-13		7: 1-10		8: 5-13		7: 1-10	
		7: 11-17				7: 11-17				7: 11-17	
11: 2-19		7: 18-35		11: 2-19		7: 18-35		11: 2-19		7: 18-35	
11: 20-30										16: 16	
		7: 36-50				7: 36-50				7: 36-50	
		8: 1-3				8: 1-3				8: 1-3	
				12: 22-37	3: 20-30	11: 17-23, 6: 43-45		12: 22-37	3: 20-30	11: 14-23, 12: 10	
								12: 38-45 6: 22, 23		11: 24-36	
				12: 46-50	3: 31-35	8: 19-21		12: 46-50	3: 31-35	8: 19-21	

few passages are transferred to the parallel places in St. Luke; they are, v. 24, 25; vi. 22-34; vii. 7-11.

GRESWELL.				STROUD.				ROBINSON.			
Matth.	Mark.	Luke.	John.	Matth.	Mark.	Luke.	John.	Matth.	Mark.	Luke.	John.
13:1-9	4:1-9	8:4-8		13:1-9	4:1-9	8:4-8		13:1-9	4:1-9	8:4-8	
13:10-17				13:10-23	4:10-25	8:9-18		13:10-23	4:10-25	8:9-18	
13:24-35	4:26-34			13:24-35	4:26-34			13:24-35	4:26-31		
13:36, 18-23	4:10-25	8:9-18									
13:36-52				13:36-52				13:36-52			
		8:19-21				8:19-21					
13:53, 8:18	4:35	8:22		8:18	4:35	8:22		8:18	4:35	8:22	
8:19-34	4:36-5:20	8:23-39		8:19-34	4:36-5:20	8:23-39		8:19-34	4:36-5:20	8:23-39 9:57-62	
9:1	5:21	8:40		9:1	5:21	8:40		9:1	5:21	8:40	
9:10-17								9:10-17	2:15-22	5:29-39	
9:18-26	5:22-43	8:41-56		9:18-26	5:22-43	8:41-56		9:18-26	5:22-43	8:41-56	
9:27-34				9:27-34				9:27-34			
13:54-58	6:1-6			13:54-58	6:1-6			13:54-58	6:1-6		
9:35-38	6:6			9:35-38	6:6			9:35-38	6:6		
10:1	6:7	9:1		10:1 10:2-4	6:7	9:1		10:1	6:7	9:1	
10:5-42, 11:1	6:8-13	9:2-6		10:5-42, 11:1	6:8-13	9:2-6		10:5-12 11:1	6:8-13	9:2-6	
14:1-2	6:14-16	9:7-9		14:1,2	6:14-16	9:7-9		14:1-2	6:14-16	9:7-9	
14:3-5	6:17-20			14:3-5	6:17-20						
14:6-12	6:21-29			14:6-12	6:21-29			14:6-12	6:21-29		
14:13-21	6:30-44	9:10-17	6:1-14	14:13-21	6:30-44	9:10-17	6:1-14	14:13-21	6:30-44	9:10-17	6:1-14
14:22-33	6:45-52		6:15-21	14:22-33	6:45-52		6:15-21	14:22-33	6:45-52		6:15-21
14:34-36	6:53-56		6:22-24	14:34-36	6:53-56			14:34-36	6:53-56		
			6:25-65				6:22-65				6:22-65
			6:66-7:1				6:66-7:1				6:66-7:1
						13:10-21					
15:1-31	7:1-37			15:1-31	7:1-37			15:1-31	7:1-37		
15:32-38	8:1-9			15:32-38	8:1-9			15:32-38	8:1-9		
15:39-16:12	8:10-21			15:39-16:12	8:10-21			15:39-16:12	8:10-21		
	8:22-26				8:22-26				8:22-26		
							7:2-11:54				
16:13-28	8:27-9:1	9:18-27		16:13-28	8:27-38	9:18-27		16:13-28	8:27-9:1	9:18-27	
17:1-27	9:2-33	9:28-45	7:1	17:1-27	9:2-32	9:28-45		17:1-27	9:2-33	9:28-45	
	9:33-37	9:46-48		18:1-5	9:33-37	9:46-48		18:1-5	9:33-37	9:46-48	

BY SEVERAL OF THE MORE RECENT HARMONISTS.

	THOMSON.				TISCHENDORF.						
Matth.	Mark.	Luke.	John.	Matth.	Mark.	Luke.	John	Matth.	Mark.	Luke.	John.
13:1-9	4:1-9	8:4-8		13:1-9	4:1-9	8:4-8		13:1-9	4:1-9	8:4-8	
13:10-23	4:10-25	8:9-18		13:10-23	4:10-25	8:9-18 (6:38)		13:1-15, 18-23	4:10-25	8:9-18	
13:24-35	4:26-34	13:18-21		13:24-35	4:26-34	13:18-21		13:24-35	4:26-34	13:18-21	
13:36-52				13:36-52				13:36-52			
12:46-50	3:31-35	8:19-21									
				8:18	4:35	8:22		8:18	4:35	8:22	
				8:23-34	4:36-5:20	8:23-39		8:23-34	4:36-5:20	8:23-39	
					5:21	8:40			5:21	8:40	
				9:18-26	5:22-43	8:41-56		9:18-26 9:27-34	5:22-43	8:41-56	
13:53-58	6:1-6			13:53-58	6:1-5			13:53-58	6:1-6		
9:35-38, 11:1	6:6			9:35-38	6:6			9:35-38	6:6		
10:1	6:7	9:1		10:1	6:7	9:1		10:1	6:7	9:1	
10:2-4											
10:5-42	6:8-13	9:2-6		10:5-42, 11:1	6:8-13, 9:41, 13:9-12	9:2-6 (10:3,5, 6,12,16,12:2-9, 11, 12, 51-53, 14:26-27, 17: 33, 21:12-17)		10:5-16, 11:1	6:8-13	9:2-6	
14:1-2	6:14-16	9:7-9						14:1-2	6:14-16	9:7-9	
14:3-5	6:17-20										
14:6-12	6:21-29			14:6-12	6:21-29			14:6-12	6:21-29		
				14:1,2	6:14-16	9:7-9					
14:13-21	6:30-44	9:10-17	6:1-11	14:13-21	6:30-44	9:10-17	6:1-14	14:13-21	6:30-44	9:10-17	6:1-14
14:22-33	6:45-52		6:15-21	14:22-33	6:45-52		6:15-21	14:22-33	6:45-52		6:15-21
14:34-36	6:53-56			14:34-36	6:53-56			14:34-36	6:53-56		
			6:22-65				6:22-65				6:22-65
											6:66-7:1
15:1-31	7:1-37			15:1-31	7:1-37			15:1-31	7:1-37		
15:32-38	8:1-9			15:32-38	8:1-9			15:32-38	8:1-9		
15:39- 16:12	8:10-21			15:39- 16:12	8:10-21			15:39- 16:12	8:10-21		
	8:22-36				8:22-36				8:22-36		
16:13-28	8:27-9:1	9:18-27		16:13-28	8:27-9:1	9:18-27		16:13-28	8:27-9:1	9:18-27	
			6:66-71				6:66-71				
17:1-27	9:2-32	9:28-45		17:1-27	9:2-33	9:28-45		17:1-27	9:2-33	9:28-45	
18:1-5	9:33-37	9:46-48		18:1-5	9:33-37	9:46-48		18:1-5	9:33-37	9:46-48	

xxxiv   TABULAR VIEW OF THE ARRANGEMENT ADOPTED

GRESWELL.				STROUD.				ROBINSON.			
Matth.	Mark.	Luke.	John.	Matth.	Mark.	Luke.	John.	Matth.	Mark.	Luke.	John.
	9:38–41	9:49,50			9:38–41	9:49,50			9:38–41	9:49,50	
	9:42–50										
18:1–5											
18:6–9				18:6–9	9:42–50	17:1–3		18:6–9	9:42–50		
18:10–11				18:10–14				18:10–14			
18:15–20				18:15–20		17:3,4		18:15–20			
18:21–35				18:21–35				18:21–35			
			7:2–11:54								
						17:5–10					
										10:1–16	
		9:51–56		19:1	10:1	9:51–56				9:51–56	7:2–10
		9:57–62				9:57–62					
										17:11–19	
											7:11–8:59
		10:1–16				10:1–16					
		10:17–24				10:17–24					
		10:25–42				10:25–37				10:25–42	
		11:1–13								11:1–13	
		11:14–23									
		11:24–28									
		11:29–32									
		11:33–36									
		11:37–54									
										10:17–24	
											9:1–11:54
		12:1–12									
		12:13–31									
		12:32–53									

THOMSON.				TISCHENDORF.							
Matth.	Mark.	Luke.	John.	Matth.	Mark.	Luke.	John	Matth.	Mark.	Luke.	John.
	9:38-41	9:49,50			9:38-41	9:49,50		10:12	9:38-41	9:49,50	
18:6-9	9:42-48	17:2		18:6-9	9:42-50	17:1,2, 15:3-7		18:6-9	9:42-50	17:1,2	
18:10-14		15:4-7		18:10-14				18:10-14			
18:15-20				18:15-20				18:15-20			
18:21-35				18:21-35		17:3,4		18:21-35			
	9:49,50										
		9:51-56	7:1-10			9:51-56	7:1-10			9:51-56	7:2-10
8:19-22		9:57-62		8:19-22		9:57-62		8:19-22		9:57-62	
		10:1-11								10:1-11	
		10:12-16						11:20-24		10:12-16	
										17:11-19	
			7:11- 8:59 9:1- 10:21				7:11- 8:59 9:1- 10:21				7:11- 8:59 9:1- 10:21
				11:20-24		10:1-16					
		10:17-24		11:25-30		10:17-24		11:25-30, 13:16,17		10:17-24	
		10:25-42				10:25-42				10:25-42	
6:9-13. 7:7-11		11:1-13		7:7-11, 6:9-13		11:1-13		7:7-11		11:1-13	
12:22-37	3:20-30	11:14-23		9:27-31		11:14,15					
12:43-45		11:24-28		12:43-45		11:17-28					
12:38-42		11:29-32		12:38-42		11:16,29-36					
5:15, 6:22, 23		11:33-36									
				23:23-25, 29-31, 34-36							
23:1-29		11:37-54				11:37-54		23:4-39		11:37-54, 13:31,35	
								10:26-33, 40,41,17-20		12:1-9, 11, 12	
10:26-33		12:1-12				12:1-12					
6:25-33		12:13-31				12:13-31		6:25-34		12:13-31	
		12:32-53		24:43-51		12:32-53		24:43-51, 10:34-36		12:32-53	

TABULAR VIEW OF THE ARRANGEMENT ADOPTED

GRESWELL.				STROUD.				ROBINSON.			
Matth.	Mark.	Luke.	John.	Matth.	Mark.	Luke.	John.	Matth.	Mark.	Luke.	John.
		12:54-59									
		13:1-17									
		13:18-21						19:1,2	10:1	13:10-21	
		13:22-35								13:22-35	
		14:1-24								14:1-24	
		14:25-35								14:25-35	
		ch. 15, 16								ch. 15, 16	
		17:1-4								17:1-4	
		17:5-10								17:5-10	
		17:11				17:11					
		17:12-19				17:12-19					
19:1,2	10:1										
		17:20-37				17:20-37				17:20-37	
		18:1-14				18:1-14				18:1-14	
				19:1-2	10:1						
19:3-12	10:2-12			19:3-12	10:2-12			19:3-12	10:2-12		
										13:22-16:31	
19:13-31	10:13-31	18:15-30		19:13-30	10:13-31	18:15-30		19:13-30	10:13-31	18:15-30	
20:1-16				20:1-16				20:1-16			
20:17-19	10:32-34	18:31-34		20:17-19	10:32-34	18:31-31		20:17-19	10:32-34	18:31-34	
20:20-28	10:35-45			20:20-28	10:35-45			20:20-28	10:35-45		
		18:35-43				18:35-43				18:35-43	
20:29-34	10:46-52	19:1		20:29-34	10:46-52	19:1		20:29-34	10:46-52	19:1	
		19:2-27				19:2-28				19:2-28	
		19:28	11:55-57				11:55-57				11:55-57
			12:1								
						10:38-42	12:1				
26:6-13	14:3-9		12:2-11	26:6-13	14:3-9		12:2-11				12:1,9-11
21:1-11, 14-17		19:29-44	12:12-19	21:1-11, 14-17		11:1-10	19:29-44	12:12-19	21:1-11, 14-17	11:1-10	19:29-44	12:12-19
	11:11				11:11				11:11		
			12:20-36								
21:18,19	11:12-14			21:18,19	11:12-14			21:18,19	11:12-14		
21:12,13, 20-22	11:15-19	19:45-48		21:12,13	11:15-19	19:45-48		21:12-13	11:15-19	19:45-48, 21:37,38	
						11:1-13					

THOMSON.				TISCHENDORF.							
Matth.	Mark.	Luke.	John.	Matth.	Mark.	Luke.	John	Matth.	Mark.	Luke.	John.
		12:54-59		16:2,3, 5:25,26		12:54-59		5:25,26		12:54-59	
		13:1-17				13:1-17				13:1-17	
13:31-33	4:30-32	13:18-21									
							10:22-42				10:22-42
23:37-39		13:22-35				13:22-33		19:1,2	10:1	13:22-33	
22:1-14		14:1-24				14:1-24				14:1-24	
10:37-38		14:25-35				14:25-35		10:37-39		14:25-35	
		ch. 15, 16		5:18-32, 11:12,13		ch. 15, 16				ch. 15, 16	
18:6-15		17:1-4									
17:20		17:5-10				17:(1-4) 5-10				17:5-10	
							11:1-54				11:1-54
		17:11		19:1-2	10:1	17:11					
		17:12-19				17:12-19					
		17:20-37		24:23-28, 37-41	13:21-23	17:20-37		24:26-28, 37-41		17:20-37	
		18:1-14				18:1-14				18:1-14	
19:1,2	10:1										
19:3-12	10:2-12			19:3-12	10:2-12			19:3-12	10:2-12		16:18
19:13-30	10:13-31	18:15-30		19:13-30	10:13-31	18:15-30		19:13-30	10:13-31	18:15-30	
20:1-16				20:1-16				20:1-16			
20:17-19	10:32-34	18:31-34		20:17-19	10:32-34	18:31-34		20:17-19	10:32-34	18:31-34	
20:20-28	10:35-45			20:20-28	10:35-45			20:20-28	10:35-45		
20:29-34	10:46-52	18:35-43		20:29-34	10:46-52	18:35-43		20:29-34	10:46-52	18:35-43	
	19:1				19:1				19:1		
25:14-30	19:2-28			25:14-30		19:2-28		25:14-30		19:2-28	
			10:22- 11:54								
			11:55-57				11:55-57				11:55-57
26:6-13	14:3-9	7:36-50	12:1-11	26:6-13	14:3-9		12:1-11	26:6-13	14:3-9		12:1-11
21:1-11	11:1-10	19:29-44	12:12-19	21:1-11	11:1-10	19:29-44	12:12-19	21:1-11	11:1-10	19:29-44	12:12-19
					11:11				11:11		
				21:18,19	11:12-14			21:18,19	11:12-14		
21:12-16	11:15-18	19:45-48		21:12-17	11:15-19	19:45-48, 21:37,38		21:12-17	11:15-19	19:45-48, 21:37,38	

xxxviii TABULAR VIEW OF THE ARRANGEMENT ADOPTED

GRESWELL.				STROUD.				ROBINSON.			
Matth.	Mark.	Luke.	John.	Matth.	Mark.	Luke.	John.	Matth.	Mark.	Luke.	John.
	11:20-26			21:20-22	11:20-26			21:20-22	11:20-26		
21:23-27	11:27-33	20:1-8		21:23-27	11:27-33	20:1-8		21:23-27	11:27-33	20:1-8	
21:28-32				21:28-32				21:28-32			
21:33-46	12:1-12	20:9-19		21:33-46	12:1-12	20:9-19		21:33-46	12:1-12	20:9-19	
22:1-14				22:1-14				22:1-14			
22:15-33	12:13-27	20:20-39		22:15-33	12:13-27	20:20-39		22:15-33	12:13-27	20:20-39	
		20:40								20:40	
22:34-40	12:28-34			22:34-40	12:28-34			22:34-40	12:28-34		
22:41-46	12:35-37, 31	20:41-44, 40		22:41-46	12:35-37	20:41-44		22:41-46	12:35-37	20:41-44	
	12:38-40	20:45-47		23:1-39	12:38-40	20:45-47		23:1-39	12:38-40	20:45-47	
	12:41-44	21:1-4	12:37-50		12:41-44	21:1-4			12:41-44	21:1-4	12:20-50
23:1-39											
24:1-42	13:1-37	21:5-36		24:1-42	13:1-37	21:5-36		21:1-42	13:1-37	21:5-36	
24:43-51				24:43-51				21:43-51			
25:1-46				25:1-46				25:1-46			
				26:1,2			12:20-50				
26:1-5	14:1,2	22:1,2		26:3-5	14:1,2	22:1,2		26:1-5	14:1,2	22:1,2	
								26:6-13	14:3-9		12:2-8
26:14-16	14:10,11	22:3-6		26:14-16	14:10,11	22:3-6		26:14-16	14:10,11	22:3-6	
		21:37,38									
26:17-19	14:12-16	22:7-13		26:17-19	14:12-16	22:7-13	13:1	26:17-19	14:12-16	22:7-13	
26:20	14:17	22:14-18		26:20	14:17	22:14-18		26:20	14:17	22:14-18	
						22:21				22:24-30	
			13:1,2-17 (1 Cor.11: 23, 24)			13:2-20					13:1,2-20
26:26	14:22	22:19				22:25-30					
						22:15-18					
				26:26-29	14:22-25	22:19,20	(1 Cor.11: 23-25)				
			13:18-20								
26:21-25	14:18-21	22:21-23	13:21-35	26:21-25	14:18-21	22:21-23	13:21-35	26:21-25	14:18-21	22:21-23	13:21-35
		22:24-38	13:36-38			22:31-38	13:36-38				
26:27-29	14:23-25	22:20	(1 Cor.11: 25)								

BY SEVERAL OF THE MORE RECENT HARMONISTS.

THOMSON.				TISCHENDORF.							
Matth.	Mark.	Luke.	John.	Matth.	Mark.	Luke.	John	Matth.	Mark.	Luke.	John.
21:17-19	11:11-14, 19										
21:20-22	11:20-23			21:20-22 (6:14-15)	11:20-26			21:20-22	11:20-26		
6:14,15	11:24-26										
21:23-27	11:27-33	20:1-8		21:23-27	11:27-33	20:1-8		21:23-27	11:27-33	20:1-8	
21:28-32				21:28-32				21:28-32			
21:33-46	12:1-12	20:9-19		21:33-46	12:1-12	20:9-19		21:33-46	12:1-12	20:9-19	
22:1-14				22:1-14				22:1-14			
22:15-33	12:13-27	20:20-39 20:40		22:15-33	12:13-27	20:20-39		22:15-33	12:13-27	20:20-39	
22:34-40	12:28-31			22:34-40	12:28-31	20:40		22:34-40	12:28-34	20:40	
22:41-46	12:35-37	20:41-44		22:41-46	12:35-37	20:41-44		22:41-46	12:35-37	20:41-44	
23:1-39	12:38-40	20:45-47		23:1-39	12:38-40	20:45-47		23:1-3	12:38-40	20:45-47	
	12:41-44	21:1-4			12:41-44	21:1-4			12:41-44	21:1-4	
							12:20-50				12:20-50
								24:1-25, 29-36,42, 10:21-25			
24:1-42	13:1-37	21:5-36		24:1-42	13:1-37	21:5-36			13:1-37	21:5-36	
24:43-51		21:37-38									
25:1-46				25:1-46		(12:39-46, 19:11-28)		25:1-13, 31-46			
			12:20-50								
26:1-5	14:1,2	22:1,2		26:1-5	14:1,2	22:1,2		26:1-5	14:1,2	22:1,2	
26:14-16	14:10,11	22:3-6		26:14-16	14:10,11	22:3-6		26:14-16	14:10,11	22:3-6	
26:17-19	14:12-16	22:7-13		26:17-19	14:12-16	22:7-13		26:17-19	14:12-16	22:7-13	
26:20	14:17	22:14-18		26:20	14:17	22:14-18 22:24-30		26:20	14:17	22:14-18 22:24-30	
			13:1,2-20				13:1,2-20				13:1,2-20
26:21-29	14:18-25	22:21-23	13:21-35	26:21-25	14:18-21	22:21-23	13:21-35	26:21-25	14:18-21	22:21-23	13:21-35
	22:24-30			26:26-29	14:22-25	22:19,20	(1 Cor.11: 23-25)	26:26-29	14:22-25	22:19,20	(1 Cor.11: 23-25)

TABULAR VIEW OF THE ARRANGEMENT ADOPTED

GRESWELL.				STROUD.				ROBINSON.			
Matth.	Mark.	Luke.	John.	Matth.	Mark.	Luke.	John.	Matth.	Mark.	Luke.	John.
								26:31-35	14:27-31	22:31-38	13:36-38
								26:26-29	14:22-25	22:19-20	(1 Cor.11: 23-25)
		14:1– 17:26				14:1– 17:26					14:1– 17:26
26:30-35	14:26-31	22:39	18:1	26:30-35	14:26-31	22:39	18:1	26:30	14:26	22:39	18:1
26:36-56	14:32-52	22:40-53	18:1,2-11	26:36-56	14:32-52	22:40-53	18:1,2-11, 12	26:36-56	14:32-52	22:40-53	18:2-11, 12
			18:19-21				18:13-16				18:13-16,
26:57,58	14:53,54	22:54,55	18:12, 13-16	26:57,58	14:53,54	22:54,55	17,18,24	26:57,58	14:53,54	22:54,55	18
26:59-68	14:55-65	22:63-65									18:17,25 26,27
				26:69-72	14:66-70	22:56-58	18:19-23	23:69-75	14:66-72	22:56-62	
				26:59-66	14:55-64						
				26:73-75	14:70-72	22:59-62	18:25-27				
				26:67,68	14:65	22:63-65		26:59-68	14:55-65	22:63-71	18:19-21
26:69-75	14:66-72	22:56-62	18:17,18, 25-27								
		22:66-71									
27:1,2	15:1	23:1	18:28	27:1,2	15:1,2	22:66-71, 23:1		27:1,2 / 11-14	15:1-5	23:1-5	18:28-38
27:3-10				27:3-10							
			18:28-38 18:39– 19:14	27:11-14	15:2-5	23:2-5	18:28-38				
27:11-14	15:2-5	23:2-5 23:6-16				23:6-16				23:6-16	
27:15-23 24-26	15:6-11, 15	23:17-23 24,25	19:14-16	27:15-23	15:6-11	23:17-23	18:39,40 19:1-15	27:15-23 24-26	15:6-14, 15	23:17-23 24,25	18:39– 19:1
				27:28-30	15:17-19						
				27:24-26	15:15	23:23-25	19:16				
27:27-30	15:16-19							27:27-30	15:16-19		19:2,3 19:4-16
27:31-34	15:20-28	23:26-34	19:16-24	27:31-34 35-38	15:20-28	23:26-34, 38	19:16-24	27:31-34 35-38	15:20-28	23:26-34, 38	19:16-24
				27:36		23:36					
27:39-44	15:29-32	23:35-37, 38,39		27:39-44	15:29-32	23:35-37, 39		27:39-44	15:29-32	23:35-37, 39	
		23:40-43				23:40-43				23:40-43	
			19:25-27				19:25-27				19:25-27
27:45-56	15:33-41	23:44-49	19:28-30	27:45-56	15:33-41	23:44-49	19:28-30	27:45-56	15:33-41	23:44,45 47-49	19:28-30

THOMSON.				TISCHENDORF.							
Matth.	Mark.	Luke.	John.	Matth.	Mark.	Luke.	John.	Matth.	Mark.	Luke.	John.
26:30-35	14:26-31	22:31-39	13:36-38	26:31-35	14:27-31	22:31-38	13:36-38	26:31-35	14:27-31	22:31-38	13:36-38
			14:1-17:26				14:1-17:26				14:1-17:26
				26:30	14:26	22:39	18:1	26:30	14:26	22:39	18:1
26:36-56	14:32-52	22:40-53	18:1,2-11	26:36-56	14:32-52	22:40-53	18:2-11	26:36-56	14:32-52	22:40-53	18:2-11, 12
26:57,58	14:53,54	22:51,55	18:12, 13-16	26:57,58	14:53,54	22:54,55	18:12,13-16,17,18	26:57,58	14:53,54	22:54,55	18:13-16, 18
26:69-75	14:66-72	22:56-62	18:17-27	26:69-75	14:66-72	22:56-62	18:25-27	26:69-75	14:66-72	22:56-62	18:17,19, 26,27
26:59-68	14:55-65	22:63-71		26:59-68	14:55-65	22:63-71	18:19-24	26:59-68	14:55-65	22:63-65, 67-71	
27:1,2, 11-14	15:1-5	23:1-3	18:28	27:1,2	15:1	23:1	18:28	27:1,2	15:1	22:66, 23:1	18:28
27:3-10				27:3-10				27:3-10		(Acts 1:18,19)	
				27:11-14	15:2-5	23:2-5	18:29-38	27:11-14	15:2-5	23:2-5	18:29-38
		23:4,5 23:6-16				23:6-16				23:6-16	
27:15-23, 24-26	15:6-14, 15	23:17-23, 24,25	18:29-19:16	27:15-23, 24-26	15:6-14, 15	23:17-23, 24,25	18:39,40	27:15-23, 24-26	15:6-14, 15	23:17-23, 24,25	18:39-19:1
27:27-31	15:16-20	23:36,37	19:2,3	27:27-30	15:16-19		19:1-3, 19:4-16	27:27-30	15:16-19		19:2-3, 19:4-16
27:32-34, 35-38	15:21-28	23:26-34	19:17-24	27:31-34, 35-38	15:20-27	23:26-34, 38	19:16-24	27:31-34, 35-38	15:20-27	23:26-34, 38	19:16-21
			19:25-27								
27:39-44	15:29-32	23:35-37, 38,39 23:40-43		27:39-44	15:29-32	23:35-37, 39 23:40-43		27:39-44	15:29-32	23:35-37, 39 23:40-43	
							19:25-27				19:25-27
27:50	15:37	23:46	19:28-30								
27:45-56	15:33-41	23:44,45, 47-49		27:45-56	15:33-41	23:44-49	19:28-30	27:45-56	15:33-41	23:44-49	19:28-30

TABULAR VIEW OF THE ARRANGEMENT ADOPTED

GRESWELL.				STROUD.				ROBINSON.			
Matth.	Mark.	Luke.	John.	Matth.	Mark.	Luke.	John.	Matth.	Mark.	Luke.	John.
			19:31-37				19:31-37				19:31-37
27:57-61	15:42-47	23:50-56	19:38-42	27:57-61	15:42-47	23:50-56	19:38-42	27:57-61	15:42-47	23:50-56	19:38-42
27:62-66				27:62-66				27:62-66			
28:1-8	16:1-8			28:1-8	16:1-8	24:1-8	20:1,2	28:1-8	16:1-8	24:1-8	20:1,2
28:11-15								28:9,10		24:9-11	
		24:1-9,11								24:12	
		24:10-12	20:3-10				20:3-10				20:3-10
	16:9-11		20:11-18		16:9		20:11-17		16:9-11		20:11-18
				28:9-15				28:11-15			
					16:10,11	24:9-12	20:18				
	16:12,13	24:13-35	(1 Cor.15:5)		16:12,13	24:13-35	(1 Cor.15:5)		16:12,13	24:13-35	(1 Cor.15:5)
			20:19-29								
	16:14	24:36-43	(1 Cor.15:5)	28:5	16:14	24:36-43	20:19-29		16:14-18	24:36-49	20:19-29
28:9,10							21:1-23	28:16			21:1-24
							(1 Cor.15:7, Acts 1:1-3)				
28:16-20			(1 Cor.15:6)	28:16-20	16:6,15-18		(Acts 1:4)	28:16-20			(1 Cor.15:6)
			(1 Cor.15:7)								(1 Cor.15:7)
			21:1-24								(Acts 1:3-8)
		24:44-49	(Acts1:4-8, 1 Cor.15:7)			24:44-49	(Acts 1:4,5)				
	16:15-18	21:50									
	16:19	21:50-53	(Acts 1:9-12)		16:19,20	24:50-53	(Acts 1:9-14)		16:19,20	24:50-53	(Acts 1:9-12)
			20:30,31								20:30,31
			21:25								21:25
	16:20										

BY SEVERAL OF THE MORE RECENT HARMONISTS.

THOMSON.				TISCHENDORF.							
Matth.	Mark.	Luke.	John.	Matth.	Mark.	Luke.	John	Matth.	Mark.	Luke.	John.
			19:31-37				19:31-37				19:31-37
27:57-61	15:42-47	23:50-56	19:38-42	27:57-61	15:42-47	23:50-56	19:38-42	27:57-61	15:42-47	23:50-56	19:38-42
27:62-66				27:62-66				27:62-66			
28:11-15											
28:1-8	16:1-8	24:1-8	20:1,2	28:1-8	16:1-8	24:1-11	20:1,2	28:1-8	16:1-8	24:1-8	20:1,2
						24:12	20:3-10			24:12	20:3-10
28:9,10	16:9-11	24:9-12	20:3-10, 11-18	28:9,10	16:9-11		20:11-18		16:9-11		20:11-18
				28:11-15				28:9-10		24:9-11	
								28:11-15			
	16:12,13	24:13-35			16:12,13	24:13-35			16:12,13	24:13-35	
	16:14-18	24:36-49	20:19-29		16:14	24:36-43	20:19-29		16:14	24:36-43	20:19-29
			21:1-23				21:1-24	28:16			21:1-24
28:16-20				28:16-20	16:15-18			28:16-20	16:15-18		
			20:30,31, 21:24,25								
						24:44-49				24:44-49	
	16:19,20	24:50-53			16:19,20	24:50-53	(Acts 1: 3-12) 20:30,31, 21:25		16:19,20	24:50-53	(Acts 1: 3-12) 20:30,31, 21:25

INTRODUCTORY NOTE TO PART I.

§ 9. THE Genealogies. I. Some points require to be noted, especially concerning the genealogy given by St. Matthew, before comparing this with the one given by St. Luke. 1. The first division ends with David, including him in the number 14; the second division begins with David, including him also in the second 14. This is in accordance with usage, but shows that the statement in Matt. i. 17, as to the number of the generations is meant to apply only to the list given, and not to the number which had actually existed. 2. The same thing appears from the fact that in v. 8, three names of Jewish kings are omitted between Joram and Ozias (Uzziah), viz.: Ahaziah, Joash, and Amaziah (2 Kings viii. 25, and 2 Chron. xxii. 1; 2 Kings xi. 2, 21, and 2 Chron. xxii. 11; 2 Kings xii. 21; xiv. 1, and 2 Chron. xxiv. 27). Also, between Josiah and Jechoniah in v. 11, the name of Jehoiakim is omitted (2 Kings xxiii. 34; 2 Chron. xxxvi. 4; Cf. 1 Chron. iii. 15, 16). Of the existence of these intermediate generations St. Matthew, regarded simply as a pious Jew, could not have been ignorant. Such omissions in genealogies abound in Scripture. Thus, Ezra (vii. 1–5), in recording his own genealogy, omits six or seven of the names given in 1 Chron. vi. 3–15. (Cf. also, 1 Chron. iv. 1, with ii. 50, etc.). The descent of David as given by St. Matthew (5, 6), is identical with that in Ruth. iv. 20–22, and in 1 Chron. ii. 10–12; but the Salmon mentioned in all was contemporary with Joshua and married Rahab. Three names only are given between him and David, which, in view of the time embraced, implies that as many more must have been omitted.

Again, from David at the time of Solomon's birth, to Christ, was above a thousand years, giving, according to St. Matthew's genealogy, about thirty-six years to a generation: but the same period in St. Luke has forty-three generations, or fifteen more, making less than twenty-four years to a generation. It is hardly possible that in two parallel lines there could have been so great a difference in the average time of a generation. It is apparent therefore, that St. Matthew has given simply a copy of the official register, without alteration, as was plainly required in a Gospel designed to show the Jews that Jesus was the Messiah.

II. We come now to the comparison of this genealogy with that of St. Luke. Before David they differ only in going back to different starting-points, in accordance with the different objects of the writers; but after David the two lines part, and it is plain that they can never come together again simply by natural descent. They can only unite by a constructive or legal sonship in one or the other. Again: both are in form the genealogies of Joseph; but as he could not have had two natural fathers, this must be a case of *legal* in contradistinction to natural paternity, or else of double names. The latter hypothesis may be at once set aside as involving a complicated series of suppositions applying not merely to the father, but also to the ancestors, of Joseph for many generations. Since, then, the parted lines can come together only by a case of legal paternity; since they do come together in Joseph; and since there must be a legal paternity in his case, it is obvious that the simplest possible supposition is that the lines are distinct to that point, and then unite by a legal or constructive sonship.

Assuming that one of the genealogies is intended to give the descent of Joseph from the official record, there can be little difficulty in determining that this has been done by St. Matthew. Moreover, it is noticeable that while he concurs with the Old Testament genealogies until after the captivity, and afterwards uses the same phrase, "begat," as far as Joseph, he then changes it in the most marked way. It is no longer Joseph who "begat;" but Joseph "the husband of Mary, of whom was born Jesus." It is unnecessary to pursue the point; there is a general agreement in considering the genealogy given by St. Matthew to be that of Joseph.

2. Is that of St. Luke the same? Some writers have so supposed, and a variety of learned and ingenious, but for the most part, cumbrous suppositions have been made to sustain this view. The student is referred to the article *Genealogy*, in Smith's Bible Dictionary, for one of the latest arguments (by Lord A. C. Hervey) in favor of this theory. But if St. Matthew has given the official descent of Joseph, why should St. Luke have traced another descent through an inferior line? The only assignable reason would be to furnish the *actual* in contradistinction to the *official* descent of Christ; but for this purpose the actual descent of Joseph would have been of no use whatever, inasmuch as Jesus was only legally his son. On the supposition, however, that St. Luke gives the genealogy of Mary, all becomes clear. The lines parting from David, do not need to be again joined, except officially in Joseph; and a sufficient reason appears for St. Luke's choice of a different line.

To this hypothesis there is but one objection, and it requires but one unproved assumption. The objection is, that the names of Salathiel and Zorobabel as father and son, occur in both genealogies, and may be supposed to belong to the same persons. This, however, is by no means necessary. Similar names are common in different genealogies, as may be seen even from the first in Gen. iv. and v.; and when it is remembered that in St. Matthew's genealogy there are but fourteen names between David and Salathiel, while in St. Luke's there are twenty, it seems probable that these names belong to different persons. The unproved assumption is, that Joseph by his marriage to Mary, became the heir, and therefore legally the son of Heli. And this, though not positively proved, is rendered probable by a variety of circumstances. The language of the angel in Lk. i. 32, implies that Mary was herself of the lineage of David; and the words of Lk. ii. 5, "to be enrolled with Mary," etc., seem to indicate that Mary was to be enrolled with Joseph, — a circumstance most readily explained on the supposition that she also represented a family of the descendants of David. There is no allusion in the New Testament to her having had brothers; and as St. Luke, in his diligent inquiries, must have derived his account of the circumstances connected with the birth of Jesus directly or indirectly from the Virgin Mary, it seems altogether likely that he would at the same time have obtained this, her private genealogical tree.

But even this supposition, probable as it is, is not necessary. The words of St. Luke admit perfectly well of being read — "being (as was supposed son of Joseph) son of Eli"; i.e. he was supposed to be the son of Joseph, but was really the son (grandson) of Eli. In this case the whole clause "as was supposed of Joseph," is parenthetical, and the grandfather's name is given because, there being no natural father, he was the nearest male progenitor. This view is ably defended by Andrews (Life of our Lord, 4th ed., pp. 57–59) and is that of Lightfoot and many others. Lightfoot refers to a similar instance in Gen. xxxvi. 2, "Aholibamah the daughter of Anah the daughter of Libeon." As it appears from vv. 24, 25, that Anah was a man and the father of children, it is evident that the second *daughter* must be connected, like the first, with Aholibamah and must mean grand-daughter. Lightfoot also finds some evidence in Jewish tradition that Mary was the daughter of Heli.

PART I.

THE INCARNATION, BIRTH, AND CHILDHOOD OF OUR LORD.

§ 1. Preface to St. John's Gospel.
ST. JOHN I. 1–18.

1 In the beginning was the Word, and the Word was with God, and the
2 Word was God. The same was in the beginning with God. All things were
3
4 made by him; and without him was not anything made that was made. In
5 him is life: and the life was the light of men. And the light shineth in
darkness; and the darkness comprehended it not.
6 There was a man sent from God, whose name *was* John. The same came
7
for a witness, to bear witness of the Light, that all *men* through him might
8 believe. He was not that Light, but *was sent* to bear witness of that Light.
9 *That* was the true Light, which lighteth every man that cometh into the
10 world. He was in the world, and the world was made by him, and the world
11
12 knew him not. He came unto his own, and his own received him not. But
as many as received him, to them gave he power to become the sons of God,
13 *even* to them that believe on his name: which were born, not of blood, nor
14 of the will of the flesh, nor of the will of man, but of God. And the Word
was made flesh, and dwelt among us, (and we beheld his glory,[a] the glory as
of the only-begotten of the Father,) full of grace and truth.
15 John bare witness of him, and cried, saying, This was he of whom I spake,
He that cometh after me is preferred before me: for he was before me.
16
17 Because[2] of his fulness have all we received, and grace for grace. For the
18 law was given by Moses, *but* grace and truth came by Jesus Christ. No man
hath seen God at any time; the only-begotten Son, which is in the bosom of
the Father, he hath declared *him*.

§ 2 Preface to St. Luke's Gospel.
ST. LUKE I. 1–4.

1 Forasmuch as many have taken in hand to set forth in order a declaration
2 of those things which are most surely believed among us, [1]even as they
delivered them unto us, which from the beginning were eye-witnesses, and

---

[1] was life   [2] And of his

[a] Comp. Matt. xvii. 1–8; Mar. ix. 2–8; Lk. ix. 28–36.

ST. LUKE I.

3 ministers of the word; it seemed good to me also, having had perfect understanding of all things from the very first, to write unto thee in order, most
4 excellent Theophilus, 'that thou mightest know the certainty of those things, wherein thou hast been instructed.

§ 3. Gabriel announces to Zacharias the Birth of John.—*Jerusalem.*
St. Luke i. 5–25.

5 There was in the days of Herod, the king of Judæa, a certain priest named Zacharias, of the course of Abia: and his wife *was* of the daughters of Aaron,
6 and her name *was* Elizabeth. And they were both righteous before God, walking in all the commandments and ordinances of the Lord blameless.
7 And they had no child, because that Elizabeth was barren, and they both
8 were *now* well stricken in years. And it came to pass, that while he executed
9 the priest's office before God in the order of his course, 'according to the custom of the priest's office, his lot was to burn incense when he went into
10 the temple of the Lord. And the whole multitude of the people were praying
11 without at the time of incense. And there appeared unto him an angel of
12 the Lord standing on the right side of the altar of incense. And when
13 Zacharias saw *him*, he was troubled, and fear fell upon him. But the angel said unto him, Fear not, Zacharias: for thy prayer is heard; and thy wife
14 Elizabeth shall bear thee a son, and thou shalt call his name John. And
15 thou shalt have joy and gladness; and many shall rejoice at his birth. For he shall be great in the sight of the Lord, and shall drink neither wine nor strong drink; and he shall be filled with the Holy Ghost, even from his
16 mother's womb. And many of the children of Israel shall he turn to the
17 Lord their God. And he shall go before him in the spirit and power of Elias, to turn the hearts of the fathers to the children, and the disobedient to the
18 wisdom of the just; to make ready a people prepared for the Lord. And Zacharias said unto the angel, Whereby shall I know this? for I am an old
19 man, and my wife well stricken in years. And the angel answering said unto him, I am Gabriel, that stand in the presence of God; and am sent to speak
20 unto thee, and to shew thee these glad tidings. And, behold! thou shalt be dumb, and not able to speak, until the day that these things shall be performed, because thou believest not my words, which shall be fulfilled in their season.
21 And the people waited for Zacharias, and marvelled that he tarried so long
22 in the temple. And when he came out, he could not speak unto them: and they perceived that he had seen a vision in the temple; for he beckoned unto them, and remained speechless.
23 And it came to pass, that, as soon as the days of his ministration were

---

§ 3. It has hitherto been found impracticable to determine the time of the service of Zacharias from the order of the courses of the priests. After their original appointment by David (1 Chron. xxiv. 7–18) and Solomon (2 Chron. viii. 14), the disorders of the times and consequent changes in those courses were so great, that it is impossible to rely upon such calculations.

ST. LUKE I.

24 accomplished, he departed to his own house. And after those days his wife
25 Elizabeth conceived, and hid herself five months, saying, 'Thus hath the Lord dealt with me in the days wherein he looked on *me*, to take away my reproach among men.

§ 4. Gabriel announces to the Virgin Mary the Conception and Birth of Jesus. *Nazareth.*

ST. LUKE I. 26–38.

26 And in the sixth month the angel Gabriel was sent from God unto a city
27 of Galilee, named Nazareth, 'to a virgin espoused to a man whose name was
28 Joseph, of the house of David; and the virgin's name *was* Mary. And the angel came in unto her, and said, Hail! *thou that art* highly favored, the Lord
29 *is* with thee.' And she was troubled at the² saying, and cast in her mind
30 what manner of salutation this should be. And the angel said unto her, Fear
31 not, Mary: for thou hast found favor with God. And, behold! thou shalt conceive in thy womb, and bring forth a son,ᵃ and shalt call his name JESUS.
32 He shall be great, and shall be called the Son of the Highest: and the Lord
33 God shall give unto him the throne of his father David: and he shall reign over the house of Jacob for ever; and of his kingdom there shall be no end.ᵇ
34 Then said Mary unto the angel, How shall this be, seeing I know not a man?
35 And the angel answered and said unto her, The Holy Ghost shall come upon thee, and the power of the Highest shall overshadow thee: therefore also that holy thing which shall be born of thee shall be called the Son of God.
36 And, behold! thy cousin Elizabeth, she hath also conceived a son in her old
37 age: and this is the sixth month with her, who was called barren. For with
38 God nothing shall be impossible. And Mary said, Behold the handmaid of the Lord; be it unto me according to thy word. And the angel departed from her.

§ 5. Mary visits Elizabeth. — *Hill Country of Judæa.*

ST. LUKE I. 39–56.

39 And Mary arose in those days, and went into the hill country with haste,
40 into a city of Juda; and entered into the house of Zacharias, and saluted
41 Elizabeth. And it came to pass, that, when Elizabeth heard the salutation of Mary, the babe leaped in her womb; and Elizabeth was filled with the Holy
42 Ghost: 'and she spake out with a loud cry,³ and said, Blessed *art* thou among
43 women! and blessed *is* the fruit of thy womb! 'and whence *is* this to me,
44 that the mother of my Lord should come to me? 'for lo! as soon as the voice of thy salutation sounded in mine ears, the babe leaped in my womb for joy.

¹ blessed art thou among women. And when she saw *him*,   ² at his saying,   ³ loud voice
  ᵃ Isa. vii. 14.   ᵇ Dan. ii. 44; Jno. xii. 34.

ST. LUKE I.

⁴⁵ And blessed *is* she that believed: for there shall be a performance of those ⁴⁶ things which were told her from the Lord. And Mary said,ᵃ

⁴⁷ My soul doth magnify the Lord,
And my spirit hath rejoiced in God my Saviour.
⁴⁸ For he hath regarded the low estate of his handmaiden:
For, behold! from henceforth all generations shall call me blessed.
⁴⁹ For he that is mighty hath done to me great things;
And holy *is* his name.
⁵⁰ And his mercy *is* on them that fear him
From generation to generation.
⁵¹ He hath shewed strength with his arm;
He hath scattered the proud in the imagination of their hearts.
⁵² He hath put down the mighty from *their* seats,
And exalted them of low degree.
⁵³ He hath filled the hungry with good things;
And the rich he hath sent empty away.
⁵⁴ He hath holpen his servant Israel,
In remembrance of *his* mercy,
⁵⁵ As he spake to our fathers,
To Abraham, and to his seed for ever.ᵇ

⁵⁶ And Mary abode with her about three months, and returned to her own house.

§ 6. Birth of John the Baptist. — *Hill Country of Judea.*
ST. LUKE I. 57–80.

⁵⁷ Now Elizabeth's full time came that she should be delivered; and she brought ⁵⁸ forth a son. And her neighbors and her cousins heard how the Lord had shewed great mercy upon her; and they rejoiced with her.

⁵⁹ And it came to pass, that on the eighth day they came to circumcise the ⁶⁰ child;ᶜ and they called him Zacharias, after the name of his father. And his ⁶¹ mother answered and said, Not *so;* but he shall be called John. And they ⁶² said unto her, There is none of thy kindred that is called by this name. And ⁶³ they made signs to his father, how he would have it¹ called. And he asked for a writing-table, and wrote, saying, His name is John. And they marvelled ⁶⁴ all. And his mouth was opened immediately, and his tongue *loosed,* and he ⁶⁵ spake, and praised God. And fear came on all that dwelt round about them; and all these sayings were noised abroad throughout all the hill country of ⁶⁶ Judæa. And all they that heard *them* laid *them* up in their hearts, saying, What manner of child shall this be! For truly² the hand of the Lord was ⁶⁷ with him. And his father Zacharias was filled with the Holy Ghost, and prophesied, saying,

¹ him   ² And
ᵃ Comp. 1 Sam. ii. 1.   ᵇ Gen. xxii. 16 etc.   ᶜ Gen. xvii. 12; Lev. xii. 3.

ST. LUKE I.

68 Blessed *be* the Lord God of Israel!
For he hath visited and redeemed his people.
69 And hath raised up an horn of salvation for us
In the house of his servant David,
70 (As he spake by the mouth of his holy prophets,
Which have been since the world began,)
71 That we should be saved from our enemies,
And from the hand of all that hate us;
72 To perform the mercy *promised* to our fathers,
And to remember his holy covenant;
73 The oath which he sware to our father Abraham,[a]
74 That he would grant unto us,
That we being delivered out of the hand of [1] enemies
Might serve him without fear,
75 In holiness and righteousness before him,
All our [2] days.
76 And thou also,[3] child,
Shalt be called the prophet of the Highest:
For thou shalt go before the face of the Lord to prepare his ways;[b]
77 To give knowledge of salvation unto his people
By the remission of their sins,
78 Through the tender mercy of our God;
Whereby the dayspring from on high hath visited us,
79 To give light to them that sit in darkness, and *in* the shadow of death,
To guide our feet into the way of peace.
80 And the child grew, and waxed strong in spirit, and was in the deserts till the day of his shewing unto Israel.

§ 7. *An Angel appears to Joseph in a dream.*—*Nazareth.*
ST. MATT. I. 18-25[a].

18 Now the birth of Jesus Christ was on this wise: When as his mother Mary was espoused to Joseph, before they came together, she was found with child
19 of the Holy Ghost. Then Joseph her husband, being a just *man*, and not
20 willing to make her an [4] example, was minded to put her away privily.[c] But while he thought on these things, behold! the angel of the Lord appeared unto him in a dream, saying, Joseph, thou son of David, fear not to take unto thee Mary thy wife: for that which is conceived in her is of the Holy Ghost.
21 And she shall bring forth a son, and thou shalt call his name JESUS; for he
22 shall save his people from their sins. (Now all this was done, that it might
23 be fulfilled which was spoken by [5] the Lord by the prophet, saying,[d] Behold!

---

[1] our enemies   [2] all the days of our life   [3] and thou, child   [4] a public example   [5] of
[a] Gen. xxii. 16, etc.   [b] Isa. xl. 3; Mal iii. 1.   [c] Deut. xxxiv. 1.   [d] Isa. vii. 14
" Behold! a virgin shall conceive, and bear a son, and shall call his name Immanuel.

ST. MATT. I.

a virgin shall be with child, and shall bring forth a son, and they shall call
24 his name Emmanuel, which being interpreted is, God with us.) Then Joseph
being raised from sleep did as the angel of the Lord had bidden him, and
25 took unto him his wife: And knew her not till she brought forth a son:[1]

§ 8. Jesus is born.—*Bethlehem.*

ST. MATT. I. 25.[b]	ST. LUKE II. 1–7.
	1 And it came to pass in those days, that there went out a decree from Cæsar Augustus, that 2 all the world should be taxed. (*And* this taxing was first made when Cyrenius was governor of 3 Syria.) And all went to be taxed, every one 4 into his own city. And Joseph also went up from Galilee, out of the city of Nazareth, into Judæa, unto the city of David, which is called Bethlehem; (because he was of the house and 5 lineage of David:) to be taxed with Mary his 6 espoused,[2] being great with child. And so it was, that, while they were there, the days were 7 accomplished that she should be delivered. And
—she brought forth a [1] son: and he called his name JESUS.	she brought forth her first-born son, and wrapped him in swaddling clothes, and laid him in a manger; because there was no room for them in the inn.

[1] had brought forth her first-born son   [2] espoused wife

§ 8. The question of the date of the birth of Christ cannot be here discussed. A large collection of authorities on the subject may be found in Jarvis's Introd. to the Hist. of the Ch. The most commonly accepted date is B C. 4, some scholars placing it a year or two earlier, others a little later. The present era was fixed by Dionysius Exiguus in the sixth century, was first used in history by Bede early in the eighth, and soon after introduced into public transactions by Pepin and Charlemagne.

Discussions have been almost endless also in regard to the time of the year of our Lord's birth; and the subject must be passed by with the same general reference. Meantime there seems no sufficient reason for giving up the date, Dec. 25th, so long and so generally observed, and which agrees well with such indications as we have of the time, even though it be now impossible to decide positively upon its accuracy on other than traditional grounds. It appears from St. Augustine that this day was observed in the West in his time as an ancient custom; and from St. Chrysostom — who glowingly advocates the accuracy of the date — that it was introduced into the East from the West about A.D. 376 and its observance spread rapidly and widely. Some evidence in its favor may be found collected in Selden's very learned work, "A Tract proving the Nativity of our Saviour to be on the 25th of December."

The clause in Luke ii. 2, "this taxing was first made," has also occasioned discussion. Suffice it here to say that *taxing* and *to be taxed* may, and probably must, mean *enrolment* with a view to taxation. See J. Von Gumpach's "The Gospel Narrative vindicated, or the Roman Census, Lk. ii. 1–5, explained, etc." (London: S. Bagster and Sons). He argues that by a colla-

§ 9. The Genealogies.

St. Matt. i. 1–17.	St. Luke iii. 23–38 (inverted).
1 The book of the generation of Jesus Christ, the son of David, the son of Abraham.	
	38 Of God, of Adam, of Seth, 37 of Enos, 'of Cainan, of Maleleel, of Jared, of Enoch, of 36 Mathusala,'of Lamech, of Noe, of Sem, of Arphaxad, of Cai- 35 nan, 'of Sala, of Heber, of Phalec, of Ragan, of Saruch, 34 'of Nahor, of Thara, of Abra-
2 Abraham begat Isaac; and Isaac begat Jacob; and Jacob begat Judas and his brethren; 3 'and Judas begat Phares and Zara of Thamar; and Phares begat Esrom; and Esrom begat 4 Aram; 'and Aram begat Aminadab; and Aminadab begat Naasson; and Naasson 5 begat Salmon; 'and Salmon begat Booz of Rachab; and Booz begat Obed of Ruth; 6 and Obed begat Jesse; 'and Jesse begat David the king. And David² begat Solomon of her *that* 7 *had been the wife* of Urias; and Solomon begat Roboam; and Roboam begat Abia; 8 and Abia begat Asa; 'and Asa begat Josaphat; and Josaphat begat Joram; and Joram	33 ham, of Isaac, of Jacob, 'of Juda, of Phares, of Esrom, of Arnei, of Admein,¹ of Aminadab, 32 'of Naasson, of Salmon, of Booz, of Obed, 31 of Jesse, of David,

¹ of Esrom, of Aram, of Aminadab. The ancient manuscripts vary very much from one another in the spelling of the names in these Genealogies; the spelling of the Authorized Version is here retained throughout. ² David the King

tion of several statements of ancient authors, the fact of such an enrolment at this very time is proved. He also notes that the census being Roman, yet carried into effect under Herod, was necessarily marked by both Roman and Jewish characteristics; the former in the registration of women and children, the latter in obliging each one to be registered "in his own city." Cyrenius, or as the name reads in the Latin records, Publius Sulpicius Quirinus, under whom St. Luke says the enrolment took place, was made governor of Syria after the banishment of Archelaus, in A.D. 6 (Joseph. Ant. xvii. [xv] 13, § 5; xviii. 1, § 1); thus apparently showing an anachronism of some ten years. The researches of Zumpt, however, have made it highly probable that Cyrenius was *twice* governor of Syria, and that his first governorship extended from about B.C. 4 to B.C. 1.

§ 9. For remarks on these Genealogies see Introductory note to Part I. pp. 1–4. An incidental advantage of the reversion of the order of St. Luke is that it allows of the omission of the words "which was the son" with each name. These are not contained in the Greek; and when omitted, it is easier to see the ground of that interpretation which considers the Evangelist as saying that "Jesus was (as was supposed) the son of Joseph; but really of Heli, of Melchi, of Janna, ... of God."

ST. MATT. I.

9 begat Ozias; ¹and Ozias begat Joatham; and Joatham begat Achaz; and Achaz begat
10 Ezekias; ¹and Ezekias begat Manasses; and Manasses begat Amon; and Amon begat
11 Josias; and Josias begat Jechonias and his brethren, about the time they were carried away to Babylon:
12 And after they were brought to Babylon, Jechonias begat Salathiel; and Salathiel begat
13 Zorobabel; ¹and Zorobabel begat Abiud; and Abiud begat Eliakim; and Eliakim
14 begat Azor; ¹and Azor begat Sadoc; and Sadoc begat Achim; and Achim begat Eliud;
15 ¹and Eliud begat Eleazar; and Eleazar begat
16 Matthan; and Matthan begat Jacob; ¹and Jacob begat Joseph the husband of Mary, of whom was born Jesus, who is called Christ.

17 So all the generations from Abraham to David *are* fourteen generations; and from David until the carrying away into Babylon *are* fourteen generations; and from the carrying away into Babylon unto Christ *are* fourteen generations.

ST. LUKE III.

of Nathan, of Mattatha, of
30 Menan, of Melea, ¹of Eliakim, of Jonan, of Joseph, of Juda,
29 of Simeon, ¹of Levi, of Matthat, of Jorim, of Eliezer, of Jose,
28 ¹of Er, of Elmodam, of Cosam,
27 of Addi, ¹of Melchi, of Neri, of Salathiel, of Zorobabel, of
26 Rhesa, of Joanna, ¹of Juda, of Joseph, of Semei, of Matta-
25 thias, of Maath, ¹of Nagge, of Esli, of Naum, of Amos, of
24 Mattathias, ¹of Joseph, of Janna, of Melchi, of Levi, of Mat-
23 that, of Heli. And Jesus himself began to be about thirty years of age, being (as was supposed) the son of Joseph, —

§ 10. An Angel announces the Birth to the Shepherds. — *Near Bethlehem.*
ST. LUKE II. 8–20.

8 And there were in the same country shepherds abiding in the field, keeping
9 watch over their flock by night. And¹ the angel of the Lord came upon them, and the glory of the Lord shone round about them: and they were sore

¹ and lo! the angel

ST. LUKE II.

10. afraid. And the angel said unto them, Fear not: for, behold! I bring you
11. good tidings of great joy, which shall be to all people. For unto you is born
12. this day in the city of David a Saviour, which is Christ the Lord. And this *shall be* a sign unto you; Ye shall find the babe wrapped in swaddling clothes,[1]
13. in a manger. And suddenly there was with the angel a multitude of the
14. heavenly host praising God, and saying, 'Glory to God in the highest, and on
15. earth peace to men of good will!'[2] And it came to pass, as the angels were gone away from them into heaven, the shepherds said one to another, Let us now go even unto Bethlehem, and see this thing which is come to pass, which
16. the Lord hath made known unto us. And they came with haste, and found
17. Mary, and Joseph, and the babe lying in a manger. And when they had seen *it* they made known abroad the saying which was told them concerning
18. this child. And all they that heard, wondered at those things which were
19. told them by the shepherds. But Mary kept all these things, and pondered
20. *them* in her heart. And the shepherds returned, glorifying and praising God for all the things that they had heard and seen, as it was told unto them.

§ 11. The Circumcision and Presentation in the Temple.—*Bethlehem and Jerusalem.*

St. Luke ii. 21-38.

21. And when eight days were accomplished for the circumcising of him,[3] his name was called JESUS, which was so named of the angel before he was conceived in the womb.
22. And when the days of their[4] purification according to the law of Moses [a] were accomplished, they brought him to Jerusalem, to present *him* to the Lord;
23. (as it is written in the law of the Lord,[b] Every male that openeth the womb
24. shall be called holy to the Lord;) and to offer a sacrifice according to that which is said in the law of the Lord,[c] A pair of turtledoves, or two young
25. pigeons. And, behold! there was a man in Jerusalem, whose name *was* Simeon; and the same man *was* just and devout, waiting for the consolation
26. of Israel: and the Holy Ghost was upon him. And it was revealed unto him by the Holy Ghost, that he should not see death, before he had seen the
27. Lord's Christ. And he came by the Spirit into the temple: and when the parents brought in the child Jesus, to do for him after the custom of the law,
28. Then took he him up in his arms, and blessed God, and said,

---

[1] lying in a manger.   [2] good will toward men.   [3] the child.   [4] her

§ 11. See Gal. iv. 4.   [a] Lev. xii. 4-6. She shall then continue in the blood of her purifying three and thirty days ..... and when the days of her purifying are fulfilled .....
[b] Ex. xiii. 2. Sanctify unto me all the first-born, whatsoever openeth the womb among the children of Israel, *both* of man and of beast; it is mine. See ver. 12, etc.; xxxiv. 19; Num iii. 12, 13; viii. 16, 17, etc.   [c] Lev. xii. 8. If she be not able to bring a lamb, then she shall bring two turtles, or two young pigeons.

ST. LUKE II.

29 Lord! now lettest thou thy servant depart
In peace, according to thy word:
30 For mine eyes have seen thy salvation,
31 Which thou hast prepared before the face of all people;
32 A light to lighten the Gentiles,[a]
And the glory of thy people Israel.

33 And his father[1] and his mother marvelled at those things which were
34 spoken of him. And Simeon blessed them, and said unto Mary his mother, Behold! this *child* is set for the fall and rising again of many in Israel; and
35 for a sign which shall be spoken against, '(yea, a sword shall pierce through thy own soul also,) that the thoughts of many hearts may be revealed.

36 And there was one Anna, a prophetess, the daughter of Phanuel, of the tribe of Aser: she was of a great age, and had lived with an husband seven
37 years from her virginity; and she *was* a widow of about fourscore and four years, which departed not from the temple, but served *God* with fastings and
38 prayers night and day. And she coming in that instant gave thanks likewise unto God[2] and spake of him to all them that looked for the redemption of[3] Jerusalem.

§ 12. Visit of the Magi. — *Jerusalem, Bethlehem.*
ST. MATT. II. 1–12.

1 Now when Jesus was born in Bethlehem of Judæa in the days of Herod
2 the king, behold! there came wise men from the east to Jerusalem, 'saying, Where is he that is born King of the Jews? for we have seen his star[b] in the
3 east, and are come to worship him. When Herod the king had heard *these*
4 *things*, he was troubled, and all Jerusalem with him. And when he had gathered all the chief priests and scribes of the people together, he demanded
5 of them where Christ should be born. And they said unto him, In Bethlehem
6 of Judæa: for thus it is written by the prophet,[c] 'And thou Bethlehem, *in* the land of Juda, art not the least among the princes of Juda: for out of thee
7 shall come a Governor, that shall rule my people Israel. Then Herod, when he had privily called the wise men, enquired of them diligently what time the

[1] Joseph and his mother   [2] the Lord   [3] for redemption in

[a] See Isa. xlix. 6; Acts xiii. 47.   [b] See Num. xxiv. 17.   [c] Micah v 2. Thou, Bethlehem Ephratah! (*though* thou be little among the thousands of Judah) *yet* out of thee shall he come forth unto me, *that is*, to be ruler in Israel.

---

§ 12. The presentation (§ 11) is placed before the visit of the Magi, because it could hardly have taken place after the events connected with that visit. St. Luke passes over all that occurred between the presentation and the return to Nazareth; but it would be an excessive precision which should consider '*when*' in v. 39 as precluding those occurrences. As Bethlehem was but a couple of hours walk from Jerusalem, a departure from the one is much the same as from the other in view of a more distant journey. A comparison of both narratives is very necessary to a full knowledge of the events. Each is the complement of the other.

ST. MATT. II.

8 star appeared. And he sent them to Bethlehem, and said, Go and search diligently for the young child; and when ye have found *him*, bring me word 9 again, that I may come and worship him also. When they had heard the king, they departed; and, lo! the star, which they saw in the east, went 10 before them, till it came and stood over where the young child was. When 11 they saw the star, they rejoiced with exceeding great joy. And when they were come into the house, they saw the young child with Mary his mother, and fell down, and worshipped him: and when they had opened their treasures, 12 they presented unto him gifts; gold, and frankincense, and myrrh. And being warned of God in a dream that they should not return to Herod, they departed into their own country another way.

§ 13. The Flight into Egypt: Herod's Cruelty.
St. Matt. ii. 13–18.

13 And when they were departed, behold! the angel of the Lord appeareth to Joseph in a dream, saying, Arise, and take the young child and his mother, and flee into Egypt, and be thou there until I bring thee word: for Herod 14 will seek the young child to destroy him. When he arose, he took the young 15 child and his mother by night, and departed into Egypt: and was there until the death of Herod: that it might be fulfilled which was spoken of the Lord by the prophet, saying, Out of Egypt have I called my Son.[a]

16 Then Herod, when he saw that he was mocked of the wise men, was exceeding wroth, and sent forth, and slew all the children that were in Bethlehem, and in all the coasts thereof, from two years old and under, according to the 17 time which he had diligently enquired of the wise men. Then was fulfilled 18 that which was spoken by Jeremy the prophet, saying,[b] In Rama was there a voice heard,[1] weeping, and great mourning: Rachel weeping *for* her children, and would not be comforted, because they are not.

§ 14. The Return, and Settlement at Nazareth.

St. Matt. ii. 19–23.	St. Luke ii. 39–40.
	39 And when they had performed all things according to the law of the Lord,
19 But when Herod was dead, behold! an angel of the Lord appeareth in a dream to 20 Joseph in Egypt. Saying, Arise, and take the young child and his mother, and go into	

---

[1] lamentation and weeping.

[a] Hos. xi. 1. When Israel *was* a child, then I loved him, and called my son out of Egypt.

[b] Jer. xxxi. 15. Thus saith the Lord; A voice was heard in Ramah, lamentation, *and* bitter weeping; Rachel weeping for her children refused to be comforted for her children, because they *were* not.

ST. MATT. II.	ST. LUKE II.
the land of Israel; for they are dead which ²¹ sought the young child's life. And he arose, and took the young child and his mother, ²² and came into the land of Israel. But when he heard that Archelaus did reign in Judæa in the room of his father Herod, he was afraid to go thither: and¹ being warned of God in a dream, he turned aside into the parts of Gali-²³ lee: and he came and dwelt in a city called Nazareth: that it might be fulfilled which was spoken by the prophets,ᵃ He shall be called a Nazarene.	they returned into Galilee, to their own city Nazareth. ⁴⁰ And the child grew, and waxed strong,² filled with wisdom: and the grace of God was upon him.

§ 15. Jesus in the Temple when Twelve Years old.

St. Luke ii. 41–52.

⁴¹ Now his parents went to Jerusalem every year at the feast of the passover. ⁴² And when he was twelve years old, they went up³ after the custom of the ⁴³ feast. And when they had fulfilled the days, as they returned, the child ⁴⁴ Jesus tarried behind in Jerusalem; and his parents⁴ knew not *of it*. But they, supposing him to have been in the company, went a day's journey; and they ⁴⁵ sought him among *their* kinsfolk and acquaintance. And when they found *him*⁵ not, they turned back again to Jerusalem, seeking him.

⁴⁶ And it came to pass, that after three days they found him in the temple, sitting in the midst of the doctors, both hearing them, and asking them questions. ⁴⁷ And all that heard him were astonished at his understanding and answers. ⁴⁸ And when they saw him, they were amazed: and his mother said unto him, Son, why hast thou thus dealt with us? behold! thy father and I have sought ⁴⁹ thee sorrowing. And he said unto them, How is it that ye sought me? ⁵⁰ wist ye not that I must be about my Father's business? And they understood ⁵¹ not the saying which he spake unto them. And he went down with them, and came to Nazareth, and was subject unto them; but his mother kept all these sayings in her heart.

⁵² And Jesus increased in wisdom and stature, and in favor with God and man.

¹ notwithstanding ² strong in spirit. ³ went up to Jerusalem
⁴ Joseph and his mother ⁵ him

ᵃ See Isa. liii. 1, 2, etc.

PART II.

FROM THE BEGINNING OF JOHN THE BAPTIST'S MINISTRY TO OUR LORD'S FIRST PASSOVER.

§ 16. The Ministry of John the Baptist. — *The Desert. The Jordan.*

St. Matt. iii. 1–12.	St. Mark. i. 1–8.	St. Luke iii. 1–18.
	1 The beginning of the gospel of Jesus Christ.¹	
		1 Now in the fifteenth year of the reign of Tiberius Cæsar, (Pontius Pilate being governor of Judæa, and Herod being tetrarch of Galilee, and his brother Philip tetrarch of Ituræa and of the region of Trachonitis, and Lysanias the tetrarch of Abilene, Annas being the high priest, and Caiaphas,²) the word of God came unto John the son of Zacharias in the wilderness.
1 In those days came John the Baptist, preaching in the wilderness of Judæa, saying,³ Repent ye: for the kingdom of heaven	4 John did baptize in the wilderness, and preach the baptism of repentance for the remission of sins; as it is written in Esaias⁴	3 And he came into all the country about Jordan, preaching the baptism of repentance for the remission of sins: 4 as it is written in the

¹ Christ, the Son of God   ² Annas and Caiaphas being the high priests
³ and, saying,   ⁴ in the prophets

§ 16. For the time of the beginning of John's ministry reference must again be made to the numerous works which treat of the subject. It is placed by Jarvis and others in September, A.D. 24.

ST. MATT. III.	ST. MARK I.	ST. LUKE III.
3 is at hand! For this is he that was spoken of by the prophet Esaias, saying,[b] The voice of one crying in the wilderness, Prepare ye the way of the Lord! make his paths straight!	the prophet, Behold! I send my messenger[a] before thy face, which shall prepare thy way.[2] 3 [b]The voice of one crying in the wilderness, Prepare ye the way of the Lord! make his paths straight!	book of the words of Esaias the prophet,[1] [b]The voice of one crying in the wilderness, Prepare ye the way of the Lord! make his paths straight! 5 Every valley shall be filled, and every mountain and hill shall be brought low; and the crooked shall be made straight, and the rough ways *shall be* made 6 smooth; And all flesh shall see the salvation of God.
4 And the same John had his raiment of camel's hair, and a leathern girdle about his loins;[c] and his meat was locusts and wild honey. 5 Then went out to him Jerusalem and all Judæa, and all the region round about 6 Jordan, and were baptized of him in the river[4] Jordan, confess-7 ing their sins. But when he saw many of the Pharisees and Sadducees come to the[5] baptism, he said unto	6 And John was clothed with camel's hair, and with a girdle of a skin about his loins;[c] and he did eat locusts and wild honey. 5 And there went out unto him all the land of Judæa, and all[3] they of Jerusalem, and were baptized of him in the river Jordan, confessing their sins.	7 Then said he to the multitude that came forth to be baptized of him, O

[1] the prophet, saying,   [2] thy way before thee
[3] and they of Jerusalem, and were all baptized   [4] in Jordan   [5] to his baptism
[a] Mal. iii. 1 (Cf. Matt. xi. 10; Lk. vii. 27). Behold! I will send my messenger, and he shall prepare the way before me.
[b] Isa. xl. 3–5 (Cf. Jno. i. 23). The voice of him that crieth in the wilderness, prepare ye the way of the Lord; make straight in the desert a highway for our God! Every valley shall be exalted, and every mountain and hill shall be made low: and the crooked shall be made straight, and the rough places plain: and the glory of the Lord shall be revealed, and all flesh shall see it together. Cf. Acts xiii. 24; xix. 4.   [c] Cf. 2 Kings i. 8.

ST. MATT. III.	ST. MARK I.	ST. LUKE III.
them, O generation of vipers! who hath warned you to flee from the wrath to 8 come? Bring forth therefore fruit[1] meet 9 for repentance: and think not to say within yourselves, We have Abraham to *our* father: for I say unto you, that God is able of these stones to raise up children unto Abra-10 ham. And now[2] the axe is laid unto the root of the trees; therefore every tree which bringeth not forth good fruit is hewn down, and cast into the fire.		generation of vipers! who hath warned you to flee from the wrath to come? 8 Bring forth therefore fruits worthy of repentance, and begin not to say within yourselves, We have Abraham to *our* father; for I say unto you, That God is able of these stones to raise up children unto 9 Abraham. And now also the axe is laid unto the root of the trees; every tree therefore which bringeth not forth good fruit is hewn down and cast into the fire. 10 And the people asked him, saying, What shall 11 we do then? He answereth and saith unto them, He that hath two coats, let him impart to him that hath none; and he that hath meat, let 12 him do likewise. Then came also publicans to be baptized, and said unto him, Master, what shall 13 we do? And he said unto them, Exact no more than that which is 14 appointed you. And the soldiers likewise demanded of him, saying, And what shall we do?

[1] fruits   [2] And now also

ST. MATT. III.	ST. MARK I.	ST. LUKE III.
		And he said unto them, Do violence to no man, accuse none[1] falsely; and be content with your wages.
		15 And as the people were in expectation, and all men mused in their hearts of John, whether he were the Christ, or not; 16 John answered, saying unto *them* all, I indeed baptize you with water; but One mightier than I cometh, the latchet of whose shoes I am not worthy to unloose: he shall baptize you with the Holy Ghost and with fire:
11 I indeed baptize you with water unto repentance; but he that cometh after me is mightier than I, whose shoes I am not worthy to bear: he shall baptize you with the Holy Ghost, and *with* fire;	7 And preached, saying, There cometh One mightier than I after me, the latchet of whose shoes I am not worthy to stoop down and 8 unloose. I[2] have baptized you with water: but he shall baptize you with the Holy Ghost.	
12 Whose fan *is* in his hand, and he will throughly purge his floor, and gather his wheat into the garner; but he will burn up the chaff with unquenchable fire.		17 Whose fan *is* in his hand, to[3] throughly purge his floor and to gather the wheat into his garner: but the chaff he will burn with fire unquenchable.
		18 And many other things in his exhortation preached he unto the people.

§ 17. The Baptism of our Lord. — *The Jordan.*

St. Matt. iii. 13–17.	St. Mark i. 9–11.	St. Luke iii. 21–23.
13 Then cometh Jesus from Galilee to Jordan	9 And it came to pass in those days, that Jesus came from Nazareth of	21 Now when all the people were baptized, it came

[1] neither accuse *any* falsely
[2] I indeed have baptized
[3] and he will throughly purge his floor, and will gather

---

§ 17. There is a difference of opinion as to the time of our Lord's baptism. All probabilities concur in pointing to the early part of January. That there is no difficulty from the tempe-

ST. MATT. III.	ST. MARK I.	ST. LUKE III.
unto John, to be baptized of him. But he[1] forbad him, saying, I have need to be baptized of thee, and comest thou to me! And Jesus answering said unto him, Suffer *it to be so* now: for thus it becometh us to fulfil all righteousness. Then he suffered him. And Jesus, when he was baptized, went up straightway out of the water; and, lo! the heavens were opened,[2] and he saw the Spirit of God descending like a dove,[3] lighting upon him; and lo! a voice from heaven, saying, This is my beloved Son, in whom I am well pleased.	Galilee, and was baptized of John in Jordan. And straightway coming up out of the water, he saw the heavens opened, and the Spirit like a dove descending unto[4] him: and[5] a voice from heaven, *saying*, Thou art my beloved Son, in thee[6] I am well pleased.	to pass, that Jesus also being baptized, and praying, the heaven was opened, and the Holy Ghost descended in a bodily shape like a dove upon him, and a voice came from heaven,[7] Thou art my beloved Son; in thee I am well pleased.

Verse numbers: Matt. 14, 15, 16, 17; Mark 10, 11; Luke 22.

[1] but John forbad [2] were opened unto him [3] and lighting [4] upon
[5] and there came a voice [6] in whom [7] from heaven, which said, Thou art

---

rature of the air and the water at that season, is abundantly shown by Andrews, Life of our Lord, pp. 33–35 (4th ed.). The traditional day (January 6th) seems quite as likely as any other suggested. The difference in the record of the words pronounced by the heavenly voice in Matt. iii. 17, as compared with the parallel places, seems almost too slight to require notice. It is, however, made the occasion, by Robinson, for the following excellent note which is quoted from his Harmony (p. 187): "A like difference is seen in the four copies of the title on the cross, Matt. xxvii. 37; Mar. xv. 26; Lk. xxiii. 38; Jno. xix. 19. And still more, in the solemn words of our Lord at the institution of the cup, Matt. xxvi. 28; Mar. xiv. 24; Lk. xxii. 20; 1 Cor. xi. 25. Similar varieties of expression in the different reports of the same language are found in the following passages, as well as very many others: Matt. iii. 11 = Mar. i. 7 = Lk. iii. 16 = Jno. i. 27. Matt. ix 11 = Mar. v. 16 = Lk v. 30. Matt xv. 27 = Mar. vii. 28. Matt. xvi. 6–9 = Mar. viii. 17–19. Matt. xx. 33 = Mar. x. 51 = Lk. xviii. 41. Matt. xxi. 9 = Mar. xi. 9 = Lk. xix. 38. Matt. xxvi. 39 = Mar. xiv. 36 = Lk. xxii. 42. Matt. xxviii. 5, 6 = Mar. xvi. 6 = Lk. xxiv. 5, 6. All these examples go only to show that when the Evangelists profess to record the expressions used by our Lord and others, they usually give them according to the *sense*, and not according to the letter. As Le Clerc expresses it: 'The Apostles seek rather to express the sense than the words.' Harm. p. 518." Of course some allowance is to be made for the transfer of the original expressions into Greek; but an examination of the above passages abundantly shows that this alone will not fully explain the facts.

§ 18. The Temptation. — *Desert of Judæa.*

St. Matt. iv. 1–11.	St. Mark i. 12, 13.	St. Luke iv. 1–13.
1 Then was Jesus led up of the Spirit into the wilderness to be tempted of the devil. 2 And when he had fasted forty days and forty nights, he was afterward an hungered.	12 And immediately the Spirit driveth him into 13 the wilderness. And he was in[1] the wilderness forty days, tempted of Satan: and was with the wild beasts;	1 And Jesus being full of the Holy Ghost returned from Jordan, and was led by the Spirit into the 2 wilderness, being forty days tempted of the devil. And in those days he did eat nothing: and when they were ended, he[2]
3 And when the tempter came to him, he said, If thou be the Son of God, command that these stones be made 4 bread. But he answered and said, It is written,[a] Man shall not live by bread alone, but by every word that proceedeth out of the mouth of God.		3 hungered. And the devil said unto him, If thou be the Son of God, command this stone, that it be made bread. 4 And Jesus answered him,[3] *It is written, That man shall not live by bread alone.[4]
5 Then the devil taketh him up into the holy city, and set[5] him on a pinnacle of the 6 temple, and saith unto him, If thou be the Son of God cast thyself down: for it is written.[b] He shall give his angels charge concerning thee: and in		9 And he brought him to Jerusalem, and set him on a pinnacle of the temple, and said unto him, If thou be the Son of God, cast thyself down 10 from hence: for it is written,[b] He shall give his angels charge over thee, to keep thee:

[1] was there in the wilderness   [2] he afterward hungered   [3] saying, It is written
[4] by bread alone, but by every word of God.   [5] setteth

[a] Deut. viii. 3. Man doth not live by bread only, but by every word that proceedeth out of the mouth of the Lord doth man live.
[b] Ps. xci. 11. For he shall give his angels charge over thee, to keep thee in all thy ways.

---

§ 18. The occurrence of the temptation immediately after the baptism seems indicated by the narrative, Jno. i. 29–44, as well as by the 'immediately' of St. Mark. The difference in the order of the temptations in St. Matthew and St. Luke is perhaps designed to show that these are but instances of the multitude of temptations with which our Lord was assailed.

ST. MATT. IV.	ST. MARK I.	ST. LUKE IV.
their hands they shall bear thee up, lest at any time thou dash thy foot against a stone.		11 and in *their* hands they shall bear thee up, lest at any time thou dash thy 12 foot against a stone. And Jesus answering said unto him, It is said,^a Thou shalt not tempt the Lord thy God.
7 Jesus said unto him, It is written again,^a Thou shalt not tempt the Lord thy God.		
8 Again, the devil taketh him up into an exceeding high mountain, and sheweth him all the kingdoms of the world, and the glory 9 of them; and said² unto him, All these things will I give thee, if thou wilt fall down 10 and worship me. Then saith Jesus unto him, Get thee hence, Satan:		5 And the devil taking him up,¹ shewed unto him all the kingdoms of the world in a moment 6 of time. And the devil said unto him, All this power will I give thee: and the glory of them, for that is delivered unto me, and to whomsoever I will I give it. 7 If thou therefore wilt worship me, all shall be 8 thine. And Jesus answered and said unto him,³ It is written,^b Thou
for it is written,^b Thou shalt worship the Lord thy God, and him only 11 shalt thou serve. Then the devil leaveth him,		shalt worship the Lord thy God, and him only 13 shalt thou serve. And when the devil had ended all the temptation, he departed from him for a season.
and, behold! angels came and ministered unto him.	and the angels ministered unto him.	

§ 19. Testimony of John the Baptist. — *Bethany beyond Jordan.*

ST. JOHN I. 19–34.

19 And this is the record of John, when the Jews sent priests and Levites from
20 Jerusalem to ask him, Who art thou? And he confessed, and denied not;

---

¹ taking him up into an high mountain   ² saith
³ Get thee behind me, Satan! for it is written

^a Deut. vi. 16. Ye shall not tempt the LORD your God.
^b Deut. vi. 13. Thou shalt fear the LORD thy God, and serve him, and shalt swear by his name. Cf. x. 20.

ST. JOHN I.

21 but confessed, I am not the Christ. And they asked him, What then? Art thou Elias? ¹He saith, I am not. Art thou that* prophet? And he an-
22 swered, No. Then said they unto him, Who art thou? that we may give an
23 answer to them that sent us. What sayest thou of thyself? He said, I am the voice of one crying in the wilderness, Make straight the way of the Lord,
24,25 as said the prophet Esaias.ᵇ And they² were sent of the Pharisees. And they asked him, and said unto him, Why baptizest thou then, if thou be not
26 that Christ, nor Elias, neither that prophet? John answered them, saying, I baptize with water: but there standeth one among you, whom ye know not;
27 who cometh after me,³ whose shoe's latchet I am not worthy to unloose.ᶜ
28 These things were done in Bethany⁴ beyond Jordan, where John was baptizing.
29 The next day he⁵ seeth Jesus coming unto him, and saith, Behold the Lamb
30 of God, which taketh away the sin of the world! This is he of whom I said, After me cometh a man which is preferred before me: for he was before me.
31 And I knew him not; but that he should be made manifest to Israel, therefore
32 am I come baptizing with water. And John bare record, saying, I saw the
33 Spirit descending from heaven like a dove, and it abode upon him. And I knew him not: but he that sent me to baptize with water, the same said unto me, Upon whom thou shalt see the Spirit descending, and remaining on him,
34 the same is he which baptizeth with the Holy Ghost. And I saw, and bare record that this is the Son of God.

§ 20. Interview of John's Disciples with our Lord. — *The Jordan.*

St. John i. 35–42.

35,36 Again the next day after John stood, and two of his disciples; and looking
37 upon Jesus as he walked, he saith, Behold the Lamb of God! The⁶ two disciples heard him speak, and they followed Jesus.
38 Jesus⁷ turned, and saw them following, and saith unto them, What seek ye? They said unto him, Rabbi, (which is to say, being interpreted, Master), where
39 dwellest thou? He saith unto them, Come and ye shall see.⁸ They came, therefore⁹ and saw where he dwelt, and abode with him that day: it¹⁰ was about
40 the tenth hour. One of the two which heard John *speak*, and followed him,
41 was Andrew, Simon Peter's brother. He first findeth his own brother Simon, and saith unto him, We have found the Messias, which is, being interpreted,

---

¹ and he saith ² they which were sent were
³ He it is, who coming after me, is preferred before me, whose shoe's ⁴ Bethabara
⁵ John ⁶ and the two ⁷ Then Jesus ⁸ Come and see ⁹ came and saw
¹⁰ for it was

ᵃ Cf. Lk. i. 17; Matt. xi. 14; xvii. 11–13. ᵇ Isa. xl. 3. ᶜ Cf. Acts xiii. 25.

---

§ 19. ver. 33. The Baptist's saying that he "knew not Jesus" must be taken, consistently with Matt. iii. 14 (§ 17), to mean that he did not *officially* know him, so that he could declare him to be the one whose way he had come to prepare.

ST. JOHN I.

42 Christ.[1] He[2] brought him to Jesus. When[3] Jesus beheld him, he said, Thou art Simon the son of John:[4] thou shalt be called Cephas, which is by interpretation, A stone.

§ 21. Jesus going into Galilee, takes with him Philip. Interview with Nathanael.

ST. JOHN I. 43–51.

43 The day following he[5] would go forth into Galilee, and findeth Philip, and
44 Jesus[6] saith unto him, Follow me. Now Philip was of Bethsaida, the city
45 of Andrew and Peter. Philip findeth Nathanael, and saith unto him, We have found him, of whom Moses in the law, and the prophets did write, Jesus of
46 Nazareth, the son of Joseph. Nathanael[7] said unto him, Can there any good thing come out of Nazareth? Philip saith unto him, Come and see!
47 Jesus saw Nathanael coming to him, and saith of him, Behold an Israelite
48 indeed, in whom is no guile! Nathanael saith unto him, Whence knowest thou me? Jesus answered and said unto him, Before that Philip called
49 thee, when thou wast under the fig tree, I saw thee. Nathanael answered
50 him,[8] Rabbi! thou art the Son of God; thou art the King of Israel. Jesus answered and said unto him, Because I said unto thee, I saw thee under the
51 fig tree, believest thou? thou shalt see greater things than these. And he saith unto him, Verily, verily, I say unto you,[9] ye shall see heaven open, and the angels of God ascending and descending upon the Son of Man.

§ 22. The Marriage at Cana, and Departure to Capernaum.

ST. JOHN II. 1–12.

1 And the third day there was a marriage in Cana of Galilee; and the mother
2 of Jesus was there: and both Jesus was called, and his disciples, to the mar-
3 riage. And[10] they had no wine, because the wine of the marriage was finished.
4 Then the mother of Jesus saith unto him, There[11] is no wine. Jesus saith unto her, Woman, what have I to do with thee? mine hour is not yet come.
5/6 His mother saith unto the servants, Whatsoever he saith unto you, do. And there were set there six waterpots of stone, after the manner of the purifying
7 of the Jews, containing two or three firkins apiece. Jesus saith unto them,
8 Fill the waterpots with water. And they filled them up to the brim. And he saith unto them, Draw out now, and bear unto the governor of the feast.

---

[1] the Christ [2] And he brought [3] and when
[4] Jona [5] Jesus would go [6] and saith unto him
[7] And Nathanael [8] answered and saith unto him [9] hereafter ye shall see
[10] And when they wanted wine, the mother of Jesus saith [11] They have no wine

---

§ 22. The *third day* may refer back to i. 44, as two days would suffice for the journey, which could not have been above fifty miles; or it may have reference to the time of his arrival in Galilee. "Cana, now *Kâna el-Jelîl*, was situated about seven miles north of Nazareth, and about three miles N. by E. of Sepphoris." See Robinson's Bibl. Res. in Palest. III. p. 204.

ST. JOHN II.

9 And they bare *it*. When the ruler of the feast had tasted the water that was made wine, and knew not whence it was: (but the servants which drew the
10 water knew;) the governor of the feast called the bridegroom, and saith unto him, Every man at the beginning doth set forth good wine; and when men have well drunk,[1] that which is worse; *but* thou hast kept the good wine
11 until now. This beginning of miracles did Jesus in Cana of Galilee, and manifested forth his glory; and his disciples believed on him.
12 After this he went down to Capernaum, he, and his mother, and his brethren, and his disciples: and they continued there not many days.

[1] then that which.

PART III.

OUR LORD'S FIRST PASSOVER AND THE EVENTS UNTIL HIS SECOND.

§ 23. At the Passover Jesus purifies the Temple. — *Jerusalem.*
ST. JOHN II. 13–25.

13 And the Jews' passover was at hand, and Jesus went up to Jerusalem,
14 and found in the temple those that sold oxen and sheep and doves, and the
15 changers of money sitting: And when he had made a scourge of small cords, he drove them all out of the temple, and the sheep, and the oxen; and poured
16 out the changer's money, and overthrew the tables; And said unto them that sold doves, Take these things hence! make not my Father's house an house
17 of merchandise. His[1] disciples remembered that it was written,[a] The zeal of thine house eateth me up.[2]
18 Then answered the Jews and said unto him, What sign shewest thou unto
19 us, seeing that thou doest these things? Jesus answered and said unto them,
20 Destroy this temple, and in three days I will raise it up. Then said the Jews, Forty and six years was this temple in building, and wilt thou rear it up in
21 three days? But he spake of the temple of his body. When therefore he
22 was risen from the dead, his disciples remembered that he had said this;[3] and they believed the scripture, and the word which Jesus had said.
23 Now when he was in Jerusalem at the passover, in the feast *day*, many
24 believed in his name, when they saw the miracles which he did. But Jesus
25 did not commit himself unto them, because he knew all *men*, And needed not that any should testify of man; for he knew what was in man.

[1] And his disciples   [2] hath eaten   [3] had said this unto them.
[a] Ps. lxix 9. The zeal of thine house hath eaten me up.

---

§ 23. In Matt. iv. 12; Mar. i. 14; Lk. iv. 14 (§ 26) it is said that Jesus *returned into Galilee*, implying a previous absence. This succeeds the account of the temptation, but evidently did not immediately follow it; for the two former Gospels say expressly that it was *after* the imprisonment of John the Baptist. Now St. John tells us (§ 19) that our Lord went into Galilee on the next day after the Baptist's public testimony to him. The Baptist, therefore, had not then been imprisoned, nor was he for some time afterwards. Cf. Jno. iii. 22–24; iv. 1–3. Hence the *return* mentioned by the other Evangelists refers to some subsequent return, and most probably to that from the Passover of Jno. ii. 13. Thus they imply the attendance at the Passover which St. John alone mentions.

In regard to the purification of the temple here mentioned and that recorded by the other

§ 24. Interview with Nicodemus. — *Jerusalem.*
St. John iii. 1–21.

1 There was a man of the Pharisees named Nicodemus, a ruler of the Jews:
2 The same came to him[1] by night, and said unto him, Rabbi, we know that thou art a teacher come from God: for no man can do these miracles that thou doest, except God be with him.
3 Jesus answered and said unto him, Verily, verily, I say unto thee, Except a man be born again, he cannot see the kingdom of God.
4 Nicodemus saith unto him, How can a man be born when he is old? can he
5 enter the second time into his mother's womb, and be born? Jesus answered, Verily, verily, I say unto thee, Except a man be born of water and *of* the
6 Spirit, he cannot enter into the kingdom of God. That which is born of the
7 flesh is flesh; and that which is born of the Spirit is spirit. Marvel not
8 that I said unto thee, Ye must be born again. The wind bloweth where it listeth, and thou hearest the sound thereof, but canst not tell whence it cometh, and whither it goeth: so is every one that is born of the Spirit.
9 Nicodemus answered and said unto him, How can these things be?
10 Jesus answered and said unto him, Art thou a master of Israel, and knowest
11 not these things? Verily, verily, I say unto thee, We speak that we do know,
12 and testify that we have seen; and ye receive not our witness. If I have told you earthly things, and ye believe not, how shall ye believe, if I tell you *of*
13 heavenly things? And no man hath ascended up to heaven, but he that came
14 down from heaven, *even* the Son of man which is in heaven. And as Moses lifted up the serpent in the wilderness,[a] even so must the Son of man be lifted
15,16 up: that whosoever believeth in him[2] should have eternal life. For God so loved the world, that he gave the[3] only begotten Son, that whosoever believeth
17 in him should not perish, but have everlasting life. For God sent not the[3] Son into the world to condemn the world; but that the world through him
18 might be saved. He that believeth on him is not condemned:[4] he that believeth not is condemned already, because he hath not believed in the name
19 of the only begotten Son of God. And this is the condemnation, that light is come into the world, and men loved darkness rather than light, because their

---

[1] came to Jesus   [2] should not perish, but have   [3] his   [4] but he that believeth
[a] See Num. xxi. 8, 9.

Evangelists (see § 114) it must now be considered as settled by common agreement that they refer to different events. The notes of time, in either case, are sufficiently definite, this being placed by St. John near the beginning, and that by the Synoptical Evangelists at the close, of our Lord's ministry. The distinguishing circumstances are somewhat different, and there is no improbability that there should have been occasion for the repetition of such an act after so long an interval, nor that it should have been repeated. That St. John should have mentioned only one, while the earlier Evangelists mention only the other, is a natural consequence of the supplementary character of his Gospel, for the most part forbearing to repeat what has been already told by them, and calling attention to such important incidents as they had left unnoticed.

St. John III.

20 deeds were evil. For every one that doeth evil hateth the light, neither 21 cometh to the light, lest his deeds should be reproved. But he that doeth truth cometh to the light, that his deeds may be made manifest, that they are wrought in God.

§ 25. Our Lord Baptizes in the Country of Judæa. Further Testimony of John, while still Baptizing.
St. John III. 22–36.

22 After these things came Jesus and his disciples into the land of Judæa; and 23 there he tarried with them and baptized. And John also was baptizing in Ænon near to Salim, because there was much water there: and they came 24 and were baptized. For John was not yet cast into prison.

25 Then there arose a question between *some* of John's disciples and a Jew[1] 26 about purifying. And they came unto John, and said unto him, Rabbi, he that was with thee beyond Jordan, to whom thou barest witness, behold! the 27 same baptizeth, and all *men* come to him. John answered and said, A man 28 can receive nothing except it be given him from heaven. Ye yourselves bear me witness, that I said, I am not the Christ, but that I am sent before 29 him. He that hath the bride is the bridegroom: but the friend of the bridegroom, which standeth and heareth him, rejoiceth greatly because of the 30 bridegroom's voice: this my joy therefore is fulfilled. He must increase, but 31 I *must* decrease. He that cometh from above is above all: he that is of the earth is earthly, and speaketh of the earth: he that cometh from heaven 32 testifieth[2] what he hath seen and heard, and no man receiveth his testimony. 33 He that hath received his testimony hath set to his seal that God is true. 34 For he whom God hath sent speaketh the words of God: for he[3] giveth not 35 the Spirit by measure *unto him*. The Father loveth the Son, and hath given 36 all things into his hand. He that believeth on the Son hath everlasting life: he[4] that believeth not the Son shall not see life; but the wrath of God abideth on him.

§ 26. (A) John the Baptist is seized.

St. Matt. xiv. 3–5.	St. Mark vi. 17–20.	St. Luke iii. 19, 20.
3 For Herod had laid hold on John, and	17 For Herod himself had sent forth and laid hold	19 But Herod the tetrarch, being reproved by him

---

[1] the Jews
[2] he that cometh from heaven is above all. And what he hath seen and heard, that he testifieth; and no man   [3] God giveth   [4] and he

§ 25. After the Passover Jesus went into the country and continued there until John was seized. Then he went through Samaria (§ 27) into Galilee (§ 28).

§ 26. The seizing of John the Baptist is mentioned by St. Mark as having taken place some time before. The account is placed here because of its parallelism with the other Evangelists; but, of course, this is not to be considered as any real exception to the accuracy of chronological sequence preserved throughout by St. Mark.

ST. MATT. XIV.	ST. MARK VI.	ST. LUKE III.
bound him, and put *him* in prison for Herodias' sake, his brother Philip's wife.	upon John, and bound him in prison for Herodias' sake, his brother Philip's wife: for he ¹⁸ had married her. For John had said unto Herod, It is not lawful for thee to have thy ¹⁹ brother's wife. Therefore Herodias had a quarrel against him, and would have killed him; but she could ²⁰ not: for Herod feared John, knowing that he was a just man and an holy, and observed him; and when he heard him, he hesitated much,² and heard him gladly.	for Herodias his brother's¹ wife, and for all the evils which Herod had done, added yet this ²⁰ above all, that he shut up John in prison.
⁴ For John said unto him, It is not lawful for thee to have her.		
⁵ And when he would have put him to death, he feared the multitude, because they counted him as a prophet.		

(B.) Our Lord afterwards departs into Galilee.

Matt. iv. 12.   Mar. i. 14.ᵃ   Lk. iv. 14.ᵃ   Jno. iv. 1–3.

			¹ When therefore Jesus³ knew how the Pharisees had heard that Jesus made and baptizedᵃ more disci-
¹² Now when he⁴ had heard that John was cast into prison, he departed into Galilee.	¹⁴ Now after that John was put in prison, Jesus came into Galilee,—	¹⁴ And Jesus returned in the power of the Spirit into Galilee:—	² ples than John, (though Jesus himself baptized not, ³ but his disciples,) he left Judæa, and departed again into Galilee.

§ 27. Discourse with the Woman of Samaria. Many Samaritans believe on him. — *Shechem*.

St. John iv. 4–42.

⁴⁄₅ And he must needs go through Samaria. Then cometh he to a city of Samaria, which is called Sychar, near to the parcel of ground that Jacob gave

---

ᵃ See iii. 22–26.

¹ his brother Philip's wife   ² did many things   ³ the Lord knew   ⁴ when Jesus

ST JOHN IV.

6 to his son Joseph.^a Now Jacob's well was there. Jesus therefore, being wearied with *his* journey, sat thus on the well: *and* it was about the sixth hour.
7 There cometh a woman of Samaria to draw water: Jesus saith unto her,
8 Give me to drink. (For his disciples were gone away unto the city to buy
9 meat.) Saith[1] the woman of Samaria unto him, How is it that thou, being a Jew, askest drink of me, which am a woman of Samaria?[2]
10 Jesus answered and said unto her, If thou knewest the gift of God, and who it is that saith to thee, Give me to drink; thou wouldest have asked of him,
11 and he would have given thee living water. The woman saith unto him, Sir, thou hast nothing to draw with, and the well is deep: from whence then hast
12 thou that living water? Art thou greater than our father Jacob, which gave us the well, and drank thereof himself, and his children, and his cattle?
13 Jesus answered and said unto her, Whosoever drinketh of this water shall
14 thirst again; but whosoever drinketh of the water that I shall give him shall never thirst; but the water that I shall give him shall be in him a well of
15 water springing up into everlasting life. The woman saith unto him, Sir, give me this water, that I thirst not, neither come hither to draw.
16/17 He[3] saith unto her, Go, call thy husband, and come hither. The woman answered and said, I have no husband.
18 Jesus said unto her, Thou hast well said, I have no husband: for thou hast had five husbands; and he whom thou now hast is not thy husband: in
19 that saidst thou truly. The woman saith unto him, Sir, I perceive that thou
20 art a prophet. Our fathers worshipped in this mountain: and ye say, that in Jerusalem is the place where men ought to worship.
21 Jesus saith unto her, Woman, believe me, the hour cometh, when ye shall
22 neither in this mountain, nor yet at Jerusalem, worship the Father. Ye worship ye know not what: we know what we worship: for salvation is of the
23 Jews. But the hour cometh, and now is, when the true worshippers shall worship the Father in spirit and in truth: for the Father seeketh such to
24 worship him. God *is* a spirit; and they that worship[4] must worship in spirit
25 and in truth. The woman saith unto him, I know that Messias cometh, (which is called Christ:) when he is come, he will tell us all things.
26/27 Jesus saith unto her, I that speak unto thee am *he*. And upon this came his disciples, and marvelled that he talked with the woman: yet no man said,
28 What seekest thou? or, Why talkest thou with her? The woman then left
29 her waterpot, and went her way into the city, and saith to the men, Come, see a man, which told me all things that ever I did: is not this the Christ?
30 They[5] went out of the city, and came unto him.
31/32 In the mean while his disciples prayed him, saying, Master, eat. But

---

^a See Gen. xlviii. 22; Josh. xvii. 14–18; xxiv. 32.

[1] Then saith   [2] a woman of Samaria? for the Jews have no dealings with the Samaritans.
[3] Jesus saith   [4] they that worship him must worship *him*   [5] Then they went

ST. JOHN IV.

33 he said unto them, I have meat to eat that ye know not of. Therefore said
34 the disciples one to another, Hath any man brought him *aught* to eat? Jesus saith unto them, My meat is to do the will of him that sent me, and to finish
35 his work. Say not ye, There are yet four months, and *then* cometh harvest? behold, I say unto you, Lift up your eyes, and look on the fields; for they
36 are white to harvest. Already[1] he that reapeth receiveth wages, and gathereth fruit unto life eternal; that both he that soweth and he that reapeth may
37 rejoice together. And herein is that saying true, One soweth, and another
38 reapeth. I sent you to reap that whereon ye bestowed no labor: other men labored, and ye are entered into their labors.
39 And many of the Samaritans of that city believed on him for the saying of
40 the woman, which testified, He told me all that ever I did. So when the Samaritans were come unto him, they besought him that he would tarry with
41 them: and he abode there two days. And many more believed because of
42 his own word; and said unto the woman, Now we believe, not because of thy saying: for we have heard *him* ourselves, and know that this is indeed[2] the Saviour of the world.

§ 28. Our Lord teaches publicly in Galilee.

MATT. IV. 17.	MAR. I. 14^b 15.	LK. IV. 14^b 15.	JNO. IV. 43–45.
12 (Now when Jesus had heard that John was cast into prison, he departed into Galilee.—) 17 From that time Jesus began to preach,	14 (Now after that John was put in prison, Jesus came into Galilee.—) Preaching the gospel[4] of God: 15 [5] The time is	14 (And Jesus returned in the power of the Spirit into Galilee.) And there went out a fame of him through	43 Now after two days he departed thence[3] into Galilee. 44 For Jesus himself testified,[a] that a prophet hath no honor in his own country. 45 Then when he was come into Galilee,

[1] they are white already to harvest. And he that reapeth
[2] is indeed the Christ, the Saviour
[3] departed thence, and went into
[4] of the kingdom of God
[5] and saying, the time is

[a] Matt. xiii. 57; Mar. vi. 4; Lk. iv. 24.

---

§ 27. ver. 35. This gives an important, though not very precise, indication of the time. The first-fruits of the harvest were by the law (Lev. xxiii. 5, 10, 11, etc.) to be offered on the morrow after the paschal Sabbath. This is said to refer to the barley harvest (Robinson, Bibl. Res. in Palest. II. p. 99 sq.), the wheat harvest being two or three weeks later. The reference here must be to the earlier harvest, *the* harvest, of which mention is made in Leviticus. Hence this journey, four months before, took place somewhere about the beginning of December. This gives a probable duration of a year and six months to the ministry of John before his imprisonment.

§ 28. On the parallelism of the three Synoptical Gospels with Jno. iv. 43–45 there is a difference of opinion, not without its bearing on the question of the length of our Lord's

ST. MATT. IV.	ST. MARK I.	ST. LUKE IV.	ST. JOHN IV.
and to say, Repent: for the kingdom of heaven is at hand.	fulfilled, and the kingdom of God is at hand! repent ye, and believe the gospel.	all the region round about. 5 And he taught in their synagogues, being glorified of all.	the Galilæans received him, having seen all the things that he did at Jerusalem at the feast: for they also went unto the feast.

§ 29. The healing of the Son of a Nobleman of Capernaum at Cana.
St. John IV. 46–54.

46 So he[1] came again into Cana of Galilee, where he made the water wine.[a]
[a] And there was a certain nobleman, whose son was sick at Capernaum.
47 When he heard that Jesus was come out of Judæa into Galilee, he went unto him and besought *him*[2] that he would come down, and heal his son: for he 48 was at the point of death. Then said Jesus unto him, Except ye see signs 49 and wonders, ye will not believe. The nobleman saith unto him, Sir, come 50 down ere my child die. Jesus saith unto him, Go thy way: thy son liveth. [3]The man believed the word that Jesus had spoken unto him, and he went 51 his way. And as he was now going down, the[4] servants met him, and told 52 *him*, that his[5] son liveth. Then enquired he of them the hour when he began to amend. And they said unto him, Yesterday at the seventh hour the fever 53 left him. So the father knew that *it was* at the same hour, in the which Jesus said unto him, Thy son liveth: and himself believed, and his whole 54 house. This *is* again the second miracle *that* Jesus did, when he was come out of Judæa into Galilee.

§ 30. Our Lord teaches at Nazareth, and is rejected.
St. Luke IV. 16–30.

16 And he came to Nazareth, where he had been brought up; and, as his custom was, he went into the synagogue on the sabbath day, and stood up for 17 to read. And there was delivered unto him the book of the prophet Esaias. And when he had opened the book, he found the place where it was written,

---

[1] So Jesus came   [2] him   [3] And the man   [4] his servant   [5] told *him*, saying, thy son
[a] Chap. ii. 1–11.

---

ministry. The arrangement of Robinson and Thomson is here followed, in opposition to that of Tischendorf, inasmuch as all the accounts seem to present this as the entrance, in Galilee, of our Lord upon his public work of preaching, and it seems more natural to place this before the miracle mentioned in § 29.

§ 30. This visit to Nazareth was before our Lord's taking up his abode at Capernaum (Matt. iv. 13; Lk. iv. 31). In Matt. xiii. 54–58; Mar. vi. 1–6 (§ 58) we have the record of a subsequent visit, and repeated rejection. It is very noticeable that this is the first record of any open opposition to our Lord, and occurred in the town in which he had been brought up. Hitherto, whatever dislike any had felt to his teaching, there had been no public manifestation of it.

ST. LUKE IV.

18 ^a"The Spirit of the Lord is upon me, because he hath anointed me to preach the gospel to the poor; he hath sent me¹ to preach deliverance to the captives, and recovering of sight to the blind, to set at liberty them that are bruised, 19 to preach the acceptable year of the Lord. And he closed the book, and he 20 gave it again to the minister, and sat down. And the eyes of all them that were in the synagogue were fastened on him.

21 And he began to say unto them, This day is this scripture fulfilled in your 22 ears. And all bare him witness, and wondered at the gracious words which 23 proceeded out of his mouth. And they said, Is not this Joseph's son? And he said unto them, Ye will surely say unto me this proverb, Physician, heal thyself: whatsoever we have heard done in Capernaum, do also here in thy 24 country. And he said, Verily I say unto you, No prophet is accepted in his 25 own country. But I tell you of a truth, many widows were in Israel in the days of Elias, when the heaven was shut up three years and six months,^b when 26 great famine was throughout all the land; but unto none of them was Elias sent, save unto Sarepta,^c a city of Sidon, unto a woman that was a widow. 27 And many lepers were in Israel in the time of Eliseus the prophet; and none 28 of them was cleansed, saving^d Naaman the Syrian. And all they in the syn- 29 agogue, when they heard these things, were filled with wrath, and rose up, and thrust him out of the city, and led him unto the brow of the hill whereon 30 their city was built, that they might cast him down headlong. But he passing through the midst of them went his way.^e

§ 31. Leaving Nazareth, he fixes his Abode at Capernaum.

ST. MATT. IV. 13–16.	ST. LUKE IV. 31.
13 And leaving Nazareth, he came and dwelt in Capernaum, which is upon the sea coast, in the borders 14 of Zabulon and Nephthalim: that it might be fulfilled which was spoken by Esaias the prophet, 15 saying, ^fThe land of Zabulon, and the land of Nephthalim (by the way of the sea beyond Jordan, 16 Galilee of the Gentiles;) the people which sat in darkness saw great light: and to them which sat in the region and shadow of death light is sprung up.	31 And came down to Capernaum, a city of Galilee, —

¹ hath sent me to heal the broken-hearted, to preach

^a Isa. lxi. 1, 2 (Comp. lviii. 6.) The Spirit of the Lord God is upon me; because the Lord hath anointed me to preach good tidings unto the meek; he hath sent me to bind up the broken-hearted, to proclaim liberty to the captives, and the opening of the prison to them that are bound; to proclaim the acceptable year of the Lord.

^b 1 Kings xvii. 1.
^c 1 Kings xvii. 9.
^d 2 Kings v.
^e Comp. Jno. viii. 59; x. 39.
^f Isa. ix. 1, 2. Nevertheless the dimness shall not be such as was in her vexation, when at the

§ 32. The Call of Peter and Andrew, of James and John, with the miraculous Draught of Fishes. — *Near Capernaum.*

St. Matt. iv. 18–22.   St. Mark i. 16–20.   St. Luke v. 1–11.

1 And it came to pass, that, as the people pressed upon him to hear the word of God, he stood by the lake of Gennesaret, 2 and saw two ships standing by the lake: but the fisherman were gone out of them, and were washing 3 *their* nets. And he entered into one of the ships, which was Simon's,[a] and prayed him that he would thrust out a little from the land. And he sat down in the ship,[1] and taught the people.

[1] he sat down, and taught the people out of the ship

first he lightly afflicted the land of Zebulon and the land of Naphtali, and afterwards did more grievously afflict *her by* the way of the sea, beyond Jordan, in Galilee of the nations. The people that walked in darkness — have seen a great light: they that dwell in the land of the shadow of death — upon them hath the light shined.

[a] Jno. i. 40–44.

---

§ 32. How long subsequent this primary call of the four apostles was to the interview with three of them mentioned in Jno. i. 40–42, it would be difficult to determine with precision, as well as how long it preceded the final definite choice of the twelve from among the whole number of the disciples (Matt. x. 2–4; Mar. iii. 13–19; vi. 12–19), because data are wanting for the exact determination of the time of the events in this section. It is evident, however, that this was not our Lord's first meeting with these disciples, and it may very naturally have happened that they had had many other interviews with him besides the one recorded by St. John.

There must probably have been a peculiar intimacy between those thus for a time associated with Jesus before others were called (with which also their natural relationship to each other harmonized) and a peculiar relation to their Lord. Accordingly it is found in many of the subsequent events that three of them, Peter, James, and John, were singled out from among the rest of the Apostles to stand especially near to Jesus.

On the differences in this narrative between St. Luke and the other Evangelists, the remark here quoted by Robinson from Spanheim (Dubia Evang. Tom. III. Dub. 72. vii.) is excellent: "The things related by St. Luke are not denied by St. Matthew, but only passed over. Nothing indeed is more common than that what is passed over by one, is supplied by another; lest, either the sacred writers should seem to have written by agreement, or the readers should cling to one of them, the others being despised."

ST. MATT. IV.	ST. MARK I.	ST. LUKE V.

4 Now when he had left speaking, he said unto Simon, Launch out into the deep, and let down your nets for a draught. 5 And Simon answering said, [1] Master, we have toiled all the night, and have taken nothing; nevertheless at thy word I will let down the nets.[2] 6 And when they had this done, they inclosed a great multitude of fishes: and their nets were breaking.[3] 7 And they beckoned unto *their* partners[4] in the other ship, that they should come and help them. And they came, and filled both the ships, so that they began to sink. 8 When Simon Peter saw *it*, he fell down at Jesus' knees, saying, Depart from me; for I am a sinful man, O Lord! 9 For he was astonished, and all that were with him, at the draught of the fishes which they had taken: 10 and so *was* also James, and John, the sons of Zebedee, which were partners with Simon.

18 And[5] walking by the sea of Galilee, he saw two brethren, Simon called Peter,[a] and Andrew his broth-	16 Now as he went along by the sea of Galilee, he saw Simon and the brother of Simon[7] Andrew, casting about	

[1] said unto him   [2] net   [3] their net brake   [4] which were in the
[5] And Jesus, walking ..... saw   [6] as he walked by   [7] Andrew his brother
[a] Comp. Jno. i. 40–42.

ST. MATT. IV.	ST. MARK I.	ST. LUKE V.
er, casting a net into the sea: for they were ¹⁹ fishers. And he saith unto them, Follow me, and I will make you ²⁰ fishers of men. And they straightway left *their* nets, and fol- ²¹ lowed him. And going on from thence, he saw other two brethen, James *the son* of Zebedee, and John his brother, in a ship with Zebedee their father, mending their nets; and he called them. ²² And they immediately left the ship and their father, and followed him.	*nets* in¹ the sea: for ¹⁷ they were fishers. And Jesus said unto them, Come ye after me, and I will make you to become fishers of ¹⁸ men. And straightway they forsook the ² nets, and followed him. ¹⁹ And when he had gone a little farther,³ he saw James the *son* of Zebedee, and John his brother, who also were in the ship mending ²⁰ their nets. And straightway he called them; and they left their father Zebedee in the ship with the hired servants, and went after him.	And Jesus said unto Simon, Fear not; from henceforth thou shalt catch men. ¹¹ And when they had brought their ships to land, they forsook all, and followed him.

§ 33. The healing of a Demoniac in the Synagogue. — *Capernaum.*

ST. MARK I. 21–28.   ST. LUKE IV. 31ᵇ–37.

²¹ And they went into Capernaum; and straightway on the sabbath day ²² he taught in⁴ the synagogue. And they were astonished at his doctrine: for he taught them as one that had authority, and not as the scribes. ²³ And straightway⁵ there was in their synagogue a man with an unclean ²⁴ spirit; and he cried out, saying,⁶ What have we to do with thee, thou Jesus of Nazareth? art thou come to destroy us? we⁸ know thee who thou art, the Holy One of God! ²⁵ And Jesus rebuked him:⁹ Hold

[He came down to Capernaum, a city of Galilee], and taught them on ³² the sabbath days. And they were astonished at his doctrine: for his word was with power. ³³ And in the synagogue there was a man, which had a spirit of an unclean devil, and cried out with a ³⁴ loud voice,⁷ Let *us* alone; what have we to do with thee, *thou* Jesus of Nazareth? art thou come to destroy us? I know thee who thou art, the ³⁵ Holy One of God! And Jesus rebuked him, saying, Hold thy peace,

---

¹ casting a net into   ² their nets   ³ farther thence
⁴ he entered into the synagogue, and taught   ⁵ *omit* straightway.
⁶ Saying, Let us alone! what have we   ⁷ Saying, Let us alone!
⁸ I know   ⁹ rebuked him, saying,

ST. MARK I.	ST. LUKE IV.

²⁶ thy peace, and come out of him. And when the unclean spirit had torn him, and cried with a loud voice, he came ²⁷ out of him. And they were all amazed, insomuch that they questioned among themselves, saying, What is this? a new doctrine with authority! He[1] commandeth even the unclean spirits, and they do ²⁸ obey him! And immediately his fame spread abroad everywhere[2] throughout all the region round about Galilee.

and come out of him. And when the devil had thrown him in the midst, he came out of him, and hurt ³⁶ him not. And they were all amazed, and spake among themselves, saying,

What a word *is* this! for with authority and power he commandeth the unclean spirits, and they come out!

³⁷ And the fame of him went out into every place of the country round about.

§ 34. *The healing of Peter's Wife's Mother, and of many others.*—*Capernaum.*

ST. MATT. VIII. 14–17.	ST. MARK I. 29–34.	ST. LUKE IV. 38–41.
¹⁴ And when Jesus was come into Peter's house, he saw his wife's mother laid, and ¹⁵ sick of a fever. And he touched her hand, and the fever left her: and she arose, and ministered unto him.[3] ¹⁶ When the even was come, they brought unto him many that were possessed with devils: and he cast out the spirits with *his*	²⁹ And forthwith, when they were come out of the synagogue, they entered into the house of Simon and Andrew, with James and John. ³⁰ But Simon's wife's mother lay sick of a fever, and anon they ³¹ tell him of her. And he came and took her by the hand, and lifted her up; and [4] the fever left her: and she ministered unto them. ³² And at even, when the sun did set, they brought unto him all that were diseased, and them that were possessed with devils. ³³ And all the city was gathered together at ³⁴ the door. And he healed many that were	³⁸ And he arose out of the synagogue, and entered into Simon's house.

And Simon's wife's mother was taken with a great fever; and they besought ³⁹ him for her. And he stood over her, and rebuked the fever; and it left her; and immediately she arose and ministered unto them. ⁴⁰ Now when the sun was setting, all they that had any sick with divers diseases brought them unto him; and he laid his hands on every one of |

---

[1] What thing is this? what new doctrine is this? for with authority commandeth he even
[2] *omit* everywhere
[3] unto them
[4] and immediately the fever

ST. MATT. VIII.	ST. MARK I.	ST. LUKE IV.
word, and healed all 17 that were sick: that	sick of divers diseases, and cast out many devils;	them, and healed them. 41 And devils also came out of many, crying out, and saying, Thou art[1] the Son of God. And he rebuking *them*
	and suffered not the devils to speak, because they knew him.	suffered them not to speak: for they knew
it might be fulfilled which was spoken by Esaias the prophet, saying,[a] Himself took our infirmities, and bare *our* sicknesses.		that he was Christ.

§ 35. Our Lord preaches and heals throughout Galilee; particularly, He heals a Leper.

MATT. IV. 23, VIII. 2–4.	MAR. I. 35–45.	LK. IV. 42–44, v. 12–16.
	35 And in the morning, rising up a great while before day, he went out, and departed into a solitary place, and 36 there prayed. And Simon and they that were with him followed 37 after him. And when they had found him, they said unto him, All *men* seek for thee. 38 And he said unto them, Let us go elsewhere[4]	42 And when it was day, he departed and went into a desert place: and the people sought him, and came unto him, and stayed him, that he should not depart from them. 43 And he said unto them, I must preach the king-
23 And he[3] went about all Galilee, teaching in their synagogues, and preaching the gospel of the kingdom, and healing all manner of sickness and all manner of disease among the people.	into the next towns, that I may preach there also: for therefore came I forth. 39 And he came preaching[5] in their synagogues throughout all Galilee, and cast out devils.	dom of God to other cities also: for therefore 44 was[2] I sent. And he preached in the synagogues of Galilee.

[1] Thou art Christ, the Son.   [2] am I sent   [3] And Jesus went
[4] *omit* elsewhere   [5] And he preached

[a] Isa. liii. 4. Surely he hath borne our griefs, and carried our sorrows.

ST. MATT. VIII.	ST. MARK I.	ST. LUKE V.
2 And, behold! there came a leper and worshipped him, saying, Lord, if thou wilt, thou canst make me clean. 3 And he[3] put forth *his* hand, and touched him, saying, I will; be thou clean. And immediately his leprosy was cleansed. 4 And Jesus saith unto him, See thou tell no man; but go thy way, shew thyself to the priest, and offer the gift that Moses commanded, for a testimony unto them.[a]	40 And there came a leper to him, beseeching him, and kneeling down,[1] saying unto him, If thou wilt, thou canst make me 41 clean. And he,[2] moved with compassion, put forth *his* hand, and touched *him*,[4] and saith[5] I will; be thou clean. 42 And[6] immediately the leprosy departed from him, and he was 43 cleansed. And he straitly charged him, and forthwith sent him 44 away; and saith unto him, See thou say nothing to any man: but go thy way, shew thyself to the priest, and offer for thy cleansing those things which Moses commanded, for a testimony unto them.[a] 45 But he went out, and began to publish *it* much, and to blaze abroad the matter, insomuch that Jesus could no more openly enter into the city, but was without in desert places: and they came to him from every quarter.	12 And it came to pass, when he was in a certain city, behold a man full of leprosy: who seeing Jesus fell on *his* face, and besought him, saying, Lord, if thou wilt, thou canst make me clean. 13 And he put forth *his* hand, and touched him, saying, I will: be thou clean. And immediately the leprosy departed from him. 14 And he charged him to tell no man: but go, and shew thyself to the priest, and offer for thy cleansing, according as Moses commanded, for a tes-15 timony unto them.[a] But so much the more went there a fame abroad of him: and great multitudes came together to hear, and to be healed[7] of their infirmities. 16 And he withdrew himself into the wilderness, and prayed.

[1] kneeling down to him, and saying [2] and Jesus, moved [3] And Jesus put forth
[4] him [5] saith unto him, I will
[6] And as soon as he had spoken, immediately   [7] to be healed by him

[a] Lev. xiv. 2, etc. This shall be the law of the leper in the day of his cleansing; he shall be brought unto the priest. Cf. Lk. xvii. 14.

§ 36. The healing of a Paralytic. — *Capernaum*.

St. Matt. ix. 1ᵇ–8.	St. Mark ii. 1—12.	St. Luke v. 17–26.
		17 And it came to pass on a certain day, as he was teaching, that there were Pharisees and doctors of the law sitting by, which were come out of every town of Galilee, and Judæa, and Jerusalem: and the power of the Lord was *present* to heal.¹
1ᵇ — And came into his own city.	1 And again he entered into Capernaum after *some* days; and it was noised that he was in the house. 2 And² many were gathered together, insomuch that there was no room to receive *them*, no, not so much as about the door: and he preached the word 3 unto them. And they come unto him, bringing one sick of the palsy, which was borne	
2 And, behold! they brought to him a man sick of the palsy, lying on a bed:	4 of four. And when they could not bring *him*³ unto him for the press, they uncovered the roof where he was: and when they had broken *it* up, they let down the bed where⁴ the sick of the palsy	18 And, behold! men brought in a bed a man which was taken with a palsy: and they sought *means* to bring him in, and to lay *him* before 19 him. And when they could not find by what *way* they might bring him in because of the multitude, they went upon the housetop, and let him down through the tiling with *his* couch into the midst before

---

¹ to heal them   ² and straightway many   ³ could not come nigh unto him   ⁴ wherein

ST. MATT. IX.	ST. MARK II.	ST. LUKE V.
and Jesus seeing their faith said unto the sick of the palsy; Son, be of good cheer; thy sins be forgiven.[2] 3 And, behold! certain of the scribes said within themselves, This *man* blasphemeth.	5 lay. When Jesus saw their faith, he said unto the sick of the palsy, Son, thy sins be forgiven.[2] 6 But there were certain of the scribes sitting there, and reasoning in their 7 hearts, Why doth this *man* thus speak? He blasphemeth.[3] who can forgive sins but 8 God only? And im-	20 Jesus. And when he saw their faith, he said,[1] Man, thy sins are forgiven 21 thee. And the scribes and the Pharisees began to reason, saying, Who is this which speaketh blasphemies? Who can forgive sins, but God 22 alone? But when Jesus
4 And Jesus knowing their thoughts said, Wherefore think ye evil in your hearts? 5 For whether is easier, to say, Thy sins be forgiven;[2] or to say, 6 Arise, and walk? But that ye may know that the Son of man hath power on earth to forgive sins, (then saith he to the sick of the palsy,) Arise, take up thy bed, and go unto 7 thine house. And he arose, and departed to 8 his house. But when the multitudes saw *it*, they were afraid,[7] and	mediately when Jesus perceived in his spirit that they so reasoned within themselves, he saith[4] unto them, Why reason ye these things 9 in your hearts? Whether is it easier to say to the sick of the palsy, *Thy* sins be forgiven;[2] or to say, Arise, and take up thy bed, and 10 walk? But that ye may know that the Son of man hath power on earth to forgive sins, (he saith to the sick 11 of the palsy,) I say unto thee, Arise,[5] take up thy bed, and go thy way into thine 12 house. And he arose, and immediately[6] took up the bed, and went forth before them all; insomuch that they were all amazed, and	perceived their thoughts, he answering said unto them, What reason ye in 23 your hearts? Whether is easier, to say, Thy sins be forgiven thee; or to say, Rise up and walk? 24 But that ye may know that the Son of man hath power upon earth to forgive sins, (he said unto the sick of the palsy,) I say unto thee, Arise, and take up thy couch, and go unto thine house. 25 And immediately he rose up before them, and took up that whereon he lay, and departed to his own house, glorifying God. 26 And they were all amazed,

---

[1] said unto him, Man [2] forgiven thee [3] thus speak blasphemies? who can forgive
[4] he said [5] Arise, and take up [6] And immediately he arose, took up
[7] they marvelled

St. Matt. ix.	St. Mark ii.	St. Luke v.
glorified God, which had given such power unto men.	glorified God, saying, We never saw it on this fashion!	and they glorified God, and were filled with fear, saying, We have seen strange things to day!

§ 37. The Call of Levi (Matthew), and his Feast. — *Capernaum.*

St. Matt. ix. 9–13.	St. Mark ii. 13–17.	St. Luke v. 27–32.
	13 And he went forth again to[1] the sea; and all the multitude resorted unto him, and he taught them. And as he passed by, he saw Levi the son of Alphaeus sitting at the receipt of custom: and said unto him, Follow me. And he arose and followed him.	
9 And as Jesus passed forth from thence, he saw a man, named Matthew, sitting at the receipt of custom: and he saith unto him, Follow me. And he arose, and followed him.		27 And after these things he went forth, and saw a publican, named Levi, sitting at the receipt of custom: and he said unto him, Follow me. 28 And he left all, rose up, and followed him.
10 And it came to pass, as Jesus sat at meat in the house, behold! many publicans and sinners came and sat down with him and 11 his disciples. And when the Pharisees saw *it*, they said unto his disciples, Why eat-	15 And it came to pass, that he[2] sat at meat in his house, and[3] many publicans and sinners sat also together with Jesus and his disciples: for there were many. 16 And there followed him[4] also scribes of the Pharisees. And seeing that he eat with publicans and sinners, they said unto his disciples, *How is it*[6] that	29 And Levi made him a great feast in his own house: and there was a great company of publicans and of others that sat 30 down with them. But the Pharisees and[5] their scribes murmured against his disciples, saying, Why do ye eat and

[1] by the sea side
[2] as Jesus sat
[3] *omit* and
[4] and they followed him. And when the scribes and Pharisees saw him eat with
[5] But their scribes and Pharisees
[6] How is it

§ 37. The feast of Levi is here placed next after his call (although it may not have occurred on the same day), in accordance with the order of the narrative in all three Evangelists, which order seems also in itself the most natural and probable. There is no reason to suppose that the teaching at this feast extended beyond the limits of this section; indeed the circumstances which led to the discourse on fasting render it more likely that this discourse was held on another occasion. It is accordingly placed by itself in the following section.

ST. MATT. IX.	ST. MARK II.	ST. LUKE V.
eth your Master with publicans and sinners? 12 But when he¹ heard *that*, he said,² They that be whole need not a physician, but they 13 that are sick. But go ye and learn what *that* meaneth, I will have mercy, and not sacrifice:ª for I am not come to call the righteous, but sinners.³	he eateth and drinketh with publicans and 17 sinners? When Jesus heard *it*, he saith unto them, They that are whole have no need of the physician, but they that are sick: I came not to call the righteous, but sinners.³	drink with publicans 31 and sinners? And Jesus answering said unto them, They that are whole need not a physician; but they that are sick. 32 I came not to call the righteous, but sinners to repentance.

§ 38. Answer to Questions about Fasting. — *Galilee?*

St. Matt. ix. 14–17.	St. Mark. ii. 18–22.	St. Luke v. 33–39.
14 Then came to him the disciples of John, saying, Why do we and the Pharisees fast,⁶ but thy disciples fast not?	18 And the disciples of John and the Pharisees were fasting:⁵ and they come and say unto him, Why do the disciples of John and the disciples⁷ of the Pharisees fast, but thy disciples fast not?	33 And they said unto him,⁴ The disciples of John fast often, and make prayers, and likewise the *disciples* of the Pharisees; but thine eat and drink.

¹ when Jesus heard ² he said unto them ³ but sinners to repentance
⁴ Why do the disciples ⁵ of John and of the Pharisees used to fast
⁶ fast oft ⁷ *omit* the disciples

ª Hos. vi. 6. For I desired mercy; and not sacrifice. Cf. Matt. xii. 7.

---

§ 38. The discourse concerning fasting here follows in the order in which it is placed by all the Evangelists who record it. It is, however, very difficult to determine the time when it was uttered. Were this to be decided by a reference exclusively to St. Matthew it must be placed just before the healing of the daughter of Jairus, inasmuch as he says (ix. 18) that Jairus came to him "while he spake these things." But the healing of Jairus' daughter did not take place until a long time after this, when Jesus had crossed the sea of Galilee and returned (Mar. v. 21, 22; Lk. viii. 40, 41). On the other hand, if this discourse be placed there, the order of both St. Mark and St. Luke would be disturbed; and St. Mark is always careful to observe chronological order. Perhaps the true solution is to be found in the fact that our Lord often encountered this same attempt to mingle the dead letter of the old ceremonial with the living spirit of his Gospel, and may therefore have repeated these same comparisons more than once. St. Matthew, like the other Evangelists, has recorded them only as they were uttered in answer to the question about fasting, and then very naturally goes on to speak of what happened on occasion of a subsequent repetition of them; cf. note on §§ 51, 52.

It having been assumed that § 38 formed part of the same discourse with that in § 37, great difficulty has generally been felt by Harmonists. Robinson, like Newcome, postpones the feast

ST. MATT. IX.	ST. MARK II.	ST. LUKE V.
15 And Jesus said unto them, Can the children of the bridechamber mourn, as long as the bridegroom is with them?	19 And Jesus said unto them, Can the children of the bridechamber fast, while the bridegroom is with them? as long as they have the bridegroom [2] they 20 cannot fast. But the	34 And Jesus[1] said unto them, Can ye make the children of the bridechamber fast, while the bridegroom is with
but the days will come, when the bridegroom shall be taken from them, and then shall they fast.	days will come, when the bridegroom shall be taken away from them, and then shall they fast in that day.[3]	35 them? But the days will come, when the bridegroom shall be taken away from them, and then shall they fast in those days.
		36 And he spake also a parable unto them; No
16 No man putteth a piece of new cloth unto an old garment, for that which is put in to fill it up taketh from the garment, and the rent 17 is made worse. Neither do men put new wine into old bottles: else the bottles break, and the wine runneth out, and the bottles perish: but they put new wine into new bottles, and both are preserved.	21 No man also seweth a piece of new cloth on an old garment: else the new piece that filled it up taketh away from the old, and the rent is made 22 worse. And no man putteth new wine into old bottles: else the wine will[7] burst the bottles, and the wine perisheth,[8] and the bottles.	man rending a piece from a new garment putteth it[4] upon an old: if otherwise, then both the new will make[5] a rent and the piece from the new will not[6] agree with 37 the old. And no man putteth new wine into old bottles: else the new wine will burst the bottles, and be spilled, and the bottles shall 38 perish. But new wine must be put into new 39 bottles.[9] No man also having drunk old *wine*[10] desireth new: for he saith, the old is good.[11]

[1] And he said   [2] have the bridegroom with them   [3] in those days
[4] No man putteth a piece of a new garment upon an old   [5] maketh a rent
[6] the piece that was *taken* out of the new agreeth not with the old   [7] the new wine doth burst
[8] the wine is spilled, and the bottles will be marred; but new wine must be put into new bottles.
[9] into new bottles; and both are preserved.   [10] straightway desireth   [11] the old is better.

---

of Levi until just before the healing of Jairus' daughter, which seems unnatural, and disturbs the order of all the Evangelists at once. Greswell (Dissert. vol. II. diss. x. p. 358–368) considers St. Matthew's narrative to relate to a different feast and different discourse from that of the other Evangelists. It is hoped the above suggestions may at least lessen the difficulty.

PART IV.

OUR LORD'S SECOND PASSOVER, AND THE EVENTS UNTIL THE THIRD.

§ 39. Our Lord comes to Jerusalem at the Feast; heals an infirm man at the Pool of Bethesda; and teaches.

St. John v. 1–47.

1 After this there was the[1] feast of the Jews; and Jesus went up to Jerusalem.
2 Now there is at Jerusalem by the sheep *market* a pool, which is called in the
3 Hebrew tongue Bethesda, having five porches. In these lay a[2] multitude of
5 impotent folk, of blind, halt, withered.[3] And a certain man was there, which
6 had his[4] infirmity thirty and eight years. When Jesus saw him lie, and knew
that he had been now a long time *in that case*, he saith unto him, Wilt thou
7 be made whole? The impotent man answered him, Sir, I have no man, when
the water is troubled, to put me into the pool: but while I am coming, another
8 steppeth down before me. Jesus saith unto him, Rise, take up thy bed, and
9 walk. And[5] the man was made whole, and took up his bed, and walked: and
on the same day was the Sabbath.
10 The Jews therefore said unto him that was cured, It is the Sabbath day,
11 and[6] it is not lawful for thee to carry *thy* bed. He answered them, He that
12 made me whole, the same said unto me, Take up thy bed, and walk. They[7]
asked him, What man is that which said unto thee, Take up,[8] and walk?
13 And he that was sick[9] wist not who it was: for Jesus had conveyed himself

---

[1] a feast
[2] a great multitude
[3] halt, withered, waiting for the moving of the water. For an angel went down at a certain season into the pool, and troubled the water: whosoever then first after the troubling of the water stepped in was made whole of whatsoever disease he had.

| [4] an infirmity | [5] And immediately the man | [6] *omit* and |
| [7] Then asked they him | [8] Take up thy bed, and walk | [9] he that was healed |

---

§ 39. On the important question as to the meaning of 'the feast' of ver. 1, see the general Introduction pp. vii–ix. It is here understood of the Passover, the second since our Lord's baptism; the reasons for this will be found in the Introduction.

The latter part of ver. 3, and the whole of ver. 4, are retained in much the greater number of existing Greek manuscripts, but are omitted in the two most ancient, as well as in several others of great authority. The balance of evidence was against their genuineness before the discovery of the Sinaitic manuscript; and this also rejects them.

ST. JOHN V.

14 away, a multitude being in *that* place. Afterward Jesus findeth him in the temple, and said unto him, Behold! thou art made whole; sin no more, lest
15 a worse thing come unto thee. The man departed, and told the Jews that it
16 was Jesus, which had made him whole. And therefore did the Jews persecute Jesus,[1] because he did[2] these things on the Sabbath day.
17 But he[3] answered them, My Father worketh hitherto, and I work.
18 Therefore the Jews sought the more to kill him, because he not only had broken the Sabbath, but said also that God was his own[4] Father, making himself equal with God.
19 Then answered Jesus and said unto them, Verily, verily, I say unto you, The Son can do nothing of himself, but what he seeth the Father do: for
20 what things soever he doeth, these also doeth the Son likewise. For the Father loveth the Son, and sheweth him all things that himself doeth: and
21 he will shew him greater works than these, that ye may marvel. For as the Father raiseth up the dead, and quickeneth *them*; even so the Son quickeneth
22 whom he will. For the Father judgeth no man, but hath committed all
23 judgment unto the Son: That all *men* should honor the Son, even as they honor the Father. He that honoreth not the Son honoreth not the Father
24 which hath sent him. Verily, verily, I say unto you, He that heareth my word, and believeth on him that sent me, hath everlasting life, and shall not
25 come into condemnation; but is passed from death unto life. Verily, verily, I say unto you, The hour is coming, and now is, when the dead shall hear
26 the voice of the Son of God: and they that hear shall live. For as the Father hath life in himself; so hath he given to the Son to have life in
27 himself; and hath given him authority to execute judgment,[5] because he is
28 the Son of man. Marvel not at this: for the hour is coming, in the which
29 all that are in the graves shall hear his voice, 'and shall come forth; they that have done good, unto the resurrection of life:[6] they that have done evil,
30 unto the resurrection of damnation. I can of mine own self do nothing: as I hear, I judge: and my judgment is just; because I seek not mine own will,
31 but the will of him[7] which hath sent me. If I bear witness of myself, my
32 witness is not true. There is Another that beareth witness of me; and ye[8] know that the witness which he witnesseth of me is true.
33
34 Ye sent unto John, and he bare witness unto the truth. But I receive not testimony from man: but these things I say, that ye might be saved.
35 He was a burning and a shining light: and ye were willing for a season to
36 rejoice in his light. But I have greater witness than *that* of John: for the works which the Father hath given me to finish, the same works that I do,
37 bear witness of me, that the Father hath sent me. And the Father[9] which

---

[1] persecute Jesus, and sought to slay him,
[2] he had done these things
[3] But Jesus answered
[4] *omit* own
[5] also, because
[6] and they that have
[7] the will of the Father
[8] and I know
[9] the Father himself which hath sent me, hath

ST. JOHN V.

hath sent me, he¹ hath borne witness of me. Ye have neither heard his voice
38 at any time, nor seen his shape. And ye have not his word abiding in you:
39 for whom he hath sent, him ye believe not. Search the scriptures; for in
them ye think ye have eternal life: and they are they which testify of me.
40,41 And ye will not come to me, that ye might have life. I receive not honor
42 from men. But I know you, that ye have not the love of God in you.
43 I am come in my Father's's name, and ye receive me not: if another shall
44 come in his own name, him ye will receive. How can ye believe, which
receive honor one of another, and seek not the honor that *cometh* from God
45 only? Do not think that I will accuse you to the Father; there is *one* that
46 accuseth you, *even* Moses, in whom ye trust. For had ye believed Moses,
47 ye would have believed me: for he wrote of me. But if ye believe not his
writings, how shall ye believe my words?

§ 40. The Disciples pluck Ears of Grain on the Sabbath.

St. Matt. xii. 1–8.	St. Mark. ii. 23–28.	St. Luke vi. 1–5.
1 At that time Jesus went on the Sabbath day through the corn; and his disciples were an hungred and began to pluck the ears of 2 corn, and to eat. But when the Pharisees saw *it*, they said unto him, Behold! thy disciples do that which is not lawful to do upon 3 the Sabbath day. But he said unto them, Have ye not read what David did, when he was an hungred, and they that were with 4 him; how he entered into the house of God.ᵃ	23 And it came to pass, that he went through the corn fields on the Sabbath day; and his disciples began, as they went, to pluck the ears 24 of corn. And the Pharisees said unto him, Behold! why do they on the Sabbath day that which is not 25 lawful? And he saith³ unto them, Have ye never read what David did, when he had need, and was an hungred, he, and they that were 26 with him: how he went into the house of Godᵃ in the days	1 And it came to pass on the second Sabbath after the first, that he went through the corn fields; and his disciples plucked the ears of corn, and did eat, rubbing 2 *them* in *their* hands. And certain of the Pharisees said,² Why do ye that which is not lawful to do on the Sabbath days? 3 And Jesus answering them said, Have ye not read so much as this, what David did, when himself was an hungred, and they which were 4 with him; how he went into the house of God,ᵃ

¹ the Father himself which hath sent me, hath   ² said unto them, Why   ³ he said
ᵃ 1 Sam. xxi. 3–6.

§ 40. It is not easy to determine certainly the meaning of the expression 'the second Sabbath after the first.' In the Greek there are but two words, literally 'the second first Sabbath.' Probably it means *the first Sabbath after the second day of unleavened bread*, from which the seven Sabbaths were reckoned to Pentecost. See Lev. xxiii. 15, etc.

ST. MATT. XII.	ST. MARK II.	ST. LUKE VI.
and did eat the shewbread,[a] which was not lawful for him to eat, neither for them which were with him, but only for the priests?[b] 5 Or have ye not read in the law, how that on the Sabbath days the priests in the temple profane the Sabbath,[c] and are blameless? 6 But I say unto you, That in this place is *one* greater than the temple.[d] 7 But if ye had known what *this* meaneth, I will have mercy, and not sacrifice,[e] ye would not have condemned the guiltless.	of Abiathar the high priest, and did eat the shewbread,[a] which is not lawful to eat but for the priests,[b] and gave also to them which were with him? 27 And he said unto them, The Sabbath was made for man, and not man 28 for the Sabbath. Therefore the Son of man is Lord also of the Sabbath.	and did take and eat the shewbread,[a] and gave also to them that were with him; which it is not lawful to eat but for the priests alone?[b] 5 And he said unto them, That the Son of man is Lord also of the Sabbath.
8 For the Son of man is Lord[1] of the Sabbath day.		

§ 41. On another Sabbath the withered Hand is healed.

St. Matt. xii. 9–14.	St. Mark iii. 1–6.	St. Luke vi. 6–11.
9 And when he was departed thence, he went into their synagogue: 10 And, behold, *there was*[3] a man which had	1 And he entered again into the synagogue: and there was a man there which had a	6 And it came to pass[2] on another Sabbath, that he entered into the synagogue and taught: and there was a man whose right hand was withered.

[1] Lord even of the
[2] came to pass also
[3] there was
[a] Lev. xxiv. 5, 6.
[b] Ib. 9.
[c] Num. xxviii. 9, 10. Cf. Jno. vii. 22.
[d] 2 Chron. vi. 18.
[e] Hos. vi. 6 : For I desired mercy, and not sacrifice.

ST. MATT. XII.	ST. MARK III.	ST. LUKE VI.
his hand withered. And they asked him, saying, Is it lawful to heal on the Sabbath days? that they might 11 accuse him. And he said unto them, What man shall there be among you, that shall have one sheep, and if it fall into a pit on the Sabbath day, will he not lay hold on it, and 12 lift *it* out? How much then is a man better than a sheep! Wherefore it is lawful to do well on the Sabbath days.	2 withered hand. And they watched him, whether he would heal him on the Sabbath day; that they might accuse him.	7 And the scribes and Pharisees watched,[1] whether he healeth[2] on the Sabbath day; that they might find an accusation against him.
	3 And he saith unto the man which had the withered hand, Stand 4 forth. And he saith unto them, Is it lawful to do good on the Sabbath days, or to do evil? to save life, or to kill? But they held 5 their peace. And when he had looked round about on them with anger, being grieved for the hardness of their hearts, he saith unto the man, Stretch forth thine hand. And he stretched *it* out: and his hand was restored.[5]	8 But he knew their thoughts, and said to the man which had the withered hand, Rise up, and stand forth in the midst. And he arose 9 and stood forth. And[3] Jesus said unto them, I ask you whether it is[4] lawful on the Sabbath days to do good, or to do evil? to save life, or to 10 destroy *it*? And looking round about upon them all, he said unto the man, Stretch forth thy hand.
13 Then saith he to the man, Stretch forth thine hand. And he stretched *it* forth; and it was restored whole, like as the other. 14 Then the Pharisees went out, and held a		And he did so: and his hand was restored.[5] 11 And they were filled with madness; and com-
	6 And the Pharisees went forth, and straight-	

[1] watched him [2] whether he would heal on the [3] Then
[4] I will ask you one thing; Is it lawful [5] was restored whole as the other.

ST. MATT. XII.	ST. MARK III.	ST. LUKE VI.
council against him, how they might destroy him.	way took counsel with the Herodians against him, how they might destroy him.	muned one with another what they might do to Jesus.

§ 42. The Fame of Jesus is spread abroad. He performs many Cures. — Sea of Galilee.

MATT. XII. 15–21. IV. 24, 25.	ST. MARK III. 7–12.	ST. LUKE VI. 17ᵇ–19.
15 But when Jesus knew *it*, he withdrew himself from thence: and great multitudes IV. followed him, and he 24 healed them all; and his fame went throughout all Syria: and they brought unto him all sick people that were taken with divers diseases and torments, and those which were possessed with devils, and those which were lunatick, and those that had the palsy; and 25 he healed them. And there followed him great multitudes of people from Galilee, and *from* Decapolis, and *from* Jerusalem, and *from* Judæa, and *from* beyond Jordan. XII. 16 And charged them that they should not	7 But Jesus withdrew himself with his disciples to the sea: and a great multitude from Galilee followed,² and 8 from Judæa, and from Jerusalem, and from Idumæa, and *from* beyond Jordan; and *they*³ about Tyre and Sidon, a great multitude, hearing⁴ what great things he did, came unto him. 9 And he spake to his disciples, that a small ship should wait on him because of the multitude, lest they should throng him. 10 For he had healed many; insomuch that they pressed upon him for to touch him, as many as had plagues. 11 And unclean spirits, when they saw him, fell down before him, and cried, saying, Thou art the Son of God! 12 And he straitly charged them that they should	And a great¹ company of his disciples, and a great multitude of people out of all Judæa and Jerusalem, and from the sea coast of Tyre and Sidon, which came to hear him, and to be healed of their diseases; 18 And they that were vexed with unclean spirits⁵ 19 were healed. And the whole multitude sought to touch him; for there went virtue out of him, and healed *them* all.

---

¹ and the company of his disciples   ² followed him   ³ they
⁴ a great multitude, when they had heard what great things
⁵ with unclean spirits: and they were healed.

ST. MATT. XII.	ST. MARK III.	ST. LUKE VI.
17 make him known: That it might be fulfilled which was spoken by Esaias the prophet, 18 saying, *Behold my servant, whom I have chosen; my beloved, in whom my soul is well pleased: I will put my spirit upon him, and he shall shew judgment to the Gentiles. 19 He shall not strive, nor cry; neither shall any man hear his voice in the streets. 20 A bruised reed shall he not break, and smoking flax shall he not quench, till he send forth judgment unto victory. 21 And in his name shall the Gentiles trust.	not make him known.	

§ 43. He withdraws to the Mountain, and chooses the Twelve. — *Near Capernaum*

ST. MATT. x. 2-4.	ST. MARK III. 13-19.	ST. LUKE VI. 12-17.
	13 And he goeth up into a mountain, and	12 And it came to pass in those days, that he went out into a mountain

---

^a Isa. xlii. 1-4. Behold my servant, whom I uphold! mine elect, *in whom* my soul delighteth: I have put my Spirit upon him: he shall bring forth judgment to the Gentiles. He shall not cry, nor lift up, nor cause his voice to be heard in the street. A bruised reed shall he not break, and the smoking flax shall he not quench: he shall bring forth judgment unto truth. He shall not fail nor be discouraged, till he have set judgment in the earth: and the isles shall wait for his law.

---

§ 43. The time of the appointment of the twelve is nowhere indicated by St. Matthew, who merely mentions their names (x. 2), as of those previously chosen. The appointment is here given in the order of St. Mark, with which St. Luke substantially agrees.

Although the phrase in Matt. x. 3, "whose surname was Thaddeus," appears to be a gloss, yet the Vatican and Sinaitic MSS. and some others read *Thaddeus* instead of *Lebbeus* (a read-

PART IV. § 43.]   AND THE EVENTS UNTIL THE THIRD.   53

ST. MATT. X.	ST. MARK III.	ST. LUKE VI.
		to pray, and continued all night in prayer to God.
	calleth *unto him* whom he would: and they 14 came unto him. And he ordained twelve, that they should be with him, and that he might send them forth 15 to preach, and to have power to¹ cast out devils.	13 And when it was day, he called *unto him* his disciples; and of them he chose twelve, whom also he named apostles;
2 Now the names of the twelve apostles are these; the first, Simon, who is called Peter, and Andrew his brother; and³ James *the son* of Zebedee, and John his brother;	16 And he appointed the² twelve, and Simon he surnamed Peter; 17 and James the *son* of Zebedee, and John the brother of James; and he surnamed them Boanerges, which is, The 18 sons of thunder: and Andrew, and Philip, and Bartholomew, and Matthew, and Thomas, and James the *son* of Alphæus, and Thaddæus, and Simon the 19 Cananite,⁵ and Judas	14 Simon, whom he also named Peter, and Andrew his brother, and³ James and John,
3 Philip, and Bartholomew; Thomas, and Matthew the publican; James *the son* of Alphæus, and Lebbæus,⁴ 4 Simon the Cananite,⁵		and³ Philip and Bartholomew, ¹and³ Matthew and Thomas, and³ James the *son* of Alphæus, and Simon called Zelotes, 16 and Judas *the brother* of James, and Judas Is-

¹ power to heal sicknesses, and to cast out
² *omit* And he appointed the twelve,
⁴ Lebbæus, whose surname was Thaddæus,

³ *omit* and
⁵ Canaanite

ing adopted by Lachmann and Tregelles), and the two names, as well as the Judas the *brother* [son] of James, of the third Evangelist, plainly indicate the same person. Bartholomew is also supposed to be the same with Nathanael of Jno. xxi. 2.

The differences in the order of the names are less than might at first appear. Peter is named first by all, and the traitor last. The four first called are placed first by all, and in the same order, except that Andrew is placed after the three chief apostles by St. Mark, while he is very naturally mentioned next to his brother by the others. The couple, Thomas and Matthew, is placed together by all, although St. Matthew, perhaps from modesty, places his own name after that of his companion. There is no other variation except the putting of the two Judases together by St. Luke.

ST. MATT. X.	ST. MARK III.	ST. LUKE VI.
and Judas Iscariot, who also betrayed him.	Iscariot, which also betrayed him.	cariot, which[1] was the traitor. 17 And he came down with them, and stood in the plain.

§ 44. The Sermon on the Mount.—*Near Capernaum*.

MATT. v. 1–24, 27–vi. 21, 34–vii. 1–6, 12–viii. 1.   LK. vi. 20–49, xvi. 17.

1 And seeing the multitudes, he went up into a mountain: and when he was set, his disciples came unto 2 him: and he opened his mouth, and taught them, saying, 3 Blessed *are* the poor in spirit! for their's is the kingdom of heaven. 5 Blessed *are* the meek! for they shall 4 inherit the earth. Blessed *are* they that mourn! for they shall be com-6 forted.[2] Blessed *are* they which do hunger and thirst after righteous-7 ness! for they shall be filled. Blessed *are* the merciful! for they shall 8 obtain mercy. Blessed *are* the pure in heart! for they shall see God. 9 Blessed *are* the peacemakers! for they shall be called the children of 10 God. Blessed *are* they which are persecuted for righteousness' sake! for their's is the kingdom of heaven.	20 And he lifted up his eyes on his disciples, and said, Blessed *be ye* poor! for your's is the 21 kingdom of God. Blessed *are ye* that hunger now! for ye shall be filled. Blessed *are ye* that weep now! for ye shall laugh.

[1] which also was the traitor.   [2] *transpose* verses 4 and 5

§ 44. The place of the delivery of the Sermon on the Mount must have been some high land in the neighborhood of Capernaum, though there is nothing to identify the precise locality, nor is there any early tradition on the subject.

The question as to whether the discourse as given by St. Matthew is the same with the much shorter form contained in St. Luke, is one which, as we learn from St. Augustine, has divided opinion from very early times. The following are briefly, some of the reasons for supposing them to be the same, as indeed they are now almost universally considered to be:

1. The choice of the twelve is expressly mentioned by St. Luke as the occasion of the discourse. St. Matthew nowhere mentions their appointment, but in v. 13, 14; vii. 6, and elsewhere, the language seems to imply their previous selection.

2. The beginning and end of both discourses, the circumstances under which they were spoken, and the general course of thought, are the same.

3. The events immediately following both discourses, the entrance into Capernaum, and the healing of the centurion's servant, are the same.

St. Matthew has given a much fuller report of the discourse than St. Luke. It has been

ST. MATT. V.

11 Blessed are ye, when *men* shall revile you, and persecute *you*, and shall say all manner of evil against you falsely,

12 for my sake. Rejoice, and be exceeding glad! for great *is* your reward in heaven: for so persecuted they the prophets which were before you.

13 Ye are the salt of the earth: but if the salt have lost his savor, wherewith shall it be salted? it is thenceforth good for nothing, but to be cast out [3] to be trodden under foot of men.

14 Ye are the light of the world. A city that is set on an hill cannot be hid.

15 Neither do men light a candle, and put it under a bushel, but on a candlestick;[a] and it giveth light unto all

ST. LUKE VI.

22 Blessed are ye, when men shall hate you, and when they shall separate you *from their company*, and shall reproach *you*, and cast out your name as evil, for the Son of man's sake.

23 Rejoice ye in that day, and leap for joy! for, behold, your reward *is* great in heaven: for in the like manner did their fathers unto the prophets.

24 But woe unto you that are rich! for ye have received your consolation.

25 Woe unto you that are full now![1] for ye shall hunger. Woe unto you that laugh now! for ye shall mourn and

26 weep. Woe,[2] when all men shall speak well of you! for so did their fathers to the false prophets.

[1] *omit* now   [2] Woe unto you, when all   [3] **cast out, and to be trodden**
[a] Mar. iv. 21; Lk. viii. 16; xi. 33.

---

suggested that as he wrote especially for the Jews, he was particularly careful to record our Lord's exposition of the spiritual nature of his dispensation and doctrine, in opposition to the technicalities of the Scribes and Pharisees; while St. Luke, writing more particularly for the Gentiles, has mentioned only what was of more general importance to all. However this may be, few things can less need explanation than a difference in the fulness of two reports of the same discourse. There are a few parts of the discourse as it stands in St. Matthew (v. 25, 26; vi. 22–34, and vii. 7–11), which are somewhat apart, less intimately joined with the context, but which are given by St. Luke in connection with circumstances minutely detailed by him. As these circumstances are not mentioned by St. Matthew at all, it was natural that he should have added the teaching connected with them to the Sermon on the Mount, although not spoken just at that time. These passages are transferred to the connection in which they are given by St. Luke.

Putting together the two accounts, it would appear that our Lord retired to the mountain to pray, and then chose the twelve; descending with them to the plain, he performed many cures; and then, the crowd pressing upon him, he again drew back to the mountain, where he uttered the discourse.

ST. MATT. V.	ST. LUKE XVI.
16 that are in the house. Let your light so shine before men, that they may see your good works, and glorify your Father which is in heaven.	
17 Think not that I am come to destroy the law, or the prophets: I am not come to destroy, but to fulfil.	
18 For verily I say unto you, Till heaven and earth pass, one jot or one tittle shall in no wise pass from the	17 And it is easier for heaven and earth to pass, than one tittle of the law to fail.
19 law, till all be fulfilled. Whosoever therefore shall break one of these least commandments, and shall teach men so, he shall be called the least in the kingdom of heaven; but whosoever shall do and teach *them*, the same shall be called great in the kingdom	
20 of heaven. For I say unto you, That except your righteousness shall exceed *the righteousness* of the scribes and Pharisees, ye shall in no case enter into the kingdom of heaven.	
21 Ye have heard that it was said by them of old time,^a Thou shalt not kill; and whosoever shall kill shall	
22 be in danger of the judgment: but I say unto you, That whosoever is angry with his brother¹ shall be in danger of the judgment: and whosoever shall say to his brother, Raca!	

[1] with his brother without a cause

a Exod. xx. 13; Deut. v. 17; comp. Matt. xix. 18; Mar. x. 19; Lk. xviii. 20; Rom. xiii. 9; Jas. ii. 11 etc.

---

§ 44. Lk. xvi. 17 is here widely separated from its context. The sixteenth chapter of St. Luke, with the exception of verses 16–18, is peculiar to him; the connection of the part before these verses with the parable immediately after them is very close; while the three verses interposed are not intimately connected with either what precedes or what follows, but are parallel to passages of the other Evangelists, and those passages are closely connected with a context which is nowhere given by St. Luke. Under these circumstances, while it is plain that the words contained in these verses were uttered in the connections given by the other Evangelists, it is unnecessary to suppose that they were repeated at the time when they are introduced by St. Luke. There is no other indication of such repetition, and they have altogether the air of detached utterances. St. Luke could not, of course, give them in their connection, as he does not record that connection.

ST. MATT. V.

shall be in danger of the council: but whosoever shall say, Thou fool![a] shall 23 be in danger of hell fire. Therefore if thou bring thy gift to the altar, and there rememberest that thy brother 24 hath ought against thee; leave there thy gift before the altar, and go thy way; first be reconciled to thy brother, and then come and offer thy gift.

27 Ye have heard that it was said[1] [b]Thou shalt not commit adultery; 28 but I say unto you, That whosoever looketh on a woman to lust[2] hath committed adultery with her already 29 in his heart. And if thy right eye offend thee, pluck it out, and cast *it* from thee: for it is profitable for thee that one of thy members should perish, and not *that* thy whole body 30 should be cast into hell.[c] And if thy right hand offend thee, cut it off, and cast *it* from thee; for it is profitable for thee that one of thy members should perish, and not *that* thy whole body should depart[3] into hell.

31 It hath been said,[d] Whosoever shall put away his wife, let him give her a 32 writing of divorcement: but I say unto you, That every one who putteth[4] away his wife, saving for the cause of fornication, causeth her to commit adultery: and whosoever shall marry her that is divorced committeth adultery.

33 Again, ye have heard that it hath been said by them of old time,[e] Thou

ST. LUKE XVI.

---

[1] was said by them of old time
[3] should be cast into hell
[2] to lust after her
[4] that whosoever shall put away

[a] See 2 Sam. vi. 20.
[b] Exod. xx. 14; Deut. v. 18. Comp. Matt. xix. 18; Mar. x. 19; Lk. xviii. 20; Rom. ii. 22; xiii. 9, etc.
[c] Comp. Matt. xviii. 8, 9; Mar. ix. 43–47.
[d] Deut. xxiv. 3. Comp. Matt. xix. 7; Mar. x. 4; Lk. xvi. 18.
[e] Comp. Exod. xx. 7; Lev. xix. 12.

ST. MATT. V.

shalt not forswear thyself, but shalt perform unto the Lord thine oaths:
34 but I say unto you, Swear not at all; neither by heaven; for it is God's
35 throne: nor by the earth; for it is his footstool: neither by Jerusalem; for it is the city of the great King.
36 Neither shalt thou swear by thy head, because thou canst not make one hair
37 white or black. But let your communication be, Yea, yea; Nay,[a] nay: for whatsoever is more than these cometh of evil.

38 Ye have heard that it hath been said,[b] An eye for an eye, and a tooth
39 for a tooth: but I say unto you, That ye resist not evil: but whosoever smiteth[1] thee on the[2] right cheek,
40 turn to him the other also. And if any man will sue thee at the law, and take away thy coat, let him have
41 *thy* cloke also. And whosoever shall compel thee to go a mile, go with
42 him twain. Give[c] to him that asketh thee, and from him that would borrow of thee turn not thou away.

43 Ye have heard that it hath been said,[d] Thou shalt love thy neighbor,
44 and hate thine enemy: but I say unto you, Love your enemies,[4] and pray for them which[5] persecute you;
45 that ye may be the children of your Father which is in heaven: for he maketh his sun to rise on the evil and on the good, and sendeth rain on

ST. LUKE VI.

27 But I say unto you which hear, Love your enemies, do good to them
28 which hate you, bless them that curse you,[3] pray for them that de-
29 spitefully use you. And unto him that smiteth thee on the *one* cheek, offer also the other; and him that taketh away thy cloke forbid not *to*
30 *take thy* coat also. Give[c] to every man that asketh of thee; and of him that taketh away thy goods ask *them* not again.

---

[1] shall smite [2] thy right cheek [3] and pray for them
[4] Love your enemies, bless them that curse you, do good to them that hate you, and pray
[5] which despitefully use you, and persecute you.

[a] Jas. v. 12.
[b] Exod. xxi. 24; Lev. xxiv. 20; Deut. xix. 21. Comp. Prov. xx. 22; xxiv. 29.
[c] Deut. xv. 8-10; Acts xx. 35.
[d] Comp. Lev. xix. 18; Matt. xix. 19; xxii. 39; Mar. xii. 31; Lk. x. 27; Rom. xiii. 9; Gal. v. 14; Jas. ii. 8.

ST. MATT. V.

46 the just and on the unjust. For if ye love them which love you, what reward have ye? do not even the 47 publicans the same? And if ye salute your brethren only, what do ye more *than others*? do not even the heathen[3] so?

54 Be ye therefore perfect, even as your heavenly[4] Father is perfect.

ST. MATT. VI.

1 But[7] take heed that ye do not your righteousness[8] before men, to be seen of them: otherwise ye have no reward of your Father which is in 2 heaven. Therefore when thou doest *thine* alms, do not sound a trumpet before thee, as the hypocrites do in the synagogues and in the streets, that they may have glory of men. Verily I say unto you, They have 3 their reward. But when thou doest alms, let not thy left hand know what 4 thy right hand doeth: that thine alms may be in secret: and thy Father which seeth in secret shall reward thee.[9]

5 And when ye pray, ye[10] shall not be as the hypocrites *are:* for they love to pray standing in the synagogues and in the corners of the

ST. LUKE VI.

32 For if ye love them which love you, what thank have ye? for sinners also 33 love those that love them. For if also[1] ye do good to them which do good to you, what thank have ye? 34 sinners[2] also do even the same. And if ye lend *to them* of whom ye hope to receive, what thank have ye? for sinners also lend to sinners, to receive 35 as much again. But love ye your enemies, and do good, and lend, hoping for nothing again; and your reward shall be great, and ye shall be the children of the Highest: for he is kind unto the unthankful and *to* the 36 evil. Be ye [5] merciful, as your Father[6] is merciful.

---

[1] And if ye do　　[2] for sinners also　　[3] the publicans
[4] your Father which is in heaven　　[5] Be ye therefore merciful　　[6] also is merciful
[7] *omit* But　　　　[8] your alms before men
[9] which seeth in secret himself shall reward thee openly
[10] when thou prayest, thou shalt not

ST. MATT. VI.	ST. LUKE VI.

streets, that they may be seen of men. Verily I say unto you, They have 6 their reward. But thou, when thou prayest, enter into thy closet, and when thou hast shut thy door, pray to thy Father which is in secret; and thy Father which seeth in secret 7 shall reward thee.[1] But when ye pray, use not vain repetitions,[a] as the heathen *do:* for they think that they shall be heard for their much speak- 8 ing. Be not ye therefore like unto them: for your Father knoweth what things ye have need of, before ye ask 9 him. After this manner therefore pray ye: [b]Our Father which art in 10 heaven. Hallowed be thy name. Thy kingdom come. Thy will be done 11 in earth, as *it is* in heaven. Give us 12 this day our daily bread. And forgive us our debts, as we have forgiven [2] 13 our debtors. And lead us not into temptation, but deliver us from evil.[3] 14 For if ye forgive men their tres- passes, your heavenly Father will 15 also forgive you: but if ye forgive not men,[4] neither will your Father forgive your trespasses.

16 Moreover when ye fast, be not, as the hypocrites, of a sad countenance: for they disfigure their faces, that they may appear unto men to fast. Verily I say unto you, They have 17 their reward. But thou, when thou fastest, anoint thine head, and wash

---

[1] reward thee openly.   [2] as we forgive our
[3] from evil: For thine is the kingdom, and the power, and the glory, for ever. Amen.
[4] forgive not men their trespasses
[a] Comp. Eccl. v. 2.   [b] Lk. xi. 2–4.

---

§ 44. vi. 9. The Lord's prayer is given here, and also again where it occurs in Lk. xi. There seems no reason why it may not have been repeated, especially as it is given by St. Luke in a somewhat shorter form, and it is in each case so intimately connected with the context as not to be easily separated.

ST. MATT. VI., VII.	ST. LUKE VI.
18 thy face; that thou appear not unto men to fast, but unto thy Father, which is in secret: and thy Father, which seeth in secret, shall reward thee.[1]	
19 Lay not up for yourselves treasures upon earth, where moth[a] and rust doth corrupt, and where thieves break	
20 through and steal: but lay up for yourselves treasures in heaven, where neither moth nor rust doth corrupt, and where thieves do not break	
21 through nor steal: for where thy[2] treasure is, there will thine[2] heart be also. **VII.**	
1 Judge not, that ye be not judged.	37 Judge not, and ye shall not be judged: and[3] condemn not, and ye shall not be condemned: forgive, and
2 For with what judgment ye judge, ye shall be judged:	38 ye shall be forgiven: give, and it shall be given unto you; good measure, pressed down,[4] shaken together, running over, shall men give into your bosom. For with what[5] measure ye
and with what measure ye mete, it shall be measured to you.[6][b]	mete it shall be measured to you 39 again.[b] And he spake also[7] a parable unto them. Can the blind lead the blind? shall they not both fall 40 into the ditch? The disciple is not above the[8] master: but every one that is perfect shall be as his master.
3 And why beholdest thou the mote that is in thy brother's eye, but considerest not the beam that is in thine 4 own eye? Or how wilt thou say to thy brother, Let me pull out the mote out of thine eye; and, behold,	41 And why beholdest thou the mote that is in thy brother's eye, but perceivest not the beam that is in thine 42 own eye? [9]How canst thou say to thy brother, Brother, let me pull out the mote that is in thine eye, when thou thyself beholdest not the beam that is in thine own eye? Thou
5 a beam *is* in thine own eye? Thou hypocrite, first cast out the beam out	hypocrite! cast out first the beam out

[1] reward thee openly [2] your treasure ..... your heart [3] *omit* and
[4] and shaken together, and [5] For with the same measure that ye mete withal it shall be
[6] measured to you again [7] *omit* also [8] his master [9] Either how canst thou
[a] See Lk. xii. 33, 34. [b] Mar. iv. 24.

ST. MATT. VII.	ST. LUKE VI.

of thine own eye; and then shalt thou see clearly to cast out the mote out of thy brother's eye.

6 Give not that which is holy unto the dogs, neither cast ye your pearls before swine, lest they trample them under their feet, and turn again and 12 rend you. Therefore all things whatsoever ye would that men should do to you, do ye even so to them: for this is the law[a] and the prophets.

13 Enter ye in at the straight gate: [b]for wide *is* the gate, and broad *is* the way, that leadeth to destruction, and many there be which go in 14 thereat: because strait *is* the gate, and narrow *is* the way, which leadeth unto life, and few there be that find it.

15 Beware of false prophets, which come to you in sheep's clothing, but inwardly they are ravening wolves. 16 Ye shall know them by their fruits. [c]Do men gather grapes of thorns, or 17 figs of thistles? Even so every good tree bringeth forth good fruit; but a corrupt tree bringeth forth evil fruit. 18 A good tree cannot bring forth evil fruit, neither *can* a corrupt tree bring 19 forth good fruit. Every tree that bringeth not forth good fruit is hewn 20 down, and cast into the fire. Wherefore by their fruits ye shall know them.[c]

21 Not every one that saith unto me, Lord! Lord! shall enter into the kingdom of heaven; but he that doeth the will of my Father which 22 is in heaven. Many will say to me in that day, Lord! Lord! have we not

---

of thine own eye, and then shalt thou see clearly to pull out the mote that is in thy brother's eye.

31 And as ye would that men should do to you, do ye also to them likewise.

43 For a good tree bringeth not forth corrupt fruit; neither again[1] doth a corrupt tree bring forth good fruit. 44 For every tree is known by his own fruit.[c] For of thorns men do not gather figs, nor of a bramble bush 45 gather they grapes. A good man out of the good treasure of the[2] heart bringeth forth that which is good; and an evil out of the evil[3] bringeth forth that which is evil; for of the abundance of the heart his mouth speaketh.

46 And why call ye me, Lord! Lord! and do not the things which I say?

---

[1] *omit* again   [2] his heart
[3] an evil man out of the evil treasure of his heart bringeth forth

[a] Lev. xix. 18.   [b] Lk. xiii. 24.   [c] Matt. xii. 33; Comp. Jas. iii. 12.

ST. MATT. VII.

prophesied in thy name? and in thy name have cast out devils? and in thy name done many wonderful 23 works? And then will I profess unto them, I never knew you: depart from me, ye that work iniquity!

24 Therefore whosoever heareth these sayings of mine, and doeth them, shall be likened¹ unto a wise man, which 25 built his house upon a rock: and the rain descended, and the floods came, and the winds blew, and beat upon that house; and it fell not: for it 26 was founded upon a rock. And every one that heareth these sayings of mine, and doeth them not, shall be likened unto a foolish man, which 27 built his house upon the sand: and the rain descended, and the floods came, and the winds blew, and beat upon that house; and it fell: and great was the fall of it.

28 And it came to pass, when Jesus had ended these sayings, the people were astonished* at his doctrine: 29 for he taught them as *one* having authority, and not as their ³ scribes.

ST. MATT. VIII.

1 When he was come down from the mountain, great multitudes followed him.

ST. LUKE VI.

47 Whosoever cometh to me, and heareth my sayings, and doeth them, I will shew you to whom he is like: 48 He is like a man which built an house, and digged deep, and laid the foundation on a rock: and when the flood arose, the stream beat vehemently upon that house, and could not shake it: because it was well 49 built.² But he that heareth, and doeth not, is like a man that without a foundation built an house upon the earth; against which the stream did beat vehemently, and immediately it fell; and the ruin of that house was great.

§ 45. The Healing of the Centurion's Servant. — *Capernaum.*

ST. MATT. VIII. 5–13.   ST. LUKE VII. 1–10.

5 And when he⁴ was entered into Capernaum, there came unto him a

1 Now when he had ended all his sayings in the audience of the people,

---

¹ I will liken him   ² for it was founded upon a rock.   ³ the scribes   ⁴ when Jesus was
ᵃ Matt. xiii. 54; Mar. i. 22; vi. 2; Lk. iv. 32; see Jno. vii. 46.

---

§ 45. The excellent note of Robinson may well be quoted here. "In Matthew the Centurion seems to come in person to Jesus, in Luke, he sends the elders of the Jews. This diversity is satisfactorily explained by the old law-maxim: *Qui facit per alium, facit per se.* Matthew narrates briefly; Luke gives the circumstances more fully. In like manner, in Jno. iv. 1, Jesus is said to baptize, when he did it by his disciples. In Jno. xix. 1, and elsewhere,

ST. MATT. VIII.

6 centurion, beseeching him, ¹and saying, Lord, my servant lieth at home sick of the palsy, grievously tor‑
7 mented. He¹ saith unto him, I will come and heal him.

8 But⁴ the centurion answered and said, Lord, I am not worthy that thou shouldest come under my roof: but speak by⁵ word only, and my
9 servant shall be healed. For I am a man under authority, having soldiers under me: and I say to this *man*, Go, and he goeth; and to another, Come, and he cometh; and to my servant, Do this, and he doeth *it*.
10 When Jesus heard *it*, he marvelled, and said to them that followed, Verily I say unto you, I have not found so
11 great faith, no, not in Israel. And I say unto you, That many shall come from the east and west, and shall sit down with Abraham, and Isaac, and Jacob, in the kingdom of heaven.
12 But the children of the kingdom shall go forth⁷ into outer darkness: there

ST. LUKE VII.

2 he entered into Capernaum. And a certain centurion's servant, who was dear unto him, was sick, and ready
3 to die. And when he heard of Jesus, he sent unto him the elders of the Jews, beseeching him that he would
4 come and heal his servant. And when they came to Jesus, they asked² him instantly, saying, That he was worthy for whom he should do this:
5 for he loveth our nation, and he hath
6 built us a synagogue. Then Jesus went with them. And when he was now not far from the house, the centurion sent friends,³ saying, Lord, trouble not thyself: for I am not worthy that thou shouldest enter under
7 my roof: wherefore neither thought I myself worthy to come unto thee: but say in a word, and let⁶ my servant
8 be healed. For I also am a man set under authority, having under me soldiers, and I say unto one, Go, and he goeth; and to another, Come, and he cometh; and to my servant, Do
9 this, and he doeth *it*. When Jesus heard these things, he marvelled at him, and turned him about, and said unto the people that followed him, I say unto you, I have not found so great faith, no, not in Israel.

---

¹ And Jesus saith   ² they besought him
⁴ *omit* But   ⁵ speak the word only
⁷ shall be cast out into
³ sent friends to him, saying unto him, Lord,
⁶ and my servant shall be

Pilate is said to have scourged Jesus; certainly not with his own hands. In Mar. x. 35, James and John come to Jesus with a certain request; in Matt. xx. 20. it is their mother who prefers the request. In 2 Sam. xxix. 1, God moves David to number Israel; in 1 Chron. xxi. 1, it is Satan who provokes him."

ST. MATT. VIII.	ST. LUKE VII.
shall be weeping and gnashing of teeth. 13 And Jesus said unto the centurion, Go thy way; as thou hast believed, *so* be it done unto thee. And the [1] servant was healed in the self same hour.	10 And they that were sent, returning to the house, found the servant whole.[2]

§ 46. Our Lord raises the only Son of a Widow. — *Near Nain.*

St. Luke vii. 11–17.

11 And it came to pass the day after, that he went into a city called Nain;
12 and many of his disciples went with him, and much people. Now when he came nigh to the gate of the city, behold, there was a dead man carried out, the only son of his mother, and she was a widow: and much people of the
13 city was with her. And when the Lord saw her, he had compassion on her,
14 and said unto her, Weep not. And he came and touched the bier: and they that bare *him* stood still. And he said, Young man, I say unto thee, Arise!
15 And he that was dead sat up, and began to speak. And he delivered him to
16 his mother. And there came a fear on all: and they glorified God, saying, That a great prophet is risen up among us; and, That God hath visited his
17 people. And this rumor of him went forth throughout all Judæa, and throughout all the region round about.

§ 47. John the Baptist in Prison sends to Jesus; His Testimony concerning John.

St. Matt. xi. 2–19.	St. Luke vii. 18–35; xvi. 16.
2 Now when John had heard in the prison the works of Christ, he sent 3 by [3] his disciples, and said unto him, Art thou he that should come, or do we look for another?	18 And the disciples of John shewed him of all these things. 19 And John calling *unto him* two of his disciples sent *them* to the Lord.[4] saying, Art thou he that should come? 20 or look we for another? When the men were come unto him, they said, John Baptist hath sent us unto thee, saying, Art thou he that should come? 21 or look we for another? In that [5] hour he cured many of *their* infirmi-

[1] his servant   [2] the servant whole that had been sick   [3] sent two of his disciples
[4] sent *them* to Jesus,   [5] And in that same hour

§ 47. This narrative is plainly not in chronological order in St. Matthew. He places it after the mission of the twelve, x. 5 ss.; whereas it appears by comparing Matt. xiv. 1 and 13, with Mar. vi. 14; vii. 30, 31, that John was beheaded during their absence. The continuous order of St. Luke is therefore followed.

ST. MATT. XI.

4 Jesus answered and said unto them,
Go and shew John again those things
5 which ye do hear and see:[a] the
blind receive their sight, and the
lame walk, the lepers are cleansed,
and the deaf hear, and[2] the dead are
raised up, and the poor have the gos-
6 pel preached to them. And blessed
is *he*, whosoever shall not be offended
in me.

7 And as they departed, Jesus began
to say unto the multitudes concerning
John, What went ye out into the
wilderness to see? A reed shaken
8 with the wind? But why went ye
out?[3] for to see a man clothed in soft
raiment[4]? Behold! they that wear soft
9 *clothing* are in king's houses. But
why went ye out?[5] for to see a
prophet? yea, I say unto you, and
10 more than a prophet! This[6] is *he*,
of whom it is written, [b]Behold! I send
my messenger before thy face, which
shall prepare thy way before thee.
11 Verily I say unto you, Among them
that are born of women there hath
not risen a greater than John the
Baptist: notwithstanding he that is
least in the kingdom of heaven is
12 greater than he. And from the days
of John the Baptist until now the
kingdom of heaven suffereth violence,
13 and the violent take it by force. For

ST. LUKE VII.

ties and plagues, and of evil spirits;
and unto many *that were* blind he
22 gave sight. Then he[1] answering
said unto them, Go your way, and
tell John what things ye have seen
and heard;[a] how that the blind see,
the lame walk, the lepers are cleansed,
the deaf hear, the dead are raised,
to the poor the gospel is preached.
23 And blessed is *he*, whosoever shall
not be offended in me.

24 And when the messengers of John
were departed, he began to speak
unto the people concerning John,
What went ye out into the wilderness
for to see? A reed shaken with the
25 wind? But what went ye out for to
see? A man clothed in soft raiment?
Behold! they which are gorgeously
apparelled, and live delicately, are
26 in kings' courts. But what went ye
out for to see? A prophet? Yea,
I say unto you, and much more than
27 a prophet! This is *he*, of whom it is
written,[b] Behold! I send my messenger before thy face, which shall
28 prepare thy way before thee. [7]I say
unto you, Among those that are born
of women there is not a greater
prophet than John:[8] but he that is
least in the kingdom of God is greater
than he.

[1] Then Jesus answering
[2] *omit* and
[3] But what went ye out to see? A man clothed
[4] raiment
[5] But what went ye out for to see? A prophet?
[6] For this is
[7] For I say unto you
[8] John the Baptist

[a] Isa. xxxv. 4–6; xlii. 7; lxi. 1.

[b] Mal. iii. 1. Behold! I will send my messenger, and he shall prepare the way before me. See Mar. i. 2; Lk. i. 76.

ST. MATT. XI.

all the prophets and the law proph-
14 esied until John. And if ye will
receive *it*, this is Elias,[a] which was
15 for to come. He that hath ears[1] let
him hear!

16 But whereunto shall I liken this
generation? It is like unto children
sitting in the markets, and calling
17 unto others,[3] saying, We have piped
unto you, and ye have not danced;
we have mourned,[5] and ye have not
18 lamented. For John came neither
eating nor drinking, and they say,
19 He hath a devil. The Son of man
came eating and drinking, and they
say, Behold a man gluttonous, and a
winebibber, a friend of publicans and
sinners! But wisdom is justified of
her works.[6]

ST. LUKE XVI.

16 The law and the prophets *were* until
John: since that time the kingdom
of God is preached, and every man
presseth into it.

ST. LUKE VII.

29 (And all the people that heard *him*,
and the publicans, justified God, being
baptized with the baptism of John. But
30 the Pharisees and lawyers rejected
the counsel of God against themselves, being not baptized of him.)
31 [2]Whereunto then shall I liken the
men of this generation? and to what
32 are they like? They are like unto
children sitting in the market-place,
and calling one to another,[4] saying,
We have piped unto you, and ye
have not danced; we have mourned,
33 and ye have not wept. For John
the Baptist came neither eating bread
nor drinking wine; and ye say, He
34 hath a devil. The Son of man is
come eating and drinking; and ye
say, Behold a gluttonous man, and
a winebibber, a friend of publicans
35 and sinners! But wisdom is justified
of all her children.

§ 48. Our Lord, at meat with Simon a Pharisee, is anointed by a Woman that was a Sinner.

ST. LUKE VII. 36-50.

36 And one of the Pharisees desired him that he would eat with him. And
37 he went into the Pharisee's house, and sat down to meat. And, behold, a
woman which was in the city, a sinner, and knowing[1] that *Jesus* sat at meat

---

[1] hath ears to hear, let him hear.
[3] calling unto their fellows, and saying,
[5] mourned to you
[7] a woman in the city, which was a sinner, when she knew that

[2] And the Lord said, Whereunto
[4] and saying
[6] of her children

[a] Mal. iv. 5, 6. See Matt. xvii. 11-13; Mar. ix. 12, 13; Lk. i. 16, 17.

---

§ 48. The anointing here recorded is obviously a different one from that recorded of Mary, the sister of Lazarus, in Jno. xii. 1-11, and which was certainly the same with that mentioned in Matt. xxvi. 6-13; Mar. xiv. 3-9. In both cases, indeed, there was an anointing while Jesus was at meat, and in both cases the name of his host was Simon; but in that case he is

St. Luke VII.

38 in the Pharisee's house, brought an alabaster box of ointment, and stood at his feet behind *him* weeping, and began to wash his feet with tears, and did wipe *them* with the hairs of her head, and kissed his feet, and anointed 39 *them* with the ointment. Now when the Pharisee which had bidden him saw *it*, he spake within himself, saying, This man, if he were a prophet, would have known who and what manner of woman *this is* that toucheth him: for she is a sinner.

40 And Jesus answering said unto him, Simon, I have somewhat to say unto 41 thee. And he saith, Master, say on. There was a certain creditor which had two debtors: the one owed five hundred pence, and the other fifty. 42 [1] When they had nothing to pay, he frankly forgave them both. Which of 43 them therefore [2] will love him most? Simon answering [3] said, I suppose that *he*, to whom he forgave most. And he said unto him, Thou hast rightly 44 judged. And he turned to the woman, and said unto Simon, Seest thou this woman? I entered into thine house, thou gavest me no water for my feet: but she hath washed my feet with tears, and wiped *them* with her hairs.[4] 45 Thou gavest me no kiss: but this woman since the time I came in hath not 46 ceased to kiss my feet. My head with oil thou didst not anoint: but this 47 woman hath anointed my feet with ointment. Wherefore I say unto thee, Her sins, which are many, are forgiven; for she loved much: but to whom 48 little is forgiven, *the same* loveth little. And he said unto her, Thy sins are 49 forgiven. And they that sat at meat with him began to say within themselves, 50 Who is this that forgiveth sins also? And he said to the woman, Thy faith hath saved thee; go in peace.

§ 49. Our Lord makes another circuit of Galilee with the Twelve.

St. Luke viii. 1–3.

1 And it came to pass afterward, that he went throughout every city and village, preaching and shewing the glad tidings of the kingdom of God: and 2 the twelve *were* with him, and certain women, which had been healed of evil spirits and infirmities, Mary called Magdalene, out of whom went seven devils, 3 and Joanna, the wife of Chuza Herod's steward, and Susanna, and many others, which ministered unto them [5] of their substance.

[1] And when they had
[3] answered and said
[5] unto him

[2] Tell me therefore, which of them will love
[4] the hairs of her head

---

distinguished as Simon "the leper," (Matt. xxvi. 6; Mar. xiv. 3), in this as "the Pharisee." Again, in that case the woman was the sister of Lazarus, and seems to have been held in much esteem among the Jews; in this case she was "a sinner," and it is on that ground that Simon bases his objection, while in the other instance it is the disciples who are offended, and that simply because of the waste.

The passage Matt. xi. 20–30, inserted by several harmonists before this section, is here transferred to the parallel passages in St. Luke.

§ 50. A Demoniac being healed, the Scribes and Pharisees blaspheme, and seek a Sign. Our Lord's Replies. — *Galilee.*

MATT. XII. 22–45. VI. 22, 23.   MAR. III. 19^b–30.   LK. XI. 14–36. XII. 10.

	And he cometh[1] into 20 an house. And the multitude cometh together again, so that they could not so much 21 as eat bread. And when his friends heard *of it,* they went out to lay hold on him: for they said, He is beside himself.	
22 Then was brought unto him one possessed with a devil, blind, and dumb: and he healed him, insomuch that the dumb[2] spake and saw. 23 And all the people were amazed, and said, Is not this the son 24 of David? But when the Pharisees heard *it,* they said, This *fellow* doth not cast out devils, but by Beelzebub[a] the prince of the devils. 25 And he[3] knew their	22 And the scribes which came down from Jerusalem said, He hath Beelzebub,[a] and by the prince of the devils casteth he out devils. 23 And he called them *unto him,* and said unto	14 And he was casting out a devil, and it was dumb. And it came to pass, when the devil was gone out, the dumb spake; and the people wondered. 15 But some of them said, He casteth out devils through Beelzebub[a] the 16 chief of the devils. And others, tempting *him,* sought of him a sign[b] 17 from heaven. But he, knowing their thoughts,

[1] And they went into an house   [2] the blind and dumb both spake and saw.
[3] And Jesus knew
[a] See Matt. ix. 32–34.   [b] Matt. xvi. 1; Mar. viii. 11; Jno. ii. 18.

---

§ 50. The parallelism of the three Evangelists is obvious, and as neither St. Matthew nor St. Luke furnish any definite note of time, the order of St. Mark is observed. St. Mark passes over in silence all the matters which occurred between the appointment of the twelve and this miracle. What is commonly divided into two sections is here thrown into one as really forming one continuous narrative, although only the former part of it is given by St. Mark.

Two verses from the Sermon on the Mount are added at the close of this section, as being parallel to St. Luke, and not closely attached to the context in St. Matthew.

ST. MATT. XII.	ST. MARK III.	ST. LUKE XI.
thoughts, and said unto them, Every kingdom divided against itself is brought to desolation; and every city or house divided against itself ²⁶ shall not stand: and if Satan cast out Satan, he is divided against himself; how shall then his kingdom stand?	them in parables, How can Satan cast out ²⁴ Satan? And if a kingdom be divided against itself, that kingdom ²⁵ cannot stand. And if a house be divided against itself, that house will not be able ²⁶ to¹ stand. And if Satan rise up against himself, he is² divided, and cannot stand, but hath an end.	said unto them, Every kingdom divided against itself is brought to desolation; and a house *divided* against a house ¹⁸ falleth. If Satan also be divided against himself, how shall his kingdom stand? because ye say that I cast out devils through Beelzebub.
²⁷ And if I by Beelzebub cast out devils, by whom do your children cast *them* out? therefore they shall be your ²⁸ judges. But if I cast out devils by the Spirit of God, then the kingdom of God is come unto you.		¹⁹ And if I by Beelzebub cast out devils, by whom do your sons cast *them* out? therefore shall they be ²⁰ your judges. But if I with the finger of God cast out devils, no doubt the kingdom of God is come upon you.
²⁹ Or else how can one enter into a strong man's house, and spoil his goods, except he first bind the strong man? and then he will spoil his house.	²⁷ But³ no man can enter into a strong man's house, and spoil his goods, except he will first bind the strong man; and then he will spoil his house.	²¹ When a strong man armed keepeth his palace, his goods are in peace: ²² but when a stronger than he shall come upon him, and overcome him, he taketh from him all his armor wherein he trusted, and divideth his spoils.
³⁰ He that is not with me is against me; and he that gathereth not with me scattereth abroad.		²³ He that is not with me is against me: and he that gathereth not with me scattereth.
³¹ Wherefore I say unto you, All manner of sin and blasphemy shall be forgiven unto men:	²⁸ Verily I say unto you, All sins shall be forgiven unto the sons of men, and the⁴ blasphe-	

¹ that house cannot stand
³ *omit* But

² and be divided, he cannot stand
⁴ *omit* the

ST. MATT. XII.	ST. MARK III.	ST. LUKE XII.
but the blasphemy *against* the *Holy* Ghost shall not be forgiven[1].	mies wherewithsoever they shall blaspheme:	
32 And whosoever speaketh a word against the Son of man, it shall be forgiven him: but whosoever speaketh against the Holy Ghost, it shall not be forgiven him, neither in this world, neither in the *world* to come.	29 But he that shall blaspheme against the Holy Ghost hath never forgiveness, but shall be[2] in danger of eternal sin?[3] Because they 30 said, He hath an unclean spirit.	10 And whosoever shall speak a word against the Son of man, it shall be forgiven him: but unto him that blasphemeth against the Holy Ghost, it shall not be forgiven.
33 Either make the tree good, and his fruit good[a]; or else make the tree corrupt, and his fruit corrupt: for the tree is known by 34 *his* fruit. O generation of vipers![b] how can ye, being evil, speak good things? for out of the abundance of the heart the mouth 35 speaketh.[c] A good man out of the good treasure[4] bringeth forth good things: and an evil man out of the evil treasure bringeth 36 forth evil things. But I say unto you, That every idle word that men shall speak, they shall give account thereof in the day of 37 judgment. For by thy words thou shalt be		

[1] not be forgiven unto men.
[2] but is in danger
[3] of eternal damnation
[4] out of the good treasure of the heart
[a] See Matt. vii. 17–20; Lk. vi. 43, 44.   [b] See Matt. iii. 7; xxiii. 33.   [c] See Lk. vi. 45.

ST. MATT. XII.	ST. MARK III.	ST. LUKE XI.
justified, and by thy words thou shalt be condemned. 38 Then certain of the scribes and of the Pharisees answered him,[1] saying, Master, we would see a sign from thee. 39 But he answered and said unto them, An evil and adulterous generation seeketh after a sign; and there shall no sign be given to it, but the sign of the prophet 40 Jonas:[a] For as Jonas was three days and three nights in the whale's belly[b]; so shall the Son of man be three days and three nights in the 41 heart of the earth. The men of Nineveh shall rise in judgment with this generation, and shall condemn it: because they repented at the preaching of Jonas[c]; and, behold, a greater than Jonas is 42 here. The queen of the south shall rise up in the judgment with this generation, and shall condemn it: for she came from the uttermost parts of the earth to hear the wisdom of Solomon[d]; and, behold, a greater than Solomon is here. 43 When the unclean spirit is gone out of a		29 And when the people were gathered thick together, he began to say, This generation[2] is an evil generation: they seek a sign; and there shall no sign be given it, but the sign of Jonas.[a][3] 30 For as Jonas was a sign unto the Ninevites, so shall also the Son of man be to this generation. 32 The men of Nineveh shall rise up in the judgment with this generation, and shall condemn it: for they repented at the preaching of Jonas[c]; and, behold, a greater than Jonas is 31 here. The queen of the south shall rise up in the judgment with the men of this generation, and condemn them: for she came from the utmost parts of the earth to hear the wisdom of Solomon[d]; and, behold, a greater than Solomon is here. 24 When the unclean spirit is gone out of a man,

[1] omit him   [2] omit first generation.   [3] Jonas the prophet
[a] See Matt. xvi. 4.   [b] Jonah ii. 1.   [c] Jonah iii. 5–10.   [d] 1 Kings x. 1; 2 Chron. ix. 1.

PART IV. § 50.]   AND THE EVENTS UNTIL THE THIRD.   73

ST. MATT. XII.	ST. MARK III.	ST. LUKE XI.
man, he walketh through dry places, seeking rest, ⁴⁴ and findeth none. Then he saith, I will return into my house from whence I came out; and when he is come, he findeth *it* empty, and¹ swept, ⁴⁵ and garnished. Then goeth he, and taketh with himself seven other spirits more wicked than himself, and they enter in and dwell there: and the last *state* of that man is worse than the first. Even so shall it be also unto this wicked generation.		he walketh through dry places, seeking rest; and finding none, he saith, I will return unto my house whence I came out; ²⁵ and when he cometh, he findeth *it* swept and ²⁶ garnished. Then goeth he, and taketh *to him* seven other spirits more wicked than himself; and they enter in, and dwell there: and the last *state* of that man is worse than the first.
		²⁷ And it came to pass, as he spake these things, a certain woman of the company lifted up her voice, and said unto him, Blessed *is* the womb that bare thee, and the paps which thou hast sucked! ²⁸ But he said, Yea rather, blessed *are* they that hear the word of God and keep *it!* ²
		³³ No man, when he hath lighted a candle, putteth *it* in a secret place, neither under a bushel, but on a candlestick,ᵃ that they which come in may see the
ST. MATT. VI. ²² The light of the body is the eye: if³ thine eye		³⁴ light. The light of the body is thine⁴ eye: when

¹ *omit* and *before* swept,   ² keep it   ³ if therefore thine eye
⁴ is the eye: therefore when
ᵃ See Matt. v. 15; Mar. iv. 21; Lk. viii. 16.

St. Matt. VI.	St. Mark III.	St. Luke XI.
be single, thy whole body shall be full of light. 23 But if thine eye be evil, thy whole body shall be full of darkness. If therefore the light that is in thee be darkness, how great *is* that darkness!		thine eye is single, thy whole body also is full of light; but when *thine eye* is evil, thy body also 35 *is* full of darkness. Take heed therefore that the light which is in thee be 36 not darkness. If thy whole body therefore *be* full of light, having no part dark, the whole shall be full of light, as when the bright shining of a candle doth give thee light.

§ 51. Our Lord describes his Disciples as his true Kinsmen.

St. Matt. XII. 46–50.	St. Mark III. 31–35.	St. Luke VIII. 19–21.
46 While he yet talked to the people, behold, *his* mother and his brethren stood without, desiring to speak 47 with him. Then one said unto him, Behold, thy mother and thy brethren stand without, desiring to speak	31 And his mother cometh and his brethren,[2] and standing without, sent unto 32 him, calling him. And the multitude sat about him, and they say [4] unto him, Behold, thy mother and thy brethren and thy sisters [5]	19 Then came to him his[1] mother and his brethren, and could not come at 20 him for the press. And it was told him that[3] Thy mother and thy brethren stand without,

---

[1] *his* mother   [2] There came then his brethren and his mother
[3] told him *by certain* which said, Thy mother   [4] they said   [5] *omit* and thy sisters

---

§§ 51. 52. The beginning of Matt. xii. 46 connects § 51 intimately with what precedes, and this is also in accordance with the order of St. Mark. So also the first words of Matt. xiii. give a definite note of time connecting § 52 with the previous section; and this also is the order of St. Mark. On the other hand, the observance of this order makes it necessary to defer the narrative beginning with Lk. xi. 37. That passage, however, begins with the words, *And as he spake;* and we are therefore brought to the conclusion that such expressions may be used by the Evangelist simply to designate the circumstances under which Jesus was invited by the Pharisee — that is, while he was in the midst of discoursing — without special reference to the particular discourse recorded in the preceding verses. The difficulty, though of less importance, is similar to the one already noticed in regard to the time of the healing of Jairus' daughter, and the solution is in either case substantially the same. Compare the remarks on § 38.

ST. MATT. XII.	ST. MARK III.	ST. LUKE VIII.
48 with thee. But he answered and said unto him that told him, Who is my mother? and who are my 49 brethren? And he stretched forth the [3] hand toward his disciples, and said, Behold my mother and my 50 brethren! For whosoever shall do the will of my Father which is in heaven, the same is my brother, and sister, and mother.	without seek for thee. 33 And answering them, he saith,[1] Who is my mother and [2] my 34 brethren? And he looked round about on them which sat about him, and said, Behold my mother and my brethren! 35 [4]Whosoever shall do the will of God, the same is my brother, and [5] sister, and mother.	desiring to see thee. 21 And he answered and said unto them, My mother and my brethren are these which hear the word of God, and do *it*.[6]

§ 52. The Parable of the Sower, and its Interpretation. — *The Sea of Galilee.*

MATT. XIII. 1-15, 18-23.	MARK IV. 1-25.	LUKE VIII. 4-18.
1 The same day went Jesus out of the house, and sat by the sea side. 2 And great multitudes were gathered together unto him, so that he went into a ship, and sat; and the whole multitude stood on the 3 shore. And he spake many things unto them in parables, saying,	1 And he began again to teach by the sea side: and there gathereth unto him a very [7] great multitude, so that he entered into a ship, and sat in the sea; and the whole multitude were [8] by the sea on the land. 2 And he taught them many things by parables, and said unto them in his doctrine, 3 Hearken! Behold, there went out a sower	4 And when much people were gathered together, and were come to him out of every city, he spake by a parable:
4 Behold, a sower went forth to sow: and when he sowed, some *seeds* fell by the way	4 to sow: and it came to pass, as he sowed, some fell by the way	5 A sower went out to sow his seed: and as he sowed, some fell by the way side; and it was

---

[1] And he answered them, saying, [2] or my brethren [3] his hand
[4] For whosoever [5] and my sister [6] and do it.
[7] there was gathered unto him a great multitude [8] the whole multitude was

ST. MATT. XIII.	ST. MARK IV.	ST. LUKE VIII.
side, and the fowls came and devoured ⁵ them up: some fell upon stony places, where they had not much earth: and forthwith they sprung up, because they had no ⁶ deepness of earth: and when the sun was up, they were scorched; and because they had no root, they withered ⁷ away. And some fell among thorns; and the thorns sprung up, and ⁸ choked them. But other fell into good ground, and brought forth fruit, some an hundredfold,⁸ some sixtyfold, some thirty- ⁹ fold. Who hath ears,⁴ let him hear! ¹⁰ And the disciples came, and said unto him, Why speakest thou unto them in par- ¹¹ ables? He answered and said,⁸ Because it is given unto you to know the mysteries of the kingdom of heaven; but to them it is ¹³ not given. Therefore	side, and the fowls¹ came and devoured it ⁵ up. And some fell on stony ground, where it had not much earth; and immediately it sprang up, because it had no depth of earth: ⁶ but when the sun was up, it was scorched; and because it had no root it withered away. ⁷ And some fell among thorns, and the thorns grew up, and choked it, and it yielded no ⁸ fruit. And other fell on good ground, and did yield fruit that sprang up and increased: and brought forth, unto thirty, and unto sixty, and unto³ ⁹ an hundred.ᵃ And he said, Whosoever⁵ hath ears to hear, let him hear! ¹⁰ And when he was alone, they that were about him with the twelve asked of him ¹¹ the parables.⁷ And he said unto them, Unto you is given⁹ the mystery of the kingdom of God: but unto them that are without, all *these* things	trodden down, and the fowls of the air devoured ⁶ it. And some fell upon a rock; and as soon as it was sprung up, it withered away, because it ⁷ lacked moisture. And some fell among thorns; and the thorns sprang up with it, and choked ⁸ it. And other fell into² good ground, and sprang up, and bare fruit an hundredfold.ᵃ And when he had said these things, he cried, He that hath ears to hear, let him hear! ⁹ And his disciples asked him,⁶ What might this ¹⁰ parable be? And he said, Unto you it is given to know the mysteries of the kingdom of God; but to others in parables;

---

¹ the fowls of the air came   ² fell on good ground   ³ *thrice* some *for* unto
⁴ ears to hear, let him hear.   ⁵ And he said unto them He that hath ears
⁶ asked him, saying,   ⁷ the parable   ⁸ said unto them
⁹ Unto you it is given to know the mystery
ᵃ See Gen. xxvi. 12.

ST. MATT. XIII.	ST. MARK IV.	ST. LUKE VIII.
speak I to them in parables: because they seeing see not; and hearing they hear not, neither do they under-14 stand. And by[1] them is fulfilled the prophecy of Esaias, which saith,[a] By hearing ye shall hear, and shall not understand; and seeing ye shall see, and shall 15 not perceive: for this people's heart is waxed gross, and *their* ears are dull of hearing, and their eyes they have closed; lest at any time they should see with *their* eyes, and hear with *their* ears, and should understand with *their* heart, and should be converted, and I shall[3] heal them.	are done in parables: 12 That seeing they may see, and not perceive; and hearing they may hear, and not understand; lest at any time they should be converted, and it[2] should be forgiven them. 13 And he said unto them, Know ye not this parable? and how then will ye know all parables?	that seeing they might not see, and hearing they might not understand.
18 Hear ye therefore the parable of the 19 sower. When any one	14 The sower soweth	11 Now the parable is this: The seed is the

[1] And in them is fulfilled   [2] and *their* sins should be   [3] I should heal

[a] Isa. vi. 9, 10. Hear ye indeed, but understand not; and see ye indeed, but perceive not. Make the heart of this people fat, and make their ears heavy, and shut their eyes; lest they see with their eyes, and hear with their ears, and understand with their heart, and convert, and be healed. Compare Jno. xii. 39–41; Acts xxviii. 25–27.

§ 52. The sixteenth and seventeenth verses of St. Matthew are indeed appropriate in this connection; but yet not more so than to the connection in which the same language is given by St. Luke (x. 23, 24). Since therefore there is nothing here to absolutely fasten them to the context, and the language of Lk. x. 23 does not allow of their being removed thence, it has seemed better to place them in parallelism with that passage.

ST. MATT. XIII.	ST. MARK IV.	ST. LUKE VIII.
heareth the word of the kingdom, and understandeth *it* not, then cometh the wicked *one*, and catcheth away that which was sown in his heart. This is he which received seed by the 20 way side. But he that received the seed into stony places, the same is he that heareth the word, and anon with 21 joy receiveth it; Yet hath he not root in himself, but dureth for a while: for when tribulation or persecution ariseth because of the word, by and by 22 he is offended. He also that received seed among the thorns is he that heareth the word; and the care of the [3] world, and the deceitfulness of riches, choke the word, and he becometh unfruit-23 ful. But he that received seed into the good ground is he that heareth the word, and understandeth *it;* which also beareth fruit, and bringeth forth, some an hun-	15 the word. And these are they by the way side, where the word is sown; but when they have heard, Satan cometh immediately, and taketh away the word that was sown 16 in them.[1] And these are they likewise which are sown on stony ground; who, when they have heard the word, immediately receive it with gladness; 17 and have no root in themselves, and so endure but for a time: afterward, when affliction or persecution ariseth for the word's sake, immediately they are 18 offended. And there are others [2] which are sown among thorns; such as hear the word, and the cares of the[3] world, and the deceitfulness of riches, and the lusts of other things entering in, choke the word, and it becometh unfruitful. 20 And these are they which are sown on good ground; such as hear the word, and receive *it*, and bring forth fruit, some thirty-	12 word of God. Those by the way side are they that hear; then cometh the devil, and taketh away the word out of their hearts, lest they should believe and be saved. 13 They on the rock *are they*, which, when they hear, receive the word with joy; and these have no root, which for a while believe, and in time of temptation fall 14 away. And that which fell among thorns are they, which, when they have heard, go forth, and are choked with cares and riches and pleasures of *this* life, and bring no 15 fruit to perfection. But that on the good ground are they, which in an honest and good heart, having heard the word, keep *it*, and bring forth fruit with patience.

[1] sown in their hearts   [2] And these are they which   [3] of this world

ST. MATT. XIII.	ST. MARK IV.	ST. LUKE VIII.
dredfold, some sixty, some thirty.	fold, some sixty, and some an hundred. 21 And he said unto them, Is a candle brought to be put under a bushel, or under a bed? and not to be set on a candlestick?ᵃ 22 For there is nothing hid, which shall not be manifested; neither was anything kept secret, but that it should come abroad.ᵇ 23 If any man have ears to hear, let him hear! 24 And he said unto them, Take heed what ye hear; with what measure ye mete, it shall be measured to you:ᶜ and unto you¹ shall more be given.	16 No man, when he hath lighted a candle, covereth it with a vessel, or putteth *it* under a bed; but setteth it on a candlestick,ᵃ that they which enter in may see the 17 light. For nothing is secret, that shall not be made manifest; neither *anything* hid, that shall not be known, and come 18 abroad.ᵇ Take heed therefore how ye hear:
12 For whosoever hath to him shall be given, and he shall have more abundance: but whosoever hath not, from him shall be taken away even that he hath.ᵈ	25 For he that hath, to him shall be given: and he that hath not, from him shall be taken even that which he hath.ᵈ	for whosoever hath, to him shall be given: and whosoever hath not. from him shall be taken even that which he seemto have.ᵈ

§ 53. Parable of the Tares, and other Parables.

ST. MATT. XIII. 24–53.	ST. MARK IV. 26–34.	ST. LUKE XIII. 18–21.
24 Another parable put he forth unto them, saying, The kingdom of heaven is likened unto a man which sowed good seed in		

¹ unto you that hear

ᵃ Matt. v. 15; Lk. xi. 33.   ᵇ Matt. x. 26; Lk. xii. 2.   ᶜ Matt. vii. 2; Lk. vi. 38.
ᵈ Matt. xxv 29; Lk. xix. 26.

ST. MATT. XIII.	ST. MARK IV.	ST. LUKE XIII.

25 his field: but while men slept, his enemy came and sowed tares among the wheat, and 26 went his way. But when the blade was sprung up, and brought forth fruit, then appeared the tares also. 27 So the servants of the householder came and said unto him, Sir, didst not thou sow good seed in thy field? from whence then hath 28 it tares? He said unto them, An enemy hath done this. The servants said unto him, Wilt thou then that we go and gather them 29 up? But he saith,[1] Nay; lest while ye gather up the tares, ye root up also the 30 wheat with them. Let both grow together until the harvest: and in the time of harvest I will say to the reapers, Gather ye together first the tares, and bind them in bundles to burn them; but gather the wheat into my barn.

26 And he said, So is the kingdom of God, as if a man should cast seed into the 28 ground; And should sleep, and rise night

---

[1] But he said

ST. MATT. XIII.	ST. MARK IV.	ST. LUKE XIII.
	and day, and the seed should spring and grow up, he knoweth 28 not how. [1] The earth bringeth forth fruit of herself; first the blade, then the ear, after that the full corn in the 29 ear. But when the fruit is brought forth, immediately he putteth in the sickle, because the harvest is come.	
	30 And he said, How [2] shall we liken the kingdom of God? or with what comparison shall we set it forth? [3]	18 Then said he, Unto what is the kingdom of God like? and whereunto shall I resemble 19 it? It is like a grain of mustard seed, which a man took, and cast into his garden; and it grew, and waxed a[4] tree.
31 Another parable put he forth unto them, saying, The kingdom of heaven is like to a grain of mustard seed, which a man took, and sowed in his field: 32 which indeed is the least of all seeds: but when it is grown, it is the greatest among herbs, and becometh a tree, so that the birds of the air come and lodge in the branches thereof.	31 *It is* like a grain of mustard seed, which, when it is sown in the earth, is less than all the seeds that be in 32 the earth: But when it is sown, it groweth up, and becometh greater than all herbs, and shooteth out great branches; so that the fowls of the air may lodge under the shadow of it.	and the fowls of the air lodged in the branches of it.
33 Another parable spake he unto them; The kingdom of heaven is like unto leaven which a woman took, and hid in three measures of meal, till the whole was leavened.		20 And again he said, Whereunto shall I liken the kingdom of God? 21 It is like leaven, which a woman took and hid in three measures of meal, till the whole was leavened.

[1] For the earth   [2] Whereunto shall we liken   [3] shall we compare it?   [4] waxed a great tree

ST. MATT. XIII.	ST. MARK IV.	ST. LUKE XIII.
34 All these things spake Jesus unto the multitude in parables;	33 And with many such parables spake he the word unto them, as they were able to 34 hear *it*. But without	
and without a parable spake he nothing [1] unto	a parable spake he not unto them: and when they were alone, he expounded all things to his own [2] disciples.	
35 them: that it might be fulfilled which was spoken by Esaias [3] the prophet, saying,[a] I will open my mouth in parables; I will utter things which have been kept secret from the foundation *of the world*.[4]		
36 Then he [5] sent the multitude away, and went into the house: and his disciples came unto him, saying, Declare unto us the parable of the tares of the		
37 field. He answered and said,[6] He that soweth the good seed is		
38 the Son of man; the field is the world; the good seed are the children of the kingdom: but the tares are the children of the wicked		
39 *one*; the enemy that sowed them is the		

[1] spake he not unto them   [2] *omit* own   [3] *omit* Esaias
[4] foundation of the world.   [5] Then Jesus sent   [6] and said unto them
[a] Ps. lxxviii. 2. I will open my mouth in a parable: I will utter dark sayings of old.

| ST. MATT. XIII. | ST. MARK IV. | ST. LUKE XIII. |

devil; the harvest is the end of the world;
40 and the reapers are the angels. As therefore the tares are gathered and burned in the fire; so shall it be in the end of the [1]
41 world. The Son of man shall send forth his angels, and they shall gather out of his kingdom all things that offend, and them
42 which do iniquity; and shall cast them into a furnace of fire: there shall be wailing
43 and gnashing of teeth. Then shall the righteous shine forth as the sun in the kingdom of their Father. Who hath ears,[2] let him hear!
44 [3]The kingdom of heaven is like unto treasure hid in a field; the which when a man hath found, he hideth, and for joy thereof goeth and selleth all that he hath, and buyeth that field.
45 Again, the kingdom of heaven is like unto a merchant man, seeking goodly pearls: but,[4]
46 when he had found one pearl of great price, went and sold all that he had, and bought it.
47 Again, the kingdom of heaven is like unto a net, that was cast into the sea, and gath
48 ered of every kind: which, when it was full, they drew to shore, and sat down, and gathered the good into vessels, but cast the
49 bad away. So shall it be at the end of the world: the angels shall come forth, and
50 sever the wicked from among the just: and shall cast them into the furnace of fire, there shall be wailing and gnashing of teeth.
51 [5]Have ye understood all these things?
52 They say unto him, Yea.[6] Then said he unto them. Therefore every scribe *which is* instructed unto the kingdom of heaven is like unto a man *that is* an householder, which bringeth forth out of his treasure *things* new and old.
53 And it came to pass, *that* when Jesus had finished these parables, he departed thence.

---

[1] end of this world   [2] who hath ears to hear   [3] Again, the kingdom
[4] who, when he had found   [5] Jesus saith unto them, Have ye understood
[6] They say unto him, Yea, Lord.

§ 54. Our Lord stills the Tempest on the Lake of Galilee.

St. Matt. viii. 18, 23–27.	St. Mark iv. 35–41.	St. Luke viii. 22–25.
18 Now when Jesus saw great multitudes about him, he gave commandment to depart unto the other side. 23 And when he was entered into a ship, his disciples followed him. 24 And, behold, there arose a great tempest in the sea, insomuch that the ship was covered with the waves: but he was asleep. 25 And they[3] came to *him*, and awoke him, saying, Lord, save![4] we perish! And he 26 saith unto them, Why are ye fearful, O ye of little faith? Then he arose, and rebuked the winds and the sea; and there was a great calm. 27 But the men marvelled, saying, What manner of man is this, that even the winds and the sea obey him!	35 And the same day, when the even was come, he saith unto them, Let us pass over unto the other 36 side. And when they had sent away the multitude, they took him even as he was in the ship. And there were also with him 37 other[1] ships. And there arose a great storm of wind, and the waves beat into the ship, so that the ship[2] 38 was now full. And he was in the hinder part of the ship, asleep on a pillow: and they awake him, and say unto him, Master! carest thou not that we perish? 39 And he arose, and rebuked the wind, and said unto the sea, Peace! be still! And the wind ceased, and there was a great calm. 40 And he said unto them, Why are ye so fearful? how is it that ye have no faith? 41 And they feared exceedingly, and said one to another, What manner of man is this, that even the wind and the sea obey him!	22 Now it came to pass on a certain day, that he went into a ship with his disciples: and he said unto them, Let us go over unto the other side of the lake. And they 23 launched forth. But as they sailed he fell asleep: and there came down a storm of wind on the lake; and they were filled *with water*, and 24 were in jeopardy. And they came to him, and awoke him, saying, Master! master! we perish! Then he arose, and rebuked the wind and the raging of the water: and they ceased, and there 25 was a calm. And he said unto them, Where *is*[5] your faith? And they being afraid wondered, saying one to another, What manner of man is this! for he commandeth even the winds and water, and they obey him.

[1] other little ships   [2] so that it was now full   [3] And his disciples came
[4] save us   [5] Where is

§ 55. The Demoniacs of Gadara.

St. Matt. viii. 28–ix. 1.	St. Mark v. 1–21.	St. Luke viii. 26–40.
28 And when he was come to the other side into the country of the Gadarenes,[1] there met him two possessed with devils, coming out of the tombs, exceeding fierce, so that no man might pass by that way.	1 And they came over unto the other side of the sea, into the country of the Gerasenes.[2] 2 And when he was come out of the ship, immediately there met him out of the tombs a man with an unclean spirit, who had *his* dwelling among the tombs: and no man could bind him, no, not with a[4] chain: 4 Because that he had been often bound with fetters and chains, and the chains had been plucked asunder by him, and the fetters broken in pieces: neither could any *man* tame him. And always, night and day, he was in the mountains, and in the tombs, crying, and cutting himself with stones. 6 And[5] when he saw Jesus afar off, he ran and worshipped him,	26 And they arrived at the country of the Gergesenes,[2] which is over against Galilee. And when he went forth to land, there met him out of the city a certain man, having devils,[3] and long time he ware no clothes, neither abode in *any* house, but in the tombs.
29 And, behold, they cried out, saying, What have we to do with thee,[7] thou Son of God? art thou come to torment us before the time?	7 And cried with a loud voice, and saith,[6] What have I to do with thee, Jesus, *thou* Son of the most high God? I abjure thee by God, that thou torment me	28 When he saw Jesus, he cried out, and fell down before him, and with a loud voice said, What have I to do with thee, Jesus, *thou* Son of God most high? I beseech thee, torment me not.

[1] Gergesenes   [2] Gadarenes   [3] which had devils long time, and ware
[4] with chains   [5] But when   [6] and said   [7] Jesus, thou Son of God

ST. MATT. VIII.	ST. MARK V.	ST. LUKE VIII.
	8 not! For he said unto him, Come out of the man, *thou* unclean spirit.	29 (For he had commanded the unclean spirit to come out of the man. For oftentimes it had caught him: and he was kept bound with chains and in fetters; and he brake the bands, and was driven of the devil in-
	9 **And** he asked him, what *is* thy name? And he saith unto him,[1] My name *is* Legion: for we are 10 many. And he besought him much that he would not send them away out of the	30 to the wilderness.) And Jesus asked him, saying, What is thy name? And he said, Legion: because many devils were en- 31 tered into him. And they besought him that he would not command them to go out into the
30 And there was a good way off from them an herd of many swine 31 feeding. So the devils besought him, saying, If thou cast us out, send us forth[4] into the herd of swine. 32 And he said unto them, Go. And when they were come out, they went into the swine:[6] and, behold, the whole herd[7] ran violently down a steep place into the sea, and perished in the waters. 33 And they that kept them fled, and went	11 country. Now there was there nigh unto the mountain[2] a great herd of swine feeding. 12 And they[3] besought him, saying, Send us into the swine, that we may enter into 13 them. And he[5] gave them leave. And the unclean spirits went out, and entered into the swine: and the herd ran violently down a steep place into the sea ([8]about two thousand) and were choked in the 14 sea. And they that fed the swine fled,	32 deep. And there was there an herd of many swine feeding on the mountain: and they besought him that he would suffer them to enter into them. And he suffered 33 them. Then went the devils out of the man, and entered into the swine: and the herd ran violently down a steep place into the lake, and 34 were choked. When they that fed *them* saw what

[1] And he answered, saying, My name
[2] mountains
[3] And all the devils besought
[4] suffer us to go away into the herd
[5] and forthwith Jesus gave
[6] the herd of swine
[7] whole herd of swine
[8] they were about

ST. MATT. VIII.	ST. MARK V.	ST. LUKE VIII.
their ways into the city, and told everything, and what was befallen to the possessed of the devils. 34 And, behold, the whole city came out to meet Jesus: and when they saw him, they besought *him* that he would depart out of their coasts.	and told *it* in the city, and in the country. And they went² to see what it was that 15 was done. And they come to Jesus, and see him that was possessed with the devil, and had the legion, sitting,³ clothed, and in his right mind: and they 16 were afraid. And they that that saw *it* told them how it befel to him that was possessed with the devil, and *also* concerning 17 the swine. And they began to pray him to depart out of their 18 coasts. And when he cometh⁶ into the ship, he that had been possessed with the devil prayed him that he might be with him. 19 And he⁸ suffered him not, but saith unto him, Go home to thy friends, and tell them how great things the Lord hath done for thee, and hath had compassion on thee. 20 And he departed, and	was done, they fled,¹ and told *it* in the city and in 35 the country. Then went they out to see what was done; and came to Jesus, and found the man, out of whom the devils were departed, sitting at the feet of Jesus, clothed, and in his right mind: and they were afraid. 36 And⁴ they which saw *it* told them by what means he that was possessed of the devils was healed. 37 Then the whole multitude of the country of the Gergesenes⁵ round about besought him to depart from them; for they were taken with great fear: and he went up into a⁷ ship, and re- 38 turned back again. Now the man out of whom the devils were departed besought him that he might be with him; but he⁹ sent him away, saying, 39 Return to thine own house, and shew how great things God hath done unto thee. And he went his way, and pub-

¹ and went, and told
⁴ They also which
⁷ the ship

² went out to see
⁵ Gadarenes
⁸ Howbeit Jesus suffered

³ sitting and clothed
⁶ when he was come
⁹ but Jesus sent

ST. MATT. IX.	ST. MARK V.	ST. LUKE VIII.
	began to publish in Decapolis how great things Jesus had done for him: and all *men* did marvel.	lished throughout the whole city how great things Jesus had done unto him.
1 And he entered into a ship, and passed over,—	21 And when Jesus was passed over again by ship unto the other side, —	40 And it came to pass, that when Jesus[1] returned, —

§ 56. The Woman with a bloody Flux is healed, and Jairus's Daughter is raised.
Capernaum.

St. Matt. ix. 18–26.	St. Mark v. 21[b]–43.	St. Luke viii. 40[b]–56.
18 While he spake these things unto them, behold! a ruler, coming in,[2]	— Much people gathered unto him; and he was nigh unto 22 the sea. And, behold! there cometh one of the rulers of the synagogue, Jairus by name; and when he saw him, he falleth[3] 23 at his feet, And beseecheth[4] him greatly, saying, My little daughter lieth at the point of death: *I pray thee*, come and lay thy hands on her, that she may be healed 24 and[5] live. And *Jesus* went with him; and much people followed him, and thronged him.	— The people *gladly* received him; for they were all waiting for him. 41 And, behold! there came a man named Jairus, and he was a ruler of the synagogue: and he fell down at Jesus' feet, and besought him that he would come in- 42 to his house: For he had one only daughter, about twelve years of age, and she lay a dying.
worshipped him, saying, My daughter is even now dead: but come and lay thy hand upon her, and 19 she shall live. And Jesus arose, and followed him, and *so did* his disciples.		
		But as he went the people thronged him.
20 And, behold, a woman, which was diseased with an issue	25 And a[6] woman, which had an issue of blood twelve years,	43 And a woman having an issue of blood twelve years, which had spent

[1] when Jesus was returned   [2] there came a certain ruler and worshipped   [3] fell
[4] besought   [5] may be healed; and she shall live   [6] a certain woman

---

§ 56. On the chronological position of this narrative see note on § 38, and on the phrase "*while he spake these things*" of Matt. ix. 18 see note on §§ 51, 52.

ST. MATT. IX.	ST. MARK V.	ST. LUKE VIII.
of blood twelve years,	26 and had suffered many things of many physicians, and had spent all that she had, and was nothing bettered, but rather grew worse, 27 when she had heard the things concerning[1] Jesus, came in the press behind, and touched 28 his garment. For she said, If I may touch but his clothes, I shall be whole. 29 And straightway the fountain of her blood was dried up; and she felt in her body that she was healed of that 30 plague. And Jesus, immediately knowing in himself that virtue had gone out of him, turned him about in the press, and said, Who touched my 31 clothes? And his disciples said unto him, Thou seest the multitude thronging thee, and sayest thou, Who 32 touched me? And he looked round about to see her that had 33 done this thing. But the woman fearing and trembling, knowing what was done in her, came and fell down before him, and told him all the truth.	all her living upon physicians, neither could be healed of any,
came behind *him*, and touched the hem of 21 his garment: For she said within herself, If I may but touch his garment, I shall be whole.		44 came behind *him* and touched the border of his garment:
		and immediately her issue of blood stanched.
		45 And Jesus said, Who touched me? When all denied, Peter and they that were with him said, Master, the multitude throng thee and press 46 *thee*.[2] And Jesus said, Somebody hath touched me; for I perceive that virtue is gone out of me. 47 And when the woman saw that she was not hid, she came trembling, and falling down before him, she declared[3] before all the people for what cause she had

[1] heard of Jesus

[2] and press *thee*, and sayest thou, who touched me?
[3] declared unto him

ST. MATT. IX.	ST. MARK V.	ST. LUKE VIII.
22 But he[1] turned him about, and when he saw her, he said, Daughter, be of good comfort: thy faith hath made thee whole. And the woman was made whole from that hour.	34 And he said unto her, Daughter, thy faith hath made thee whole; go in peace, and be whole of thy plague.	touched him, and how she was healed immediately. 48 And he said unto her, Daughter,[2] thy faith hath made thee whole: go in peace.
	35 While he yet spake, there came from the ruler of the synagogue's *house certain* which said, Thy daughter is dead: why troublest thou the Master any further? But Jesus having casually[4] heard the word that was spoken, he saith unto the ruler of the synagogue, Be not afraid, only believe.	49 While he yet spake, there cometh one from the ruler of the synagogue's *house*, saying to him, Thy daughter is dead; trouble the 50 Master no longer.[3] But when Jesus heard *it*, he answered him,[5] Fear not: believe only, and she shall be made whole.
	37 And he suffered no man to follow with[6] him, save Peter, and James, and John the brother of James.	51 And when he came into the house, he suffered not any to go in with him,[7] save Peter, and James, and John, and the father and the mother
23 And when Jesus came into the ruler's house, and saw the minstrels and the people making a noise,	38 And they[8] come to the house of the ruler of the synagogue, and he seeth the tumult, and them that wept and wailed greatly.	52 of the maiden. And all wept, and bewailed her:
24 He said,[9] Give place! for the maid is not dead, but sleepeth.	39 And when he was come in, he saith unto them, Why make ye this ado, and weep? the damsel is not dead,	but he said, Weep not; she is not dead, but

[1] But Jesus turned
[3] trouble not the Master
[5] saying, Fear not
[7] he suffered no man to go in, save
[2] Daughter, be of good comfort: thy faith
[4] As soon as Jesus heard
[6] *omit* with
[8] And he cometh,..... and seeth

ST. MATT. IX.	ST. MARK V.	ST. LUKE VIII.
And they laughed him to scorn. But when the people were put forth, he went in,	40 but sleepeth. And they laughed him to scorn. But when he had put them all out, he taketh the father and the mother of the damsel, and them that were with him, and entereth in where the 41 damsel was.[1] And he took the damsel by the hand, and said unto her, Talitha cumi! which is, being interpreted, Damsel, I say unto thee, arise!	53 sleepeth. And they laughed him to scorn, knowing that she was 54 dead. And he[2] took her by the hand, and
25		
and took her by the hand,		
and the maid arose.	42 And straightway the damsel arose, and walked; for she was *of the age* of twelve years. And they were straightway[3] astonished with a great astonishment. 43 And he charged them straitly that no man should know it: and commanded that something should be given her to eat.	55 called, saying, Maid, arise! And her spirit came again, and she arose straightway; and he commanded to give 56 her meat. And her parents were astonished: but he charged them that they should tell no man what was done.
26 And the fame hereof went abroad into all that land.[a]		

§ 57. Two Blind Men healed, and a Spirit cast out of one Dumb.

St. Matt. ix. 27–34.

27 And when Jesus departed thence, two blind men followed him, crying, and
28 saying, *Thou* son of David, have mercy on us! And when he was come into the house, the blind men came to him: and Jesus saith unto them, Believe ye

---

[1] was lying   [2] and he put them all out, and took   [3] omit straightway
[a] See Lk. vii. 17.

---

§ 57. There seems no good reason for disturbing the order of St. Matthew, and the account of these miracles is therefore placed, as he has given it, immediately after the raising of Jairus' daughter. Verses 32–34 are sometimes arranged in parallelism with Lk. xi. 14–17, the incidents recorded in both being much alike; but these have been already (§ 50) given in connection with Matt. xii. 22–25, with which they still more closely correspond.

ST. MATT. IX.

29 that I am able to do this? They said unto him, Yea, Lord. Then touched
30 he their eyes, saying, According to your faith be it unto you. And their eyes were opened; and Jesus straitly charged them, saying, See *that* no man know
31 it. But they, when they were departed, spread abroad his fame in all that country.
32 As they went out, behold, they brought to him a dumb man possessed with
33 a devil.[a] And when the devil was cast out, the dumb spake; and the multi-
34 tudes marvelled, saying, It was never so seen in Israel! But the Pharisees said, He casteth out devils through the prince of the devils.

§ 58. Our Lord, teaching at Nazareth, is again rejected.

ST. MATT. XIII. 54–58.　　　　ST. MARK VI. 1–6.

54 And when he was come into his own country, he taught them in their synagogue, insomuch that they were astonished, and said, Whence hath this *man* this wisdom,
55 and *these* mighty works? Is not this the carpenter's son? is not his mother called Mary? and his brethren, James, and Joseph,[3] and Simon, and Judas? And his sisters, are they not all with us? Whence then hath this *man* all these things?
57 And they were offended in him. But Jesus said unto them, A prophet is not without honor, save in his own
58 country, and in his own house. And he did not many mighty works there because of their unbelief.

1 And he went out from thence, and cometh[1] into his own country; and
2 his disciples follow him. And when the sabbath day was come, he began to teach in the synagogue: and many hearing *him* were astonished, saying, From whence hath this *man* these things? and what wisdom *is* this which is given unto this one? and[2] such mighty works are wrought
3 by his hands? Is not this the carpenter, the son of Mary, the brother of James, and Joses, and of Juda, and Simon? and are not his sisters here with us? And they were offended at
4 him. But Jesus said unto them, A prophet is not without honor, but in his own country, and among his own
5 kin, and in his own house. And he could there do no mighty work, save that he laid his hands upon a few
6 sick folk, and healed *them*. And he marvelled because of their unbelief.

---

[1] and came into　　　[2] given unto him, that even such　　　[3] Joses

[a] Matt. xii. 22–25; Lk. xi. 14–17.

§ 59. A third Circuit in Galilee. The Twelve instructed and sent forth.

MATT. IX. 35–X. 1, 5–16, XI. 1.   MAR. VI. 6ᵇ–13.   LK. IX. 1–6.

35 And Jesus went about all the cities and villages, teaching in their synagogues, and preaching the gospel of the kingdom, and healing every sickness and every disease.[1]

36 But when he saw the multitudes, he was moved with compassion on them, because they were harassed,[2] and were scattered abroad, as sheep having no shepherd.[a]

37 Then saith he unto his disciples, The harvest truly is plenteous, but the laborers are few;

38 pray ye therefore the Lord of the harvest, that he will send forth laborers into his harvest.

6ᵇ And he went round about the villages, teaching.

---

[1] and every disease among the people   [2] because they fainted

[a] Comp. Mar. vi. 34; 1 Pet. ii. 25.

---

§ 59. The charge to the Twelve, as they were sent forth two and two, is in some points much like the corresponding charge to the Seventy (Lk. x. 1-16), as they also were sent forth in like manner. Of the latter St. Luke gives the only account, and some of his language there is quite parallel to that of the Evangelists in the present passage. From a comparison, however, of Lk. ix. 4 with x. 5, it is plain that something of the same instruction, as might indeed have been expected, was given on both occasions.

On the other hand, much of the latter part of the charge, as given by St. Matthew (vs. 17–42), seems to have more distinctly in view the Apostolic work at a later period, after Christ's own ascension, inasmuch as it refers to trials and persecutions which could not have occurred at this time. St. Matthew appears therefore, to have here followed his custom of grouping like things together, without especial regard to their chronological connection, and has thus collected together in one, instructions given at different times to the Apostles. The portion of the charge indicated is therefore detached from the former part, and inserted at a later period, in accordance with the order of both St. Mark and St. Luke (§§ 90, 92, 97, and 126).

In regard to the superficial discrepancy between the language of Matt. x. 10, and that of Mar. vi. 8, 9; Lk. ix. 3, it is enough to say that the *thought* in all is identical — they should make no preparation for the journey. They were to go as they were, in the clothes and with the staff and the sandals they had with them, providing nothing further.

ST. MATT. X.	ST. MARK VI.	ST. LUKE IX.
1 And when he had called unto *him* his twelve disciples, he gave them power *against* unclean spirits, to cast them out, and to heal all manner of sickness and all manner of disease.	7 And he called *unto him* the twelve, and began to send them forth by two and two; and gave them power over unclean spirits;	1 Then he called the[1] twelve together, and gave them power and authority over all devils, and to cure diseases.
5 These twelve Jesus sent forth, and commanded them, saying, Go not into the way of the Gentiles, and into *any* city of the Samaritans enter ye not; 6 but go rather to the lost sheep of the house 7 of Israel. And as ye go, preach, saying, The kingdom of heaven is at 8 hand. Heal the sick, cleanse the lepers, raise the dead, cast out devils: freely ye have received, 9 freely give. Provide neither gold, nor silver, nor brass in your purses, 10 nor scrip for *your* journey, neither two coats, neither shoes, nor yet staves: for the workman is worthy of his meat. 11 And into whatsoever city or town ye shall enter, enquire who in it is worthy; and there abide till ye go thence. 12 And when ye come into 13 an house,[a] salute it. And if the house be worthy, let your peace come upon it: but if it be not worthy,	8 And commanded them that they should take nothing for *their* journey, save a staff only; no scrip, no bread, no money in *their* purse; 9 But *be* shod with sandals; and not put on 10 two coats. And he said unto them, In what place soever ye enter into an house,[a] there abide till ye depart from that place.	2 And he sent them to preach the kingdom of God, and to heal the sick. 3 And he said unto them, Take nothing for *your* journey, neither staff,[1] nor scrip, neither bread, neither money; neither have two coats apiece. 4 And whatsoever house ye enter into,[a] there abide, and thence depart.

[1] called his twelve disciples

[a] Comp. Lk. x. 5, 6.

[2] neither staves,

ST. MATT. X.	ST. MARK VI.	ST. LUKE IX.
let your peace return to 14 you. And whosoever shall not receive you, nor hear your words, when ye depart out of that house or city, shake off the dust of your feet. 15 Verily I say unto you, It shall be more tolerable for the land of Sodom and Gomorrha in the day of judgment than for that city.ª 16 Behold, I send you forth as sheep in the midst of wolves:ᵇ be ye therefore wise as serpents, and harmless as doves.ᶜ	11 And whosoever shall not receive you, nor hear you, when ye depart thence, shake off the dust under your feet for a testimony against them.³ 12 And they went out, and preached that men 13 should repent. And they cast out many devils, and anointed with oil many that were sick, and healed *them.*	5 And whosoever receive you not,¹ when ye go out of that city, shake off the² dust from your feet for a testimony against them. 6 And they departed, and went through the towns, preaching the gospel, and healing everywhere.

ST. MATT. XI.

1 And it came to pass, when Jesus had made an end of commanding his twelve disciples, he departed thence to teach and to preach in their cities.

§ 60. Herod believes Jesus to be John the Baptist, whom he had beheaded.

ST. MATT. XIV. 1, 2, 6–12.   ST. MARK VI. 14–16, 21–29.   ST. LUKE IX. 7–9.

| 1 At that time Herod the tetrarch heard of the | 14 And king Herod heard *of him*; (for | 7 Now Herod the tetrarch heard of all that |

---

¹ whosoever will not receive you   ² shake off the very dust
³ *add to ver.* 11. Verily I say unto you, It shall be more tolerable for Sodom and Gomorrha in the day of judgment, than for that city.

ª Comp. Lk. x. 12, 14.   ᵇ Comp. Lk. x. 3.   ᶜ Comp. Rom. xvi. 19.

ST. MATT. XIV.	ST. MARK VI.	ST. LUKE IX.
2 fame of Jesus. And said unto his servants, This is John the Baptist; he is risen from the dead; and therefore mighty works do show forth themselves in him.	his name was spread abroad:) and he said, That John the Baptist was risen from the dead, and therefore mighty works do shew forth themselves in him. And[2] others said, That it is Elias. And others said, That *it is*[3] a prophet,[4] as one of 10 the prophets. But when Herod heard *thereof*, he said, It is John, whom I beheaded: he is risen.[5]	was done:[1] and he was perplexed, because that it was said of some, that John was risen from the dead; 8 and of some, that Elias had appeared; and of others, that one of the old prophets was risen 9 again. And Herod said, John have I beheaded: but who is this, of whom I hear such things? And he desired to see him.
6 But when Herod's birthday was come,[6] the	21 And when a convenient day was come, that Herod on his birthday made a supper to his lords, high captains, and chief *estates* of 22 Galilee; and when the daughter of the	
daughter of Herodias danced before them, and 7 pleased Herod. Whereupon he promised with an oath to give her whatsoever she would ask.	said Herodias came in, and danced, she[7] pleased Herod and them that sat with him; and[8] the king said unto the damsel, Ask of me whatsoever thou wilt, and I will give *it* thee. 23 And he sware unto her, Whatsoever thou shalt ask of me, I will give	

[1] *omit* all that was done by him. [2] *omit* and [3] That it is [4] or as one
[5] he is risen from the dead [6] birth-day was kept [7] danced and pleased [8] *omit* and

§ 60. John the Baptist was beheaded by Herod in the castle of Machærus (Joseph. Ant. 18, 5, 2.) at the southern extremity of Perea, near the Dead Sea. It appears to have occurred during the absence of the Twelve, and from the mention by St. John in the next section (vi. 4) of the approach of the Passover, must have been near eighteen months from the time of his imprisonment. The account of his imprisonment, which is mentioned by St. Matthew and St. Mark only in connection with his execution, has been transferred to its chronological position (§ 26). Both evangelists narrate the execution in explanation of Herod's remark.

ST. MATT. XIV.	ST. MARK VI.	ST. LUKE IX.
8 And she, being before instructed of her mother, said, Give me here John Baptist's head in a charger. 9 And the king was sorry: nevertheless for the oath's sake, and them which sat with him at meat, he commanded it 10 to be given her. And he sent, and beheaded 11 John in the prison. And his head was brought in a charger, and given to the damsel: and she brought it to her mother. 12 And his disciples came, and took up the body, and buried him,[3] and went and told Jesus.	it thee, unto the half of 24 my kingdom. And she went forth, and said unto her mother, What shall I ask? And she said, The head of John the Baptist. 25 And she came in straightway with haste unto the king, and asked, saying, I will that thou give me by and by in a charger the head 26 of John the Baptist. And the king was exceeding sorry; *yet* for his oath's sake, and for their sakes which sat *with him*,[1] he 27 would not reject her. And immediately the king sent an executioner, and commanded to bring [2] his head: and he went and beheaded him 28 in the prison; and brought his head in a charger, and gave it to the damsel: and the damsel gave it to her 29 mother. And when his disciples heard *of it*, they came and took up his corpse, and laid him [4] in a tomb.	

§ 61. The Twelve having returned, Jesus crosses the Lake with them, and there feeds the Five Thousand. — *N. W. and N. E. Coasts of Sea of Galilee.*

MATT. XIV. 13–21.   MAR. VI. 30–44.   LK. IX. 10–17.   JNO. VI. 1–14.

	30 And the apostles gathered them-	10 And the apostles, when they

[1] sat with him   [2] commanded his head to be brought   [3] and buried it   [4] laid it in a tomb.

§ 61. The feeding of the five thousand evidently took place on the N. E. side of the Sea of Galilee, in Perea. Tischendorf makes the time to have been just that at which the Passover was celebrated at Jerusalem, considering the remark in Jno. vi. 4 as referring to the assembling of the multitudes. The coincidence would be a most interesting one, if it could be distinctly established. Certainly the two events were in close proximity, and the relation between them ought not to pass unnoticed.

ST. MATT. XIV.	ST. MARK VI.	ST. LUKE. IX.	ST. JOHN VI.
	selves together unto Jesus, and told him all things, whatsoever[2] they had done and taught. And he saith[3] unto them, Come ye yourselves apart into a desert place, and rest a while: for there were many coming and going, and they had no leisure so much as	were returned, told him what[1] they had done.	
13 When Jesus heard *of it*, he departed thence by ship into a desert place apart: and when the people had heard *thereof*, they followed him on foot out of the cities.	32 to eat. And they departed into a desert place by ship privately. 33 And they[5] saw them departing, and many knew them,[6] and ran afoot thither out of all cities, and outwent them.[7]	And he took them, and went aside privately into[4] the city called Beth- 11 saida. And the people, when they knew *it*, followed him:	1 After these things Jesus went over the sea of Galilee, which is *the sea of* Tiberias. 2 And a great multitude followed him, because they saw the[8] miracles which he did on them that were diseased. 3 And Jesus went up into a mountain, and there he sat with his disci- 4 ples. And the passover, the[9] feast of the Jews, was nigh.
14 And he[10] went	34 And when he	and he received	5 When Jesus

[1] told him all that they [2] both what they had done, and what they had taught.
[3] said unto them [4] into a desert place belonging to the city [5] the people saw them
[6] knew him [7] outwent them, and came together unto him. [8] saw his miracles
[9] a feast [10] and Jesus went forth

ST. MATT. XIV.	ST. MARK VI.	ST. LUKE IX.	ST. JOHN VI.
forth, and saw a great multitude, and was moved with compassion toward them, and he healed their sick.	came out, he[1] saw much people, and was moved with compassion toward them, because they were as sheep not having a shepherd: and he began to teach them many things.	them, and spake unto them of the kingdom of God, and healed them that had need of healing.	then lifted up *his* eyes, and saw a great company come unto him, he
15 And when it was evening, the[2] disciples came to him, saying, This is a desert place, and the time is now past; send therefore[4] the multitude away, that they may go into the villages, and buy themselves victuals. But he[6] said unto them, They need not depart; give ye them to eat. 17 And they say unto him, we	35 And when the day was now far spent, his disciples came[3] and said, This is a desert place, and now the time *is* far passed: 36 Send them away, that they may go into the country round about, and into the villages, and buy themselves something to eat.[5] He answered and said unto them, Give ye them to eat. And they say unto him, Shall we go and buy two hundred pennyworth of bread, and give 38 them to eat? He saith unto them, How many loaves have ye? go and[9]	12 And when the day began to wear away, then came the twelve, and said unto him, Send the multitude away, that they may go into the towns and country round about, and lodge, and get victuals: for we are here in a desert place. 13 But he said unto them, Give ye them to eat.	saith unto Philip, Whence shall we buy bread, that these may eat? 6 And this he said to prove him: for he himself knew what he would do. 7 Philip answereth[7] him. Two hundred pennyworth of bread is not sufficient for them, that every one[8] may take 8 a little. One of his disciples, Andrew, Simon Peter's brother, saith 9 unto him. There

[1] And Jesus, when he came out, saw   [2] his disciples   [3] came unto him, and said
[4] *omit* therefore   [5] buy themselves bread; for they have nothing to eat.
[6] But Jesus said   [7] answered   [8] every one of them   [9] go and see

ST. MATT. XIV.	ST. MARK VI.	ST. LUKE IX.	ST. JOHN VI.
have here but five loaves, and 14 two fishes. He said, Bring them hither to me.	see. And when they knew, they say, Five, and two 39 fishes. And he	And they said, We have no more but five loaves and two fishes; except we should go and buy meat for all this peo- 14 ple. And [2] they were about five thousand men. And he said to his disciples, Make them sit down by fifties in a company. 15 And they did so, and made them all sit 16 down. Then he took the five loaves and the two fishes, and looking up to heaven, he blessed them, and brake, and gave to the dis- ciples to set be- fore the multi- 17 tude. And they did eat, and were all filled: and there was taken up of fragments that remained to them twelve baskets.	is a lad here, who[1] hath five barley loaves, and two small fishes: but what are they among 10 so many? And Jesus said, Make the men sit down. Now there was much grass in the place. So the men sat down, in number a- bout five thou- 11 sand. Jesus therefore[3] took the loaves; and gave thanks, and gave[5] to them that were set down; and likewise of the fishes as much as they would. 12 When they were filled he said unto his disciples. Gath- er up the frag- ments that re- main, that no- thing be lost. 13 Therefore they gathered *them* together, and filled twelve baskets with
19 And he com- manded the multitude to sit down on the grass, and took the five loaves, and the two fishes, and look- ing up to heaven, he blessed, and brake, and gave the loaves to *his* disciples, and the disciples to the multitude. 20 And they did all eat, and were filled: and they took up of the fragments that remained twelve baskets full. 21 And they that had eaten were	commanded them to make all sit down by com- panies upon the 40 green grass. And they sat down in ranks, by hun- dreds, and by fif- 41 ties. And when he had taken the five loaves and the two fishes, he looked up to heav- en, and blessed, and brake the loaves, and gave *them* to the[4] dis- ciples to set be- fore them; and the two fishes divided he among them 42 all. And they did all eat, and were filled. 43 And they took up twelve baskets full of fragments, and of the fishes. 44 And they that did eat of the loaves		

[1] which hath
[2] For they were
[3] And Jesus took
[4] his disciples
[5] and when he had given thanks, he distributed to the disciples, and the disciples to them

ST. MATT. XIV.	ST. MARK IV.	ST. LUKE IX.	ST. JOHN VI.
about five thousand men, besides women and children.	were[1] five thousand men.		the fragments of the five barley loaves, which remained over and above unto them that had eaten.
14 Then those men, when they had seen the miracle that he[2] did, said, This is of a truth that prophet that should come into the world.

§ 62. Our Lord walks upon the Water, and performs Cures. — *Lake of Galilee. Gennesaret.*

ST. MATT. XIV. 22–36.	ST. MARK VI. 45–56.	ST. JOHN VI. 15–21.
22 And he constrained the[3] disciples to get into a ship, and to go before him unto the other side, while he sent the multitudes	45 And straightway he constrained his disciples to get into the ship, and to go to the other side before unto Bethsaida, while he	15 When Jesus therefore perceived that they would come and take him by force, to make *him*[4] king, he fleeth again into a mountain himself alone.

[1] were about five thousand   [2] the miracle that Jesus did
[3] And straightway Jesus constrained his disciples   [4] to make him a king, he departed again

---

§ 62. There is a seeming discrepancy between the point at which the Apostles aimed in Mark vi. 45, *Bethsaida*, and in Jno. vi. 17, *Capernaum*. Attention to the geographical features removes this. From Lk. ix. 10, compared with the other evangelists, it appears that the place of the feeding of the five thousand was an appurtenance of Bethsaida, as indeed is expressly asserted in the reading of the *text. rec*. Bethsaida, according to the best authorities, was situated just at the northern junction of the Jordan with the sea of Galilee, probably occupying both banks of the river; from it stretches eastward a triangular plain having the Jordan for one side, the sea for another, and the barren eastern mountains for the third. At the S. E. corner of this plain Thomson (ii. 29) locates the miracle, the distance from Bethsaida being about three miles. From Bethsaida to Tell Hum, the probable site of Capernaum, was about the same distance along the N. W. coast of the lake, the plain of Gennesaret lying just south of it. The disciples therefore in going from the place of the miracle to Capernaum would necessarily pass close by Bethsaida and would naturally try to make it, both that they might keep as much as possible in the lee of the land on that stormy night, and also that they might then take in their master if he pleased, as he also must pass through Bethsaida. The

ST. MATT. XIV.	ST. MARK VI.	ST. JOHN VI.
23 away. And when he had sent the multitudes away, he went up into a mountain apart to pray: and when the evening was come, he 24 was there alone. But the ship was now in the midst of the sea, tossed with waves: for the wind was contrary. 25 And in the fourth watch of the night he[3] went unto them, walk-26 ing on the sea. And when they[4] saw him walking on the sea, they were troubled, saying, It is a spirit! and they cried out for 27 fear. But straightway he[5] spake unto them, saying, Be of good cheer: it is I; be not 28 afraid. And Peter answered him and said, Lord, if it be thou, bid me come unto thee on 29 the water. And he	sent away the people. 46 And when he had sent them away, he departed into a moun-47 tain to pray. And when even was come, the ship was in the midst of the sea, and he alone on the land. 48 And he, seeing them toiling in rowing, (for the wind was contrary unto them,[2]) about the fourth watch of the night he cometh unto them, walking upon the sea, and would have passed by them. 49 But when they saw him walking upon the sea, they supposed it had been a spirit, and 50 cried out: for they all saw him, and were troubled. And immediately he talked with them, and saith unto them, Be of good cheer: it is I; be not afraid.	16 And when even was *now* come, his disciples went 17 down unto the sea, and entered into a ship, and went over the sea toward Capernaum. And the darkness overtook them, and Jesus was not yet[1] 18 come to them. And the sea arose by reason of a great wind that blew. 19 So when they had rowed about five and twenty or thirty furlongs, they see Jesus walking on the sea, and drawing nigh unto the ship: and they were afraid. 20 But he saith unto them, It is I; be not afraid.

[1] And it was now dark, and Jesus was not come
[2] And he saw them..... and about the fourth watch
[3] Jesus went
[4] when the disciples saw
[5] Jesus spake

---

storm, however, made this impossible and even drove them south of Capernaum to the shore of Gennesaret. Thomson (ii. 32) experienced a furious storm just in this locality, continuing for three days, during which it would have been impossible for a boat to make the northern shore. The width of the sea opposite Gennesaret is about six miles; the disciples therefore (Jno. vi. 19), rowed somewhat more than half the distance, having struggled with the winds and waves (Mar. vi. 48) some eight or ten hours.

ST. MATT. XIV.	ST. MARK VI.	ST. JOHN VI.
said, Come. And when Peter was come down out of the ship, he walked on the water, and came¹ to Jesus. 30 But when he saw the wind,² he was afraid; and beginning to sink, he cried, saying, Lord, 31 save me! And immediately Jesus stretched forth *his* hand, and caught him, and said unto him, O thou of little faith, wherefore 32 didst thou doubt? And when they were come into the ship, the wind 33 ceased. Then they that were in the ship³ worshipped him, saying, Of a truth thou art the Son of God.	51 And he went up unto them into the ship; and the wind ceased: and they were sore amazed in themselves 52 beyond measure.⁴ For they considered not *the miracle* of the loaves: but⁵ their heart was hardened.	21 Then they willingly received him into the ship: and immediately the ship was at the land whither they went.
34 And when they were gone over, they came to land unto⁶ Gennes-35 aret. And when the men of that place had knowledge of him, they sent out into all that country round about, and brought	53 And when they had passed over to the land they came unto⁶ Gennesaret, and drew 54 to the shore. And when they were come out of the ship, straightway they knew 55 him, and ran through that whole region,⁷ and began to carry about in beds those	

¹ to go to Jesus   ² the wind boisterous   ³ came and worshipped
⁴ beyond measure and wondered.   ⁵ for their heart
⁶ they came into the land of Gennesaret   ⁷ whole region round about

ST. MATT. XIV.	ST. MARK VI.	ST. JOHN VI.
unto him all that were	that were sick, where they heard he was.	
	56 And whithersoever he entered, into villages, or cities, or country, they laid the sick in the streets, and be-	
36 diseased; and besought him that they might only touch the hem of his garment: and as many as touched were made perfectly whole.	sought him that they might touch if it were but the border of his garment: and as many as touched him were made whole.	

§ 63. Our Lord's Discourse concerning the Bread of Life. — *Capernaum.*
St. John vi. 22–vii. 1.

22 The day following, when the people which stood on the other side of the sea saw that there was none other boat there, save one,[1] and that Jesus went not with his disciples into the ship,[2] but *that* his disciples were gone away 23 alone: (howbeit there came other boats from Tiberias nigh unto the place 24 where they did eat bread, after that the Lord had given thanks): when the people therefore saw that Jesus was not there, neither his disciples, they took 25 boats[3] and came to Capernaum, seeking for Jesus. And when they had found him on the other side of the sea, they said unto him, Rabbi, when camest thou hither?

26 Jesus answered them and said, Verily, verily, I say unto you, Ye seek me, not because ye saw the miracles, but because ye did eat of the loaves, and 27 were filled. Labor not for the meat which perisheth, but for that meat which endureth unto everlasting life, which the Son of man giveth[4] unto you: for 28 him hath God the Father sealed. Then said they unto him, What shall we 29 do, that we might work the works of God? Jesus answered and said unto them, 30 This is the work of God, that ye believe on him whom he hath sent. They said therefore unto him, What sign shewest thou then, that we may see, and 31 believe thee? what dost thou work? Our fathers did eat manna in the desert: as it is written, He gave them bread from heaven to eat.ᵃ

32 Then Jesus said unto them, Verily, verily, I say unto you, Moses gave you not that bread from heaven; but my Father giveth you the true bread from 33 heaven. For the bread of God is he which cometh down from heaven, and

---

[1] none other boat there, save that one whereinto his disciples were entered, and that
[2] boat   [3] they also took shipping   [4] shall give unto you

ᵃ Exod. xvi. 4, 15. Behold, I will rain bread from heaven for you..... This *is* the bread which the Lord hath given you to eat. Ps. lxxviii. 24. Comp. Neh. ix. 15; Ps. cv. 40; Wisd. xvi. 20.

ST. JOHN VI.

34 giveth life unto the world. Then said they unto him, Lord, evermore give
35 us this bread. And Jesus said unto them, I am the bread of life:[a] he that cometh to me shall never hunger: and he that believeth on me shall never
36 thirst.[b] But I said unto you, that ye also have seen me, and believe not.
37 All that the Father giveth me shall come to me; and him that cometh to me
38 I will in no wise cast out. For I came down from heaven, not to do mine
39 own will, but the will[c] of him that sent me. And this is the will of him [1] which hath sent me, that of all which he hath given me I should lose nothing, but
40 should raise it up again at the last day. For this is the will of my Father,[2] that every one which seeth the Son, and believeth on him, may have everlasting life: and I will raise him up at the last day.

41 The Jews then murmured at him, because he said, I am the bread which
42 came down from heaven. And they said, Is not this Jesus, the son of Joseph, whose father and mother we know? how is it now [3] that he saith, I came down
43 from heaven? Jesus [4] answered and said unto them, Murmur not among
44 yourselves. No man can come to me, except the Father which hath sent me
45 draw him: and I will raise him up at the last day. It is written in the prophets, And they shall be all taught of God.[d] Every man [5] that hath heard,
46 and hath learned of the Father, cometh unto me. Not that any man hath
47 seen the Father, save he which is of God.[e] he hath seen God.[6] Verily, verily,
48 I say unto you, He that believeth [7] hath everlasting life. I am that bread of
49/50 life. Your fathers did eat manna in the wilderness, and are dead. This is the bread which cometh down from heaven, that a man may eat thereof and
51 not die. I am the living bread which came down from heaven: if any man eat of my [8] bread, he shall live forever: and the bread that I will give for the life of the world is my flesh.[9]

52 The Jews therefore strove among themselves, saying, how can [f] this man
53 give us his flesh to eat? Then Jesus said unto them, Verily, verily, I say unto you, Except ye eat the flesh of the Son of man, and drink his blood, ye
54 have no life in you. Whoso eateth my flesh, and drinketh my blood, hath
55 eternal life: and I will raise him up at the last day. For my flesh is true [10]
56 meat, and my blood is true drink. He that eateth my flesh, and drinketh my
57 blood, dwelleth in me, and I in him. As the living Father hath sent me, and I live by the Father: so he that eateth me, even he shall live by me.

---

[1] the Father's will which hath   [2] And this is the will of him that sent me
[3] how is it then   [4] Jesus therefore answered
[5] Every man therefore   [6] the Father
[7] believeth on me   [8] of this bread
[9] the bread that I will give is my flesh, which I will give for the life of the world.
[10] is meat indeed..... is drink indeed

[a] See ver. 48, 58.   [b] Comp. iv. 14; vii. 37.   [c] Comp. Heb. x. 7, 9.
[d] Isa. liv. 13. And all thy children *shall be* taught of the LORD. Comp. Jer. xxxi. 34; Mic. iv. 2; Heb. viii. 10; x. 16.   [e] Comp. i. 18.   [f] Comp. iii. 9.

ST. JOHN VI.

58 This is that bread which came down from heaven: not as the [1] fathers did eat, and are dead: he that eateth of this bread shall live forever.
59/60 These things said he in the synagogue, as he taught in Capernaum. Many therefore of his disciples, when they had heard *this*, said, This is an hard
61 saying; who can hear it? When Jesus knew in himself that his disciples
62 murmured at it, he said unto them, Doth this offend you? *What* and if ye
63 shall see the Son of man ascend up where he was before? It is the spirit that quickeneth; the flesh profiteth nothing; the words that I have spoken [2] unto
64 you, *they* are spirit, and *they* are life. But there are some of you that believe not. For Jesus knew from the beginning who they were that believed not,
65 and who should betray him. And he said, Therefore said I unto you, that no man can come unto me, except it were given unto him of the [3] Father.
66 From that *time* many of his disciples went back, and walked no more with
67/68 him. Then said Jesus unto the twelve, will ye also go away? [4] Simon Peter answered him, Lord, to whom shall we go? thou hast the words of eternal life.
69/70 And we believe and are sure that thou art the Holy One of God.[5][a] He[6] an-
71 swered them, have not I chosen you twelve, and one of you is a devil? He spake of Judas *the son* of Simon Iscariot;[7] for he it was that should betray him, being one of the twelve.

ST. JOHN VII.

1 After these things Jesus walked in Galilee; for he would not walk in Jewry, because the Jews sought to kill him.

[1] as your fathers did eat manna, and are dead
[2] that I speak unto you
[3] of my Father
[4] Then Simon Peter
[5] that thou art that Christ, the Son of the living God.
[6] Jesus answered
[7] Judas Iscariot *the son* of Simon.

[a] Matt. xvi. 16; Mar. viii. 29; Lk. ix. 20.

§ 63. In Jno. vii. 1, a sufficient reason is given for our Saviour's non-attendance at the Passover mentioned in vi. 4. According to the chronological order here adopted he must have absented himself from Jerusalem for about a year and a half. It is not inconsistent with Jno. vii. 1, that after the lapse of so much time he should again have gone up to the Holy City.

It enables us the better to appreciate the significance of the Saviour's teaching concerning the Bread of Life to remember that it was uttered during the Paschal week, and certainly while the feast of the Passover was going on at Jerusalem,—perhaps, at the hour of the sacrifice of the Paschal Lamb itself (between three o'clock and sunset), but hardly, as Tischendorf (following Wieseler) supposes, at the very time of eating it, which was later in the evening.

PART V.

FROM OUR LORD'S THIRD PASSOVER TO HIS FINAL DEPARTURE FROM GALILEE, JUST BEFORE THE FEAST OF TABERNACLES.

§ 64. The Pharisees, accusing the Disciples for eating with unwashen Hands, are confuted. — *Capernaum.*

St. Matt. xv. 1–20.	St. Mark vii. 1–23.
1 Then came to Jesus from Jerusalem, scribes and Pharisees, saying.[1]	1 Then came together unto him the Pharisees, and certain of the scribes, 2 which came from Jerusalem. And when they saw that[2] some of his disciples eat bread with defiled, that is 3 to say, with unwashen hands.—([3] For the Pharisees, and all the Jews, except they wash *their* hands oft, eat not, holding the tradition of the elders. 4 And *when they come* from the market, except they wash, they eat not. And many other things there be, which they have received to hold, *as* the washing of cups, and pots, brazen vessels.)—[4] 5 Then the Pharisees and scribes asked him, Why walk not thy disciples according to the tradition of the elders, but 6 eat bread with defiled[6] hands? He 7 said unto them, Well hath Esaias prophesied of you hypocrites, as it is written, that[8] This people honoreth me with *their* lips, but their heart is 7 far from me. Howbeit in vain do they
2 Why do thy disciples transgress the tradition of the elders? for they wash not the[5] hands when they eat 3 bread. But he answered and said 7 unto them, *Ye hypocrites!* well did Esaias prophecy of you, saying. 8 This people honoreth me with the[9] lips; but their heart is far from me.	

[1] Then came to Jesus scribes and Pharisees, which were of Jerusalem,
[2] *omit* that   [3] with unwashen hands, they found fault.
[4] brazen vessels, and of tables.   [5] their hands
[6] with unwashen hands   [7] He answered and said   [8] *omit* that
[9] This people draweth nigh unto me with their mouth, and honoreth me with *their* lips

§ 64. The time is probably after the close of the Paschal feast, and *which came from Jerusalem* (Mar. vii. 1), refers to those who had been in attendance upon it in the holy city.

ST. MATT. XV.	ST. MARK VII.

9 But in vain do they worship me, teaching *for* doctrines the command-
4 ments of men.[a] Why do ye also transgress the commandment of God by your tradition? For God commanded, saying, Honor[3] father and mother;[b] and, He that curseth father or mother, let him die the
5 death.[c] But ye say, Whosoever shall say to *his* father or *his* mother, *It is* a gift, by whatsoever thou
6 mightest be profited by me:—he shall not honor[5] his father or his mother. Thus have ye made the law of God of none effect by your tradition.

10 And he called the multitude, and said unto them, Hear, and under-
11 stand: Not that which goeth into the mouth defileth a man; but that which cometh out of the mouth, this defileth a man.

12 Then came the[10] disciples, and said unto him, Knowest thou that the Pharisees were offended, after

worship me, teaching *for* doctrines the
8 commandments of men.[a] [1] Laying aside the commandment of God, ye
9 hold the tradition of men.[2] And he said unto them, Full well ye reject the commandment of God, that ye may
10 keep your own tradition. For Moses said, Honor thy father and thy mother:[b] and, Whoso curseth father or mother,
11 let him die the death:[c] But ye say, If a man shall say to his father or mother, *It is* Corban, that is to say, a gift, by whatsoever thou mightest
12 be profited by me;[4]— ye suffer him no more to do ought for father or
13 mother;[6] making the word of God of none effect through your tradition, which ye have delivered; and many such like things do ye.

14 And when he had called the people again[7] *unto him*, he said unto them, Hearken unto me every one *of you*,
15 and understand: There is nothing from without a man, that entering into him, can defile him; but the things which come out of a man[8] are they that defile the man.[9]

[1] For laying aside
[2] tradition of men, *as* the washing of pots and cups; and many other such like things do ye.
[3] thy father
[4] be profited by me; *he shall be free.* And ye suffer
[5] and honor not his father or his mother, *he shall be free.* Thus have ye made the commandment
[6] his father or his mother
[7] called all the people *unto him*
[8] which come out of him, those are they
[9] ver. 16. If any man have ears to hear, let him hear.
[10] his disciples

[a] Isa. xxix. 13. Forasmuch as this people draw near *me* with their mouth: and with their lips do honor me, but have removed their heart far from me, — Comp. Col. ii. 22.
[b] Ex. xx. 12; Deut. v. 16.   [c] Ex. xxi. 17.

ST. MATT. XV.	ST. MARK VII.
13 they heard this saying? But he answered and said, Every plant, which my heavenly Father hath not planted, shall be rooted up. 14 Let them alone: they be blind leaders of the blind. And if the blind lead the blind, both shall fall 15 into the ditch. Then answered Peter and said unto him, Declare 16 unto us the[1] parable. And he[2] said, Are ye also yet without un-17 derstanding? Do not ye[4] understand, that whatsoever entereth in at the mouth goeth into the belly, and is cast out into the draught? 18 But those things which proceed out of the mouth come forth from the heart: and they defile the man. 19 For out of the heart proceed evil thoughts, murders, adulteries, fornications, thefts, false witness, 20 blasphemies: these are *the things* which defile a man; but to eat with unwashen hands defileth not a man.	17 And when he was entered into the house from the people, his disciples 18 asked of him[3] the parable. And he saith unto them, are ye so without understanding also? Do ye not perceive, that whatsoever thing from without entereth into the man, *it* can-19 not defile him; because it entereth not into his heart, but into the belly, and goeth out into the draught, purging 20 all meats? And he said, That which cometh out of the man, that defileth 21 the man. For from within, out of the heart of men, proceed evil thoughts, adulteries, fornications, murders, 22 thefts, covetousness, wickedness, deceit, lasciviousness, an evil eye, blas-23 phemy, pride, foolishness: all these evil things come from within, and defile the man.

§ 65. The Daughter of a Syrophenician Woman is healed. — *Land of Tyre.*

St. Matt. xv. 21-28.	St. Mark vii. 24-30.
21 Then Jesus went thence, and departed into the coasts of Tyre and 22 Sidon. And, behold, a woman of Canaan came out of the same coasts, and cried,[6] saying, Have mercy on me, O Lord, *thou* son of David! my daughter is grievously vexed 23 with a devil. But he answered her	24 And from thence he arose, and went into the coasts[5] of Tyre and Sidon, and entered into an house, and would have no man know *it*: but he 25 could not be hid. But straightway[7] a woman, whose young daughter had an unclean spirit, heard of him, and 26 came in[8] and fell at his feet: (the

[1] this parable [2] Jesus said [3] asked him concerning the parable
[4] Do not ye yet understand [5] the borders of [6] cried unto him
[7] For *a certain* woman [8] came and fell

ST. MATT. XV.

not a word. And his disciples came and besought him, saying, Send her 24 away; for she crieth after us. But he answered and said, I am not sent but unto the lost sheep of the house 25 of Israel. Then came she and worshipped him, saying, Lord, help me. 26 But he answered and said, It is not meet to take the children's bread, 27 and to cast it to dogs. And she said, Truth, Lord: yet the dogs eat of the crumbs which fall from their 28 master's table. Then Jesus answered and said unto her, O woman, great is thy faith! be it unto thee even as thou wilt. And her daughter was made whole from that very hour.

ST. MARK VII.

woman was a Greek, a Syrophenician by nation;) and she besought him that he would cast forth the devil out of 27 her daughter. But he[1] said unto her, Let the children first be filled: for it is not meet to take the children's bread, and to cast it unto the dogs. 28 And she answered and said unto him, Yes, Lord: yet the dogs under the table eat of the children's crumbs. 29 And he said unto her, For this saying go thy way; the devil is gone out of 30 thy daughter. And when she was come to her house, she found the child laid upon the bed,[2] and the devil gone out.

§ 66. A Deaf and Dumb Man is healed, and many others; the Four Thousand fed. — *The Decapolis.*

ST. MATT. XV. 29–38.

29 And Jesus departed from thence, and came nigh unto the sea of Galilee; and went up into a mountain, and sat down there.

ST. MARK VII. 31–VIII. 9.

31 And again, departing from the coasts of Tyre he came through Sidon,[3] unto the sea of Galilee, through the 32 midst of the coasts of Decapolis. And they bring unto him one that was deaf, and had an impediment in his speech; and they beseech him to put his[4] hand 33 upon him. And he took him aside from the multitude, and put his fingers

---

[1] But Jesus said [2] she found the devil gone out, and her daughter laid upon the bed.
[3] departing from the coasts of Tyre and Sidon, he came unto the sea of Galilee
[4] to put his hand

---

§ 66. The name Decapolis, which in Scripture occurs elsewhere only in Matt. iv. 25 (§ 42) and Mar. v. 20 (§ 55), is frequently used by Josephus and other ancient writers. The names of the ten cities are very variously given by different authors, but they agree in placing them all, except Scythopolis, on the east of the Jordan. The tract of country included under the name was not clearly defined, but lay on the east and southeast of the Sea of Galilee.

Accepting the reading in Mar. vii. 31, *through Sidon*, it appears that after the miracle narrated in § 65, our Lord went on still to the northward, and from Sidon probably went along the Phenician border to Dan, and thence turned to the southward on the eastern side of the river and lake and thus "came to the Sea of Galilee through the midst of the coasts of Decapolis."

| ST. MATT. XV. | ST. MARK VII. |

<table>
<tr><td></td><td>into his ears, and he spit, and touched
34 his tongue: And looking up to heaven, he sighed, and saith unto him, Eph-
35 phatha, that is, Be opened. And[1] his ears were opened, and straightway[2] the string of his tongue was loosed,
36 and he spake plain. And he charged them that they should tell no man: but the more he charged them, so much the more a great deal they published *it;*</td></tr>
</table>

30 And great multitudes came unto him, having with them *those that were* lame, blind, dumb, maimed, and many others, and cast them down at his[3] feet; and he healed
31 them: insomuch that the multitude wondered, when they saw the dumb to speak, the maimed to be whole, the lame to walk, and the blind to see: and they glorified the God of Israel.

and were beyond measure astonished, saying, He hath done all things well: he maketh both the deaf to hear, and the dumb to speak.

ST. MARK VIII.

1 In those days the multitude being again[4] great, and having nothing to eat, he[5] called the disciples *unto him,* and
2 saith unto them, I have compassion on the multitude, because they have now been with me three days, and
3 have nothing to eat: and if I send them away fasting to their own houses, they will faint by the way: and[6] divers
4 of them came from far. And his disciples answered him, From whence can a man satisfy these *men* with bread
5 here in the wilderness? And he asked them, How many loaves have
6 ye? And they said, Seven. And he commandeth[8] the people to sit down on the ground: and he took the seven

32 Then Jesus called his disciples *unto him,* and said, I have compassion on the multitude, because they continue with me now three days, and have nothing to eat: and I will not send them away fasting, lest they faint in the way.
33 And the[7] disciples say unto him, Whence should we have so much bread in the wilderness, as to fill
34 so great a multitude? And Jesus saith unto them, How many loaves have ye? And they said, Seven,
35 and a few little fishes. And he commanded the multitude to sit
36 down on the ground. And he took

---

[1] and straightway his ears   [2] and the string   [3] at Jesus' feet
[4] being very great   [5] Jesus called his disciples   [6] for divers of them
[7] his disciples   [8] commanded

ST. MATT. XV.	ST. MARK VIII.
the seven loaves and the fishes, and gave thanks, and brake *them*, and gave to his disciples, and the disci- ³⁷ ples to the multitudes.² And they did all eat, and were filled: and they took up of the broken *meat* that was left seven baskets full. ³⁸ And they that did eat were four thousand men, beside women and children.	loaves, and gave thanks, and brake, and gave to his disciples to set before *them*; and they did set *them* before ⁷ the people. And they had a few small fishes: and he blessed and¹ set them ⁸ before *them*. And³ they did eat, and were filled: and they took up of the broken *meat* that was left seven bas- ⁹ kets. And they⁴ were about four thousand: and he sent them away.

§ 67. The Pharisees and Sadducees again demand a Sign.—*West Coast of Sea of Galilee.*

ST. MATT. XV. 39–XVI. 4ᵃ.	ST. MARK VIII. 10–12.
³⁹ And he sent away the multitude, and took ship, and came into the coast of Magadan.⁵	¹⁰ And straightway he entered into a ship with his disciples, and came into the parts of Dalmanutha.
ST. MATT. XVI.	
¹ The Pharisees also with the Sadducees came, and, tempting, desired him that he would shew them a sign ² from heaven.ᵃ He answered and said unto them, [⁶When it is evening, ye say, *It will be* fair weather: ³ for the sky is red. And in the morning, *It will be* foul weather to-day: for the sky is red and lowring.⁷ Ye can discern the face of the sky; but can ye not *discern* the signs of ⁴ the times?] A wicked and adulterous generation seeketh after a sign; and there shall no sign be given unto it, but the sign of⁸ Jonas.	¹¹ And the Pharisees came forth, and began to question with him, seeking of him a sign from heaven,ᵃ tempting ¹² him. And he sighed deeply in his spirit, and saith, Why doth this generation seek after a sign? verily I say unto you, There shall no sign be given unto this generation.

---

¹ he blessed, and commanded to set them also before *them*. ² multitude
³ So they did eat ⁴ they that had eaten were about
⁵ Magdala ⁶ When it is evening, *etc., to* end of ver. 3 is omitted in several early MSS.
⁷ O *ye* hypocrites, ye can discern ⁸ the prophet Jonas

ᵃ See Matt. xii. 38, 39; Lk. xi. 16.

§ 68. Warnings against the Leaven of the Pharisees. — *North East Coast of Sea of Galilee.*

St. Matt. xvi. 4ᵇ–12.	St. Mark viii. 13–21.
4ᵇ And he left them, and departed. 5 And when the² disciples were come to the other side, they had 6 forgotten to take bread. Then Jesus said unto them, Take heed and beware of the leaven of the Pharisees 7 and of the Sadducees. And they reasoned among themselves, saying, *It is* because we have taken no 8 bread. *Which* when Jesus perceived, he said,⁵ O ye of little faith! why reason ye among yourselves, because ye have brought no bread? 9 Do ye not yet understand, neither remember the five loaves of the five thousand, and how many bas-10 kets ye took up?ᵃ Neither the seven loaves of the four thousand, and how many baskets ye took up?ᵇ 11 How is it that ye do not understand that I spake *it* not to you concerning bread? but¹⁰ beware of the leaven of the Pharisees and of the 12 Sadducees? Then understood they how that he bade *them* not beware of the leaven of the Pharisees and Sadducees,¹¹ but of the doctrine of the Pharisees and Sadducees.	13 And he left them, and embarking¹ again departed to the other side. 14 Now *the disciples* had forgotten to take bread, neither had they in the ship with them more than one loaf. 15 And he charged them, saying, Take heed, beware of the leaven of the Pharisees, and *of* the leaven of Herod. 16 And they reasoned among themselves,³ *It is* because we have no 17 bread. And when he⁴ knew *it*, he saith unto them, Why reason ye, because ye have no bread? perceive ye not yet, neither understand? have 18 ye your heart hardened?⁶ Having eyes, see ye not? and having ears, hear ye not? and do ye not remember 19 when I brake the five loaves among five thousand, and⁷ how many baskets full of fragments ye took up?ᵃ 20 They say unto him, Twelve. And when the seven among four thousand, how many baskets full of fragments took ye up?ᵇ And they say,⁸ Seven. 21 And he said unto them, Do ye not yet⁹ understand?

¹ and entering into the ship again   ² his disciples
³ saying, *It is* because   ⁴ when Jesus knew
⁵ he said unto them   ⁶ have ye your heart yet hardened?
⁷ *omit* and   ⁸ they said, Seven
⁹ How is it that ye do not understand?   ¹⁰ concerning bread, that ye should beware
¹¹ of the leaven of bread, but of the doctrine

ᵃ Matt. xiv. 16–21; Mar. vi. 37–44; Lk. ix. 13–17; Jno. vi. 5–13.   ᵇ Matt. xv. 32–38; Mar. viii. 1–9.

§ 69. A blind Man healed. — *Bethsaida.*
St. Mark viii. 22–26.

22 And they[1] come to Bethsaida; and they bring a blind man unto him, and
23 besought him to touch him. And he took the blind man by the hand, and led him out of the town; and when he had spit on his eyes, and put his
24 hands upon him, he asked him if he saw ought. And he looked up, and
25 said, I see men, because I see *them*[2] as trees walking. After that he put *his* hands again upon his eyes, and[3] he saw and was restored, and saw every-
26 thing clearly. And he sent him away to his house, saying, go not[4] into the town.

§ 70. The Confession of Peter: Christ foretells His own Passion and the Sufferings of His Followers. — *Region of Cæsarea Philippi.*

St. Matt. xvi. 13–28.	St. Mark viii. 27–ix. 1.	St. Luke ix. 18–27.
13 When Jesus came into the coasts of Caesarea Philippi, he asked his disciples, saying, Whom do men say that the Son of man 14 is?[5] And they said, Some *say that thou art* John the Baptist: some, Elias: and others, Jeremias, or one of 15 the prophets. He saith unto them, But whom say ye that I 16 am? And Simon Peter answered and said, Thou art the Christ the Son of the	27 And Jesus went out, and his disciples, into the town of Caesarea Philippi: and by the way he asked his disciples, saying unto them, Whom do men 28 say that I am? And they told him, saying,[6] John the Baptist: but some *say,* Elias: and others, One of the 29 prophets. And he asked[7] them, But whom say ye that I am? [8] Peter answereth and saith unto him, Thou art the Christ.	18 And it came to pass, as he was alone praying, his disciples were with him; and he asked them, saying, Whom say the 19 people that I am? They answering said, John the Baptist: but some *say,* Elias: and others *say,* that one of the old prophets is risen again. 20 He said unto them, But whom say ye that I am? Peter answering said, The Christ of God.

[1] And he cometh
[2] see men as trees, walking
[3] and made him look up: and he was restored, and saw every man clearly.
[4] Neither go into the town, nor tell *it* to any in the town.
[5] say that I, the Son of Man, am?
[6] they answered, John
[7] And he saith unto them
[8] And Peter answereth

§ 70. A somewhat similar confession of St. Peter is recorded in St. John vi. 66–71 (§ 63); but there is no sufficient reason for transferring that passage to this section, as has been done by Thomson and Tischendorf. The confession is mentioned in each place in the closest connection with the accompanying circumstances, and those circumstances are quite different in the two cases. The confession must therefore have been made more than once.

ST. MATT. XVI.	ST. MARK VIII.	ST. LUKE IX.
17 living God. And Jesus answered and said unto him, Blessed art thou, Simon Bar-Jona: for flesh and blood hath not revealed *it* unto thee, but my Father which is in heaven.		
18 And I say also unto thee, That thou art Peter [a] and upon this rock I will build my church [b]: and the gates of hell shall not prevail against it.		
19 [1] I will give unto thee the keys of the kingdom of heaven: and whatsoever thou shalt bind on earth shall be bound in heaven; and whatsoever thou shalt loose on earth shalt be loosed in heaven.[c]		
20 Then charged he the [2] disciples that they should tell no man that he was [3] the Christ.	30 And he charged them that they should tell no man of him.	21 And he straitly charged them, and commanded *them* to tell no man that thing;
21 From that time forth began Jesus to shew unto his disciples, how that he must go unto Jerusalem, and suffer many things of the elders and chief priests and scribes, and be killed, and be raised again the third	31 And he began to teach them, that the Son of man must suffer many things, and be rejected of the elders, and *of* the chief priests, and scribes, and be killed, and after three days 32 rise again. And he spake that saying	22 saying, The Son of man must suffer many things, and be rejected of the elders and chief priests and scribes, and be slain, and be raised the third day.

[1] And I will give [2] his disciples [3] he was Jesus the Christ.
[a] See Jno. i. 42. [b] Acts ii. 14, 37, 41; viii. 14, etc.; x. [c] Matt. xviii. 18; Jno. xx. 23.

ST. MATT. XVI.	ST. MARK VIII.	ST. LUKE IX.
22 day. Then Peter took him, and began to rebuke him, saying, Be it far from thee, Lord! this shall not be unto 23 thee. But he turned, and said unto Peter, Get thee behind me, Satan! thou art an offence unto me: for thou savorest not the things that be of God, but those that be of men.	openly. And Peter took him, and began 33 to rebuke him. But when he had turned about and looked on his disciples, he rebuked Peter, and saith,¹ Get thee behind me, Satan! for thou savorest not the things that be of God, but the things that be of men. 34 And when he had called the people *unto him* with his disciples	
24 Then said Jesus unto his disciples, If any *man* will come after me, let him deny himself, and take up his cross, and follow 25 me.ᵃ For whosoever will save his life shall lose it; and whosoever will lose his life for my sake shall find it. 26 For what shall a man be⁴ profited, if he shall gain the whole world, and lose his own soul? or what shall a man give in exchange for his soul?	also, he said unto them, Whosoever will follow² after me, let him deny himself, and take up his cross, and 35 follow me.ᵃ For whosoever will save his life shall lose it; but whosoever shall lose his life for my sake and the gospel's,³ shall 36 save it. For what profiteth it⁵ a man to gain the whole world, and lose his own soul? 37 For what giveth⁶ a man in exchange for 38 his soul? Whosoever therefore shall be ashamed of me and of my words in this adulterous and sinful generation; of him also	23 And he said to *them* all, If any *man* will come after me, let him deny himself, and take up his cross daily, and follow 24 me.ᵃ For whosoever will save his life shall lose it; but whosoever will lose his life for my sake, the same shall save 25 it. For what is a man advantaged, if he gain the whole world, and lose himself, or be cast 26 away? For whosoever shall be ashamed of me and of my words, of him

¹ saying, Get thee
³ the same shall save
⁵ what shall it profit a man, if he shall gain
ᵃ Matt. x. 38; Lk. xiv. 27.

² will come after me
⁴ what is a man profited
⁶ Or what shall a man give

ST. MATT. XVI.	ST. MARK VIII., IX.	ST. LUKE IX.
27 For the Son of man shall come in the glory of his Father with his angels; and then he shall reward every man according to his 28 works. Verily I say unto you, that [1] there be some standing here which shall not taste of death, till they see the Son of man coming in his kingdom.	shall the Son of man be ashamed, when he cometh in the glory of his Father with the 1 holy angels. And he said unto them, Verily, I say unto you, That there be some of them that stand here which shall not taste of death, till they have seen the kingdom of God come with power.	shall the Son of man be ashamed, when he shall come in his own glory, and *in his* Father's, and 27 of the holy angels. But I tell you of a truth, there be some standing here which shall not taste of death, till they see the kingdom of God.

§ 71. The Transfiguration and subsequent Discourse. — *Region of Cæsarea Philippi.*

ST. MATT. XVII. 1–13.	ST. MARK IX. 2–13.	ST. LUKE IX. 28–36.
1 And after six days Jesus taketh Peter, James, and John his brother, and bringeth them up into an high 2 mountain apart, and was transfigured before them:[a] and his face did shine as the sun, and his raiment was white as the light. 3 And, behold, there appeared unto them Moses and Elias talking with him.	2 And after six days Jesus taketh *with him* Peter, and James, and John, and leadeth them up into an high mountain apart by themselves; and he was transfigured before 3 them.[a] And his raiment became shining, exceeding white;[2] so as no fuller on earth 4 can white them. And there appeared unto them Elias with Moses; and they were talking with Jesus.	28 And it came to pass about an eight days after these sayings, he took Peter, and John, and James, and went up into a mountain to pray. 29 And as he prayed the fashion of his countenance was altered,[a] and his raiment *was* white 30 *and* glistering. And, behold, there talked with him two men, which were 31 Moses and Elias; who appeared in glory, and spake of his decease which he should accom- 32 plish at Jerusalem. But Peter and they that were with him were heavy with sleep; and

[1] *omit* that   [2] exceeding white as snow

a Jno. i. 14; 2 Pet. i. 16–18.

ST. MATT. XVII.	ST. MARK IX.	ST. LUKE IX.
		when they were awake, they saw his glory, and the two men that stood 33 with him. And it came to pass, as they departed from him, Peter said unto
4 Then answered Peter, and said unto Jesus, Lord, it is good for us to be here: if thou wilt, I will¹ make here three tabernacles, one for thee, and one for Moses, and one for 5 Elias. While he yet spake, behold, a bright cloud overshadowed them; and behold, a voice out of the cloud, which said, This is my beloved Son, in whom I am well pleased: 6 hear ye him. And when the disciples heard *it*, they fell on their face, and were 7 sore afraid. And Jesus came and touched them, and said, Arise, 8 and be not afraid. And when they had lifted up their eyes, they saw no man, save 9 Jesus only. And as they came down from the mountain, Jesus charged them, saying,	5 And Peter answered and said to Jesus, Master, it is good for us to be here; and let us make three tabernacles; one for thee, and one for Moses, and 6 one for Elias. For he wist not what to answer;² for they be-7 came sore afraid. And there was a cloud that overshadowed them; and there was³ a voice out of the cloud,⁴ This is my beloved Son: hear him. 8 And suddenly, when they had looked round about, they saw no man any more, save Jesus only with themselves. 9 And as they came down from the mountain, he charged them that they should tell no man what	Jesus, Master, it is good for us to be here; and let us make three tabernacles; one for thee, and one for Moses, and one for Elias: not knowing 34 what he said. While he thus spake, there came a cloud, and overshadowed them; and they feared as they entered 35 into the cloud. And there came a voice out of the cloud, saying, This is my chosen⁵ Son: hear him. 36 And when the voice was past, Jesus was found alone.

¹ let us make ² what to say; for they were ³ and a voice came out
⁴ saying, This is ⁵ my beloved Son

ST. MATT. XVII.	ST. MARK IX.	ST. LUKE IX.
Tell the vision to no man, until the Son of man be raised[1] again from the dead.	things they had seen, till the Son of man were risen from the 10 dead. And they kept that saying with themselves, questioning one with another what the rising from the dead should mean.	And they kept *it* close, and told no man in those days any of those things which they had seen.
10 And the[2] disciples asked him, saying, Why then say the scribes that Elias must 11 first come? And he[4] answered and said, Elias truly shall come,[6] and restore all things.[a]	11 And they asked him, saying, Why say the Pharisees and[3] the scribes that Elias must 12 first come? And he[5] told them, Elias[7] cometh first, and restoreth all things;[a] and how it is written of the Son of man, that he must suffer many things, and be set at nought.	
12 But I say unto you, That Elias is come already, and they knew him not, but have done unto him whatsoever they listed. Likewise shall also the Son of man suffer of them. 13 Then the disciples understood that he spake unto them of John the Baptist.	13 But I say unto you, That Elias is indeed come, and they have done unto him whatsoever they listed, as it is written of him.	

§ 72. The Healing of the Demoniac whom the Disciples could not heal.

ST. MATT. XVII. 14–21.	ST. MARK IX. 14–29.	ST. LUKE IX. 37–43.
14 And when *they*[8] were come to the multitude,	14 And when they[9] came to the disciples, they	37 And it came to pass, that on the next day,

[1] be risen again   [2] his disciples   [3] omit the Pharisees and
[4] And Jesus answered and said unto them, Elias   [5] And he answered and told
[6] shall first come   [7] Elias verily cometh
[8] they were   [9] And when he came to *his* disciples, he saw

[a] Mal. iv. 4, 5. Comp. Lk. i. 16, 17; Matt. xi. 14.

ST. MATT. XVII.	ST. MARK IX.	ST. LUKE IX.
	saw a great multitude about them, and the scribes questioning with 15 them. And straightway all the people, when they beheld him, were greatly amazed, and running to 16 *him*, saluted him. And he asked them,[1] What question ye with them?	when they were come down from the hill, much people met him.
there came to him a *certain* man, kneeling down to him, and say- 15 ing, Lord, have mercy on my son: for he is lunatick, and sore vexed; for ofttimes he falleth into the fire, and oft into the water.	17 And one of the multitude answered him,[2] Master, I have brought unto thee my son, which hath a 18 dumb spirit; and wheresoever he taketh him, he teareth *him*;[3] and he foameth, and gnasheth the[4] teeth, and pineth	38 And, behold, a man of the company cried out, saying, Master, I beseech thee look upon my son; for he is mine 39 only child. And, lo! a spirit taketh him, and he suddenly crieth out; and it teareth him that he foameth again, and bruising him, hardly departeth from him.
16 And I brought him to thy disciples, and they could not cure him. 17 Then Jesus answered and said, O faithless and perverse generation! how long shall I be with you? how long shall I suffer you? bring him hither to me.	away; and I spake to thy disciples that they should cast him out; and 19 they could not. He answereth them[5] and saith, O faithless generation! how long shall I be with you? how long shall I suffer you? bring him 20 unto me. And they brought him unto him; and when he saw him, straightway the spirit tare him; and he fell on the ground, and wallowed 21 foaming. And he asked his father, How long is it ago since this came unto him? And he said,	40 And I besought thy disciples to cast him out; and they could 41 not. And Jesus answering said, O faithless and perverse generation! how long shall I be with you, and suffer you? Bring thy 42 son hither. And as he was yet a coming, the devil threw him down, and tare *him*.

[1] he asked the scribes   [2] answered and said, Master   [3] teareth him
[4] gnasheth with his teeth   [5] answereth him and saith

ST. MATT. XVII.	ST. MARK VIII., IX.	ST. LUKE IX.
	22 Of a child. And ofttimes it hath cast him into the fire, and into the waters, to destroy him; but if thou canst do anything, have compassion on us, 23 and help us. Jesus said unto him, If thou canst *believe*,[1] all things *are* possible to him that be- 24 lieveth. [2] Straightway the father of the child cried out, and said,[3] I believe; help thou mine 25 unbelief. When Jesus saw that the people came running together, he re-	
18 And Jesus rebuked the devil,	buked the foul spirit, saying unto him, *Thou* dumb and deaf spirit, I charge thee, come out of him, and enter no more into him. And *the spirit* cried, and rent *him*[4] sore,	And Jesus rebuked the unclean spirit,
and he departed out of him; and the child was cured from that very	and came out of him; and he was as one dead: insomuch that many said,	and healed the child, and delivered him a- gain to his father.
		43 And they were all amazed at the mighty power of God.
	27 He is dead. But Jesus took him by the hand, and lifted him up; and 28 he arose. And when he	
20 hour. Then came the disciples to Jesus a- part, and said, Why could not we cast him 20 out? And he saith[5] unto them, Because of your little faith:[6] for	was come into the house, his disciples asked him privately, Why could not 29 we cast him out? And he said unto them, This kind can come forth by nothing, but by prayer.[7]	

[1] If thou canst believe   [2] And straightway   [3] and said with tears, Lord, I believe
[4] rent him   [5] And Jesus said   [6] your unbelief   [7] by prayer and fasting

ST. MATT. XVII.	ST. MARK IX.	ST. LUKE IX.
verily I say unto you, If ye have faith as a grain of mustard seed, ye shall say unto this mountain, Remove hence to yonder place; and it shall remove; and nothing shall be impossible unto you.¹		

§ 73. Our Lord again foretells his Death and Reserrection.

ST. MATT. XVII. 22, 23.	ST. MARK IX. 30–32.	ST. LUKE IX. 43ᵇ–45.
22 And while they abode in Galilee,	30 And they departed thence, and passed through Galilee: and he would not that any man should know it. For he taught his disciples, and said unto them, The Son of man is delivered into the hands of men, and they shall kill him; and after that he is killed, he shall rise after 32 three days.³ But they understood not that saying, and were afraid to ask him.	But while they wondered every one at all things which he² did, he said unto his disciples,
Jesus said unto them, The Son of man shall be betrayed into the 23 hands of men: and they shall kill him,		44 Let these sayings sink down into your ears; for the Son of man shall be delivered into the hands of men.
and the third day he shall be raised again. And they were exceeding sorry.		45 But they understood not this saying, and it was hid from them, that they perceived it not; and they feared to ask him of that saying.

§ 74. The Tribute-money miraculously provided. — *Capernaum.*

ST. MATT. XVII. 24–27.		ST. MARK IX. 33.ᵃ
24 And when they were come to Capernaum, they that received tribute *money* came to Peter, and said, Doth 25 not your master pay tribute? He saith, Yes. And when he was entering⁵ into the house, Jesus prevented him, saying, What thinkest thou, Simon? of whom do the kings of the earth take custom or tribute? of their own		33 And they⁴ came to Capernaum:

---

¹ ver. 21. Howbeit this kind goeth not out but by prayer and fasting.
² which Jesus did   ³ rise the third day   ⁴ and he came   ⁵ was come into

ST. MATT. XVII.		ST. MARK IX.

26 children or of strangers? And when he saith,[1] Of strangers, Jesus saith unto him, Then are the children free.
27 Notwithstanding, lest we should offend them, go thou to the sea, and cast an hook, and take up the fish that first cometh up; and when thou hast opened his mouth, thou shalt find a piece of money: that take, and give unto them for me and thee.

§ 75. Several Discourses with the Disciples. — *Capernaum.*
(A) Our Lord reproves their Ambition by the Example of a Child.

St. Matt. xviii. 1–5.	St. Mark ix. 33^b–37.	St. Luke ix. 46–48.
	And being in the house he asked them, What was it that ye disputed[2] by the way?	
1 At the same time came the disciples unto Jesus, saying, Who is the greatest in the kingdom of heaven?	34 But they held their peace: for by the way they had disputed among themselves, who *should be* the greatest.	46 Then there arose a reasoning among them, which of them should be greatest.
	35 And he sat down, and called the twelve, and saith unto them, If any man desire to be first, *the same* shall be last of all, and servant	
2 And he[4] called a little child unto him, and set him in the 3 midst of them. And said, Verily I say unto you, Except ye be converted, and become as little children, ye shall not enter into the kingdom of heav- 4 en. Whosoever therefore shall humble himself as this little child,	36 of all. And he took a child, and set him in the midst of them: and when he had taken him in his arms, he said unto them,	47 And Jesus knowing[3] the thought of their heart, took a child, and 48 set him by him, and said unto them,

[1] Peter saith unto him, of strangers.
[2] disputed among yourselves
[3] perceiving the thought
[4] And Jesus called

ST. MATT. XVIII.	ST. MARK IX.	ST. LUKE IX.
the same is greatest in the kingdom of heaven.		
5 And whoso shall receive one such little child in my name receiveth me.	37 Whosoever shall receive one of these[1] children in my name, receiveth me: and whosoever shall receive me, receiveth not me, but him that sent me.	Whosoever shall receive this child in my name receiveth me: and whosoever shall receive me receiveth him that sent me: for he that is least among you all, the same is [2] great.

(B) He directs concerning Another healing in his Name.

St. Matt. x. 42.	St. Mark ix. 38–41.	St. Luke ix. 49, 50.
	John answered him,[3] Master, we saw one casting out devils in thy name, and he followeth not us; and we forbad him, because he 39 followeth not us. But Jesus said, Forbid him not: for there is no man which shall do a miracle in my name, that can lightly speak 40 evil of me. For he that is not against us 41 is on our part. For	49 And John answered and said, Master, we saw one casting out devils in thy name; and we forbad him, because he followeth not with us. And 50 Jesus said unto him, Forbid *him* not:
42 And whosoever shall give to drink unto one of these little ones a cup of cold *water* only in the name of a disciple, verily I say unto you, he shall in no wise lose his reward.	whosoever shall give you a cup of water to drink in my name, because ye belong to Christ, verily I say unto you, that[5] he shall not lose his reward.	for he that is not against you is for you.[4]

(C) He teaches to avoid Offences.

St. Matt. xviii. 6–9.	St. Mark ix. 42–50.	St. Luke xvii. 1, 2.
6 But whoso shall offend one of these little ones	42 And whosoever shall offend one of these [6] little	1 Then said he unto his [7] disciples, It is

[1] of such children [2] shall be great [3] And John answered him, saying,
[4] against us is for us [5] *omit* that [6] *these* little ones [7] unto the disciples

ST. MATT. XVIII.	ST. MARK IX.	ST. LUKE XVII.
which believe in me, it were better for him that a millstone were hanged about his neck, and *that* he were drowned in the depth of the sea. 7 Woe unto the world because of offences! for it must needs be that offences come; but woe to the [2] man by whom the offence cometh! Wherefore 8 if thy hand or thy foot offend thee, cut it off, and cast *it* [3] from thee: it is better for thee to enter into life halt or maimed, rather than having two hands or two feet to be cast into everlasting fire. 9 And if thine eye offend thee, pluck it out, and cast *it* from thee: it is better for thee to enter into life with one eye, rather than having two eyes to be cast into hell fire.	ones that believe,[1] it is better for him that a millstone were hanged about his neck, and he were cast into the sea. 43 And if thy hand offend thee, cut it off; it is better for thee to enter into life maimed, than having two hands to go into hell, into the fire that never shall be 45 quenched.[4] And if thy foot offend thee, cut it off; it is better for thee to enter halt into life, than having two feet to be cast into hell, into the 47 fire.[5] [4] And if thine eye offend thee, pluck it out: it is better for thee to enter into the kingdom of God with one eye, than having two eyes to 48 be cast into hell:[6] where their worm dieth not, and the fire is not 49 quenched.[a] For every one shall be salted with fire.[7]	impossible but that offences will come: but woe *unto him*, through 2 whom they come! It were better for him that a millstone were hanged about his neck, and he cast into the sea, than that he should offend one of these little ones.

[1] believe in me   [2] to that man   [3] cut them off, and cast *them* from thee
[4] ver. 44 and 46. Where their worm dieth not, and the fire is not quenched.
[5] into the fire that never shall be quenched.   [6] hell fire
[7] salted with fire, and every sacrifice shall be salted with salt.
    [a] Isa. lxvi. 24. For their worm shall not die, neither shall their fire be quenched.

St. Matt. XVIII.	St. Mark IX.	St. Luke XVII.
	50 Salt *is* good: but if the salt have lost his saltness, wherewith will ye season it? have salt in yourselves, and have peace one with another.	

(D) Parable of the Sheep gone astray; Forgiveness taught; Parable of the King reckoning with his Servants.

St. Matt. XVIII. 10–35.	St. Luke XVII. 3, 4.
10 Take heed that ye despise not one of these little ones; for I say unto you, that in heaven their angels do always behold the face of my Father which is in 12 heaven.[1] How think ye?[a] if a man have an hundred sheep, and one of them be gone astray, doth he not leave the ninety and nine, and goeth into the mountains, and seeketh that which is gone 13 astray? And if so be that he find it, verily I say unto you, he rejoiceth more of that *sheep*, than of the 14 ninety and nine which went not astray. Even so it is not the will of your Father which is in heaven, that one of these little ones should perish.	
15 Moreover if thy brother shall trespass,[2] go,[3] tell him his fault between thee and him alone: if he shall hear thee, thou hast gained thy brother. 16 But if he will not hear *thee, then* take with thyself[4] one or two more more, that in the mouth of two or three witnesses every word may be established.[b]	3 Take heed to yourselves: If thy brother trespass,[2] rebuke him: and if he repent, forgive him.

[1] ver. 11. For the Son of man is come to save that which was lost.
[2] trespass against thee   [3] go and tell   [4] take with thee
[a] Comp. Lk. xv. 3–7.
[b] Deut. xix. 15. At the mouth of two witnesses, or at the mouth of three witnesses shall the matter be established.

---

§ 75. (D.) The parables in Matt. xviii. 12, 13 and Lk. xv. 3–7 have a close resemblance, but yet, on examination, show marks of distinction. Each is so closely bound in with its context that it cannot well be separated, and there is thus a considerable interval of time between them. They were uttered on different occasions, and for different purposes: the parable in St. Matthew has for its subject a sheep that has *wandered* from the fold, and is diligently sought, tenderly restored, and rejoiced over as the brother should be who has strayed into the paths of sin; the parable in St. Luke is concerned with a *lost* sheep, as the Publicans and sinners were considered to be, and whose recovery ought to be a cause of joy to all. Between the two there are necessarily strong resemblances, but they seem intended to illustrate somewhat different points.

ST. MATT. XVIII.

17 And if he shall neglect to hear them, tell *it* unto the church: but if he neglect to hear the church, let him be unto thee as an heathen man and a publican.
18 Verily I say unto you, Whatsoever ye shall bind on earth shall be bound in heaven: and whatsoever ye shall loose on earth, shall be loosed in heaven.
19 Again I say unto you, That if two of you shall agree on earth, as touching any thing that they shall ask, it shall be done for them of my Father which
20 is in heaven. For where two or three are gathered together in my name, there am I in the midst of them.
21 Then came Peter to him, and said, Lord, how oft shall my brother sin against me, and I forgive him?
22 till seven times? Jesus saith unto him, I say not unto thee, Until seven times: but, Until seventy
23 times seven. Therefore is the kingdom of heaven likened unto a certain king, which would take ac-
24 count of his servants. And when he had begun to reckon, one was brought unto him, which owed him
25 ten thousand talents; but forasmuch as he had not to pay, the [2] lord commanded him to be sold, and [3] wife and children and all that he had, and
26 payment to be made. The servant therefore fell down, and worshipped him, saying,[4] have patience
27 with me, and I will pay thee all. Then the lord of that servant was moved with compassion, and loosed
28 him, and forgave him the debt. But the same servant went out, and found one of his fellow-servants, which owed him an hundred pence; and he laid hands on him, and took *him* by the throat, say-
29 ing, Pay whatsoever [5] thou owest. And his fellow-servant fell down,[6] and besought him, saying, Have
30 patience with me, and I will pay thee.[7] And he would not: but went and cast him into prison, till
31 he should pay the debt. So when his fellow-servants saw what was done, they were very sorry, and came
32 and told unto the [8] lord all that was done. Then his

ST. LUKE XVII.

4 And if he trespass against thee seven times in a day, and seven times [1] turn again to thee, saying, I repent: thou shalt forgive him.

---

[1] seven times in a day turn again
[3] and his wife
[5] Pay me that thou
[7] pay thee all.
[2] his lord commanded
[4] saying, Lord, have patience
[6] fell down at his feet, and
[8] unto their lord

ST. MATT. XVIII.

lord, after that he had called him, said unto him, O thou wicked servant! I forgave thee all that debt,
33 because thou desiredst me; shouldest not thou also have compassion on thy fellow-servant, even as I
34 had pity on thee? And his lord was wroth, and delivered him to the tormentors, till he should pay
35 all that was due unto him. So likewise shall my heavenly Father do also unto you, if ye from your hearts forgive not every one his brother.[1]

§ 76. Our Lord's final Departure from Galilee, going up to the Feast of Tabernacles.

MATT. XIX. 1.ᵃ MAR. X. 1.ᵃ LK. IX. 51–56. JOHN VII. 2–10.

ST. LUKE XVII.

2 Now the Jews' feast of tabernacles
3 was at hand. His brethren therefore said unto him, Depart hence, and go into Judea, that thy disciples also may see the works that thou
4 doest. For *there is* no man *that* doeth any thing in secret, and he himself seeketh to be known openly. If thou do these things, shew thy-
5 self to the world. For neither did
6 his brethren believe in him. ²Jesus said unto them, My time is not yet come: but your time is alway
7 ready. The world cannot hate you; but me it hateth, because I testify of it, that the works thereof
8 are evil. Go ye up unto the ³ feast: I go not up⁴ unto this feast; for my time is not yet full come.
9 When he had said these words, he himself⁵ abode *still* in Galilee.

---

[1] his brother their trespasses.　　[2] Then Jesus said　　[3] unto this feast
　　[4] I go not up yet unto　　[5] had said these words unto them, he abode *still*

---

§ 76. The difficulties presented at this point in the chronological arrangement of the material furnished by the several Evangelists are usually thought the most considerable in the whole work of a Harmony. There is not space here to enter into the multitude of schemes which have been proposed. A very clear and succinct account of the more important of them may be found in Andrews' "Life of our Lord," pp. 345–362. Suffice it briefly to state the arrangement here adopted, with the chief reasons therefor. Lk. ix. 51 bears upon the face of it that this was our Lord's final departure from Galilee, and his entrance upon a series of jour-

ST. MATT. XIX.	ST. MARK X.	ST. LUKE IX.	ST. JOHN VII.
1 And it came to pass, *that* when Jesus had finished these sayings, he departed from Galilee.	1 And he arose from thence.	51 And it came to pass, when the time was come that he should be received up, he steadfastly set his face to go to Jerusalem, and sent messengers before his face: and they went, and entered into a city[3] of	10 But when his brethren were gone up unto the feast,[1] then went he also up, not openly, but[2] in secret.

[1] were gone up, then went he also up unto the feast   [2] but as it were in secret.
[3] into a village

---

neyings which terminated at last in his death at Jerusalem and his ascension. Any other interpretation of '*received up*' is forced; and the expression '*the time was come*' implies that this was now so near at hand that there was no longer any intervening object of magnitude, but rather that all things were rapidly converging to this consummation. The first point in this journey was the attendance upon the Feast of Tabernacles in Jerusalem, and so far, the journey appears, from Jno. vii. 9, 10, to have been made somewhat privately and rapidly. Matt. xix. 1 and Mar. x. 1 are necessarily placed in parallelism, as both mention a departure from Galilee, and this was the final one. Soon after entering upon this journey our Lord appears to have sent forth the seventy (probably wholly or chiefly into Perea); allowing them the time required for his attendance at the feast in which to prepare the people for his own journeyings in Perea. This should be particularly noted, as it forms the turning point of the arrangement. The difficulties usually found in this part of the narrative arise chiefly from supposing that our Lord followed immediately after the seventy, in the same road. If, however, as the nature of their mission seems to require, a little time be allowed for their labors by themselves before our Saviour goes over the same ground, these difficulties in great part disappear.

Having attended the Feast of Tabernacles (of which, however, the Synoptical Evangelists make no mention), our Lord retires to Perea, whence he again resumes his slow and public progress toward Jerusalem, teaching as he went in those numerous villages of Perea, hitherto little visited by him, but where the seventy had now prepared the people for his coming (Lk. xiii. 10). On this journey he was attended by great multitudes (Matt. xix. 2; Lk. xii. 1); and that it lay through Perea appears from Matt. xix. 1; Mar. x. 1, yet always tending, however circuitously, toward Jerusalem (Lk. xiii. 22). This journey appears to have been again interrupted, or perhaps it was brought to a close, by our Lord's attendance upon the Feast of the Dedication in Jerusalem. After the Dedication he "went away again beyond Jordan, into the place where John at first baptised, and there he abode" (Jno. x. 39). The question whether this sojourn is to be included in St. Luke's general account of the journey, or was subsequent thereto, is merely a formal one, and only involves the unimportant question at what point exactly Jno. x. 22–42 should be inserted.

From this retirement he is summoned to Bethany (Jno. xi. 3) and raises Lazarus from the dead. Thence he retires to Ephraim, near the wilderness, and "there continued with his disciples" (Jno. xi. 54) until the pilgrims began to gather for the Passover. He joins them, probably near the Jordan, and enters Jericho attended by the multitude, and thence goes to Jerusalem. The several narratives have now again coalesced, Lk. xvii. 11 being considered parallel with Jno. xi. 55.

ST. MATT. XIX	ST. MARK X.	ST. LUKE IX.	ST. JOHN VII.

		the Samaritans, to make
	53	ready for him. And they did not receive him, because his face was as though he would go to
	54	Jerusalem. And when the[1] disciples James and John saw *this*, they said, Lord, wilt thou that we command fire to come down from heaven and
	55	consume them?[2] But he turned and rebuked
	56	them.[3] And they went to another village.

§ 77. On the Way, the Devotion of new Disciples put to the Test.

St. Matt. viii. 19–22.   St. Luke ix. 57–62.

19 And a certain scribe came, and said unto him, Master, I will follow thee whithersoever thou goest. And
20 Jesus saith unto him, The foxes have holes, and the birds of the air *have* nests; but the Son of man hath not where to lay *his* head.
21 And another of the[5] disciples said unto him, Lord, suffer me first to
22 go and bury my father. But he saith[7] unto him, Follow me: and let the dead bury their dead.

57 And[4] as they went in the way, a certain *man* said unto him, Lord, I will follow thee withersoever thou
58 goest. And Jesus said unto him, Foxes have holes, and birds of the air *have* nests; but the Son of man
59 hath not where to lay *his* head. And he said unto another, Follow me. But he said,[6] Suffer me first to go and bury
60 my father. He[8] said unto him, Let the dead bury their dead; but go thou and preach the kingdom of God.
61 And another also said, Lord, I will follow thee; but let me first go bid them farewell, which are at home at
62 my house. And Jesus said unto him, No man, having put his hand to the plough, and looking back, is fit for the kingdom of God.

---

[1] his disciples   [2] consume them, even as Elias did?
[3] rebuked them, and said, Ye, know not what manner of spirit ye are of. For the Son of man is not come to destroy men's lives, but to save *them*. And they
[4] And it came to pass, that, as they went   [5] his disciples
[6] Lord, suffer me   [7] But Jesus said unto him   [8] Jesus said

§ 78. The Seventy sent forth.
St. Luke x. 1–11.

1 After these things the Lord appointed other seventy also, and sent them [a] two and two before his face into every city and place, whither he himself would come.
2 And he[1] said unto them, The harvest truly is great, but the laborers are few: pray ye therefore the Lord of the harvest, that he would send forth
3 laborers into his harvest.[b] Go your ways: behold I send you forth as lambs
4 among wolves. Carry neither purse, nor scrip, nor shoes: [2] salute no man by
5 the way. And into whatsoever house ye enter, first say, Peace be to this house.
6 And if a[3] son of peace be there, your peace shall rest upon it: if not, it shall
7 turn to you again. And in the same house remain, eating and drinking such things as they give: for the laborer is[4] worthy of his hire.[c] Go not from
8 house to house. And into whatsoever city ye enter, and they receive you,
9 eat such things as are set before you: and heal the sick that are therein,
10 and say unto them, The kingdom of God is come nigh unto you. But into whatsoever city ye enter, and they receive you not, go your ways out into the
11 streets of the same, and say, Even the very dust of your city, which cleaveth to us on our feet[5] we do wipe off against you: notwithstanding be ye sure of this, that the kingdom of God is come nigh.[6]

§ 79. The Doom of the Impenitent Cities.

St. Matt. xi. 20–24.	St. Luke x. 12–16.
20 Then began he to upbraid the cities wherein most of his mighty works were done, because they repented not: Woe unto thee, Chorazin! woe unto thee, Bethsaida![d] for if the mighty works, which were done in you, had been done in Tyre and Sidon, they would have repented long ago in sackcloth and ashes.	13 Woe unto thee, Chorazin! woe unto thee, Bethsaida![d] for if the mighty works had been done in Tyre and Sidon, which have been done in you, they had a great while ago repented, 14 sitting in sackcloth and ashes. But

[1] Therefore said he unto them   [2] and salute no man   [3] the son of peace
[4] is worthy   [5] cleaveth on us, we do wipe   [6] come nigh unto you

[a] Comp. Matt. x. 5, etc.; Mar. vi. 7, etc.   [b] Matt. ix. 37, 38; Jno. iv. 35.
[c] Comp. 1 Tim. v. 18; 1 Cor. ix. 14.   [d] Matt. x. 15; Mar. vi. 11.

§ 79. The order of narration in St. Luke is here also the most natural order, and is therefore retained rather than that of St. Matthew. To suppose a repetition on a different occasion of a passage so closely parallel is quite unnecessary. Our Lord had just instructed the Seventy in regard to cities which should reject them; the cities which had already rejected himself, and which he had now just left for the last time, would naturally have been present to their thoughts, and Jesus points out the fearful consequences of their folly.

ST. MATT. XI.	ST. LUKE X.
22 But I say unto you, It shall be more tolerable for Tyre and Sidon at the day of judgment, than for you. And 23 thou, Capernaum, art thou¹ exalted unto heaven? thou shalt be brought down to hell: for if the mighty works, which have been done in thee, had been done in Sodom, it would have remained until this day. 24 But I say unto you, That it shall be more tolerable for the land of Sodom in the day of judgment, than for thee.	it shall be more tolerable for Tyre and Sidon at the judgment, than for 15 you. And thou, Capernaum, art thou exalted to heaven? thou¹ shalt be thrust down to hell. 16 But I say unto you, that it shall be more tolerable in that day for Sodom, than for that city. He that heareth you heareth me;ª and he that despiseth you despiseth me; and he that despiseth me, despiseth him that sent me.

§ 80. The Ten Lepers healed.

St. Luke xvii. 11–19.

11 And it came to pass, as he went to Jerusalem, that he passed through the 12 midst of Samaria and Galilee. And as he entered into a certain village, there 13 met him ten men that were lepers, which stood afar off: and they lifted up 14 *their* voices, and said, Jesus, Master, have mercy on us. And when he saw *them*, he said unto them, Go shew yourselves unto the priests. And it came 15 to pass, that, as they went, they were cleansed. And one of them, when he saw that he was healed, turned back, and with a loud voice glorified God, 16 and fell down on *his* face at his feet, giving him thanks: and he was a Samar-17 itan. And Jesus answering said, Were there not ten cleansed? ²where *are* 18 the nine? There are not found that returned to give glory to God, save this 19 stranger. And he said unto him, Arise, go thy way: thy faith hath made thee whole.

¹ Capernaum, which art exalted unto heaven, shalt be   ² but where *are*
ª Matt. x. 40; Lk. ix. 48; Jno. xiii. 20.

---

§ 80. The record of this miracle in St. Luke, who alone mentions it, has no other note of time than that it was performed while our Lord was passing through the midst of Galilee and Samaria on his way to Jerusalem. As this was his final departure from Galilee (see note on § 76), it should be placed here (as has been done by Robinson), being narrated by St. Luke out of its chronological order. It stands in his Gospel entirely isolated from the context, a short narrative by itself, with no indication of time.

PART VI.

THE FESTIVAL OF TABERNACLES, AND THENCEFORWARD UNTIL OUR LORD'S FINAL ARRIVAL AT BETHANY.

§ 81. Our Lord at the Feast of Tabernacles. — *Jerusalem.*

St. John vii. 11–52.

11 Then the Jews sought him at the feast,[a] and said, Where is he? And there
12 was much murmuring among the multitudes [1] concerning him: for some said,
13 He is a good man; others said, Nay; but he deceiveth the people. Howbeit no man spake openly of him for fear of the Jews.
14 Now about the midst of the feast Jesus went up into the temple, and taught.
15 The Jews therefore [2] marvelled, saying, How knoweth this man letters, having
16 never learned? Jesus therefore [3] answered them, and said, My doctrine is not
17 mine, but his that sent me. If any man will do his will, he shall know of the
18 doctrine, whether it be of God, or *whether* I speak of myself. He that speaketh of himself seeketh his own glory; but he that seeketh his glory that sent
19 him, the same is true, and no unrighteousness is in him. Did not Moses give you the law,[b] and *yet* none of you keepeth the law? Why go ye about to kill
20 me? The people answered,[4] Thou hast a devil; who goeth about to kill thee?
21 Jesus answered and said unto them, I have done one work, and ye all marvel.
22 Moses [5] gave unto you circumcision;[c] not because it is of Moses, but of the
23 fathers;[d] and ye on the sabbath day circumcise a man. If a man on the sabbath day receive circumcision, that the law which is [6] of Moses should not be broken: are ye angry at me, because I have made a man every whit
24 whole on the sabbath day? Judge not according to the appearance, but judge righteous judgment.
25 Then said some of them of Jerusalem, Is not this he, whom they seek to
26 kill? But, lo, he speaketh boldly, and they say nothing unto him. Do the
27 rulers know indeed that this is the [7] Christ? Howbeit we know this man whence he is:[e] but when Christ cometh, no man knoweth whence he is.
28 Then cried Jesus in the temple as he taught, saying, Ye both know me, and ye know whence I am: and I am not come of myself, but he that sent me is

---

[1] among the people   [2] And the Jews marvelled   [3] *omit* therefore
[4] answered and said   [5] Moses therefore gave   [6] *omit* which is   [7] the very Christ
[a] Comp. Jno. xi. 56.   [b] Exod. xxiv. 3; Deut. xxvii. 1, 9, 11, etc.   [c] Lev. xii. 3.
[d] Gen. xvii. 10–14.   [e] Comp. Matt. xiii. 55; Mar. vi. 3; Lk. iv. 23, etc.

ST. JOHN VII.

29 true, whom ye know not. ¹ I know him; for I am from him, and he hath sent
30 me. Then they sought to take him: but no man laid hands on him, because
31 his hour was not yet come. And many of the people believed on him, and
said, When Christ cometh, will he do more miracles than *these* which this *man* doeth?²
32 The Pharisees heard that the people murmured such things concerning
33 him; and the Pharisees and the chief priests sent officers to take him. Then
said Jesus,³ Yet a little while am I with you, and *then* I go unto him that
34 sent me. Ye shall seek me, and shall not find *me:* and where I am, *thither*
35 ye cannot come. Then said the Jews among themselves, Whither will he go,
that we shall not find him? will he go unto the dispersed among the Gentiles,
36 and teach the Gentiles? What *manner of* saying is this that he said, Ye
shall seek me, and shall not find *me:* and where I am, *thither* ye cannot
come?
37 In the last day, that great *day* of the feast,ᵃ Jesus stood and cried, saying,
38 If any man thirst, let him come,⁴ and drink. He that believeth on me, as the
39 scripture hath said, out of his belly shall flow rivers of living water.ᵇ (But
this spake he of the Spirit,ᶜ which they that believe on him should receive:
for the Spirit⁵ was not yet *given*; because that Jesus was not yet glorified.)
40 Some⁶ of the people therefore, when they heard these sayings,⁷ said, Of a truth
41 this is the Prophet. Others said, This is the Christ. Others⁸ said, Shall
42 Christ come out of Galilee? Hath not the scripture said, That Christ cometh
of the seed of David,ᵈ and out of the town of Bethlehem,ᵉ where David was?ᶠ
43,44 So there was a division among the people because of him. And some of them
would have taken him: but no man laid hands on him.
45 Then came the officers to the chief priests and Pharisees; and they said
46 unto them, Why have ye not brought him? The officers answered, Never
47 man spake thus as this man speaketh.⁹ The Pharisees answered them,¹⁰ Are
48 ye also deceived? Have any of the rulers or of the Pharisees believed on
49,50 him? But this people who knoweth not the law are cursed. Nicodemus
51 saith unto them,¹¹ being one of them, Doth our law judge *any* man, before it
52 hear him, and know what he doeth? They answered and said unto him,
Art thou also of Galilee? Search, and look: for out of Galilee ariseth no prophet.ᵍ

---

¹ But I know   ² than these which this *man* hath done?   ³ said Jesus unto them
⁴ come unto me, and   ⁵ for the Holy Ghost was not   ⁶ Many of the people
⁷ this saying   ⁸ But some said   ⁹ Never man spake like this man
¹⁰ Then answered them the Pharisees, Are ye
¹¹ Nicodemus saith unto them, (he that came to Jesus by night, being one of them,)

ᵃ Lev. xxiii. 36.   ᵇ Isa. lv. 1.   ᶜ Comp. Joel ii. 28.
ᵈ Ps. lxxxix. 3, 4; cxxxii. 11; Jer. xxiii. 5, etc.   ᵉ Mic. v. 1, 2.
ᶠ 1 Sam. xvi. 1, 4, etc.   ᵍ Deut. xviii. 18, etc.

§ 82. The Woman taken in Adultery. — *Jerusalem.*

St. John vii. 53–viii. 11.

⁵³ [And every man went unto his own house. Jesus went unto the mount of
² Olives. And early in the morning he came again into the temple, and all the
³ people came unto him: and he sat down, and taught them. And the scribes
and Pharisees brought unto him a woman taken in adultery; and when they
⁴ had set her in the midst, they said unto him, Master, this woman was taken
⁵ in adultery, in the very act. Now Moses in the law commanded us,[a] that
⁶ such should be stoned; but what sayest thou? This they said, tempting him,
that they might have to accuse him. But Jesus stooped down, and with *his*
⁷ finger wrote on the ground, *as though he heard them not.* So when they continued asking him, he lifted up himself, and said unto them, He that is without
⁸ sin among you, let him first[b] cast a stone at her. And again he stooped down,
⁹ and wrote on the ground. And they which heard *it*, being convicted by *their
own* conscience, went out one by one, beginning at the eldest, *even* unto the
¹⁰ last: and Jesus was left alone, and the woman standing in the midst. When
Jesus had lifted up himself, and saw none but the woman, he said unto her,
Woman, where are those thine accusers? hath no man condemned thee?
¹¹ She said, No man, Lord. And Jesus said unto her, Neither do I condemn
thee: go, and sin no more.]

§ 83. Further Teaching in the Temple; the Jews attempt to stone Jesus, and He escapes. — *Jerusalem.*

St. John viii. 12–59.

¹² Then spake Jesus again unto them, saying, I am the light of the world: he
that followeth me shall not walk in darkness, but shall have the light of life.
¹³ The Pharisees therefore said unto him, Thou bearest record of thyself; thy
¹⁴ record is not true. Jesus answered and said unto them, Though I bear record
of myself, *yet* my record is true: for I know whence I came, and whither I
¹⁵ go: ²ye cannot tell whence I come, or ³whither I go. Ye judge after the
¹⁶ flesh: I judge no man. And yet if I judge, my judgment is true: for I am
¹⁷ not alone, but I and He⁴ that sent me. It is also written in your law, that
¹⁸ the testimony of two men is true.[c] I am one that bear witness of myself, and
¹⁹ the Father that sent me beareth witness of me. Then said they unto him,
Where is thy father? Jesus answered, Ye neither know me, nor my Father:
if ye had known me, ye should have known my Father also.

---

¹ vii. 53–viii. 11, is omitted by most critical editors in accordance with the earliest and best
Greek MSS. Some MSS. contain the passage marked with asterisks. The text varies very
much in the MSS. which give it. The authorized version is printed above without reference
to these variations.

² but ye cannot ³ and whither ⁴ and the Father that sent

[a] Lev. xx. 10; Deut. xxii. 22. [b] Comp. Deut. xvii. 7. [c] Deut. xvii. 6; xix. 15.

ST. JOHN VIII.

20 These words spake He[1] in the treasury, as he taught in the temple: and no man laid hands on him; for his hour was not yet come.

21 Then said He[2] again unto them, I go my way, and ye shall seek me, and
22 shall die in your sins: whither I go, ye cannot come. Then said the Jews,
23 Will he kill himself? because he saith, Whither I go, ye cannot come. And he said unto them, Ye are from beneath; I am from above: ye are of this
24 world; I am not of this world. I said therefore unto you, that ye shall die in
25 your sins: for if ye believe not that I am *He*, ye shall die in your sins. Then said they unto him, Who art thou? [3] Jesus saith unto them, Even *the same*
26 that I said unto you from the beginning. I have many things to say and to judge of you: but he that sent me is true; and I speak to the world those things
27 which I have heard of him. They understood not that he spake to them of the Father.

28 Then said Jesus,[4] When ye have lifted up the Son of man, then shall ye know that I am *He*, and *that* I do nothing of myself; but as the [5] Father hath
29 taught me, I speak these things. And he that sent me is with me: He[6] hath not left me alone; for I do always those things that please him.

30
31 As he spake these words many believed on him. Then said Jesus to those Jews which believed on him, If ye continue in my word, *then* are ye my disci-
32 ples indeed; and ye shall know the truth, and the truth shall make you free.
33 They answered him, We be Abraham's seed, and were never in bondage to any man:[a] how sayest thou, Ye shall be made free?
34 Jesus answered them, Verily, verily, I say unto you, Whosoever committeth
35 sin is the servant of sin. And the servant abideth not in the house for ever:
36 *but* the Son abideth ever. If the Son therefore shall make you free, ye shall
37 be free indeed. I know that ye are Abraham's seed; but ye seek to kill me,
38 because my word hath no place in you. I speak that which I have seen with the[7] Father; and ye do that which ye have heard with *your*[8] father.

39 They answered and said unto him, Abraham is our father.
Jesus saith unto them, If ye were Abraham's children, ye would do the
40 works of Abraham. But now ye seek to kill me, a man that hath told you the truth, which I have heard of God: this did not Abraham. Ye do the deeds of your father.
41 They[9] said to him, We be not born of fornication; we have one Father, *even* God.
42 Jesus said unto them, If God were your Father, ye would love me; for I proceeded forth and came from God; neither came I of myself, but he sent me.
43 Why do ye not understand my speech? *even* because ye cannot hear my word.
44 Ye are of *your* father the devil, and the lusts of your father ye will do. He was a murderer from the beginning, and abode not in the truth, because there

---

[1] spake Jesus   [2] said Jesus   [3] And Jesus saith
[4] Then said Jesus unto them   [5] my Father   [6] the Father hath not left
[7] my Father   [8] ye have seen with your Father   [9] Then said they
[a] Comp. Lev. xxv. 39–42.

ST. JOHN VIII.

44 is no truth in him. When he speaketh a lie, he speaketh of his own; for he
45 is a liar, and the father of it. And because I tell *you* the truth, ye believe
46 me not. Which of you convinceth me of sin? [1] If I say the truth, why do ye
47 not believe me? He that is of God heareth God's words: ye therefore hear *them* not, because ye are not of God.

48 The Jews [2] answered and said unto him, Say we not well that thou art a Samaritan, and hast a devil?

49 Jesus answered, I have not a devil; but I honor my Father, and ye do
50 dishonor me. And I seek not mine own glory: there is One that seeketh and
51 judgeth. Verily, verily, I say unto you, If a man keep my saying, he shall never see death.

52 The Jews said [3] unto him, Now we know that thou hast a devil. Abraham is dead, and the prophets: and thou sayest, If a man keep my saying, he shall
53 never taste of death! Art thou greater than our father Abraham, which is dead? and the prophets are dead: whom makest thou thyself?

54 Jesus answered, If I honor myself, my honor is nothing: it is my Father
55 that honoreth me; of whom ye say, that he is our [4] God: yet ye have not known him; but I know him: and if I should say, I know him not, I shall be
56 a liar like unto you: but I know him, and keep his saying. Your father Abraham rejoiced to see my day: and he saw *it*, and was glad.

57 Then said the Jews unto him, Thou art not yet fifty years old, and hast thou seen Abraham?

58 Jesus said unto them, Verily, verily, I say unto you, Before Abraham was,
59 I am.[a] Then took they up stones to cast at him: but Jesus hid himself, and went out of the temple.[5]

§ 84. Our Lord heals one born blind; the Good Shepherd. — *Jerusalem.*

ST. JOHN IX. 1–X. 21.

1 And as *Jesus* passed by, he saw a man which was blind from *his* birth.
2 And his disciples asked him, saying, Master, who did sin, this man, or his
3 parents, that he was born blind? Jesus answered, neither hath this man sinned, nor his parents: but that the works of God should be made manifest
4 in him. We [6] must work the works of him that sent us, while it is day: the
5 night cometh, when no man can work. As long as I am in the world, I am

---

[1] And if I say [2] Then answered the Jews [3] Then said the Jews
[4] he is your God [5] *add* going through the midst of them, and so passed by.
[6] I must work..... sent me

[a] Comp. Ex. iii. 4.

---

§ 84. This section may be placed either before or after the journey in Peræa, of which St. Luke gives so full a record. Its connection is perhaps rather more close with what precedes than with what follows, and it is accordingly here placed before the Peræan journey. The allusion in x. 26 to the discourse in x. 1–18 would be perfectly appropriate on the next occasion of addressing the people at Jerusalem after an interval of only two or three months.

ST. JOHN IX.

6 the light of the world. When he had thus spoken, he spat on the ground,
7 and made clay of the spittle, and he anointed *his* eyes with clay.[1] And said unto him, Go, wash in the pool of Siloam,[a] (which is by interpretation, Sent.) He went his way therefore, and washed, and came seeing.

8 The neighbors therefore, and they which before had seen him that he was
9 a beggar,[2] said, Is not not this he that sat and begged? Some said, this is
10 he: others said, No, but he[3] is like him: *but* he said, I am *he*. Therefore
11 said they unto him, How then[4] were thine eyes opened? He answered,[5] A man that is called Jesus made clay, and anointed mine eyes, and said unto me, Go to[6] Siloam, and wash: I went therefore,[7] and washed, and I received
12 sight. They said[8] unto him, Where is he? He said, I know not.

13
14 They brought to the Pharisees him that aforetime was blind. And it was
15 the sabbath day when Jesus made the clay, and opened his eyes. Then again the Pharisees also asked him how he had received his sight. He said unto
16 them, He put clay upon mine eyes, and I washed, and do see. Therefore said some of the Pharisees, This man is not of God, because he keepeth not the sabbath day. Others said, How can a man that is a sinner do such mira-
17 cles? And there was a division among them. They say therefore[9] unto the blind man again, What sayest thou of him, that he hath opened thine eyes?
18 He said, He is a prophet. But the Jews did not believe concerning him, that he had been blind, and received his sight, until they called the parents of him
19 that had received his sight. And they asked them, saying, Is this your son,
20 who ye say was born blind? how then doth he now see? His parents answered therefore,[10] and said, We know that this is our son, and that he was
21 born blind: but by what means he now seeth, we know not; or who hath opened his eyes, we know not: he is of age; ask him: he shall speak for
22 himself. These *words* spake his parents, because they feared the Jews: for the Jews had agreed already, that if any man did confess that he was Christ,
23 he should be put out of the synagogue. Therefore said his parents, He is of age; ask him.

24 Then again called they the man that was blind, and said unto him, Give God
25 the praise: we know that this man is a sinner. He answered,[11] whether he be a sinner *or no*, I know not: one thing I know, that, whereas I was blind,
26 now I see. They said therefore[12] to him, What did he to thee? how opened
27 he thine eyes? He answered them, I have told you already, and ye did not
28 hear: wherefore would ye hear *it* again? will ye also be his disciples? [13] They

---

[1] anointed the eyes of the blind man
[2] that he was blind
[3] others *said*, He is like
[4] *omit* then
[5] He answered and said,
[6] Go to the pool of Siloam
[7] and I went and washed
[8] Then said they unto him
[9] *omit* therefore
[10] answered them and said
[11] He answered and said,
[12] Then said they to him again
[13] Then they reviled

[a] Neh. iii. 15.

ST. JOHN IX., X.

reviled him, and said, Thou art his disciple; but we are Moses' disciples. 29 We know that God spake unto Moses: *as for* this *fellow*, we know not from 30 whence he is. The man answered and said unto them, Why herein is a marvellous thing, that ye know not from whence he is, and *yet* he hath opened 31 mine eyes. Now we know that God heareth not sinners: but if any man be 32 a worshipper of God, and doeth his will, him he heareth. Since the world began was it not heard that any man opened the eyes of one that was born 33 blind. If this man were not of God, he could do nothing. They answered 34 and said unto him, Thou wast altogether born in sins! and dost thou teach us? And they cast him out.

35 Jesus heard that they had cast him out; and when he had found him, he 36 said,[1] Dost thou believe on the Son of Man?[2] He answered and said, and[3] 37 who is he, Lord, that I might believe on him? [4] Jesus said unto him, Thou 38 hast both seen him, and it is he that talketh with thee. And he said, Lord, 39 I believe. And he worshipped him. And Jesus said, For judgment I am come into this world, that they which see not might see; and that they which see might be made blind.

40 [5] *Some* of the Pharisees which were with him heard,[6] and said unto him, 41 Are we blind also? Jesus said unto them, If ye were blind, ye should have 1 no sin: but now ye say, We see;[7] your sin remaineth. x. Verily, verily, I say unto you, He that entereth not by the door into the sheepfold, but climb- 2 eth up some other way, the same is a thief and a robber. But he that entereth 3 in by the door is the shepherd of the sheep. To him the porter openeth; and the sheep hear his voice: and he calleth his own sheep by name, and 4 leadeth them out. [8] When he putteth forth all his own,[9] he goeth before them, 5 and the sheep follow him: for they know his voice. And a stranger will they not follow, but will flee from him: for they know not the voice of stran- 6 gers. This parable spake Jesus unto them: but they understood not what things they were which he spake unto them.

7 Then said Jesus unto them again, Verily, verily, I say unto you, I am the 8 door of the sheep. All that ever came [10] are thieves and robbers: but the 9 sheep did not hear them. I am the door: by me if any man enter in, he shall 10 be saved, and shall go in and out, and find pasture. The thief cometh not but for to steal, and to kill, and to destroy: I am come that they might have life, 11 and that they might have *it* more abundantly. I am the good shepherd: the 12 good shepherd giveth his life for the sheep. But he that is an hireling, and not the shepherd, whose own the sheep are not, seeth the wolf coming, and leaveth the sheep, and fleeth; and the wolf catcheth and scattereth them,[11]

[1] he said unto him
[2] the Son of God
[3] *omit* and
[4] And Jesus said
[5] And some of the Pharisees
[6] heard these words, and said
[7] We see; therefore your sin
[8] And when he putteth
[9] forth his own sheep
[10] ever came before me are thieves
[11] catcheth them and scattereth the sheep. The hireling fleeth because he is

ST. JOHN X.

14 because he is an hireling, and careth not for the sheep. I am the good shep-
15 herd, and know mine, and mine know me.[1] As the Father knoweth me, even
16 so know I the Father: and I lay down my life for the sheep. And other sheep I have, which are not of this fold: them also I must bring, and they
17 shall hear my voice; and there shall be one fold *and* one shepherd. Therefore doth my Father love me, because I lay down my life, that I might take it
18 again. No man taketh it from me, but I lay it down of myself. I have power to lay it down, and I have power to take it again. This commandment have I received of my Father.

19
20   There was a division[2] again among the Jews for these sayings. Therefore[3]
21 many of them said, He hath a devil, and is mad; why hear ye him? Others said, These are not the words of him that hath a devil. Can a devil open the eyes of the blind?

§ 85. The Return of the Seventy. — *In or near Jerusalem.*

St. Matt. xi. 25–30, xiii. 16, 17.	St. Luke x. 17–24.
	17 And the seventy returned again with joy, saying, Lord, even the devils are subject unto us through thy
	18 name! And he said unto them, I beheld Satan as lightning fall from
	19 heaven. Behold, I have given[4] unto you power to tread on serpents and scorpions, and over all the power of the enemy; and nothing shall by any
	20 means hurt you. Notwithstanding in this rejoice not, that the spirits are subject unto you: but[5] rejoice because your names are written in heaven.
25 At that time Jesus answered and said, I thank thee, O Father, Lord of heaven and earth, because thou hast hid these things from the wise	21 In that hour He rejoiced in the Holy Spirit,[6] and said, I thank thee, O Father, Lord of heaven and earth, that thou hast hid these things from

[1] and know my *sheep*, and am known of mine   [2] a division therefore again
[3] And many of them said   [4] Behold, I give unto you
[5] but rather rejoice   [6] In that hour Jesus rejoiced in spirit, and said

---

§ 85. The return of the Seventy is shown to have occurred in or near Jerusalem by the narrative of the following sections, evidently relating to that neighborhood. Very likely our Lord waited at Jerusalem after the feast of Tabernacles until joined by them, and then set out for Perea, where they had been preparing his way.

There is no reason for disturbing the order of St. Luke, although the visit to Jerusalem at the feast (of which he makes no mention) comes between the sending forth and the return of the Seventy.

ST. MATT. XI.	ST. LUKE X.
and prudent, and hast revealed them unto babes: even so, Father; for so it seemed good in thy sight. ²⁶	the wise and prudent, and hast revealed them unto babes: even so, Father; for so it seemed good in thy sight. ²¹
27 All things are delivered unto me of my Father: and no man knoweth the Son, but the Father; neither knoweth any man the Father, save the Son, and *he* to whomsoever the Son will reveal *him*.	22 All things are delivered to me of my Father: and no man knoweth who the Son is, but the Father; and who the Father is, but the Son, and *he* to whom the Son will reveal *him*.
28 Come unto me, all *ye* that labor and are heavy laden, and I will give 29 you rest. Take my yoke upon you, and learn of me; for I am meek and lowly in heart: and ye shall 30 find rest unto your souls. For my yoke *is* easy, and my burden is light.	
ST. MATT. XIII.	
16 But blessed *are* your eyes, for they see: and your ears, for they hear! 17 ¹ Verily I say unto you, that many prophets and righteous *men* have desired to see *those things* which ye see, and have not seen *them*; and to hear *those things* which ye hear, and have not heard *them*.	23 And he turned him unto *his* disciples, and said privately, Blessed *are* the eyes which see the things that ye 24 see! for I tell you, that many prophets and kings have desired to see those things which ye see, and have not seen *them*; and to hear those things which ye hear, and have not heard *them*.

§ 86. Parable of the Good Samaritan. — *Near Jerusalem.*
ST. LUKE X. 25–37.

25 And behold, a certain lawyer stood up, tempting² him, saying, Master, what 26 shall I do to inherit eternal life? He said unto him, What is written in the 27 law? how readest thou? And he answering said, Thou shalt love the Lord thy God with all thy heart, and with all thy soul, and with all thy strength, 28 and with all thy mind; and thy neighbor as thyself. And he said unto him, 29 Thou hast answered right: this do, and thou shalt live. But he, willing to 30 justify himself, said unto Jesus, And who is my neighbor? ³ Jesus answering said, A certain *man* went down from Jerusalem to Jericho, and fell among thieves, which stripped him of his raiment, and wounded *him*, and departed, leaving 31 *him* half dead. And by chance there came down a certain priest that way: 32 and when he saw him, he passed by on the other side. And likewise a Levite, when he was at the place, came and looked *on him*, and passed by on the other 33 side. But a certain Samaritan, as he journeyed, came where he was: and when he saw *him*,⁴ he had compassion *on him*, and went to *him* and bound up

¹ For verily I say   ² and tempted him   ³ And Jesus answering   ⁴ saw him

ST. LUKE X.

his wounds, pouring in oil and wine, and set him on his own beast, and brought
35 him to an inn, and took care of him. And on the morrow [1] he took out two
pence, and gave *them* to the host, and said,[2] Take care of him : and whatsoever
36 thou spendest more, when I come again, I will repay thee. Which [3] of these
three, thinkest thou, was neighbor unto him that fell among the thieves?
37 And he said, He that shewed mercy on him. [4]And said Jesus unto him, Go,
and do thou likewise.

§ 87. The Visit to Martha and Mary. — *Bethany.*
St. Luke x. 38–42.

38 Now it came to pass, as they went, that he entered into a certain village :
39 and a certain woman named Martha received him into the [5] house. And she
had a sister called Mary, which also sat at the Lord's [6] feet, and heard his word.
40 But Martha was cumbered about much serving, and came to him, and said,
Lord, dost thou not care that my sister hath left me to serve alone? bid her
41 therefore that she help me. And the Lord [7] answered and said unto her,
42 Martha, Martha, thou art careful and troubled about many things : but one
thing is needful : for [8] Mary hath chosen that good part, which shall not be
taken away from her.

§ 88. The Disciples again taught how to pray.

St. Matt. vii. 7–11.   St. Luke xi. 1–13.

1 And it came to pass, that, as he was praying in a
certain place, when he ceased, one of his disciples said
unto him, Lord, teach us to pray, as John also taught
2 his disciples. And he said unto them, When ye pray,
say, [9] Father, Hallowed be thy name. Thy kingdom
3,4 come.[10] Give us day by day our daily bread. And
forgive us our sins ; for we also forgive every one that

---

[1] And on the morrow, when he departed, he took
[2] and said unto him, Take
[3] Which now of these
[4] Then said Jesus
[5] into her house
[6] at Jesus's feet
[7] And Jesus answered
[8] and Mary hath
[9] Our Father which art in heaven, Hallowed
[10] Thy kingdom come. Thy will be done, as in heaven, so in earth.

---

§ 87. St. Luke here mentions our Lord's acquaintance with Martha and Mary, which St. John (xi.) assumes, but does not mention, while St. Luke makes no allusion to the miracle recorded by St. John.

§ 88. The much abridged form of the Lord's prayer as given (according to the text) by St. Luke is perhaps to be considered as our Lord's recalling to the recollection of the disciples, in answer to their request, the prayer he had already long since taught them in the Sermon on the Mount (Matt. vi. 9 ss.) ; in the common version it appears almost as a full repetition of the prayer itself.

ST. MATT. VII.	ST. LUKE XI.
	is indebted to us. And lead us not 5 into temptation.¹ And he said unto them. Which of you shall have a friend, and shall go unto him at midnight, and 6 say unto him, Friend, lend me three loaves; for a friend of mine in his journey is come to me, and I have 7 nothing to set before him? And he from within shall answer and say, Trouble me not: the door is now shut, and my children are with me in bed; 8 I cannot rise and give thee. I say unto you, though he will not rise and give him, because he is his friend, yet because of his importunity[a] he will rise and give him as many as he
7 Ask, and it shall be given you; seek, and ye shall find; knock, and 8 it shall be opened unto you; for every one that asketh receiveth; and he that seeketh findeth; and to him that knocketh it shall be opened.	9 needeth. And I say unto you, Ask, and it shall be given you; seek, and ye shall find; knock, and it shall be 10 opened unto you. For every one that asketh receiveth; and he that seeketh findeth; and to him that knocketh it shall be opened.
9 Or what man is there of you, of whom his son shall² ask bread, will 10 he give him a stone? Or he shall⁴ ask a fish, will he give him a ser- 11 pent? If ye then, being evil, know how to give good gifts unto your children, how much more shall your Father which is in heaven give good things to them that ask him!	11 If a son shall ask bread of any of you that is a father, will he give him a stone? or³ *he ask* a fish, will he for 12 a fish give him a serpent? Or if he shall ask an egg, will he offer him a 13 scorpion? If ye then, being evil, know how to give good gifts unto your children: how much more shall *your* heavenly Father give the Holy Spirit to them that ask him!

§ 89. At meat in the House of a Pharisee, Jesus reproves the Pharisees.

ST. MATT. XXIII. 4–39.   ST. LUKE XI. 37–54, XIII. 34, 35.

37 And as he spake, a Pharisee beseecheth⁵ him to dine with him: and he went in, and sat down to

---

¹ not into temptation; but deliver us from evil.   ² is there of you whom if his son ask bread,
³ or if *he ask* a fish   ⁴ Or if he ask   ⁵ a certain Pharisee besought him
[a] Comp. Lk. xviii. 1–5.

ST. MATT. XXIII.	ST. LUKE XI.
25 Woe unto you, scribes and Pharisees, hypocrites! for ye make clean the outside of the cup and of the platter, but within they are full of extortion 26 and excess. *Thou* blind Pharisee! cleanse first that *which is* within the cup,[1] that the outside of it[2] may be clean also.	38 meat. And when the Pharisee saw *it*, he marvelled that he had not first 39 washed before dinner. And the Lord said unto him, Now do ye Pharisees make clean the outside of the cup and the platter; but your inward part is full of ravening 40 and wickedness. *Ye* fools! did not he that made that which is without make that which is within also? 41 But rather give alms of such things as ye have; and, behold, all things 42 are clean unto you. But woe unto you, Pharisees! for ye tithe mint and rue and all manner of herbs, and pass over judgment and the love of God: these ought ye to have done, and not to leave the other undone.
23 Woe unto you, scribes and Pharisees, hypocrites! for ye pay tithe of mint and anise and cummin, and have omitted the weighter *matters* of the law, judgment, mercy, and faith: these ought ye to have done, and not to leave the 24 other undone. *Ye* blind guides! which strain out[3] a gnat, and swallow a camel.	
5 But all their works they do for to be seen of men: for[4] they make broad their phylacteries, and enlarge the 6 borders,[5] and love the uppermost rooms at feasts, and the chief seats in 7 the synagogues, and greetings in the markets, and to be called of men, 8 Rabbi![6] But be not ye called Rabbi: for One is your Master,[7] and all ye 9 are brethren. And call no *man* your father upon the earth: for One is your	43 Woe unto you, Pharisees! for ye love the uppermost seats in the synagogues, and greetings in the markets.

[1] within the cup and platter, that   [2] outside of them   [3] *translated* at a gnat   [4] omit for
[5] the borders of their garments   [6] Rabbi, Rabbi.   [7] your Master, *even* Christ.

§ 89. This discourse, as given by the two Evangelists, is too plainly the same to allow of the separation of the two records. It is more fully recorded by St. Matthew, as is his custom in regard to the discourses of our Lord; but as he gives no account of the journey in Perea, it is placed by him in connection with the warning against the Scribes and Pharisees in xxiii. 1–3 (§ 122). The closing verses of lament over Jerusalem are commonly considered as having been twice uttered: once in the connection given by St. Matthew, and once in that mentioned by St. Luke. This is indeed probable; for if they were uttered only once, it is not easy to see why St. Luke should have omitted them here, and have inserted them there; while in St. Matthew they cannot well be separated from the context. Nevertheless, the agreement of the two passages is so close, almost verbal throughout, that for the purposes of a harmony they must be exhibited together.

ST. MATT. XXIII.	ST. LUKE XI.
10 heavenly Father.¹ Neither be ye called masters: for one is your Master, 11 *even* Christ. But he that is greatest among you shall be your servant. 12 And whosoever shall exalt himself shall be abased; and he that shall 27 humble himself shall be exalted. Woe unto you, scribes and Pharisees, hypocrites! for ye are like unto whited sepulchres, which indeed appear beautiful outward, but are within full of dead *men's* bones, and of all unclean- 28 ness. Even so ye also outwardly appear righteous unto men, but within ye are full of hypocrisy and iniquity.	
4 But³ they bind heavy burdens⁴ and lay *them* on men's shoulders; but they themselves⁵ will not move them 29 with one of their fingers. Woe unto you, scribes and Pharisees, hypocrites! because ye build the tombs of the prophets, and garnish the sepulchres 30 of the righteous, and say, If we had been in the days of our fathers, we would not have been partakers with them in the blood of the prophets. 31 Wherefore ye be witnesses unto yourselves that ye are the children of them 32 which killed the prophets. Fill ye up then the measure of your fathers. 33 *Ye* serpents! *ye* generation of vipers! how can ye escape the damnation of hell? 13 But woe unto you, scribes and Pharisees, hypocrites! for ye shut up the	44 Woe unto you,² for ye are as graves which appear not, and the men that walk over *them* are not aware of *them*. 45 Then answered one of the lawyers, and said unto him, Master, thus saying thou reproachest us also. 46 And he said, Woe unto you also, *ye* lawyers! for ye lade men with burdens grievous to be borne, and ye yourselves touch not the burdens 47 with one of your fingers. Woe unto you! for ye build the sepulchres of the prophets, and your fathers killed 48 them. Truly ye are witnesses⁶ that ye allow the deeds of your fathers: for they indeed killed them, and ye build.⁷ 52 Woe unto you, lawyers! for ye have taken away the key of knowl-

¹ your Father which is in heaven.
² Woe unto you, scribes and Pharisees, hypocrites! for ye are   ³ For they bind
⁴ heavy burdens and grievous to be borne, and lay   ⁵ *themselves*
⁶ ye bear witness that ye   ⁷ build their sepulchres.

ST. MATT. XXIII.

kingdom of heaven against men: for ye neither go in *yourselves*, neither suffer ye them that are entering to
15 go in.¹ Woe unto you, scribes and Pharisees, hypocrites! for ye compass sea and land to make one proselyte, and when he is made, ye make him twofold more the child of hell than
16 yourselves. Woe unto you, *ye* blind guides! which say, Whosoever shall swear by the temple, it is nothing; but whosoever shall swear by the gold
17 of the temple, he is a debtor. *Ye* fools and blind! for whether is greater, the gold, or the temple that sanctifieth
18 the gold? And, Whosoever shall swear by the altar, it is nothing; but whosoever sweareth by the gift that is
19 upon it, he is guilty. *Ye*² blind! for whether *is* greater, the gift, or the
20 altar that sanctifieth the gift?ᵃ Whoso therefore shall swear by the altar, sweareth by it, and by all things
21 thereon. And whoso shall swear by the temple, sweareth by it, and by
22 him that dwelleth therein. And he that shall swear by heaven, sweareth by the throne of God, and by him that sitteth thereon.

34 Wherefore, behold, I send unto you prophets, and wise men, and scribes: and *some* of them ye shall kill and crucify; ³*some* of them shall ye scourge in your synagogues, and persecute
35 *them* from city to city:ᵇ that upon you may come all the righteous blood shed upon the earth; from the blood of righteous Abelᶜ unto the blood of

ST. LUKE XI.

edge: ye entered not in yourselves, and them that were entering in ye hindered.

49 Therefore also said the wisdom of God, I will send them prophets and apostles: and *some* of them they
50 shall slay and persecute:ᵇ that the blood of all the prophets, which was shed from the foundation of the world, may be required of this gen-
51 eration; from the blood of Abelᶜ

---

¹ ver. 14. Woe unto you, scribes and Pharisees, hypocrites! for ye devour widows' houses, and for a pretence make long prayer: therefore ye shall receive the greater damnation.
² Ye fools and blind!
³ and *some* of them

ᵃ Exod. xxix. 37; xxx. 29.   ᵇ See 2 Chron. xxiv. 18–22   ᶜ Gen. iv. 8.

ST. MATT. XXIII.

Zacharias son of Barachias,ª whom ye slew between the temple and the altar. 36 Verily I say unto you, All these things shall come upon this generation.

37 O Jerusalem, Jerusalem! *thou* that killest the prophets, and stonest them which are sent unto thee, how often would I have gathered thy children together, even as a hen gathereth her chickens under *her* wings, and ye 38 would not! Behold, your house is 39 left unto you desolate.ᵇ For I say unto you, Ye shall not see me henceforth, till ye shall say, Blessed *is* he that cometh in the name of the Lord.ᶜ

ST. LUKE XI, XIII.

unto the blood of Zacharias,ª which perished between the altar and the temple: verily I say unto you, It shall be required of this generation.

ST. LUKE XIII.

34 O Jerusalem, Jerusalem! which killest the prophets, and stonest them that are sent unto thee; how often would I have gathered thy children together, as a hen *doth gather* her brood under *her* wings, 35 and ye would not! Behold, your house is left unto you:ᵇ¹ I say unto you, Ye shall not see me, until *the time* come when ye shall say, Blessed *is* he that cometh in the name of the Lord.ᶜ

ST. LUKE XI.

53 And as he went thence² the scribes and the Pharisees began to urge *him* vehemently, and to provoke 54 him to speak of many things: laying wait for him,³ to catch something out of his mouth.

§ 90. Christ teaches to avoid Hypocrisy and Timidity.

ST. MATT. X. 26–33, 40, 41, 17–20.   ST. LUKE XII. 1–9, 11, 12.

In the mean time, when there were gathered together an innumerable multitude of people, insomuch that they trode one upon another, he began to say unto his disciples first of all, Beware ye of the leaven of the Phar-26 Fear them not therefore: for 2 isees,ᵈ which is hypocrisy. For there

---

¹ is left unto you desolate: and verily I say
² And as he said these things unto them, the scribes
³ laying wait for him, and seeking to catch something out of his mouth, that they might accuse him.
ª 2 Chron. xxiv. 20, 21; See also, Zech. i. 1.   ᵇ See Ps. lxix. 25; Jer. xii. 7; xxii. 5.
ᶜ Ps. cxviii. 26.   ᵈ Matt. xvi. 6, 12.

---

§ 90. It has been already said (note to § 59) that this discourse can hardly have been originally spoken in connection with its context in St. Matthew; the order of St. Luke (except vs. 10) is therefore preserved. The remainder of the discourse as given by St. Matthew will appear still later (§§ 92, 97, 126).

ST. MATT. X.	ST. LUKE XII.

there is nothing covered, that shall not be revealed; and hid, that shall 27 not be known. What I tell you in darkness, *that* speak ye in light:

and what ye hear in the ear, *that* preach ye upon the housetops.

28 And fear not them which kill the body, but are not able to kill the

soul: but rather fear him which is able to destroy both soul and body

29 in hell. Are not two sparrows sold for a farthing? and one of them shall not fall on the ground without 30 your Father. But the very hairs of your head are all numbered. 31 Fear ye not therefore, ye are of more value than many sparrows. 32 Whosoever therefore shall confess me before men, him will I confess also before my Father which is in 33 heaven. But whosoever shall deny me before men, him will I also deny before my Father which is in heaven.ᵃ

40 He that receiveth you receiveth me, and he that receiveth me re- 41 ceiveth him that sent me. He that receiveth a prophet in the name of a prophet shall receive a prophet's reward; and he that receiveth a righteous man in the name of a righteous man shall receive a right- 17 eous man's reward. But beware of men: for they will deliver you up to the councils, and they will scourge 18 you in their synagogues; and ye shall be brought before governors and kings for my sake, for a testi-

is nothing covered, that shall not be revealed; neither hid, that shall not 3 be known. Therefore whatsoever ye have spoken in darkness shall be heard in the light; and that which ye have spoken in the ear in closets shall be proclaimed upon the housetops.

4 And I say unto you my friends, Be not afraid of them that kill the body, and after that have no more that they 5 can do. But I will forewarn you whom ye shall fear: Fear him, which after he hath killed hath power to cast into hell; yea, I say unto you, 6 Fear him. Are not five sparrows sold for two farthings? and not one of them is forgotten before God. 7 But even the very hairs of your head are all numbered. Fear not:¹ ye are

of more value than many sparrows. 8 Also I say unto you, Whosoever shall confess me before men, him shall the Son of man also confess before the 9 angels of God: but he that denieth me before men shall be denied before the angels of God.ᵃ

---

¹ Fear not therefore   ᵃ Comp. 2 Tim. ii. 12.

ST. MATT. X.	ST. LUKE XII.
mony against them and the Gentiles. 19 But when they deliver you up, take no thought how or what ye shall speak: for it shall be given you in that same hour what ye shall speak. For it is not ye that speak, but the Spirit of your Father which speaketh in you.	11 And when they bring you unto the synagogues, and *unto* magistrates, and powers, take ye no thought how or what thing ye shall answer, or what 12 ye shall say: for the Holy Ghost shall teach you in the same hour what ye ought to say.

§ 91. He refuses to divide an Inheritance. The Parable of the Rich Man.

ST. LUKE XII. 13–21.

13 And one of the company said unto him, Master, speak to my brother, that
14 he divide the inheritance with me. And he said unto him, Man, who made
15 me a judge or a divider over you? And he said unto them, Take heed, and beware of all[1] covetousness: for a man's life consisteth not in the abundance
16 of the things which he possesseth. And he spake a parable unto them, saying,
17 The ground of a certain rich man brought forth plentifully: and he thought within himself, saying, What shall I do, because I have no room where to
18 bestow my fruits? And he said, This will I do: I will pull down my barns,
19 and build greater; and there will I bestow all my fruits and my goods. And I will say to my soul, Soul, thou hast much goods laid up for many years;
20 take thine ease, eat, drink, *and* be merry. But God said unto him, *Thou* fool! this night thy soul shall be required of thee: then whose shall those
21 things be, which thou hast provided? So *is* he that layeth up treasure for himself, and is not rich toward God.

§ 92. Further Instructions and Parables.

ST. MATT. VI. 25–34, XXIV. 43–51, X. 34–36, V. 25, 26.   ST. LUKE XII. 22–59.

25 Therefore I say unto you, Take no thought for your life, what ye shall eat;[2] nor yet for your body, what ye shall put on. Is not the life more than meat, and the body 26 than raiment? Behold the fowls of the air: for they sow not, neither	22 And he said unto his disciples, Therefore I say unto you, Take no thought for the[3] life, what ye shall eat; neither for the body, what ye 23 shall put on. The life is more than meat, and the body *is more* than rai- 24 ment. Consider the ravens: for they

[1] *omit* all   [2] what ye shall eat, or what ye shall drink;   [3] for your life

§ 92. As St. Matthew gives no account of this journey through Perea, he cannot, of course, record in their connection the discourses there spoken. Such portions of them as he has preserved at all, he has placed in connection with such other teachings of our Lord, given at various times, as they most resembled. It thus happens that in order to exhibit really parallel passages in their parallelism, it is necessary to bring together matter distributed in the Gospel of St. Matthew almost from one end to the other. The present section is the most striking instance of this, and it is noticeable in several others.

ST. MATT. VI.	ST. LUKE XII

do they reap, nor gather into barns; yet your heavenly Father feedeth them. Are ye not much better than
27 they? Which of you by taking thought can add one cubit unto his
28 stature? And why take ye thought for raiment? Consider the lilies of the field, how they grow: they toil
29 not, neither do they spin; and yet I say unto you, that even Solomon in all his glory was not arrayed like
30 one of these. Wherefore, if God so clothe the grass of the field, which to day is, and to morrow is cast into the oven, *shall he* not much more
31 *clothe* you, O ye of little faith? Therefore take no thought, saying, What shall we eat? or, What shall we
32 drink? or, Wherewithal shall we be clothed? For after all these things do the Gentiles seek: for your heavenly Father knoweth that ye
33 have need of all these things. But seek ye first his [3] kingdom and righteousness; and all these things shall
34 be added unto you. Take therefore no thought for the morrow: for the morrow shall take thought for [6] itself. Sufficient unto the day *is* the evil thereof.

neither sow nor reap; which neither have storehouse nor barn; and God feedeth them: how much more are ye
25 better than the fowls? And which of you with taking thought can add to
26 his stature a[1] cubit? If ye then be not able to do that thing which is least, why take ye thought for the rest?
27 Consider the lilies how they grow: they toil not, they spin not; and yet I say unto you, that Solomon in all his glory was not arrayed like one of these.
28 If then God so clothe the grass, which is to day in the field, and to morrow is cast into the oven; how much more *will he clothe* you, O ye of little faith?
29 And seek not ye what ye shall eat, and [2] what ye shall drink, neither be
30 ye of doubtful mind. For all these things do the nations of the world seek after: and your Father knoweth that
31 ye have need of these things. But rather seek ye his [4] kingdom; and [5] these things shall be added unto you.

32 Fear not, little flock; for it is your Father's good pleasure to give
33 you the kingdom. Sell that ye have, and give alms; provide yourselves bags which wax not old, a treasure in the heavens that faileth not, where no thief approacheth, neither moth cor-
34 rupteth. For where your treasure is, there will your heart be also. Let
35 your loins be girded about, and *your*

---

[1] one cubit   [2] or what   [3] the kingdom of God and his righteousness;
[4] the kingdom of God   [5] and all these things   [6] for the things of itself

ST. MATT. XXIV.	ST. LUKE XII.
	36 lights burning; and ye yourselves like unto men that wait for their lord, when he will return from the wedding; that when he cometh and knocketh, they may open unto him 37 immediately. Blessed *are* those servants, whom the lord when he cometh shall find watching: verily I say unto you, that he shall gird himself, and make them to sit down to meat, and will 38 come forth and serve them. And if he shall come in the second watch, or come in the third watch, and find *them*
43 But know this, that if the goodman of the house had known in what watch the thief would come, he would have watched, and would not have suffered his house to be broken 44 up. Therefore be ye also ready: for in such an hour as ye think not the Son of Man cometh.	39 so, blessed are they.[1] And this know, that if the goodman of the house had known what hour the thief would come, he would[2] not have suffered his house 40 to be broken through. Be ye[3] ready also: for the Son of Man cometh at an hour when ye think not. 41 Then Peter said unto him, Lord, speakest thou this parable unto us, or
45 Who then is a faithful and wise servant, whom the[4] lord hath made ruler over his household, to give them meat in due season? 46 Blessed *is* that servant, whom his lord when he cometh shall find so 47 doing. Verily I say unto you, That he shall make him ruler over all his 48 goods. But and if the[5] evil servant shall say in his heart, My lord 49 delayeth;[6] and shall begin to smite his[7] fellow-servants, and to eat and 50 drink with the drunken; the lord of that servant shall come in a day when he looketh not for *him*, and in an hour that he is not aware of,	42 even to all? And the Lord said, Who then is that faithful and wise steward, whom *his* lord shall make ruler over his household, to give *them their* por- 43 tion of meat in due season? Blessed *is* that servant, whom his lord when 44 he cometh shall find so doing. Of a truth I say unto you, that he will make him ruler over all that he hath. 45 But and if that servant say in his heart, My lord delayeth his coming; and shall begin to beat the men-servants and maidens, and to eat and 46 drink, and to be drunken; the lord of that servant will come in a day when he looketh not for *him*, and at an hour when he is not aware, and

[1] blessed are those servants
[2] he would have watched and not have suffered
[3] Be ye therefore ready
[4] his lord
[5] that evil servant
[6] delayeth his coming
[7] *his*

ST. MATT. XXIV. X.

51 And shall cut him asunder, and appoint *him* his portion with the hypocrites: there shall be weeping and gnashing of teeth.

ST. MATT. X.

34 Think not that I am come to send peace on earth: I came not 35 to send peace, but a sword. For I am come to set a man at variance against his father, and the daughter against her mother, and the daughter-in-law against her mother-in-law. 36 And a man's foes *shall be* they of his own household.

ST. LUKE XII.

will cut him in sunder, and will appoint him his portion with the unbe-47 lievers. And that servant, which knew his lord's will, and prepared not *himself*, or [1] did according to his will, shall be beaten with many *stripes*. 48 But he that knew not, and did commit things worthy of stripes, shall be beaten with few *stripes*. For unto whomsoever much is given, of him shall be much required; and to whom men have committed much, of him they will ask the more.

49 I am come to send fire on the earth; and what will I, if it be already 50 kindled? But I have a baptism to be baptized with; and how am I straitened till it be accomplished! 51 Suppose ye that I am come to give peace on earth? I tell you, Nay; 52 but rather division: for from henceforth there shall be five in one house divided, three against two, and two 53 against three. The father shall be divided against the son, and the son against the father; the mother against the daughter, and the daughter against the mother; the mother-in-law against the [2] daughter-in-law, and the daughter-in-law against the [3] mother-in-law.

54 And he said also to the people, When ye see a cloud rise in [4] the west, straightway ye say, That [5] there 55 cometh a shower; and so it is. And when *ye see* the south wind blow, ye say, There will be heat: and it cometh 56 to pass. *Ye* hypocrites! ye can discern the face of the sky and of the earth; but how is it that ye do not discern 57 this time? Yea, and why even of yourselves judge ye not what is right?

---

[1] neither did. [2] her daughter in law [3] her mother in law
[4] rise out of the west [5] *omit* That

OUR LORD'S FINAL ARRIVAL AT BETHANY.

ST. MATT. V.

25 Agree with thine adversary quickly, whiles thou art in the way with him; lest at any time the adversary deliver thee to the judge, and the judge[1] to the officer, and thou be 26 cast into prison. Verily I say unto thee, Thou shalt by no means come out thence, till thou hast paid the uttermost farthing.

ST. LUKE XII.

58 When thou goest with thine adversary to the magistrate, *as thou art* in the way, give diligence that thou mayest be delivered from him; lest he hale thee to the judge, and the judge shall[2] deliver thee to the officer, and the officer shall[2] cast thee into 59 prison. I tell thee, thou shalt not depart thence, till thou hast paid the very last mite.

§ 93. Of the Slaughter of the Galileans; the Parable of the Fig-tree; a Woman healed on the Sabbath.

ST. LUKE XIII. 1–17.

1 There were present at that season some that told him of the Galileans,
2 whose blood Pilate had mingled with their sacrifices. And he[3] answering said unto them, Suppose ye that these Galileans were sinners above all the
3 Galileans, because they suffered these[4] things? I tell you, Nay: but, except
4 ye repent, ye shall all likewise perish. Or those eighteen, upon whom the tower in Siloam fell, and slew them, think ye that they were sinners above
5 all men that dwelt in Jerusalem? I tell you, Nay; but, except ye repent, ye shall all likewise perish.
6 He spake also this parable:[a] A certain *man* had a fig tree planted in his
7 vineyard; and he came and sought fruit thereon, and found none. Then said he unto the dresser of his vineyard, Behold, these three years since[5] I come seeking fruit on this fig-tree, and find none: cut it down; why cumbereth it
8 the ground? And he answering said unto him, Lord, let it alone this year
9 also, till I shall dig about it, and dung *it*: And if it bear fruit after that,[6] *well:* and if not, thou shalt cut it down.
10,11 And he was teaching in one of the synagogues on the sabbath. And, behold, *there was*[7] a woman which had a spirit of infirmity eighteen years,
12 and was bowed together, and could in no wise lift up *herself*. And when Jesus saw her, he called *her to him*, and said unto her, Woman, thou art
13 loosed from thine infirmity. And he laid *his* hands on her; and immediately she was made straight, and glorified God.
14 And the ruler of the synagogue answered with indignation, because that Jesus had healed on the sabbath day, and said unto the people, that[8] there are six days in which men ought to work;[b] in them, therefore, come and be

---

[1] the judge deliver thee to the
[2] *twice omit* shall
[3] And Jesus answering
[4] such things
[5] *omit* since
[6] And if it bear fruit, *well:* and if not, *then* after that thou shalt
[7] there was
[8] *omit* that

[a] Comp. Isa. v. 1–7.
[b] Ex. xx. 9.

ST. LUKE XIII.

15 healed, and not on the sabbath-day. But[1] the Lord answered him, and said,
Hypocrites![2] doth not each one of you on the sabbath[a] loose his ox or *his*
16 ass from the stall, and lead *him* away to watering? And ought not this
woman, being a daughter of Abraham, whom Satan hath bound, lo, these
17 eighteen years, be loosed from this bond on the sabbath-day? And when he
had said these things, all his adversaries were ashamed; and all the people
rejoiced for all the glorious things that were done by him.

§ 94. The Festival of the Dedication; Jesus retires beyond the Jordan.
ST. JOHN x. 22–42.

22 And it was at Jerusalem the feast of the dedication[b]:[3] it was winter. And
23
24 Jesus walked in the temple in Solomon's porch.[c] Then came the Jews round
about him, and said unto him, How long dost thou make us to doubt? If thou
25 be the Christ, tell us plainly. Jesus answered,[4] I told you, and ye believe not;
26 the works that I do in my Father's name, they bear witness of me. But ye
27 believe not, because ye are not of my sheep.[5] My sheep hear my voice, and I
28 know them, and they follow me: And I give unto them eternal life; and they
29 shall never perish, neither shall any *man* pluck them out of my hand. The[6]
Father, which gave *them* me, is greater than all; and no *man* is able to pluck
30 *them* out of the[6] Father's hand. I and *my* Father are one.
31 The[7] Jews took up stones again to stone him. Jesus answered them, Many
32 good works have I showed you from the[6] Father; for which of those works do
33 ye stone me? The Jews answered him.[8] For a good work we stone thee not;
but for blasphemy; and because that thou, being a man, makest thyself God.
34 Jesus answered them, Is it not written in your law, that[9] I said, Ye are gods?[d]
35 If he called them gods, unto whom the word of God came, and the scripture
36 cannot be broken; say ye of him, whom the Father hath sanctified, and sent
into the world, Thou blasphemest; because I said, I am the Son of God?
37 If I do not the works of my Father, believe me not. But if I do, though ye
38 believe not me, believe the works; that ye may know, and understand,[10] that
39 the Father *is* in me, and I in the Father.[11] Therefore they sought[12] to take
40 him; but he escaped out of their hand, and went away again beyond Jordan
41 into the place where John at first baptized;[e] and there he abode. And
many resorted unto him, and said, John did no miracle; but all things that
42 John spake of this man were true. And many believed on him there.

[1] The Lord then answered·	[2] *Thou* hypocrite,	[3] and it was winter
[4] answered them	[5] not of my sheep, as I said unto you	[6] my Father;
[7] then the Jews	[8] answered him, saying,	[9] *omit* that
[10] know and believe	[11] and I in him	[12] sought again to take
[a] Comp. Lk. xiv 5.	[b] See 1 Macc. iv. 59.	[c] Comp. Acts iii. 11; v. 12.
[d] Ps. lxxxii. 6.		[e] Jno. i. 28.

§ 94. St. John's narrative of our Lord's visit to Jerusalem and his discourse at the festival
of Dedication is inserted in this place, not without doubt. No mention being made of

§ 95 (A) Our Lord journeys towards Jerusalem. — *Perea.*

St. Matt. xix. 1b, 2.	St. Mark x. 1b.	St. Luke xiii. 22.
—and came into the coasts of Judæa beyond Jordan; and ² great multitudes followed him; and he healed them there.	—and cometh into the coasts of Judæa and¹ the farther side of Jordan; and the people resort unto him again; and, as he was wont, he taught them again.	²² And he went through the cities and villages, teaching, and journeying toward Jerusalem.

(B) He teaches on the way, and is warned against Herod. — *Perea.*

St. Luke xiii. 23–33.

23 Then said one unto him, Lord, are there few that be saved? And he said
24 unto them, Strive to enter in at the strait door ᵃ²; for many, I say unto you,
25 will seek to enter in, and shall not be able. When once the master of the house is risen up, and hath shut to the door, and ye begin to stand without, and to knock at the door, saying, Lord,³ open unto us; and he shall answer and
26 say unto you, I know you not whence ye are: ᵇ then shall ye begin to say, We have eaten and drunk in thy presence, and thou hast taught in our streets.
27 But he shall say, I tell you, I know you not whence ye are; depart from me,
28 all *ye* workers of iniquity. There shall be weeping and gnashing of teeth,ᶜ when ye shall see Abraham, and Isaac, and Jacob, and all the prophets, in
29 the kingdom of God, and you *yourselves* thrust out. And they shall come from the east, and *from* the west, and *from*⁴ the north, and *from* the south,

¹ by the farther side   ² the straight gate   ³ saying, Lord, Lord, open   ⁴ from the north
ᵃ Comp. Matt. vii. 13.   ᵇ Comp. Matt. vii. 22, 23.   ᶜ Matt. viii. 11, 12.

---

these things by the other Evangelists, and the Perean journey being recorded by St. Luke alone, there are no points of comparison by which to determine with certainty the chronological order. This visit and discourse, however, must have taken place not far from this time; and as St. Luke, in the next section (xiii. 22), mentions our Lord's "journeying towards Jerusalem," he may intend to designate thereby another going up to the city, besides the one of which he has already given so full an account. This cannot, however, be considered as quite decisive. As attendance at the festival of Dedication was not obligatory, it is generally considered that our Lord must have been already in the neighborhood, — as he would very probably have been at the close of his journey through Perea.

§ 95. (A) According to the arrangement given above, as on the whole more probable than any other, some time must have elapsed since the events of the previous section. During this time our Lord abode where John had baptized; and there many, prepared by his forerunner, believed on him. He now began again to move towards Jerusalem, stopping as he went, to teach in the villages along the way. Here the latter part of Matt. xix. 1 and Mar. x. 1 is introduced, although these verses must cover the whole time from our Lord's final departure from Galilee until his near approach to Jerusalem for the last Passover.

If Jno. x. 22-42 be placed elsewhere than in the previous section, then Lk. xiii. 22 will refer only to the leisurely continuance of the journey begun so long before.

ST. LUKE XIII.

30 and shall sit down in the kingdom of God. And, behold, there are last which shall be first, and there are first which shall be last.ᵃ
31 The same hour¹ there came certain of the Pharisees, saying unto him, Get
32 thee out, and depart hence; for Herod will kill thee. And he said unto them, Go ye, and tell that fox, Behold, I cast out devils, and I do cures to-day and
33 to-morrow, and the third *day* I shall be perfected. Nevertheless I must walk to-day, and to-morrow, and the *day* following; for it cannot be that a prophet perish out of Jerusalem.

§ 96. At Table with a chief Pharisee on the Sabbath; He heals the Dropsy, and teaches. — *Perea.*

St. Luke xiv. 1–24.

1 And it came to pass, as he went into the house of one of the chief Pharisees
2 to eat bread on the Sabbath-day, that they watched him. And, behold, there
3 was a certain man before him which had the dropsy. And Jesus answering spake unto the lawyers and Pharisees, saying, Is it lawful to heal on the
4 sabbath-day, or not?² And they held their peace. And he took *him*, and
5 healed him, and let him go; and answered them, saying, Which of you shall have a son³ or an ox fallen into a pit, and will not straightway pull him out
6 on the Sabbath-day?ᵇ And they could not answer⁴ again to these things.
7 And he put forth a parable to those which were bidden, when he marked
8 how they chose out the chief rooms; saying unto them, When thou art bidden of any *man* to a wedding, sit not down in the highest room; lest a more honor-
9 able man than thou be bidden of him; and he that bade thee and him come and say to thee, Give this man place, and thou begin with shame to take the
10 lowest room. But when thou art bidden, go and sit down in the lowest room; that when he that bade thee cometh, he may say unto thee, Friend, go up higher; then shalt thou have worship in the presence of all⁵ them that
11 sit at meat with thee. For whosoever exalteth himself shall be abased; and he that humbleth himself shall be exalted.ᶜ

¹ The same day   ² *omit* or not?   ³ an ass or an ox
     ⁴ answer him again   ⁵ *omit* all
ᵃ Matt. xix. 30; xx. 16; Mar. x. 31.   ᵇ Comp. Lk. xiii. 15.
ᶜ Matt. xxiii. 12; Lk. xviii. 14.

---

§ 95. (B) Several of our Lord's sayings in this passage closely resemble parts of the Sermon on the Mount. These appear to have been a partial repetition in Perea of the instruction long before given in Galilee. Although particular expressions are even verbally the same, their context is quite different.

Verses 34 and 35 of Lk. xiii. are so closely parallel to Matt. xxiii. 37–39, that they may be better studied in connection with them, and they have been therefore placed in § 89. As a matter of fact, however, it is likely that they were uttered twice, first under the circumstances mentioned by St. Matthew, and afterwards repeated as they are recorded by St. Luke. They are most closely attached to the context in St. Matthew.

ST. LUKE XIV.

12 Then said he also to him that bade him, When thou makest a dinner or a supper, call not thy friends, nor thy brethren, neither thy kinsmen, nor *thy rich neighbors*; lest they also bid thee again, and a recompence be made thee.
13 But when thou makest a feast, call the poor, the maimed, the lame, the blind:
14 and thou shalt be blessed;[a] for they cannot recompense thee; but[1] thou shalt be recompensed at the resurrection of the just.
15 And when one of them that sat at meat with him heard these things, he said unto him, Blessed *is* he whosoever[2] shall eat bread in the kingdom of
16 God. Then said he unto him,[b] A certain man made a great supper, and bade
17 many: and sent his servant at supper time to say to them that were bidden,
18 Come; for the[3] things are now ready. And they all with one *consent* began to make excuse. The first said unto him, I have bought a piece of ground,
19 and I must needs go and see it: I pray thee have me excused. And another said, I have bought five yoke of oxen, and I go to prove them: I pray thee
20 have me excused. And another said, I have married a wife, and therefore I
21 cannot come. So the[4] servant came, and showed his lord these things. Then the master of the house being angry said to his servant, Go out quickly into the streets and lanes of the city, and bring in hither the poor, and the
22 maimed, and the halt, and the blind. And the servant said, Lord, what
23 thou hast commanded is done,[5] and yet there is room. And the lord said unto the servant, Go out into the highways and hedges, and compel *them* to
24 come in, that my house may be filled. For I say unto you, That none of those men which were bidden shall taste of my supper.[c]

§ 97. What is required of Disciples. — *Perea*.

St. Matt. x. 37—39.	St. Luke xiv. 25—35.
	25 And there went great multitudes with him
37 He that loveth father or mother more than me is not worthy of me; and he that loveth son or daughter more than me is not worthy 38 of me. And he that taketh	26 and he turned, and said unto them, If any *man* come to me, and hate not his father, and mother, and wife, and children, and brethren, and sisters, yea, and his own life also, he cannot 27 be my disciple. Whosoever[6] doth not bear his cross and come after me, cannot be my

[1] for thou shalt be recompensed [2] that shall eat [3] all things [4] that servant
[5] Lord, it is done as thou hast commanded, and yet [6] And whosoever
[a] Comp. Acts xx. 35. [b] Comp. Matt. xxii. 2-14. [c] Matt. xxi. 43.

§ 97. Matt. x. 39 is allowed to stand here in its close connection with the preceding verses although it does not occur in the parallel passage of St. Luke. It occurs again in Lk. xvii. 33 (§ 102), where there is nothing to correspond in St. Matthew. But as it was often repeated by our Lord (see §§ 70, 102, 124) there seems no objection to supposing one more repetition, and thus preserve its various connections.

ST. MATT. X.

not his cross and followeth
after me, is not worthy of
39 me.[a] He that findeth his
life shall lose it; and he
that loseth his life for my
sake shall find it.[b]

ST. LUKE XIV.

28 disciple.[a] For which of you, intending to
build a tower, sitteth not down first, and
counteth the cost, whether he have *sufficient*
29 to finish *it?* Lest haply, after he hath laid
the foundation, and is not able to finish *it*, all
30 that behold *it* begin to mock him, saying,
This man began to build, and was not able to
31 finish. Or what king, going to make war
against another king, will not sit [1] down first
and consult whether he be able with ten thousand
to meet him that cometh against him
32 with twenty thousand? Or else, while the
other is yet a great way off, he sendeth an
ambassage, and desireth conditions of peace.
33 So likewise, whosoever he be of you that forsaketh
not all that he hath, he cannot be my
disciple.

34 Salt therefore *is* good: but if even [2] the salt
have lost his savor, wherewith shall it be
35 seasoned?[c] It is neither fit for the land, nor
yet for the dung-hill; *but* men cast it out.
He that hath ears,[3] let him hear!

§ 98. Parables of the Lost Sheep, the Lost Drachma, and the Prodigal Son. — *Perea.*

ST. LUKE XV. 1–32.

1 Then drew near unto him all the publicans and sinners for to hear him.
2 And both [4] the Pharisees and scribes murmured, saying, This man receiveth
sinners, and eateth with them.

3 4 And he spake this parable unto them, saying, What man of you, having an
hundred sheep, if he lose one of them, doth not leave the ninety and nine in
5 the wilderness, and go after that which is lost, until he find it? And when
6 he hath found *it*, he layeth *it* on his shoulders, rejoicing. And when he cometh
home, he calleth together *his* friends and neighbors, saying unto them, Rejoice
7 with me; for I have found my sheep which was lost.[d] I say unto you, that
likewise joy shall be in heaven over one sinner that repenteth, more than over
ninety and nine just persons, which need no repentance.

8 Either what woman having ten pieces of silver, if she lose one piece, doth
not light a candle, and sweep the house, and seek diligently till she find *it?*

[1] sitteth not down first and consulteth
[2] *omit* therefore *and* even
[3] hath ears to hear, let him
[4] *omit* both

[a] Matt. xvi. 24; Mar. viii. 34; Lk. ix. 23. [b] Matt. xvi. 25; Mar. viii. 35; Lk. ix. 24; xvii. 33; Jno. xii. 25. [c] Matt. v. 13; Mar. ix. 50. [d] Matt. xviii. 12, 13 and note.

ST. LUKE XV.

9. And when she hath found *it*, she calleth *her* friends and *her* neighbors together,
10. saying, Rejoice with me; for I have found the piece which I had lost. Likewise, I say unto you, there is joy in the presence of the angels of God over one sinner that repenteth.
11.
12. And he said, A certain man had two sons: and the younger of them said to *his* father, Father, give me the portion of goods that falleth *to me*. And
13. he divided unto them *his* living. And not many days after the younger son gathered all together, and took his journey into a far country, and there wasted
14. his substance with riotous living. And when he had spent all, there arose a
15. mighty famine in that land; and he began to be in want. And he went and joined himself to a citizen of that country; and he sent him into his fields to
16. feed swine. And he would fain have filled his belly with the husks that the
17. swine did eat; and no man gave unto him. And when he came to himself, he said, How many hired servants of my father's have bread enough and to
18. spare, and I perish here [1] with hunger! I will arise and go to my father, and
19. will say unto him, Father, I have sinned against heaven, and before thee.[2] I am no more worthy to be called thy son: make me as one of thy hired ser-
20. vants. And he arose, and came to his father. But when he was yet a great way off, his father saw him, and had compassion, and ran, and fell on his neck,
21. and kissed him. And the son said unto him, Father, I have sinned against
22. heaven, and in thy sight.[3] I am no more worthy to be called thy son. But the father said to his servants, Bring forth the best robe, and put *it* on him;
23. and put a ring on his hand, and shoes on *his* feet; and bring hither the fatted
24. calf, and kill *it*; and let us eat, and be merry: for this my son was dead, and is alive again: he was lost, and is found. And they began to be merry.
25. Now his elder son was in the field; and as he came and drew nigh to the
26. house, he heard music and dancing. And he called one of the servants, and
27. asked what these things meant. And he said unto him, Thy brother is come; and thy father hath killed the fatted calf, because he hath received him safe
28. and sound. And he was angry, and would not go in; but his father came [4]
29. out, and intreated him. And he answering said to *his* father, Lo, these many years do I serve thee, neither transgressed I at any time thy commandment; and yet thou never gavest me a kid, that I might make merry with my friends:
30. but as soon as this thy son was come, which hath devoured thy living with
31. harlots, thou hast killed for him the fatted calf. And he said unto him, Son,
32. thou art ever with me, and all that I have is thine. It was meet that we should make merry, and be glad; for this thy brother was dead, and is alive; [5] lost, and is found.

---

[1] *omit* here   [2] before thee, and am no more   [3] in thy sight, and am no more
[4] therefore came his father out   [5] and is alive again; and was lost

§ 99 (A) The Parable of the Unjust Steward. — *Perea.*

St. Luke xvi. 1–8.

1 And he said also unto the [1] disciples, There was a certain rich man, which had a steward; and the same was accused unto him that he [2] wasted his goods.
2 And he called him, and said unto him, How is it that I hear this of thee? Give an account of thy stewardship; for thou mayest be no longer steward.
3 Then the steward said within himself, What shall I do? for my lord taketh
4 away from me the stewardship: I cannot dig; to beg I am ashamed. I am resolved what to do, that, when I am put out of the stewardship, they may receive me into their own [3] houses.
5 So he called every one of his lord's debtors *unto him*, and said unto the
6 first, How much owest thou unto my lord? And he said, An hundred measures of oil. And he said unto him, Take thy bill, and sit down quickly, and write
7 fifty. Then said he to another, And how much owest thou? And he said, An hundred measures of wheat. He [4] said unto him, Take thy bill, and write
8 fourscore. And the lord commended the unjust steward, because he had done wisely; for the children of this world are in their generation wiser than the children of light.

(B) The right use of Riches. The covetous Pharisees reproved.

St. Matt. vi. 24.	St. Luke xvi. 9–15.
	9 And I say unto you, Make to yourselves friends of the mammon of unrighteousness; that when it faileth [5] they may receive you
	10 into everlasting habitations. He that is faithful in that which is least is faithful also in much; and he that is unjust in the least is
	11 unjust also in much. If therefore ye have not been faithful in the unrighteous mammon, who will commit to your trust the true *riches*?
	12 And if ye have not been faithful in that which is another man's, who shall give you that
24 No man can serve two masters: for either he will	13 which is your own? No servant can serve two masters: for either he will hate the one,

[1] his disciples   [2] *translated* had wasted   [3] *omit* own
[4] And he said   [5] when ye fail, they may

§ 99. The three verses of St. Luke xvi. (16, 17, and 18) omitted here are closely parallel to passages of St. Matthew, which are intimately joined to their context: vs. 16 with Matt. xi. 12, 13; vs. 17 with Matt. v. 18; and vs. 18 with Matt. xix. 9 (Mar. x. 11, 12). As they stand isolated here, without any reference to the circumstances under which they were severally spoken, their true chronological position is obviously determined by St. Matthew, and they have been placed accordingly.

ST. MATT. VI.	ST. LUKE XVI.
hate the one, and love the other; or else he will hold to the one, and despise the other. Ye cannot serve God and mammon.	and love the other: or else he will hold to the one, and despise the other. Ye cannot serve God and mammon.

14 And the Pharisees,[1] who were covetous, heard all these things; and they derided him.
15 And he said unto them, Ye are they which justify yourselves before men; but God knoweth your hearts: for that which is highly esteemed among men is[2] abomination in the sight of God.

(C) The Parable of Dives and Lazarus.
St. Luke xvi. 19–31.

19 There was a certain rich man, which was clothed in purple and fine linen,
20 and fared sumptuously every day. And[3] a certain beggar named Lazarus
21 was laid at his gate, full of sores, and desiring to be fed with that[4] which fell from the rich man's table: moreover the dogs came and licked his sores.
22 And it came to pass, that the beggar died, and was carried by the angels into
23 Abraham's bosom; the rich man also died, and was buried; and in hell he lift up his eyes, being in torments, and seeth Abraham afar off, and Lazarus
24 in his bosom. And he cried and said, Father Abraham, have mercy on me! and send Lazarus, that he may dip the tip of his finger in water, and cool
25 my tongue; for I am tormented in this flame. But Abraham said, Son, remember that thou in thy lifetime receivedst thy good things, and likewise Laz-
26 arus evil things: but now he is comforted here,[5] and thou art tormented. And besides all this, between us and you there is a great gulf fixed: so that they which would pass from thence to you cannot; neither can they pass to us,
27 that *would come* from thence. Then he said, I pray thee therefore, father,
28 that thou wouldst send him to my father's house: for I have five brethren; that he may testify unto them, lest they also come into this place of torment.
29 But Abraham saith,[6] They have Moses and the prophets; let them hear
30 them. And he said, Nay, father Abraham: but if one went unto them from
31 the dead, they will repent. And he said unto him, If they hear not Moses and the prophets, neither will they be persuaded, though one rose from the dead.

---

[1] And the Pharisees also
[2] is abomination
[3] And there was a certain beggar named Lazarus, which was laid
[4] with the crumbs which fell
[5] *omit* here
[6] Abraham saith unto him

§ 100. The Power of Faith, and the Duty of Humility. — *Perea.*

St. Luke xvii. 5–10.

5
6 And the apostles said unto the Lord, Increase our faith. And the Lord said, If ye have¹ faith as a grain of mustard-seed,ᵃ ye might say unto this sycamine-tree, Be thou plucked up by the root, and be thou planted in the sea; and it should obey you.

7 But which of you, having a servant ploughing, or feeding cattle, will say unto him² when he is come from the field, Go directly and sit down to meat?

8 And will not rather say unto him, Make ready wherewith I may sup, and gird thyself, and serve me, till I have eaten and drunken; and afterward thou

9 shalt eat and drink? Doth he thank the³ servant, because he did the things

10 that were commanded.⁴ So likewise ye, when ye shall have done all those things which are commanded you, say, We are unprofitable servants: we have done that which was our duty to do.

§ 101. The Resurrection of Lazarus and consequent Action of the Jews. — *Bethany, Jerusalem, and Ephraim.*

St. John xi. 1–54.

1 Now a certain *man* was sick, *named* Lazarus, of Bethany, the town of Mary

2 and her sister Martha.ᵇ (It was *that* Mary which anointedᶜ the Lord with ointment, and wiped his feet with her hair, whose brother Lazarus was sick.)

3 Therefore his sisters sent unto him, saying, Lord, Behold! he whom thou lovest is sick.

4 When Jesus heard *that*, he said, This sickness is not unto death, but for

5 the glory of God, that the Son of God might be glorified thereby. Now

6 Jesus loved Martha, and her sister, and Lazarus. When he had heard therefore that he was sick, he abode two days still in the same place where

7 he was. Then after that saith he to *his* disciples, Let us go into Judea

8 again. *His* disciples say unto him, Master, the Jews of late sought to stone

9 theeᵈ; and goest thou thither again? Jesus answered, Are there not twelve hours in the day? If any man walk in the day, he stumbleth not, because

10 he seeth the light of this world. But if a man walk in the night, he

11 stumbleth, because there is no light in him. These things said he; and after that he saith unto them, Our friend Lazarus sleepeth; but I go, that I

12 may awake him out of sleep. Then said his disciples unto him,⁵ Lord, if he

13 sleep, he shall do well. Howbeit Jesus spake of his death: but they thought that

14 he had spoken of taking of rest in sleep. Then said Jesus unto them plainly,

---

¹ If ye had faith   ² will say unto him by and by, when he is come from the field, Go and sit
³ that servant   ⁴ were commanded him? I trow not.
⁵ Then said his disciples, Lord, if he

ᵃ Matt. xvii. 20; xxi. 21; Mar. ix. 23; xi. 23.   ᵇ Lk. x. 38, 39.   ᶜ Matt. xxvi. 7;
Mar. xiv. 3; Jno. xii. 3.   ᵈ Jno. x. 31.

ST. JOHN XI.

15 Lazarus is dead. And I am glad for your sakes that I was not there, to the
16 intent ye may believe; nevertheless let us go unto him. Then said Thomas, which is called Didymus, unto his fellow disciples, Let us also go, that we may die with him.
17 Then when Jesus came, he found that he had *lain* in the grave four days
18 already. Now Bethany was nigh unto Jerusalem, about fifteen furlongs
19 off: and many of the Jews came to Martha and Mary, to comfort them con-
20 cerning *their*[1] brother. Then Martha, as soon as she heard that Jesus was
21 coming, went and met him: but Mary sat *still* in the house. Then said Martha unto Jesus, Lord, if thou hadst been here, my brother had not died.
22 Even now I know, that[2] whatsoever thou wilt ask of God, God will give
23/24 *it* thee. Jesus saith unto her, Thy brother shall rise again. Martha saith unto him, I know that he shall rise again in the resurrection at the last
25 day.[a] Jesus said unto her, I am the resurrection, and the life: he that
26 believeth in me, though he were dead, yet shall he live: and whosoever
27 liveth and believeth in me shall never die. Believest thou this? She saith unto him, Yea, Lord: I believe that thou art the Christ, the Son of God, which should come into the world.
28 And when she had said this,[3] she went her way, and called Mary her sister
29 secretly, saying, The Master is come, and calleth for thee. As soon as she
30 heard *that*, she arose quickly, and came unto him. Now Jesus was not yet
31 come into the town, but was in that place where Martha met him. The Jews then which were with her in the house, and comforted her, when they saw Mary, that she rose up hastily and went out, followed her, thinking,[4] She
32 goeth unto the grave to weep there. Then when Mary was come where Jesus was, and saw him, she fell down at his feet, saying unto him, Lord, if
33 thou hadst been here, my brother had not died. When Jesus therefore saw her weeping, and the Jews also weeping which came with her, he groaned in
34/35 the spirit, and was troubled, 'and said, Where have ye laid him? They said
36 unto him, Lord, come and see. Jesus wept. Then said the Jews, Behold
37 how he loved him! And some of them said, Could not this man, which opened the eyes of the blind, have caused that even this man should not
38 have died? Jesus therefore again groaning in himself cometh to the grave.
39 It was a cave, and a stone lay upon it. Jesus said, Take ye away the stone. Martha, the sister of him that was dead, saith unto him, Lord, by this time he stinketh: for he hath been *dead* four days. Jesus saith unto her, Said I not
40 unto thee, that, if thou wouldest believe, thou shouldest see the glory of God?
41 Then they took away the stone.[5] And Jesus lifted up *his* eyes, and said,
42 Father, I thank thee that thou hast heard me. And I knew that thou hearest me always: but because of the people which stand by I said *it*, that they

---

[1] their   [2] but I know, that even now, whatsoever   [3] she had so said
[4] followed her, saying,   [5] Then they took away the stone *from the place* where the dead was laid.

[a] Dan. xii. 2, etc.

ST. JOHN XI.

43 may believe that thou hast sent me. And when he thus had spoken, he cried
44 with a loud voice, Lazarus, come forth. He[1] that was dead came forth, bound hand and foot with grave-clothes: and his face was bound about with a napkin. Jesus saith unto them, Loose him, and let him go.
45 Then many of the Jews which came to Mary, and had seen the things
46 which he[2] did, believed on him. But some of them went their ways to the Pharisees, and told them what things Jesus had done.
47 Then gathered the chief priests and the Pharisees a council, and said,
48 What do we? for this man doeth many miracles. If we let him thus alone, all *men* will believe on him: and the Romans shall come and take away both
49 our place and nation. And one of them, *named* Caiaphas[a] being the high
50 priest that same year, said unto them, Ye know nothing at all, 'nor consider that it is expedient for you,[3] that one man should die for the people, and that
51 the whole nation perish not. And this spake he not of himself: but being high priest that year, he prophesied that Jesus should die for that nation;
52 and not for that nation only, but that also he should gather together in one
53 the children of God that were scattered abroad. Then from that day forth they took counsel[4] for to put him to death.
54 Jesus therefore walked no more openly among the Jews; but went thence unto a country near to the wilderness, into a city called Ephraim, and there continued with the[5] disciples.

§ 102. Concerning the Coming of the Kingdom of God.

ST. MATT. XXIV. 26–28, 37–41.   ST. LUKE XVII. 20–30, 32–37.

20 And when he was demanded of the Pharisees, when the kingdom of God should come, he answered them and said, The kingdom of God cometh not

[1] And he that was   [2] the things which Jesus did   [3] expedient for us
[4] took counsel together   [5] with his disciples
[a] Comp. Lk. iii. 2.

---

§ 101. Ephraim, to which our Lord retired (vs. 54), is a small, but very strong, city in the N. E. of Judah, on the confines of Samaria, and is identified with the Ephron or Ephraim of 2 Chron. xiii. 19, and is also identified by Robinson (notes in loco, p. 204) with the Ophrah in Benjamin of Josh. xviii. 23; 1 Sam. xiii. 17, and with "the lofty site of the modern et-Taiyibeh, situated two hours northeast of Bethel, and six hours and twenty minutes N. N. E. of Jerusalem (reckoning three Roman miles to the hour), adjacent to and overlooking the broad tract of desert country lying between it and the valley of the Jordan." Our Saviour appears to have remained here until the near approach of the last Passover, when he again crossed the Jordan, and joined the crowds of worshippers going up to Jerusalem. At this point the other Evangelists resume their narrative. The length of the sojourn in Ephraim we have no means of ascertaining, and there are no certain data for determining at precisely what point in St. Luke's narrative the resurrection of Lazarus occurred. It is generally

ST. MATT. XXIV.	ST. LUKE XVII.
	21 with observation: neither shall they say, Lo here! or,[1] there! for, behold! the kingdom of God is within you.
	22 And he said unto the disciples. The days will come, when ye shall desire to see one of the days of the Son of
	23 Man, and ye shall not see it. And
26 Wherefore if they shall say unto you, Behold! he is in the desert; go not forth: behold! *he is* in the secret chambers; believe *it* not.	they shall say to you. See here,[2] see there: go not after *them*, nor follow
27 For as the lightning cometh out of the east, and shineth even unto the west; so shall[4] the coming of the	24 *them*. For as the lightning[3] lighteneth out of the one *part* under heaven, shineth unto the other *part* under heaven; so shall[5] the Son of Man be
37 Son of Man be. But as the days of Noe[a] *were*, so shall[4] the coming	25 in his day. But first must he suffer many things, and be rejected of this
38 of the Son of Man be. For as in the days that were before the flood they were eating and drinking, marrying and giving in marriage, until the day that Noe entered into	26 generation. And as it was in the days of Noe,[a] so shall it be also in
	27 the days of the Son of Man. They did eat, they drank, they married wives, they were given in marriage, until the day that Noe entered into the ark, and the flood came, and de-
39 the ark, and knew not until the flood came, and took them all away; so shall also the coming of the Son of Man be.	28 stroyed them all. Likewise also as it was in the days of Lot;[b] they did eat, they drank, they bought, they
	29 sold, they planted, they builded; but the same day that Lot went out of Sodom it rained fire and brimstone from heaven, and destroyed *them* all:[c]
	30 even thus shall it be in the day when
	32 the Son of Man is revealed. Re-
	33 member Lot's wife.[d] Whosoever shall

[1] or, lo there!   [2] See here; or, see there   [3] lightning that lighteneth
[4] so shall also the coming   [5] so shall also the Son
[a] Gen. vi. vii.   [b] Gen. xix.   [c] ib. 24–26.   [d] ib. 26.

agreed, however, that it is not likely to have been later than the point here assigned, while there is no sufficient reason for putting it earlier.

§ 102. Another instance in which St. Matthew, having omitted the narrative of this period, preserves some important parts of its discourses, by connecting them with a similar discourse uttered somewhat later. By transposing these passages to this place, and into connection with the closely parallel language of St. Luke, the twenty-fourth chapter of St. Matthew may become clearer to the student. A single verse of St. Luke (31), on the other hand, requires to be transposed to that discourse by the arrangment of both St. Matthew and St. Mark. It is also intimately connected with what thus becomes its context in St. Luke.

ST. MATT. XXIV.	ST. LUKE XVII.
	seek to save his life shall lose it; and whosoever shall lose his life shall 34 preserve it. I tell you, in that night there shall be two *men* in one bed; the one shall be taken, and the other 35 shall be left. Two *women* shall be grinding together; the one shall be taken, and the other left.[1] And they answered and said unto him, Where, Lord? And he said unto them, Wheresoever the body *is*, thither also[3] will the eagles be gathered together.
40 Then shall two be in the field; the one shall be taken, and the other 41 left. Two *women shall be* grinding at the mill; the one shall be taken, and the other left.	
28 [2]Wheresoever the carcase is, there will the eagles be gathered together.	

§ 103. The Parables of the Importunate Widow, and of the Pharisee and Publican.

St. Luke XVIII. 1–14.

1 And he spake a parable unto them *to this end*, that they[4] ought always to
2 pray,[a] and not to faint; saying, There was in a city a judge, which feared not
3 God, neither regarded man: and there was a widow in that city; and she
4 came unto him, saying, Avenge me of mine adversary. And he would not for a while: but afterward he said within himself, Though I fear not God,
5 nor regard man; yet because this widow troubleth me, I will avenge her, lest
6 by her continual coming she weary me. And the Lord said, Hear what the
7 unjust judge saith. And shall not God avenge his own elect, which cry day
8 and night unto him, though he bear long with them? I tell you that he will avenge them speedily. Nevertheless when the Son of Man cometh, shall he find faith on the earth?

9 And he spake this parable unto certain which trusted in themselves that
10 they were righteous, and despised others: Two men went up into the temple
11 to pray; the one a Pharisee, and the other a publican. The Pharisee stood and prayed thus,[5] God, I thank thee, that I am not as other men *are*, extor-
12 tioners, unjust, adulterers, or even as this publican. I fast twice in the week,
13 I give tithes of all that I acquire.[6] But[7] the publican, standing afar off, would not lift up so much as *his* eyes unto heaven, but smote[8] his breast,
14 saying, God be merciful to me a sinner. I tell you, this man went down to his house justified rather[9] than the other: for every one that exalteth himself shall be abased; and he that humbleth himself shall be exalted.

[1] ver. 36 Two *men* shall be in the field; the one shall be taken, and the other left.
[2] For wheresoever   [3] *omit* also   [4] that men ought
[5] prayed thus with himself   [6] *translated* all that I possess   [7] And the publican
[8] smote upon his   [9] *rather*

[a] Cf. Lk. xi. 5–8.

§ 104. Instructions concerning Divorce.

St. Matt. xix. 3–12.	St. Mark x. 2–12.	St. Luke xvi. 18.
3 The Pharisees also came unto him, tempting him, and saying,[1] Is it lawful *for a man*[2] to put away his wife for every cause?	2 And the Pharisees came to him, and asked him, Is it lawful for a man to put away *his* wife? tempting him. 3 And he answered and said unto them, What did Moses command	
7 They say unto him, Why did Moses then command to give a writing of divorcement, and to put 8 *her*[3] away?[a] He saith unto them, Moses because of the hardness of your hearts suffered you to put away your wives: but from the beginning 4 it was not so. And he answered and said,[4] have ye not read, that he which made *them* at the beginning made them 5 male and female,[b] and said, For this cause shall a man leave father and mother, and shall cleave to his wife: and they twain shall be one flesh?[c] 6 Wherefore they are no more twain, but one flesh. What therefore God hath joined together, let not man put asunder.	4 you? And they said, Moses suffered to write a bill of divorcement, and to put *her* away.[a] 5 And Jesus[4] said unto them, For the hardness of your heart he wrote you this precept. 6 But from the beginning of the creation he[5] made them male 7 and female,[b] For this cause shall a man leave his father and his[7] 8 mother.[8] And they twain shall be one flesh: so then they are no more twain, 9 but one flesh.[c] What therefore God hath joined together, let not man put asunder.	

[1] saying unto him, Is it   [2] for a man   [3] her
[4] answered and said unto   [5] God made them   [6] and said unto them
[7] *omit* his   [8] and mother and cleave to his wife

[a] Deut. xxiv. 1.   [b] Gen. i. 27; ii. 18–25; v. 2.
[c] Gen. ii. 24. Comp. 1 Cor. vi. 16; xi. 8; Eph. v. 30, 31.

ST. MATT. XIX.	ST. MARK X.	ST. LUKE XVI.
	10 And in the house the¹ disciples asked him again concerning 11 this.² And he saith unto them, Whosoever shall put away his wife, and marry another, committeth adultery 12 against her. And if she⁴ shall put away her husband and marry⁵ another, she committeth adultery.	18 Whosoever putteth away his wife, and marrieth another, committeth adultery: and he who⁶ marrieth her that is put away from *her* husband committeth adultery.
9 And I say unto you, Whosoever shall put away his wife, except *it be* for fornication, and shall marry another, committeth adultery:³		
10 The⁷ disciples say unto him, If the case of the man be so with *his* wife, it is not good to marry. 11 But he said unto them, All *men* cannot receive this saying, save *they* to 12 whom it is given. For there are some eunuchs, which were so born from *their* mother's womb, and there are some eunuchs, which were made eunuchs of men: and there be eunuchs, which have made themselves eunuchs for the kingdom of heaven's sake. He that is able to receive *it*, let him receive *it*.		

§ 105. Our Lord receives and blesses little Children.

St. Matt. xix. 13–15.	St. Mark x. 13–16.	St. Luke xviii. 15–17.
13 Then were there brought unto him little children, that he should	13 And they brought young children to him, that he should touch	15 And they brought unto him also infants, that he would touch

¹ his disciples ² asked him again of the same *matter*.
³ committeth adultery: and whoso marrieth her which is put away doth commit adultery.
⁴ And if a woman shall ⁵ and be married to another
⁶ and whosoever marrieth ⁷ His disciples

ST. MATT. XIX.	ST. MARK. X.	ST. JOHN XVIII.
put *his* hands on them, and pray: and the disciples rebuked them.	them: and *his* disciples rebuked those that 14 brought *them*. But when Jesus saw it, he was much displeased, and said unto them, Suffer the little children to come unto me,[2] forbid them not: for of such is the 15 kingdom of God. Verily I say unto you, Whosoever shall not receive the kingdom of God as a little child, he shall not 16 enter therein. And he took them up in his arms, and blessed them,[3] and put *his* hands upon them.	them: but when *his* disciples saw *it*, they 16 rebuked them. But Jesus called them *unto him*, and said, Suffer little children to come unto me, and forbid them not: for of such is the kingdom of God. 17 Verily I say unto you, Whosoever shall not receive the kingdom of God as a little child shall in no wise enter therein.
14 But Jesus said unto them.[1] Suffer little children, and forbid them not, to come unto me: for of such is the kingdom of heaven.		
15 And he laid *his* hands on them, and departed thence.		

§ 106. (A) The Rich Young Man.

ST. MATT. XIX. 16–30.	ST. MARK X. 17–31.	ST. LUKE XVIII. 18–30.
16 And, behold, one came and said unto him,[4] Master, what good thing shall I do, that I may 17 have eternal life? And he said unto him, Why askest thou me concerning the[5] good? the good is one: but if thou wilt enter into life, keep 18 the commandments. He saith,[7] Which? Jesus said,[8] Thou shalt do no murder, Thou shalt not commit adultery, Thou	17 And when he was gone forth into the way, there came one running, and kneeled to him, and asked him, Good Master, what shall I do that I may inherit eternal life? 18 And Jesus said unto him, Why callest thou me good? *there is* none good but one, 19 *that is* God. Thou knowest the commandments,[a] Do not commit adultery, Do not kill, Do not steal,	18 And a certain ruler asked him, saying, Good Master, what shall I do to inherit 19 eternal life? And Jesus said unto him, Why callest thou me good? none *is* good, 20 save God only.[6] Thou knowest the commandments,[a] Do not commit adultery, Do not kill, Do not steal,

[1] *omit* unto them
[2] and forbid them not
[3] in his arms, put *his* hands upon them, and blessed them
[4] Good master
[5] Why callest thou me good? *there is* none good but one, *that is*, God:
[6] save one, *that is*, God.
[7] He saith unto him, Which?

[a] Ex. xx. 13, etc.; Deut. v. 17, etc.

ST. MATT. XIX.	ST. MARK X.	ST. LUKE XVIII.
shalt not steal, Thou shalt not bear false witness, Honor thy father and *thy* mother: and, Thou shalt love thy neighbor as thyself.ᵃ The young man saith unto him, All these things have I kept:² what lack I yet?	Do not bear false witness, Defraud not, Honor thy father and mother.	Do not bear false witness, Honor thy father and thy mother.
(19) (20)		
21 Jesus said unto him, If thou wilt be perfect, go *and* sell that thou hast, and give to the poor, and thou shalt have treasure in heaven: and come *and* follow me.	20 And he¹ said unto him, Master, all these have I observed from my 21 youth. Then Jesus beholding him loved him, and said unto him, One thing thou lackest: go thy way, sell whatsoever thou hast, and give to the poor, and thou shalt have treasure in heaven: and 22 come⁵ follow me. And	21 And he said, All these have I kept from³ 22 youth up. Now when Jesus heard⁴, he said unto him, Yet lackest thou one thing: sell all that thou hast, and distribute unto the poor, and thou shalt have treasure in heaven: and come, follow
22 But when the young man heard⁶ he went away sorrowful: for he had great possessions.	he was sad at that saying, and went away grieved: for he had great possessions.	23 me. And when he heard this, he was very sorrowful: for he was very rich.
23 Then said Jesus unto his disciples, Verily I say unto you, That a rich man shall hardly enter into the kingdom of heaven.	23 And Jesus looked round about, and saith unto his disciples, How hardly shall they that have riches enter into the kingdom of God! 24 And the disciples were astonished at his words. But Jesus answereth again, and saith unto them, Children, how hard is it⁸ to enter into the kingdom of God!	24 And when Jesus saw him⁷ he said, How hardly shall they that have riches enter into the kingdom of God!
24 And again I say unto you, That⁹ it is easier for a camel to	25 It is easier for a camel	25 For it is easier for a

¹ And he answered and said
² kept from my youth up
³ from my youth up
⁴ heard these things, he said
⁵ and come, take up the cross, and follow
⁶ heard that saying
⁷ when Jesus saw that he was very sorrowful, he said
⁸ how hard is it for them that trust in riches to enter
⁹ *omit* that

ᵃ Lev. xix. 18.

ST. MATT. XIX.	ST. MARK X.	ST. LUKE XVIII.
enter into[1] the eye of a needle, than for a rich man to enter into the kingdom of heaven.[2]	to go through the eye of a needle, than for a rich man to enter into the kingdom of	camel to go through a needle's eye, than for a rich man to enter into the kingdom of
25 When the[3] disciples heard *it*, they were exceedingly amazed, saying, Who then can be saved?	26 God. And they were astonished out of measure, saying among themselves, Who then 27 can be saved? [4]Jesus	26 God. And they that heard *it* said, Who then can be saved?
26 But Jesus beheld *them*, and said unto them, With men this is impossible; but with God all things *are*[5] possible.	looking upon them saith, With men *it is* impossible, but not with God: for with God all things *are*[5] possible.	27 And he said, The things which are impossible with men are possible with God.
27 Then answered Peter and said unto him, Behold! we have forsaken all, and followed thee; 28 what shall we have therefore? And Jesus said unto them, Verily I say unto you, That ye which have followed me, in the regeneration when the Son of man shall sit in the throne of his glory, ye also shall sit upon twelve thrones, judging the twelve tribes of Is-29 rael. And every one that hath forsaken houses, or brethren, or sisters, or father, or mother," or children, or lands, for my name's sake, shall receive manifold,[10] and shall in-	28 [6]Peter began to say unto him, Lo! we have left all, and have followed thee. 29 Jesus[8] said, Verily I say unto you, There is no man that hath left house, or brethren, or sisters, or father, or mother,[9] or children, or lands, for 30 my sake, and the gospel's, but he shall receive an hundredfold now in this time,	28 Then Peter said, Lo! we have left our own[7] and followed thee. 29 And he said unto them, Verily I say unto you, There is no man that hath left house, or parents, or brethren, or wife, or children, for the kingdom of 30 God's sake, who shall not receive manifold more in this present time,

[1] to go through the eye
[2] kingdom of God
[3] his disciples
[4] And Jesus
[5] are
[6] Then Peter
[7] left all
[8] And Jesus answered and said
[9] mother, or wife, or children
[10] an hundredfold

ST. MATT. XIX.	ST. MARK X.	ST. LUKE XVIII.
herit everlasting life.	houses, and brethren, and sisters, and mothers, and children, and lands, with persecutions; and in the world to come eternal life.	and in the world to come life everlasting.
30 But many *that are* first shall be last; and the last *shall be* first.ᵃ	31 But many *that are* first shall be last; and the last first.ᵃ	

(B) The Parable of the Laborers.

St. Matt. xx. 1–16.

1 For the kingdom of heaven is like unto a man *that is* an householder,
2 which went out early in the morning to hire laborers into his vineyard. And when he had agreed with the laborers for a penny a day, he sent them into
3 his vineyard. And he went out about the third hour, and saw others standing
4 idle in the marketplace, ¹and he said unto them; Go ye also into the vineyard,
5 and whatsoever is right I will give you. And they went their way. ¹And¹
again he went out about the sixth and ninth hour, and did likewise.
6 And about the eleventh² he went out, and found others standing,³ and saith
7 unto them, Why stand ye here all the day idle? They say unto him, Because no man hath hired us. He saith unto them, Go ye also into the vineyard:⁴
8 So when even was come, the lord of the vineyard saith unto his steward, Call
9 the laborers, and give the⁵ hire, beginning from the last unto the first. And when they came that *were hired* about the eleventh hour, they received every
10 man a penny. But when the first came, they supposed that they should have
11 received more; and they likewise received every man a penny. And when they had received *it*, they murmured against the goodman of the house,
12 ⁶saying, These last have wrought *but* one hour, and thou hast made them
13 equal unto us, which have borne the burden and heat of the day. But he answered one of them, and said, Friend, I do thee no wrong: didst not thou
14 agree with me for a penny? Take *that* thine *is*, and go thy way: I will give
15 unto this last, even as unto thee. Is it not lawful for me to do what I will
16 with mine own? Is thine eye evil, because I am good? So the last shall be first, and the first last.ᵇ⁶

¹ *omit* And   ² eleventh hour   ³ standing idle
⁴ into the vineyard; and whatsoever is right, *that* shall ye receive   ⁵ give them *their* hire
⁶ *add* for many be called, but few chosen.

ᵃ Matt. xx. 16.   ᵇ Matt. xix. 30; Mar. x. 31.

§ 107. On the Journey, our Lord again foretells His Death and Resurrection.
[Cf. §§ 70, 73.]

St. Matt. xx. 17–19.	St. Mark x. 32–34.	St. Luke xviii. 31–34.
17 And Jesus going up to Jerusalem took the twelve apart and[1] in the way, said 18 unto them, Behold! we go up to Jerusalem; and the Son of Man shall be betrayed unto the chief priests and unto the scribes, and they shall condemn 19 him to death, and shall deliver him to the Gentiles to mock, and to scourge, and to crucify *him*: and the third day he shall rise again.	32 And they were in the way going up to Jerusalem; and Jesus went before them: and they were amazed; and as they followed, they were afraid. And he took again the twelve, and began to tell them what things should happen 33 unto him, *saying*, Behold! we go up to Jerusalem; and the Son of Man shall be delivered unto the chief priests, and unto the scribes; and they shall condemn him to death, and shall deliver 34 him to the Gentiles: and they shall mock him, and shall scourge him, and shall spit upon him, and shall kill *him*:[2] and after three days[3] he shall rise again.	31 Then he took *unto him* the twelve, and said unto them, Behold! we go up to Jerusalem, and all things that are written by the prophets concerning the Son of Man shall 32 be accomplished. For he shall be delivered unto the Gentiles, and shall be mocked, and spitefully entreated, 33 and spitted on: and they shall scourge *him*, and put him to death: and the third day he 34 shall rise again. And they understood none of these things: and this saying was hid from them, neither knew they the things which were spoken.

§ 108. The Ambition of the Sons of Zebedee reproved.

St. Matt. xx. 20–28.	St. Mark x. 35–45.
20 Then came to him the mother of Zebedee's children with her sons,	35 And James and John, the sons of Zebedee, come unto him, saying,

[1] the twelve disciples apart in the way and said   [2] him   [3] and the third day

§ 107. How long before this our Lord had left Ephraim does not appear; but it is clear that he was now on his last journey to Jerusalem. He was probably on the other side of the Jordan, as he had not yet (§ 109) reached Jericho.

ST. MATT. XX.	ST. MARK X.

worshipping *him*, and desiring a
21 certain thing of him. And he said
unto her, What wilt thou? She saith
unto him, Grant that these my two
sons may sit, the one on the[1] right
hand, and the other on thy left, in
22 thy kingdom. But Jesus answered
and said, Ye know not what ye ask.
Are ye able to drink of the cup
that I shall drink of?[2] They say
23 unto him, We are able. [4]He saith
unto them, Ye shall drink indeed

of my cup:[6] but to sit on my right
hand, and on the left, this[7] is not
mine to give, but *it shall be given
to them* for whom it is prepared of
my Father.

24 And when the ten heard *it*, they
were moved with indignation against
25 the two brethren. But Jesus called
them *unto him*, and said, Ye know
that the princes of the Gentiles
exercise dominion over them, and
they that are great exercise au-
26 thority upon them.[a] [10]It shall not
be so among you: but whosoever
will be great among you, shall[12] be
27 your minister; and whosoever will
be chief among you, shall be[12] your

Master, we would that thou shouldest
do for us whatsoever we shall desire.
36 And he said unto them, What would
37 ye that I should do for you? They
said unto him, Grant unto us that we
may sit, one on thy right hand, and
the other on thy left hand, in thy
38 glory. But Jesus said unto them,
Ye know not what ye ask: can ye
drink of the cup that I drink of? or[3]
be baptized with the baptism that I
39 am baptized with? And they said unto
him, We can. And Jesus said unto
them, Ye shall[5] drink of the cup that
I drink of; and with the baptism that
I am baptized withal shall ye be
40 baptized: but to sit on my right hand
or[8] on my left hand is not mine to
give; but *it shall be given to them* for
whom it is prepared.

41 And when the ten heard *it*, they
began to be much displeased with
42 James and John. And[9] Jesus called
them *to him*, and saith unto them, Ye
know that they which are accounted
to rule over the Gentiles exercise
lordship over them; and their great
ones exercise authority upon them.[a]
43 But so it is not[11] among you: but
whosoever will be great among you,
44 shall be your minister: and whosoever
of you will be the chiefest, shall be

[1] thy right ..... the left
[2] drink of, and to be baptized with the baptism that I am baptized with?
[3] and be baptized   [4] And he saith   [5] shall indeed drink
[6] my cup, and be baptized with the baptism that I am baptized with   [7] and on my left, is not
[8] and on   [9] But   [10] But it shall not
[11] so shall it not be among   [12] twice let him be

[a] Comp. Lk. xxii. 25, 26.

§ 108. The very similar narrative in Lk. xxii. 25, 26, is not to be confounded with this. That occurred at the last Supper, and it does not appear that James and John were then in any way prominent. In this case, these two (St. Mark) prefer their ambitious request through their mother (St. Matthew), who certainly was not present at the last Supper.

ST. MATT. XX.	ST. MARK X.
28 servant: even as the Son of Man came not to be ministered unto, but to minister, and to give his life a ransom for many.	45 servant of all. For even the Son of Man came not to be ministered unto, but to minister, and to give his life a ransom for many.

§ 109. Two Blind Men healed near Jericho.

ST. MATT. XX. 29–34.	ST. MARK X. 46–52.	ST. LUKE XVIII. 35–43.
29 And as they departed from Jericho, a great multitude followed 30 him. And, behold, two blind men sitting by the way side, when they heard that Jesus passed by, cried out, saying, Have mercy on us[2] son of David. 31 And the multitude rebuked them, because	46 And they came to Jericho: and as he went out of Jericho with his disciples and a great number of people, the son of Timæus, Bartimæus,[1] a blind beggar, sat by the highway side. 47 And when he heard that it was Jesus of Nazareth, he began to cry out, and say, Jesus, *thou* son of	35 And it came to pass, that as he was come nigh unto Jericho, a certain blind man sat by the way side begging: and hearing the 36 multitude pass by, he asked what it meant. 37 And they told him, that Jesus of Nazareth 38 passeth by. And he cried, saying, Jesus,

[1] blind Bartimæus, the son of Timæus, sat by the highway side begging.
[2] Have mercy on us, O Lord, *thou* son of David.

---

§ 109. St. Matthew speaks of *two* blind men, St. Mark and St. Luke mention only one of them, Bartimæus, who may have been, either previously or subsequently, better known.

A more important difference is, that St. Matthew and St. Mark describe the miracle as having been performed *after our Lord's departure* from Jericho, while St. Luke says that it was *during his approach* to the city. The attempt of Grotius, and others, to explain the latter expression merely of our Lord's *being near* the city, cannot be considered as sustained by satisfactory examples of such usage. The true solution of the difficulty seems to lie in the fact that our Lord probably spent some days in Jericho or its vicinity; and while there, would naturally have made excursions into the country. Very possibly he spent his nights at some house in the country, and came into the city during the day, as was his custom at Jerusalem, and as is still often done by travellers in the East. A miracle performed when he had thus gone into the country and was nearing the city on his return, might naturally be described by one Evangelist as taking place when he had gone out of the city, and by another with more particularity, as being performed on his approach to the city.

The only objection to this solution — that St. Luke speaks as if he were now first coming near the city on his journey — quite disappears when we remember that he gives no account of the journey at all, and does not so much as mention the sojourn at Ephraim, whence it was undertaken. He merely describes the circumstances under which the miracle was performed.

From the course of the narrative this miracle may have marked our Lord's last return to Jericho; for St. Luke goes on immediately to say that "entering, he passed through Jericho," and then, without pause, he gives the account of the visit to Zacchæus (whose residence must have been in the country), and then the parable of the talents, spoken (Lk. xix. 11) "because of his being near Jerusalem."

ST. MATT. XX.	ST. MARK X.	ST. LUKE XVIII.
they should hold their	David, have mercy on	*thou* son of David, have mercy on me.
	48 me. And many charged him that he should hold	39 And they which went before rebuked him, that he should hold his
peace: but they cried the more, saying, O Lord, Have mercy on us,[1] *thou* son of David. 32 And Jesus stood still, and called them,	his peace: but he cried the more a great deal, *Thou* son of David, have 49 mercy on me. And Jesus stood still, and said, Call him.[2] And they call the blind man, saying unto him, Be of good comfort, rise; he calleth thee. 50 And he, casting away his garment, sprang up,[3] and 51 came to Jesus. And Jesus answered and said unto	peace: but he cried so much the more, *Thou* son of David, have mercy on me. 40 And Jesus stood, and commanded him to be brought unto him: and when he was come near, he asked him,
and said, What will ye that I shall do unto 33 you? They say unto him, Lord, that our 34 eyes may open.[4] So Jesus had compassion on *them*, and touched their eyes: and immediately they[5] received sight, and they followed him.	him, What wilt thou that I should do unto thee? The blind man said unto him, Lord, that I might receive my sight. 52 And Jesus said unto him, Go thy way; thy faith hath made thee whole. And immediately he received his sight, and followed him[6] in the way.	41 saying, What wilt thou that I shall do unto thee? And he said, Lord, that I may re- 42 ceive my sight. And Jesus said unto him, Receive thy sight: thy faith hath saved thee. 43 And immediately he received his sight, and followed him, glorifying God: and all the people, when they saw *it*, gave praise unto God.

§ 110. The Visit to Zacchæus.
St. Luke xix. 1–10.

½ And *Jesus* entered and passed through Jericho. And, behold, *there was a* man named Zacchæus, which was the chief among the publicans, and he was

---

[1] Have mercy on us, O Lord,
[2] stood still, and commanded him to be called.
[3] rose, and came
[4] our eyes may be opened.
[5] their eyes received sight
[6] followed Jesus in the way.

ST. LUKE XIX.

3 rich. And he sought to see Jesus who he was; and could not for the press,
4 because he was little of stature. And he ran before, and climbed up into a
5 sycamore tree to see him: for he was to pass that *way*. And when Jesus came to the place, he looked up, and¹ said unto him, Zacchæus, make haste,
6 and come down; for to day I must abide at thy house. And he made haste,
7 and came down, and received him joyfully. And when they saw *it*, they all murmured, saying, That he was gone to be guest with a man that is a sinner.
8 And Zacchæus stood, and said unto the Lord; Behold! Lord, the half of my goods I give to the poor; and if I have taken any thing from any man by
9 false accusation, I restore *him* fourfold.ᵃ And Jesus said unto him, This day is salvation come to this house, forsomuch as he also *is*² a son of Abraham.
10 For the Son of man is come to seek and to save that which was lost.

§ 111. The Parable of the Ten Minæ. — *Near Jerusalem.*

ST. MATT. XXV. 14–30.	ST. LUKE XIX. 11–28.
	11 And as they heard these things, he added and spake a parable, because he was nigh to Jerusalem, and because they thought that the kingdom of God should immediately appear. He said therefore,
14 For *the kingdom of heaven is* as a man travelling into a far country,ᵇ *who* called his own servants, and delivered unto them his goods. And unto one he gave five talents, to another two, and to another one; to every man according to his several ability; and³ took his journey.	12 A certain nobleman went into a far countryᵇ to receive for himself 13 a kingdom, and to return. And he called his ten servants, and delivered them ten pounds, and said 14 unto them, Occupy till I come. But his citizens hated him, and sent a message after him, saying, We will not have this *man* to reign over us.

¹ looked up, and saw him, and said   ² is   ³ and straightway took his journey. Then he
ᵃ Ex. xxii. 1; cf. 2 Sam. xii. 6.   ᵇ Cf. Mar. xiii. 34.

§ 111. The question, whether this parable as given by the two Evangelists is the same, must be decided in the affirmative in view of its main scope and purport. There are considerable differences in the narration of it; but these arise from the greater fulness of detail in St. Matthew, and the greater prominence given to its main teaching in St. Luke. The evident design in both is to correct the expectation of the immediate manifestation of "the kingdom of God" (Lk. xix. 11), and to teach that the way to the attainment of its rewards is through long and patient labor in the service of its Lord. This design is more distinctly brought out by St. Luke, and the part of the parable describing the fate of those who would not accept their King, is given by him alone.

St. Matthew, according to his general plan, has placed this parable in a group with others of a somewhat similar character, so that its special design is not so readily observed. On attentive consideration, however, it appears quite plainly enough to show the identity of the two.

ST. MATT. XXV.	ST. LUKE XIX.
16 Straightway he that had received the five talents went and traded with the same, and made *them* other five talents. 17 [1]Likewise he that *had received* two, 18 [2]gained other two. But he that had received one went and digged[3] the 19 earth, and hid his lord's money. After a long time the lord of those servants cometh, and reckoneth with them.	15 And it came to pass, that when he was returned, having received the kingdom, then he commanded these servants to be called unto him, to whom he had given the money, that he might know how much every 16 man had gained by trading. Then came the first, saying, Lord, thy pound hath gained ten pounds.
20 And so he that had received five talents came and brought other five talents, saying, Lord, thou deliveredst unto me five talents: behold! I have 21 gained[4] five talents more. His lord said unto him, Well done, *thou* good and faithful servant: thou hast been faithful over a few things, I will make thee ruler over many things: enter 22 thou into the joy of thy lord. He[5] that had received two talents came and said, Lord, thou deliveredst unto me two talents: behold! I have gained 23 two other talents.[6] His lord said unto him, Well done, good and faithful servant; thou hast been faithful over a few things, I will make thee ruler over many things: enter thou into 24 the joy of thy lord. Then he which had received the one talent came and said, Lord, I knew thee that thou art an hard man, reaping where thou hast not sown, and gathering where thou 25 hast not strawed: and I was afraid, and went and hid thy talent in the earth: lo, *there* thou hast *that is* thine. 26 His lord answered and said unto him,	17 And he said unto him, Well, thou good servant: because thou hast been faithful in a very little, have thou authority over ten cities. 18 And the second came, saying, Lord, thy pound hath gained five pounds. 19 And he said likewise to him, Be 20 thou also over five cities. And another came, saying, Lord, behold *here is* thy pound, which I have 21 kept laid up in a napkin: for I feared thee, because thou art an austere man: thou takest up that thou layedst not down, and reapest 22 that thou didst not sow. [7]He saith unto him, Out of thine own mouth

[1] And likewise [2] he also gained [3] in the earth [4] gained beside them five
[5] He also that had received [6] other talents beside them [7] And he saith

ST. MATT. XXV.	ST. LUKE. XIX.
Thou wicked and slothful servant, thou knewest that I reap where I sowed not, and gather where I have not ²⁷ strawed? thou oughtest therefore to have put my money to the exchangers, and *then* at my coming I should have ²⁸ received mine own with usury. Take therefore the talent from him, and give *it* unto him which hath ten talents. ²⁹ For unto every one that hath shall be given, and he shall have abundance: but from him that hath not shall be taken away even that which he hath.[a] ³⁰ And cast ye the unprofitable servant into outer darkness: there shall be weeping and gnashing of teeth.	will I judge thee, *thou* wicked servant. Thou knewest that I was an austere man, taking up that I laid not down, and reaping that I ²³ did not sow? wherefore then gavest not thou my money into the bank, that at my coming I might have required mine own with usury? ²⁴ And he said unto them that stood by, Take from him the pound, and give *it* to him that hath ten pounds. ²⁵ (And they said unto him, Lord, he ²⁶ hath ten pounds.) [1]I say unto you, That unto every one which hath shall be given; and from him that hath not, even that he hath shall be taken away.[a][2] ²⁷ But those mine enemies, which would not that I should reign over them, bring hither, and slay them[3] before me. ²⁸ And when he had thus spoken, he went before, ascending up to Jerusalem.

§ 112. Our Lord arrives at Bethany six days before the Passover, and is there entertained in the House of Simon the Leper.

ST. MATT. XXVI. 6–13.   ST. MARK XIV. 3–9.   ST. JOHN XI. 55–XII. 11.

⁵⁵ And the Jews' passover was nigh at hand: and many went out of

---

[1] For I say   [2] taken away from him   [3] them
[a] Matt. xiii. 12; Mar. iv. 25; Lk. viii. 18.

---

§ 112. St. John had apparently some reason for especially noting the time (xii. 1) of the feast at Bethany; while St. Matthew and St. Mark merely say that it was during our Lord's stay in Bethany. The two latter omit the account of it at the time of its occurrence; but afterwards, in order to explain why the Jews proceeded against Jesus at the feast, contrary to their intention, they go back to mention the circumstances under which Judas determined

ST. MATT. XXVI.	ST. MARK XIV.	ST. JOHN XI.
		the country up to Jerusalem before the passover, to purify themselves. ⁵⁶ Then sought they for Jesus, and spake among themselves, as they stood in the temple, What think ye, that he will not come ⁵⁷ to the feast? Now¹ the chief priests and the Pharisees had given commandments,² that, if any man knew where he were, he should shew *it*, that they might take him.

¹ Now both the chief   ² a commandment

upon his treachery. The account of this feast therefore, stands in the same relation to the general course of the narrative in their Gospels as their account of the apprehension of the Baptist (Matt. xiv. 3–5; Mar. vi. 17–20), and is not properly to be considered as a violation of chronological order. It is so plain that St. John has carefully noted the exact order of events, and also that the passage in Matt. xxvi. 6–13 and Mar. xiv. 3–9 is of the nature of an episode (vs. 10 in St. Mark being immediately connected with vs. 2, and vs. 14 in St. Matthew in the same way with vs. 5), that it is unnecessary to give further reasons for the arrangement adopted. The only argument of weight for a different arrangement, by which this narrative is transferred to the evening of the fourth day of the week, is drawn from the fact that on this day the question of putting Jesus to death was formally discussed (Matt. xxvi. 3, 4; Mar. xiv. 1, 2). It was after this that Judas approached the chief priests with his proposal, and this was plainly after the feast. So far there is no difficulty; for Judas may well have waited a couple of days before finding a convenient opportunity to close his guilty bargain. But it is urged that the *then* ..... *went* of Matt. xxvi. 14, implies that he went immediately. The difficulty arises only from leaving out of view the parenthetical character of vs. 6–13. The true reference of *then* is not to vs. 13, but to vs. 5.

The anointing by the woman at this feast is not to be confounded with that which occurred at an earlier period in the house of another Simon, see Lk. vii. 36–50, § 48 and notes. Nor, on the other hand, can this anointing, as narrated by St. John, be considered different from that narrated in the parallel passages by St. Matthew and St. Mark. Robinson well says "The identity of circumstances is too great, and the alleged differences too few, to leave a doubt on this point."

It is noticeable that the two first Evangelists, neither here nor elsewhere, mention either Lazarus or his sisters.

The expression in Jno. xii. 1, "*six days before the Passover*," is of great importance to the chronology of this eventful week. The Paschal lamb, according to the law, was to be killed on the fourteenth Nisan (which fell this year on Thursday), and to be eaten the same evening, i.e. according to the Jewish reckoning of the day as beginning at sunset, on the fifteenth Nisan. Now counting back six days, including both days in the six, after the Jewish custom, we are brought to the tenth, or Saturday, the Sabbath, as the day on which the feast occurred, and this accords with the ancient tradition on the subject.

OUR LORD'S FINAL ARRIVAL AT BETHANY.

ST. MATT. XXVI.	ST. MARK XIV.	ST. JOHN XII.
6 Now when Jesus was in Bethany, in the house of Simon the leper, there came unto him a woman[a] having an alabaster box of very precious ointment, and poured it on his head, as he sat 8 at meat. But when the[2] disciples saw it, they had indignation, saying, To what purpose is this waste? 9 For this[5] might have been sold for much, and given to the poor. 10 When Jesus understood it, he said unto them, Why trouble ye the woman? for she hath wrought a good	3 And being in Bethany in the house of Simon the leper, as he sat at meat, there came a woman[a] having an alabaster box of ointment of spikenard very precious: she brake the box, and poured it on his head. 4 And there were some that had indignation within themselves:[4] Why was this waste of the ointment made? 5 For this ointment[6] might have been sold for more than three hundred pence, and have been given to the poor. And they murmured against her. 6 And Jesus said, Let her alone; why trouble ye her? she hath wrought a good work	1 Then Jesus, six days before the passover, came to Bethany, where Lazarus was[1] whom Jesus raised from the dead. 2 There they made him a supper; and Martha served: but Lazarus was one of them that sat at 3 the table with him. Then took Mary[a] a pound of ointment of spikenard, very costly, and anointed the feet of Jesus, and wiped his feet with her hair: and the house was filled with the odor of 4 the ointment. But one of his disciples, Judas Iscariot,[3] which should 5 betray him, saith 'Why was not this ointment sold for three hundred pence, and given to the 6 poor? This he said, not that he cared for the poor; but because he was a thief, and having the bag,[7] bare what was 7 put therein. Then said Jesus, Let her alone, that

[1] Lazarus was which had been dead whom he raised   [2] his disciples
[3] Then saith one of his disciples, Judas Iscariot, Simon's *son*, which should betray him,
[4] within themselves, and said, Why
[5] this ointment might   [6] For it might   [7] and had the bag, and bare
[a] Comp. Lk. vii. 36–50.

ST. MATT. XXVI.	ST. MARK XIV.	ST. JOHN XII.
11 work upon me. For ye have the poor always with you; but me ye have not always.	7 on me. For ye have the poor with you always, and whensoever ye will ye may do¹ good: but me ye	
12 For in that she hath poured this ointment on my body, she did *it* 13 for my burial. Verily I say unto you, Wheresoever this gospel shall be preached in the whole world, *there* shall also this, that this woman hath done, be told for a memorial of her.	8 have not always. She hath done what she could; she is come aforehand to anoint my body to the burying. 9 But³ verily I say unto you, Wheresoever the⁴ gospel shall be preached throughout the whole world, *this* also that she hath done shall be spoken of for a memorial of her.	against the day of my burying she may keep² 8 this. For the poor always ye have with you; but me ye have not always. 9 Much people of the Jews therefore knew that he was there: and they came not for Jesus' sake only, but that they might see Lazarus also, whom he had raised from the dead. 10 But the chief priests consulted that they might put Lazarus also to 11 death; because that by reason of him many of the Jews went away, and believed on Jesus.

¹ may do them good
³ *omit* But

² alone: against the day of my burying hath she kept this.
⁴ this gospel

SCHEDULE

OF THE

EVENTS OF EACH DAY OF THE HOLY WEEK,

FOR PARTS VII. AND VIII..

[N. B. — Each day, according to Jewish usage, is reckoned from sunset to sunset; for greater clearness the days according to our reckoning are given in brackets when there is a difference.]

Days of Nisan.	Day of the Week.		
9	7	SATURDAY	The Sabbath. Our Lord, having arrived from Jericho before the Sabbath began, remains at Bethany, and is there anointed in the house of Simon, § 112.
10	1	SUNDAY	The triumphal entry into Jerusalem, § 113.
11	2	MONDAY	In the evening [Sunday] our Lord returns to Bethany, Mar. xi. 11. In the morning [Monday] the fig-tree is cursed; afterwards the Temple is cleansed, § 114.
12	3	TUESDAY	Having returned in the evening [Monday] to Bethany (Matt. xxi. 17; Mar. xi. 19), in the morning [Tuesday] the fig-tree is found withered, § 115; our Lord teaches in the Temple. §§ 116-123; and is visited by certain Greeks, § 124.
13	4	WEDNESDAY	In the evening [Tuesday] our Lord finally leaves the Temple, and on the Mount of Olives, on his way to Bethany, foretells the future, §§ 126-128; [Wednesday] the rulers conspire against him, and make agreement with Judas.
14	5	THURSDAY	"Preparation." Remaining at Bethany, our Lord sends his disciples to make ready the Passover, § 130.
15	6	FRIDAY	In the evening [Thursday] He comes with the disciples and sits down to eat the Passover; He reproves their ambition, § 131; washes their feet, § 132; points out the traitor, § 133; institutes the Lord's Supper, § 134; foretells the desertion of the Twelve and the denials of Peter, § 135; discourses at length with the disciples. § 136; offers his sacerdotal prayer, § 137; goes with the disciples to the Mount of Olives, § 138; endures the agony in the garden, § 139; [Friday] is made prisoner, § 140; taken before Annas and Caiaphas, § 141; examined, denied by Peter, § 142; further examined, condemned, mocked by the servants, and led to Pilate, §§ 143, 144; Judas hangs himself, § 145; Jesus is examined by Pilate, who seeks to release him, § 146; sent to Herod, and back to Pilate, who again seeks to release him, § 147; after further efforts for his release, He is scourged, and delivered to be crucified, § 148; is mocked by the soldiers, § 149; Pilate makes a further, final, effort for his release, § 150; then he is led forth and crucified, §§ 151-157; towards evening, his body is taken from the cross, and laid in the tomb, § 158.
16	7	SATURDAY	A watch is set at the sepulchre, § 159.
17	1	SUNDAY	The Resurrection, §§ 160, etc.

PART VII.

OUR LORD'S TRIUMPHAL ENTRY INTO JERUSALEM, AND THE EVENTS UNTIL THE LAST PASSOVER.

FIRST DAY OF THE WEEK.—SUNDAY.

§ 113. Our Lord's Triumphal Entry into Jerusalem.

MATT. XXI. 1–11. MAR. XI. 1–11. LK. XIX. 29–44. JNO. XII. 12–19.

MATT. XXI. 1–11.	MAR. XI. 1–11.	LK. XIX. 29–44.	JNO. XII. 12–19.
			12 On the next day much people that were come to the feast, when they heard that Jesus was coming to 13 Jerusalem, took branches of palm trees, and went forth to meet him,
1 And when they drew nigh unto Jerusalem, and were come to Bethphage, unto the mount of Olives, then sent Jesus two disci- 2 ples, saying unto	1 And when they came nigh to Jerusalem,[1] and unto Bethany, at the mount of Olives, he sendeth forth two of 2 his disciples, and saith unto them,	29 And it came to pass, when he was come nigh to Bethphage and Bethany, at the mount called *the mount* of Olives, he sent two of the[2] disciples,	

[1] to Jerusalem, unto Bethphage and Bethany   [2] his disciples

§ 113. The feast at Bethany having been on the Sabbath (see note § 112), the "next day" of Jno. xii. 12 must be the first day of the week, Sunday.

The topography explains this narrative. The road from Bethany to Jerusalem, as it passed along the side of the Mount of Olives, encountered a deep valley, and made a long detour around the head of the valley to avoid the ascent and descent. A short foot-path however, led directly across the valley, and it was probably from the point where this parted from the road that the disciples were sent for the ass to the village on the opposite side where the path again met the road,—"a place where two ways met"—a site still marked by ruins. The owner could here see the whole procession winding round the valley, and he must have already known from the multitudes going out from Jerusalem to meet Jesus (Jno. xii. 13) what it meant. He was therefore ready to acquiesce in the arrangement; and the disciples, taking the ass, went down the road to meet our Lord.

[PART VII. § 113.] OUR LORD'S TRIUMPHAL ENTRY INTO JERUSALEM.

ST. MATT. XXI.	ST. MARK XI.	ST. LUKE XIX.	ST. JOHN XII.
them, Go into the village over against you, and straightway ye shall find an ass tied, and a colt with her: loose *them*, and bring *them* unto me. 3 And if any *man* say ought unto you, ye shall say, The Lord hath need of them; and straightway he will send them.— 6 And the disciples went, and did as Jesus commanded them. 7 And brought the ass, and the colt, and put on them the clothes,⁷ and	Go your way into the village over against you: and as soon as ye be entered into it, ye shall find a colt tied, whereon never man yet¹ sat; loose him, and 3 bring *him*. And if any man say unto you, Why do ye this? say ye that the Lord hath need of him: and straightway he sendeth him again³ hither. 4 And they went their way, and found the colt tied by the door without in a place where two ways met; and they 5 loose him. And certain of them that stood there said unto them, What do ye, loos- 6 ing the colt? And they said unto them even as Jesus had said:⁵ and they let them 7 go. And they bring⁶ the colt to Jesus, and cast their garments	30 saying, Go ye into the village over against *you;* in the which at your entering ye shall find a colt tied, whereon yet never man sat: loose him, and bring *him hither.* 31 And if any man ask you, Why do ye loose *him?* thus shall ye say,² Because the Lord hath need of him. 32 And they that were sent went their way, and found even as he had said unto 33 them. And as they were loosing the colt, the owners thereof said unto them, Why loose ye the 34 colt? And they said, that⁴ The Lord hath need 35 of him. And they brought him to Jesus: and they cast their garments upon the colt, and they set Jesus thereon.	14 — And Jesus, when he had found a young ass, sat thereon; as it is

¹ omit yet ² say unto him ³ he will send him hither
⁴ omit that ⁵ Jesus had commanded ⁶ they brought ⁷ their clothes

ST. MATT. XXI.	ST. MARK XI.	ST. LUKE XIX.	ST. JOHN XII.
they set *him* thereon. And¹ this was done, that it might be fulfilled which was spoken by the prophet, saying, Tell ye the daughter of Sion, Behold! thy King cometh unto thee, meek, and sitting upon an ass, and upon² a colt the foal of an ass.ᵃ	on him; and he sat upon him.		15 written, Fear not, daughter of Sion: behold! thy King cometh, sitting on an ass's colt.—
8 And a very great multitude spread their garments in the way; others cut down branches from the trees, and strawed *them* in the way. And the multitudes that went before him,⁴ and that followed, cried, saying, Hosanna to the son of David: Blessed *is* he that cometh in the name of the Lord;ᵇ Ho-	8 And many spread their garments in the way: and others branches, cutting *them* out of the fields.³ 9 And they that went before, and they that followed, cried,⁵ Hosanna; Blessed *is* he that cometh 10 in the name of the Lord:ᵇ Blessed *be* the kingdom of our father David, that com-	36 And as he went, they spread their clothes in the way. And when he was come 37 nigh, even now at the descent of the mount of Olives, the whole multitude of the disciples began to rejoice and praise God with a loud voice for all the mighty works that they had 38 seen; saying, Blessed *be* the King⁶ in the name of the Lord;ᵇ peace in	13 —and cried, Hosanna: Blessed *is* he⁷ that cometh in the name of the Lord,ᵇ and the King of Israel.—

¹ All this was
² others cut down branches off the trees, and strawed *them* in the way.
⁵ cried, saying,
⁷ Blessed *is* the King of Israel that cometh in the name of the Lord.
ᵃ Zech. ix. 9. Behold, thy King cometh unto thee: he is just, and having salvation; lowly, and riding upon an ass, and upon a colt the foal of an ass. Comp. Isa. lxii. 11.
ᵇ Ps. cxviii. 26.
³ omit second upon
⁴ omit him
⁶ the King that cometh in the name

ST. MATT. XXI.	ST. MARK XI.	ST. LUKE XIX.	ST. JOHN XII.
sanna in the highest.	eth,[1] Hosanna in the highest.	heaven, and glory in the highest.	
			16 These things understood not his disciples at the first: but when Jesus was glorified, then remembered they that these things were written of him, and *that* they had done these things 17 unto him. The people therefore that was with him when he called Lazarus out of his grave, and raised him from the dead, bare 18 record. For this cause the people also met him, for that they heard that he had done 19 this miracle. The Pharisees therefore said among themselves, Perceive ye how ye prevail nothing? behold! the world is gone after him
		39 And some of the Pharisees from among the multitude said unto him, Master, rebuke thy disciples. 40 And he answered and said,[2]	

---

[1] that cometh in the name of the Lord.

[2] said unto them

ST. MATT. XXI.	ST. MARK XI.	ST. LUKE XIX.	ST. JOHN XII.
		I tell you that, if these¹ hold their peace, the stones will² immediately cry out.	
		41 And when he was come near, he beheld the city, and wept 42 over it, saying, If thou hadst known, even thou, at least in this thy day, the things *which belong* unto thy peace! but now they are hid from 43 thine eyes. For the days shall come upon thee, that thine enemies shall cast a trench about thee,ᵃ and compass thee round, and keep thee in on every side, 44 And shall lay thee even with the ground, and thy children within thee; and they shall not leave in thee one stone upon another; because thou knewest not the time of thy visitation.	
10 And when he was come into	11 And he³ entered into Jerusalem,⁴		

¹ should hold   ² stones would immediately   ³ Jesus entered   ⁴ and into the temple

ᵃ Comp. Lk. xxi. 20, etc.; Matt. xxiv. 2, etc.; Mar. xiii. 2, etc.

St. Matt. XXI.	St. Mark. XI	St. Luke. XIX.	St. John XII.
Jerusalem, all the city was moved, saying, Who is ¹¹ this? And the multitude said, This is Jesus the prophet of Nazareth of Galilee.	into the temple: and when he had looked round about upon all things, and now the eventide was come, he went out unto Bethany with the twelve.		

SECOND DAY OF THE WEEK.—MONDAY.

§ 114. The Fig-tree cursed. The Temple cleansed.

St. Matt. XXI. 12–19.	St. Mark XI. 12–19.	St. Luke XIX. 45–48, XXI. 37, 38.
18 Now in the morning as he returned into the city, he hungered. 19 And when he saw a fig tree in the way, he came to it, and found nothing thereon, but leaves only, and said unto it, Let no fruit grow on thee henceforward for ever. And presently the fig tree withered away.	12 And on the morrow, when they were come from Bethany, he was 13 hungry: and seeing a fig tree from[1] afar off having leaves, he came, if haply he might find any thing thereon: and when he came to it, he found nothing but leaves; for the time of figs was 14 not *yet*. And he[2] answered and said unto it, No man eat fruit of thee hereafter for ever. And his disciples heard *it*.	

[1] *omit* from [2] Jesus answered

§ 114. St. Matthew mentions the cursing of the fig-tree retrospectively, in connection with the surprise of the disciples at its withering. It is plain from St. Mark that the day in the temple and the night at Bethany intervened between the two. Although the tree withered immediately, as mentioned by St. Matthew, this could not have been noticed by the disciples until they again passed that way.

St. Luke xxi. 37, 38, is inserted here because it is a general statement, covering several days, and, as it stands in his Gospel, is chiefly retrospective.

ST. MATT. XXI.	ST. MARK XI.	ST. LUKE XIX.
12 And Jesus went into the temple of God, and cast out all them that sold and bought in the temple, and overthrew the tables of the money-changers, and the seats of them that 13 sold doves, and said unto them, It is written, My house shall be called the house of prayer;^a but ye make⁵ it a den of thieves.^b 14 And the blind and the lame came to him in the temple; and he⁷ 15 healed them. And when the chief priests and scribes saw the wonderful things that he did, and the children crying in the temple, and saying, Hosanna to the son of David; they were sore dis-16 pleased, and said unto him, Hearest thou what these say? And Jesus saith unto them, Yea; have ye never read, Out of the mouth of babes and sucklings thou hast perfected praise?^c	15 And they come to Jerusalem: and he¹ went into the temple, and began to cast out them that sold and bought in the temple, and overthrew the tables of the money-changers, and the seats of them that sold doves; 16 and would not suffer that any man should carry *any* vessel through the 17 temple. And he taught, and said³ unto them, Is it not written, My house shall be called of all nations the house of prayer?^a but ye have made it a den of thieves.^b 18 And the scribes and chief priests heard *it*, and sought how they might destroy him: for they feared him, because all the people were⁶ astonished at his doctrine.	45 And he went into the temple, and began to cast out them that sold.² 46 Saying unto them, It is written, My house shall be a⁴ house of prayer:^a but ye have made it a den of thieves.^b 47 And he taught daily in the temple. But the chief priests and the scribes and the chief of the people sought to destroy him: 48 and could not find what they might do: for all the people were very attentive to hear him.

¹ Jesus went
³ taught, saying,
⁵ ye have made it
^a Isa. lvi. 7.

² that sold therein, and them that bought
⁴ My house is the house
⁶ the people was
^b Jer. vii. 11.

^c Ps. viii. 2.

ST. MATT. XXI.	ST. MARK XI.	ST. LUKE XXI.
17 And he left them, and went out of the city into Bethany; and he lodged there.	19 And when even was come, he went out of the city.	37 And in the day time he was teaching in the temple; and at night he went out, and abode in the mount that is called *the mount* of 38 Olives. And all the people came early in the morning to him in the temple, for to hear him.

THIRD DAY OF THE WEEK.—TUESDAY.

§ 115. The Fig-tree found withered away.

ST. MATT. XXI. 20–22.	ST. MARK XI. 20–25.
20 And when the disciples saw *it*, they marvelled, saying, How soon 21 is the fig tree withered away! Jesus answered and said unto them, Verily I say unto you, If ye have faith, and doubt not, ye shall not only do this *which is done* to the fig tree, but also if ye shall say unto this mountain, Be thou removed, and be thou cast into the sea; it shall be done. 22 And all things, whatsoever ye shall ask in prayer, believing, ye shall receive.	20 And in the morning, as they passed by, they saw the fig tree dried up 21 from the roots. And Peter calling to remembrance saith unto him, Master, behold the fig tree which thou cursedst 22 is withered away. And Jesus answering saith unto them, Have faith 23 in God. [1]Verily I say unto you, That whosoever shall say unto this mountain, Be thou removed, and be thou cast into the sea; and shall not doubt in his heart, but shall believe that what[2] he saith shall come to pass; he shall have it.[3] Therefore I say unto 24 you, What things soever ye pray for, and desire,[4] believe that ye received[5] *them*, and ye shall have *them*. And 25 when ye stand praying, forgive, if ye have ought against any: that your Father also which is in heaven may forgive you your trespasses.[a][6]

[1] For verily   [2] that those things which he saith   [3] shall have whatsoever he saith.
[4] soever ye desire, when ye pray believe   [5] receive
[6] ver. 26. But if ye do not forgive, neither will your Father which is in heaven forgive your trespasses.

[a] Comp. Matt. vi. 14, 15; xviii. 35, etc.

§ 116. The Authority of Christ questioned.

St. Matt. xxi. 23–27.	St. Mark xi. 27–33.	St. Luke xx. 1–8.
23 And when he was come into the temple, the chief priests and the elders of the people came unto him as he was teaching, and said, By what authority doest thou these things? and who gave thee 24 this authority? And Jesus answered and said unto them, I also will ask you one thing, which if ye tell me, I in like wise will tell you by what authority I do these things: 25 the baptism of John, whence was it? from heaven, or of men? And they reasoned with themselves, saying, If we shall say, From heaven; he will say unto us, Why did ye not then believe 26 him? But if we shall say, Of men; we fear the people: for all hold John as a prophet.ᵃ 27 And they answered Jesus, and said, We cannot tell. And he said unto them, Nei-	27 And they come again to Jerusalem: and as he was walking in the temple, there come to him the chief priests, and the scribes, and 28 the elders, and said³ unto him, By what authority doest thou these things? and who gave thee this authority to do these things? 29 And Jesus⁴ said unto them, I will⁵ ask of you one question, and answer me, and I will tell you by what authority I do these 30 things: the baptism of John, was *it* from heaven, or of men? 31 answer me. And they reasoned with themselves, saying, If we shall say, From heaven; he will say, Why then did ye not believe 32 him? But if we shall say, Of men; they feared the people: for all *men* counted John, that he was a prophet 33 indeed.ᵃ And they answer⁸ and say unto Jesus, We cannot tell. And Jesus⁹ saith unto	1 And it came to pass, *that* on one of the¹ days, as he taught the people in the temple, and preached the gospel, the² priests and the scribes came upon *him* with the 2 elders, and spake unto him, saying, Tell us, by what authority doest thou these things? or who is he that gave thee 3 this authority? And he answered and said unto them, I will also ask you aᵍ thing; and answer 4 me: the baptism of John, was it from heaven, 5 or of men? And they reasoned with themselves, saying, If we shall say, From heaven; he will say, Why⁷ believed 6 ye him not? But and if we say, Of men; all the people will stone us: for they be persuaded that John was a prophet.ᵃ 7 And they answered, that they could not tell 8 whence *it was*. And Jesus said unto them,

¹ those days ² the chief priests ³ say
⁵ I will also ask   ⁶ one thing
⁸ *translated* they answered and said
ᵃ Matt. iii. 5, 6; xiv. 5, etc.
⁴ answered and said
⁷ Why then believed
⁹ answering saith

ST. MATT. XXI.	ST. MARK XI.	ST. LUKE XX.
ther tell I you by what authority I do these things.	them, Neither do I tell you by what authority I do these things.	Neither tell I you by what authority I do these things.

§ 117. The Parable of The two Sons.
ST. MATT. XXI. 28–32.

28 But what think ye? A *certain* man had two sons; ¹he came to the first,
29 and said, Son, go work to day in the² vineyard. He answered and said, I
30 will not: ³afterward he repented, and went. ¹He came to the other,⁴ and said
31 likewise. And he answered and said, I *go*, sir: and went not. ¹Whether of them twain did the will of *his* father? They say,⁵ The first. Jesus saith unto them, Verily I say unto you, That the publicans and the harlots go into
32 the kingdom of God before you. For John came unto you in the way of righteousness, and ye believed him not: but the publicans and the harlots believed him: and ye, when ye had seen *it*, repented not afterward, that ye might believe him.

§ 118. The Parable of The wicked Husbandmen.

ST. MATT. XXI. 33–46.	ST. MARK XII. 1–12.	ST. LUKE XX. 9–19.
33 Hear another parable: ªThere was a⁶ householder, which planted a vineyard, and hedged it round about, and digged a winepress in it, and built a tower, and let it out to husbandmen, and went into a far 34 country. And when the time of the fruit drew near, he sent his servants to the husbandmen, that they might receive the fruits 35 of it. And the husbandmen took his servants, and beat one,	1 And he began to speak unto them by parables. ªA *certain* man planted a vineyard, and set an hedge about *it*, and digged *a place for* the winefat, and built a tower, and let it out to husbandmen, and went into a 2 far country. And at the season he sent to the husbandmen a servant, that he might receive from the husbandmen of the fruits⁹ 3 of the vineyard. And they caught *him*, and beat him, and sent *him*	9 Then began he to speak to the people this parable; ªA ⁷man planted a vineyard, and let it forth to husbandmen, and went into a far country for a 10 long time. And at the season he sent a servant to the husbandmen, that they should give him of the fruit of the vineyard: but the husbandmen beat him, and sent *him* away

¹ *twice* and he came
⁴ to the second, and said
⁷ a certain man

² my vineyard
⁵ they say unto him
⁹ the fruit of

³ but afterwards
⁶ a certain householder

ª Comp. Ps. lxxx. 8–11; Isa. v. 1, 2, etc.

ST. MATT. XXI.	ST. MARK XII.	ST. LUKE XX.
and killed another, and stoned another. 36 Again, he sent other servants more than the first: and they did unto them likewise.	4 away empty. And again he sent unto them another servant; and they¹ wounded him in the head, and handled *him* shame- 5 fully. And² he sent another; and him they killed, and many others; beating some, and killing some.	11 empty. And again he sent another servant: and they beat him also, and entreated *him* shame- fully, and sent *him* away 12 empty. And again he sent a third: and they wounded him also, and 13 cast *him* out. Then said
37 But last of all he sent unto them his son, saying, They will rev- 38 erence my son. But when the husbandmen saw the son, they said among themselves, This is the heir; come, let us kill him, and let us have⁸ his in- 39 heritance. And they caught him, and cast *him* out of the vine- yard, and slew *him*. 40 When the lord there- fore of the vineyard cometh, what will he do unto those hus- 41 bandmen? They say unto him, He will mis- erably destroy those wicked men, and will let out *his* vineyard unto other husband- men, which shall ren-	6 Having yet therefore one well-beloved son³ he sent him⁴ last unto them, saying, They will reverence my son. 7 But those husbandmen said among themselves, This is the heir; come, let us kill him, and the inheritance shall 8 be our's. And they took him, and killed him,⁹ and cast him⁹ out 9 of the vineyard. What shall¹⁰ the lord of the vineyard do? he will come and destroy the husbandmen, and will give the vineyard unto others.	the lord of the vineyard, What shall I do? I will send my beloved son: it may be they will rever- 14 ence him.⁵ But when the husbandmen saw him, they reasoned with one another,⁶ saying, This is the heir: ⁷let us kill him, that the inheritance may 15 be our's. So they cast him out of the vineyard, and killed *him*. What therefore shall the lord of the vineyard do unto 16 them? He shall come and destroy these hus- bandmen, and shall give the vineyard to others.

¹ and at him they cast stones, and wounded *him* in the head, and sent *him* away shamefully handled.
  ² And again he sent   ³ one Son, his well-beloved, he
  ⁴ him also last   ⁵ will reverence *him* when they see him
  ⁶ reasoned among themselves, saying,   ⁷ come, let us kill
  ⁸ let us seize on his inheritance   ⁹ *twice him*
  ¹⁰ what shall therefore the lord

ST. MATT. XXI.	ST. MARK XII.	ST. LUKE XX.
der him the fruits in their seasons.		
		And when they heard *it*, they said, God forbid.
42 Jesus saith unto them, Did ye never read in the scriptures, The stone which the builders rejected, the same is become the head of the corner: this is the Lord's doing, and it is marvellous in our eyes?	10 And have ye not read this scripture; The stone which the builders rejected is become the head of the corner: 11 This was the Lord's doing, and it is marvellous in our eyes?	17 And he beheld them, and said, What is this then that is written, The stone which the builders rejected, the same is become the head of the corner?
43 Therefore say I unto you, The kingdom of God shall be taken from you, and given to a nation bringing forth the fruits thereof.[1]		
		18 Whosoever shall fall upon that stone shall be broken: but on whomsoever it shall fall, it will grind him to powder.
45 And when the chief priests and Pharisees had heard his parables, they perceived that he 46 spake of them. But when they sought to lay hands on him, they feared the multitude, because they took him for a prophet.	12 And they sought to lay hold on him, but feared the people: for they knew that he had spoken the parable against them: and they left him, and went their way.	19 And the chief priests and the scribes the same hour sought to lay hands on him; and they feared the people: for they perceived that he had spoken this parable against them.

[1] ver. 44. And whosoever shall fall on this stone shall be broken: but on whomsoever it shall fall, it will grind him to powder.

§ 119. The Parable of The Marriage of the King's Son.
St. Matt. xxii. 1–14.

1 And Jesus answered and spake unto them again by parables, and said,
2 The kingdom of heaven is, like unto a certain king, which made a marriage
3 for his son, and sent forth his servants to call them that were bidden to the
4 wedding: and they would not come. Again, he sent forth other servants,
saying, Tell them which are bidden, Behold! I have prepared my dinner:
my oxen and *my* fatlings *are* killed, and all things *are* ready: come unto the
5 marriage. But they made light of *it*, and went their ways, one to his farm,
6 another to his merchandise: and the remnant took his servants, and entreated
7 *them* spitefully, and slew *them*. But the king[1] was wroth: and he sent forth
8 his armies, and destroyed those murderers, and burned up their city. Then
saith he to his servants, The wedding is ready, but they which were bidden
9 were not worthy. Go ye therefore into the highways, and as many as ye
10 shall find, bid to the marriage. So those servants went out into the highways,
and gathered together all as many as they found, both bad and good: and the
11 bridechamber[2] was furnished with guests. And when the king came in to
see the guests, he saw there a man which had not on a wedding garment:
12 and he saith unto him, Friend, how camest thou in hither not having a
13 wedding garment? And he was speechless. Then said the king to the
servants, Bind him hand and foot,[3] and cast him into outer darkness; there
14 shall be weeping and gnashing of teeth. For many are called, but few *are*
chosen.[a]

§ 120. Insidious Questionings (A) of Pharisees, concerning Tribute to Cæsar.

St. Matt. xxii. 15–22.	St. Mark xii. 13–17.	St. Luke xx. 20–26.
15 Then went the Pharisees, and took counsel how they might entangle 16 him in *his* talk. And they sent out unto him their disciples with the Herodians, saying, Master, we know that thou art true, and teachest the way of God in truth, neither carest thou for any *man:* for thou re-	13 And they send unto him certain of the Pharisees and of the Herodians, to catch him in *his* words. 14 And when they were come, they say unto him, Master, we know that thou art true, and carest for no man: for	20 And they watched *him*, and sent forth spies, which should feign themselves just men, that they might take hold of his words, that so they might deliver him unto the power and authority 21 of the governor. And they asked him, saying, Master, we know that thou sayest and teach-

---

[1] But when the king heard *thereof*, he was wroth [2] the wedding was furnished
[3] hand and foot, and take him away, and cast *him*
[a] Matt. xx. 16.

ST. MATT. XXII.	ST. MARK XII.	ST. LUKE XX.
gardest not the person 17 of men. Tell us therefore, What thinkest thou? Is it lawful to give tribute unto Cæsar, or not? 18 But Jesus perceived their wickedness, and said, Why tempt ye me, 19 ye hypocrites? Shew me the tribute money. And they brought unto him 20 a penny. And Jesus³ saith unto them, Whose *is* this image and super21 scription? They say⁴ Cæsar's. Then saith he unto them, Render therefore unto Cæsar the things which are Cæsar's, and unto God the things 22 that are God's. When they had heard *these words*, they marvelled, and left him, and went their way.	thou regardest not the person of men, but teachest the way of God in truth: Is it lawful to give tribute to Cæsar, or not? 15 Shall we give, or shall we not give? But he, seeing¹ their hypocrisy, said unto them, Why tempt ye me? bring me a penny, that I 16 may see *it*. And they brought *it*. And he saith unto them, Whose *is* this image and superscription? And they said unto him, 17 Cæsar's. And Jesus⁶ said unto them, Render to Cæsar the things that are Cæsar's, and to God the things that are God's. And they marvelled at him.	est rightly, neither acceptest thou the person *of any*, but teachest the way of God 22 truly: Is it lawful for us to give tribute unto 23 Cæsar, or no? But he perceived their craftiness, and said unto 24 them,² Shew me a penny. Whose image and superscription hath it? and they⁵ said, Cæsar's. 25 And he said unto them, Render therefore unto Cæsar the things which be Cæsar's, and unto God the things which be 26 God's. And they could not take hold of his words before the people: and they marvelled at his answer, and held their peace.

(B) Of Sadduces, concerning the Resurrection.

ST. MATT. XXII. 23–33.	ST. MARK XII. 18–27.	ST. LUKE XX. 27–39.
23 The same day came to him Sadducees, saying⁷ that there is no resurrection, and asked 24 him, saying, Master, Moses said, If a man die, having no children,	18 Then come unto him the Sadducees, which say there is no resurrection; and they asked him, saying, 19 Master, Moses wrote unto us, If a man's	27 Then came to *him* certain of the Sadducees, which deny that there is any resurrection; and 28 they asked him, saying, Master, Moses wrote unto us, If any man's

¹ knowing their hypocrisy
³ And he saith
⁵ They answered and said
² said unto them, Why tempt ye me? Shew me
⁴ They say unto him
⁶ answering said unto them
⁷ came to him the Sadducees, which say that

OUR LORD'S TRIUMPHAL ENTRY INTO JERUSALEM, [PART VII. § 120.

ST. MATT. XXII.	ST. MARK XII.	ST. LUKE XX.
his brother shall marry his wife, and raise up seed unto his brother.ª	brother die, and leave *his* wife *behind him*, and leave no child[1] that his brother should take the[3] wife, and raise up seed unto his brother.ª	brother die, having a wife, and he be[2] without children, that his brother should take his wife, and raise up seed unto his brother.ª There were

25 Now there were with us seven brethren: and the first, when he had married a wife, deceased, and, having no issue, left his wife unto 26 his brother: likewise the second also, and the third, unto the 27 seventh. And last of all the woman died.[8] 28 Therefore in the resurrection whose wife shall she be of the seven? for they all 29 had her. Jesus answered and said unto them, Ye do err, not knowing the scriptures, nor the power 30 of God. For in the resurrection they neither marry, nor are given in marriage, but are as the angels of 31 God in heaven. But as touching the resurrection of the dead, have ye not read that which was spoken unto

20 brother.ª ⁴There were seven brethren: and the first took a wife, and dying left no seed. 21 And the second took her, and died, not leaving[5] seed: and the 22 third likewise. And the seven[7] left no seed: last of all the woman 23 died also. In the resurrection,[10] when they shall rise, whose wife shall she be of them? for the seven had her 24 to wife. Jesus[12] said unto them, Do ye not therefore err, because ye know not the scriptures, neither the pow- 25 er of God? For when they shall rise from the dead, they neither marry, nor are given in marriage; but are as[13] angels in heaven. 26 And as touching the dead, that they rise: have ye not read in the book of Moses, at

therefore seven brethren: and the first took a wife, and died without chil- 30 dren. And the second,[6] and the third took her; and in like manner the seven also: and they left no children, and died. 32 At[9] last the woman died 33 also. The woman[11] therefore in the resurrection, whose wife of them is she? for seven had her 34 to wife. And Jesus[12] said unto them, The children of this world marry, and are given in marriage: 35 but they which shall be accounted worthy to obtain that world, and the resurrection from the dead, neither marry, nor are given in marriage: 36 neither can they die any more: for they are equal unto the angels; and are the children of God, being the children of the 37 resurrection. Now that the dead are raised, even

---

[1] no children   [2] and he die without   [3] his wife
[4] Now there were   [5] and died, neither left he any seed
[6] And the second took her to wife, and he died childless. And the third
[7] the seven had her, and left   [8] died also
[9] Last of all the   [10] In the resurrection therefore, when
[11] *omit* The woman   [12] And Jesus answering said
[13] as the angels which are

Deut. xxv. 5, 6; comp. Gen. xxxviii. 8.

ST. MATT. XXII.	ST. MARK XII.	ST. LUKE XX.
you by God, saying, 32 I am the God of Abraham, and the God of Isaac, and the God of Jacob?ᵃ Heˆ² is not the God of the dead, 33 but of the living. And when the multitude heard *this*, they were astonished at his doctrine.	the bush how¹ God spake unto him, saying, I *am* the God of Abraham, and the God of Isaac, and the God of Jacob?ᵃ 27 He is not the God of the dead, but³ of the living: ye⁴ do greatly err.	Moses shewed at the bush, when he calleth the Lord the God of Abraham, and the God of Isaac, and the God of Jacob.ᵃ 38 For he is not a God of the dead, but of the living: for all live unto him.
		39 Then certain of the scribes answering said, Master, thou hast well said.

(C) Of a Lawyer, concerning the greatest Commandment.

ST. MATT. XXII. 34–40.	ST. MARK XII. 28–34.	ST. LUKE XX. 40.
34 But when the Pharisees had heard that he had put the Sadducees to silence, they were gathered together. 35 Then one of them, *which was* a lawyer, asked *him a question*, 36 tempting him,⁶ Master, which *is* the great commandment in the law? 37 And he⁷ said	28 And one of the scribes came, and having heard them reasoning together, and seeing⁵ that he had answered them well, asked him, Which is the first commandment of 29 all? Jesus answered,⁸	

¹ *translated* in the book of Moses, how in the bush God spake
³ but the God of the living
⁵ and perceiving that   ⁶ tempting him, and saying,
⁸ And Jesus answered him, The first of all the commandments *is*, Hear
² God is not
⁴ ye therefore do greatly
⁷ Jesus said unto him

ᵃ Ex. iii. 6; comp. 16.

§ 120. C. Doubtless the wily Pharisees chose to put forward as their spokesman a really ingenuous man, who had hitherto honestly rejected the claims of our Lord. Hence St. Mark describes him as answering "discreetly." He came "tempting" (St. Matthew); but being deeply impressed by our Lord's answer, he went away (St. Mark) "not far from the kingdom of God." The answer to the question was really the Lord's — whether as St. Matthew describes it, he gave the answer himself; or as St. Mark more particularly specifies, He led on the lawyer to answer it himself.

ST. MATT. XXII.	ST. MARK XII.	ST. LUKE XX.
unto him, Thou shalt love the Lord thy God with all thy heart, and with all thy soul, and with all thy mind.^a 38 This is the first and great commandment. 39 ¹The second *is* like unto it, Thou shalt love thy neighbor as 40 thyself.^b On these two commandments hang all the law and the prophets.	The first is, Hear, O Israel; The Lord our 30 God is one Lord: and thou shalt love the Lord thy God with all thy heart, and with all thy soul, and with all thy mind, and with all thy 31 strength:^{a,2} The second this, Thou shalt love thy neighbor as thyself.^b There is none other commandment greater 32 than these. And the scribes said unto him, Well, Master, thou hast said the truth: for he³ is one and there is none 33 other but he:^c and to love him with all the heart, and with all the understanding,⁴ and with all the strength, and to love *his* neighbor as himself, is more than all whole burnt offerings 34 and sacrifices.^d And when Jesus saw that he answered discreetly, he said unto him, Thou art not far from the kingdom of God. And no man after that durst ask him any *questions*.	40 For⁵ after that they durst not ask him any question at all.

¹ And the second

² thy strength: this *is* the first commandment. And the second *is* like, *namely* this, Thou shalt

³ for there is one God; and there is

⁴ understanding, and with all the soul, and with all the

⁵ And after that

^a Deut. vi. 4, 5.

^b Lev. xix. 18. Comp. Matt. v. 44; xix. 19; Lk. x. 27; Rom. xiii. 9; Gal. v. 14; Jas. ii. 8, etc.

^c Deut. iv. 35, 39; Isa. xlv. 21, etc.   ^d Hos. vi. 6.

§ 121. Our Lord's Question in return: How is Christ David's Son?

St. Matt. xxii. 41–46.	St. Mark xii. 35–37.	St. Luke xx. 41–44.
41 While the Pharisees were gathered together, 42 Jesus asked them, saying, What think ye of Christ? whose son is he? They say unto him, *the son of* 43 David. He saith unto them, How then doth David in spirit call him 44 Lord, saying, The Lord said unto my Lord, Sit thou on my right hand, till I put thine enemies 45 under thy feet?[3][a] If David then call him Lord, how is he his son? 46 And no man was able to answer him a word, neither durst any *man* from that day forth ask him any more *questions*.	35 And Jesus answered and said, while he taught in the temple, How say the scribes that Christ is the son 36 of David? [1]David himself said by the Holy Ghost, The Lord said to my Lord, Sit thou on my right hand, till I make thine enemies thy footstool.[a] 37 David[4] himself calleth him Lord, and whence is he *then* his son? And the common people heard him gladly.	41 And he said unto them, How say they that Christ is David's 42 son? For[2] David himself saith in the book of Psalms, The Lord said unto my Lord, Sit thou on 43 my right hand, till I make thine enemies 44 thy footstool.[a] David therefore calleth him Lord, how is he then his son?

§ 122. Warning against the Scribes and Pharisees.

St. Matt. xxiii. 1–3.	St. Mark xii. 38–40.	St. Luke xx. 45–47.
1 Then spake Jesus to the multitude, and 2 to his disciples, saying, The scribes and the Pharisees sit in Moses'	38 And he said[5] in his doctrine, Beware of the scribes, which love	45 Then in the audience of all the people he 46 said unto the[6] disciples, Beware of the scribes,

[1] For David
[3] till I make thine enemies thy footstool?
[6] said unto them
[a] Ps. cx. 1.
[2] And David
[4] David therefore himself
[5] his disciples

§ 122. The continuation of this discourse in St. Matthew (ver. 5–7), is very similar to the language of St. Mark and St. Luke. It is plain, however, from Lk. xi. 43, etc., that much the same discourse was uttered on more than one occasion. These verses of St. Matthew are therefore placed with the passage of St. Luke (§ 89) to which they are most closely parallel. Matt. xxiii. is apparently a collection of our Lord's sayings without mention of, or reference to, the circumstances under which they were severally uttered.

St. Matt. XXIII.	St. Mark XII.	St. Luke XX.

3 seat: All therefore whatsoever they bid you, do and observe;[1] but do not ye after their works: for they say, and do not.

<table>
<tr><td></td><td>to go in long clothing,[a] and love salutations in</td><td>which desire to walk in long robes,[a] and love greetings in the markets,[b]</td></tr>
<tr><td></td><td>39 the marketplaces,[b] and the chief seats in the synagogues, and the uppermost rooms at</td><td>and the highest seats in the synagogues, and the chief rooms at feasts;</td></tr>
<tr><td></td><td>40 feasts: which devour widows' houses, and for a pretence make long prayers: these shall receive greater damnation.</td><td>47 which devour widows' houses, and for a shew make long prayers: the same shall receive greater damnation.</td></tr>
</table>

§ 123. The Widow's Mite.

St. Mark XII. 41–44.	St. Luke XXI. 1–4.
41 And he[2] sat over against the treasury, and beheld how the people cast money into the treasury: and many that were rich cast in much. 42 And there came a certain poor widow, and she threw in two mites, which 43 make a farthing. And he called *unto him* his disciples, and said[4] unto them, Verily I say unto you, That this poor widow hath cast more in than all they which have cast into the treasury: 44 for all *they* did cast in of their abundance; but she of her want did cast in all that she had, *even* all her living.	1 And he looked up, and saw the rich men casting their gifts into the 2 treasury. And he saw[3] a certain poor widow casting in thither two 3 mites. And he said, Of a truth I say unto you, that this poor widow hath cast in more than they all: 4 for all these have of their abundance cast in unto the offerings:[5] but she of her penury hath cast in all the living that she had.

[1] bid you observe, *that* observe and do [4] and saith unto
[a] See Matt. xxiii. 5.

[2] And Jesus sat [3] saw also a certain
[5] offerings of God
[b] See Matt. xxiii. 6, 7; Lk. xi. 43.

§ 124. Our Lord speaks to certain Greeks, who desired to see Him, of His approaching Death. The Voice from Heaven.

St. John xii. 20–36.

20 And there were certain Greeks among them that came up to worship at
21 the feast: The same came therefore to Philip, which was of Bethsaida of
22 Galilee, and desired him, saying, Sir, we would see Jesus. Philip cometh and telleth Andrew: and Andrew and Philip come and[1] tell Jesus.
23 And Jesus answereth[2] them, saying, The hour is come, that the Son of
24 Man should be glorified. Verily, verily, I say unto you, Except a corn of wheat fall into the ground and die, it abideth alone: but if it die, it bringeth
25 forth much fruit. He that loveth his life loseth[3] it; and he that hateth his
26 life in this world shall keep it unto life eternal.[a] If any man serve me, let him follow me; and where I am, there shall also my servant be: if any man serve me, him will *my* Father honor.
27 Now is my soul troubled; and what shall I say? Father, save me from this hour? but for this cause came I unto this hour. Father, glorify thy
28 name. Then came there a voice from heaven,[b] *saying*, I have both glorified *it*,
29 and will glorify *it* again. The people therefore, that stood by, and heard *it*,
30 said that it thundered: others said, An angel spake to him. Jesus answered
31 and said, This voice came not because of me, but for your sakes. Now is the judgment of this world: now shall the prince of this world be cast out.
32/33 And I, if I be lifted up from the earth,[c] will draw all *men* unto me. This he said, signifying what death he should die.
34 The people therefore[4] answered him, We have heard out of the law that Christ abideth for ever:[d] and how sayest thou, The Son of Man must be
35 lifted up? who is this Son of Man? Then Jesus said unto them, Yet a little while is the light among[5] you. Walk while ye have the light, lest darkness come upon you: for he that walketh in darkness knoweth not whither he
36 goeth. While ye have light, believe in the light, that ye may be the children of light. These things spake Jesus, and departed, and did hide himself from them.

[1] and again Andrew and Philip tell Jesus   [2] answered   [3] shall lose it
     [4] *omit* therefore   [5] with you

[a] Cf. Matt. x. 39; xvi. 25; Mar. viii. 35; Lk. ix. 24; xvii. 33.
[b] Cf. Matt. iii. 17; xvii. 5; Mar. i. 11; ix. 7; Lk. iii. 22; ix. 35.
[c] Comp. Num. xxi. 8, 9; Jno. iii. 14.
[d] Comp. Ps. lxxxix 36, 37; cx. 4; Isa. ix. 7; Dan. ii. 44; vii. 14, 27; Mic. iv. 7, etc.

---

§ 124. The Greeks were probably in that precinct of the temple known as the court of the Gentiles; and as our Lord must have been sitting here when he saw the gift of the poor widow (§ 123), this, as Tischendorf has noticed, seems the proper place for the incident. Robinson well observes that after our Lord left the temple at this time, he returned to it no more. This interview therefore could not well have occurred later. The last clause of vs. 36 corresponds with Matt. xxiv. 1; Mar. xiii. 1.

§ 125. The Jews' Unbelief, notwithstanding the Words and Works of Christ

JOHN XII. 37–50.

37 But though he had done so many miracles before them, yet they believed
38 not on him: that the saying of Esaias the prophet might be fulfilled, which
he spake, Lord, who hath believed our report? and to whom hath the arm
39 of the Lord been revealed?[a] Therefore they could not believe, because that
40 Esaias said again, 'He hath blinded their eyes, and hardened their heart;
that they should not see with *their* eyes, nor understand with *their* heart, and
41 be converted, and I should heal them.[b] These things said Esaias, because[1]
he saw his glory[c] and spake of him.
42 Nevertheless among the chief rulers also many believed on him; but
because of the Pharisees they did not confess *him*, lest they should be put out
43 of the synagogue: for they loved the praise of men more than the praise of
God.
44 Jesus cried, and said, He that believeth on me, believeth not on me, but on
45 him that sent me. And he that seeth me seeth him that sent me. I am
46 come a light into the world, that whosoever believeth on me should not abide
47 in darkness. And if any man hear my words, and keep *them*[2] not, I judge
48 him not: for I came not to judge the world, but to save the world. He that
rejecteth me, and receiveth not my words, hath one that judgeth him: the
49 word that I have spoken, the same shall judge him in the last day. For I
have not spoken of myself; but the Father which sent me, he gave me a
50 commandment, what I should say, and what I should speak. And I know
that his commandment is life everlasting: whatsoever I speak therefore, even
as the Father said unto me, so I speak.

FOURTH DAY OF THE WEEK. — WEDNESDAY (BEGINNING AT SUNSET.)

§ 126. Our Lord's Prophecy of the Destruction of Jerusalem, and of the Future.

ST. MATT. XXIV. 1–25, 29–36, 42. x. 21–25.	ST. MARK XIII. 1–37.	ST. LUKE XXI. 5–36. XVII. 31.
1 And Jesus went out, and departed from the temple: and his disciples came to *him* for to shew	1 And as he went out of the temple, one of his disciples saith unto him, Master, see what	5 And as some spake of the temple, how it was adorned with

[1] when he saw [2] and believe not
[a] Isa. liii. 1; Rom. x. 16.
[b] Isa. vi. 9, 10. See Matt. xiii. 13–15; Mar. iv. 12; Lk. viii. 10; Acts xxviii. 25–27.
[c] Isa. vi. 1–10.

§ 125. After the reflections of the Evangelist in vs. 37–43, he records other words of our Lord, which are not to be considered as a later utterance, but rather as previously spoken, and now recalled and recorded, to show the authority for his own reflections.

ST. MATT. XXIV.	ST. MARK XIII.	ST. LUKE XXI.
him the buildings of 2 the temple. And he answered and[1] said unto them, See ye not all these things? verily I say unto you, There shall not be left here one stone upon another, that shall not be thrown down.[a] 3 And as he sat upon the mount of Olives, the disciples came unto him privately, saying, Tell us, when shall these things be? and what *shall be* the sign of thy coming, and of the end of the 4 world? And Jesus answered and said unto them, Take heed that no 5 man deceive you. For many shall come in my name, saying, I am Christ; and shall deceive 6 many. And ye shall hear of wars and rumors of wars: see that ye be not troubled: for *these*[5] must come to pass, but the end 7 is not yet. For nation shall rise against nation, and kingdom against kingdom: and there shall	manner of stones and what buildings *are* 2 *here!* And Jesus[2] said unto him, Seest thou these great buildings? there shall not be left one stone upon another, that shall not be thrown down.[a] 3 And as he sat upon the mount of Olives over against the temple. Peter and James and John and Andrew asked him privately, 4 Tell us, when shall these things be? and what *shall be* the sign when all these things 5 shall be fulfilled? And Jesus began to say unto them,[3] Take heed lest any *man* deceive 6 you: many shall come in my name, saying, I am *Christ;* and shall 7 deceive many. And when ye shall hear of wars and rumors of wars, be ye not troubled:[5] *such things* must needs be; but the end *shall* not be 8 yet. For nation shall rise against nation, and kingdom against kingdom:[7] there shall	goodly stones and gifts, 6 he said, *As for* these things which ye behold, the days will come, in the which there shall not be left one stone upon another, that shall not be thrown down.[a] 7 And they asked him, saying, Master, but when shall these things be? and what sign *will there be* when these things shall come 8 to pass? And he said, Take heed that ye be not deceived: for many shall come in my name, saying, I am *Christ;* and the time draweth near: go ye 9 not[4] after them. But when ye shall hear of wars and commotions, be not terrified: for these things must first come to pass; but the end *is* not by and by. 10 Then said he unto them, Nation shall rise against nation, and kingdom against king-

[1] And Jesus said
[2] And Jesus answering, said
[3] Jesus answering them began to say, Take
[4] go ye not therefore after
[5] for *such things*
[6] for all *these things* must come
[7] and there shall

[a] 1 Kings ix. 7; Jer. xxvi. 18; Mich. iii. 12, etc.

ST. MATT. XXIV.	ST. MARK XIII.	ST. LUKE XXI.
be famines,¹ and earthquakes, in divers places. ⁸ All these *are* the beginning of sorrows. Then	be earthquakes in divers places,² there shall be famines:³ these *are* the beginning⁴ of sorrows.	11 dom: and great earthquakes shall be in divers places, and famines, and pestilences; and fearful sights and great signs shall there 12 be from heaven. But
shall they deliver you up to be afflicted,ᵃ and shall kill you: and ye shall be hated of all nations for 10 my name's sake. And then shall many be offended and shall betray one another, and shall 11 hate one another. And many false prophets shall rise, and shall deceive 12 many.ᵇ And because iniquity shall abound, the love of many shall wax 13 cold. But he that shall endure unto the end, the 14 same shall be saved. And this gospel of the kingdom shall be preached in all the world for a witness unto all nations; and then shall the end come.	9 But take heed to yourselves: ⁵they shall deliver you up to councilsᵃ; and in the synagogues ye shall be beaten: and ye shall be brought before rulers and kings for my sake, for a testimony against them. 10 And the gospel must first be published among all nations. 11 Andᶜ when they shall lead *you*, and deliver you up, take no thought beforehand what ye shall speak:⁷ᶜ but whatsoever shall be	before all these, they shall lay their hands on you, and persecute *you*,ᵃ delivering *you* up to the synagogues, and into prisons, being brought before kings and rulers for my name's sake. 13 And it shall turn to you for a testimony. 14 Settle *it* therefore in your hearts, not to meditate before what 15 ye shall answer:ᶜ For I will give you a mouth

¹ famines, and pestilences, and ² and there shall ³ famines, and troubles;
⁴ beginnings ⁵ for they shall ⁶ But when they shall
⁷ shall speak, neither do ye premeditate
ᵃ See Matt. x. 17, 18; Lk. xii. 11. ᵇ Comp. 2 Thess. ii. 3, 10–12.
ᶜ Matt. x. 19, 20; Lk. xii. 11, 12.

ST. MATT. X, XXIV.	ST. MARK XIII.	ST. LUKE XXI.
	given you in that hour, that speak ye: for it is not ye that speak, but the Holy Ghost.	and wisdom, which all your adversaries shall not be able to gainsay 16 nor resist. And ye
ST. MATT. X.		
21 And the brother shall deliver up the brother to death, and the father the child: and the children shall rise up against *their* parents, and cause them 22 to be put to death. And ye shall be hated of all *men* for my name's sake: but he that endureth to the end shall be saved.	12 And[1] the brother shall betray the brother to death, and the father the son; and children shall rise up against *their* parents, and shall cause them to be put 13 to death. And ye shall be hated of all *men* for my name's sake: but he that shall endure unto the end, the same shall be saved.	shall be betrayed both by parents, and brethren, and kinsfolks, and friends; and *some* of you shall they cause to be put to death. 17 And ye shall be hated of all *men* for my 18 name's sake. But there shall not an hair of 19 your head perish. In your patience possess ye your souls.
23 But when they persecute you in this city, flee ye into another: for verily I say unto you, Ye shall not have gone over the cities of Israel, till the Son of Man be come. 24 The disciple is not above *his* master, nor the ser-25 vant above his lord.[a] It is enough for the disciple that he be as his master, and the servant as his lord. If they have called the master of the house Beelzebub, how much more *shall they call* them of his household!		
ST. MATT. XXIV.		
15 When ye therefore shall see the abomination of desolation,[b] spoken of by Daniel the prophet, stand in the holy place,	14 But when ye shall see the abomination of desolation,[b][2] standing where it ought not,	20 And when ye shall see Jerusalem compassed with armies, then know that the desolation thereof is

[1] Now the brother
[2] of desolation, spoken of by Daniel the prophet, standing
[a] Comp. Lk. vi. 40; Jno. xiii. 16; xv. 20. [b] Dan. ix. 27; Comp. viii. 13; xi. 31; xii. 11.

ST. MATT. XXIV.	ST. MARK XIII.	ST. LUKE XXI., XVII.
(whoso readeth, let him understand.) 16 then let them which be in Judæa flee into the mountains:	(let him that readeth understand,) then let them that be in Judæa flee to the mountains:	21 nigh. Then let them which are in Judæa flee to the mountains: and let them which are in the midst of it depart out; and let not them that are in the countries enter thereinto.
		ST. LUKE XVII.
17 let him which is on the housetop not come down to take the things[1] out of his house:	15 and let him that is on the housetop not go down,[2] neither enter *therein*, to take any thing out of his house:	31 In that day, he which shall be upon the housetop, and his stuff in the house, let him not come down to take it away: and he that is in the field, let him likewise not return back.
18 neither let him which is in the field return back to take his garment.[3]	16 and let him that is in the field not turn back again for to take up his garment.	
		ST. LUKE XXI.
		22 For these be the days of vengeance, that all things which are written may be fulfilled.
19 And woe unto them that are with child, and to them that give suck in 20 those days! But pray ye that your flight be not in the winter, neither on 21 the Sabbath day: for then shall be great tribulation, such as was not since the beginning of the world to this time, no, nor ever shall be. 22 And except those days should be shortened, there should no flesh be saved: but for the elect's sake	17 But woe to them that are with child, and to them that give suck 18 in those days! And pray ye that *it*[5] be not 19 in the winter. For *in* those days shall be affliction, such as was not from the beginning of the creation which God created unto this time, neither shall be. 20 And except that the Lord had shortened those days, no flesh should be saved: but for the elect's sake,	23 [4]Woe unto them that are with child, and to them that give suck, in those days! for there shall be great distress in the land, and wrath upon this people.

[1] anything [2] go down into the house, neither [3] his clothes
[4] But woe unto [5] that your flight be not

PART VII. § 126.] AND THE EVENTS UNTIL THE LAST PASSOVER. 209

ST. MATT. XXIV.	ST. MARK XIII.	ST. LUKE XXI.
those days shall be shortened. ²³ Then if any man shall say unto you, Lo, here *is* Christ, or there; ²⁴ believe *it* not. For there shall arise false Christs, and false prophets,ᵃ and shall shew great signs and wonders; insomuch that, if *it were* possible, even the very elect shall ²⁵ be deceived.³ Behold! I have told you before.	whom he hath chosen, he hath shortened the ²¹ days. And then if any man shall say to you, Lo, here *is* Christ; or, lo, *he is* there; ²² believe *him* not: and¹ false Christs and false prophets shall rise, and shall do² signs and wonders, to seduce, if *it were* possible,⁴ the ²³ elect. But take ye heed: ⁵I have foretold you all things.	
		²⁴ And they shall fall by the edge of the sword, and shall be led away captive into all nations: and Jerusalem shall be trodden down of the Gentiles, until the times of the Gentiles be fulfilled.
²⁹ Immediately after the tribulation of those days shall the sun be darkened, and the moon shall not give her light, and the stars shall fall from heaven, and the powers of the heavens shall be	²⁴ But in those days, after that tribulation, the sun shall be darkened, and the moon shall not give her light, ²⁵ and the stars shall fall from heaven⁶ and the powers that are in heaven shall be shak-	²⁵ And there shall be signs in the sun, and in the moon, and in the stars; and upon the earth distress of nations, with perplexity by reason of the noise of⁷ the sea and ²⁶ the waves; men's hearts failing them for fear, and for looking after those things which are coming on the earth: for the powers of heaven shall

¹ For false   ² shall shew signs   ³ if *it were* possible, they shall deceive the very elect.
⁴ even the elect   ⁵ behold, I have foretold
⁶ with perplexity; the sea and the waves roaring;   ⁷ the stars of heaven shall fall, and
ᵃ See ver. 11.

ST. MATT. XXIV.	ST. MARK XIII.	ST. LUKE XXI.
30 shaken.[a] And then shall appear the sign of the Son of Man in heaven: and all the tribes of the earth shall[1] mourn, and they shall see the Son of Man coming in the clouds of heaven with power and great glory. 31 And he shall send his angels with a great[3] trumpet, and they shall gather together his elect from the four winds, from one end of heaven to the other.	26 en.[a] And then shall they see the Son of Man coming in the clouds with great power and glory. 27 And then shall he send the[2] angels, and shall gather together the[4] elect from the four winds, from the uttermost part of the earth to the uttermost part of heaven.	27 be shaken.[a] And then shall they see the Son of Man coming in a cloud with power and great glory. 28 And when these things begin to come to pass, then look up, and lift up your heads; for your redemption draweth nigh.
32 Now learn a parable of the fig tree; when his branch is yet tender, and putteth forth leaves, ye know that summer is 33 nigh: so likewise ye, when ye shall see all these things, know that it is near, *even* at the 34 doors. Verily I say unto you, this generation shall not pass, till all	28 Now learn a parable of the fig tree; when her branch is yet tender, and putteth forth leaves, it is known[5] that summer is near: 29 so ye in like manner, when ye shall see these things come to pass, know that it is nigh, *even* at the doors. 30 Verily I say unto you that this generation shall not pass, till all	29 And he spake to them a parable; Behold the fig tree, and all the trees; 30 when they now shoot forth, ye see and know of your own selves that summer is now 31 nigh at hand: so likewise ye, when ye see these things come to pass, know ye that the kingdom of God is 32 nigh at hand. Verily I say unto you, this generation shall not pass away, till all be

[1] and then shall all the tribes of the earth mourn   [2] his angels
[3] a great sound of a trumpet   [4] his elect   [5] ye know that summer

[a] Isa. xiii. 10; Ezek. xxxii. 7; Joel ii. 10, 30–32; iii. 15; Amos viii. 9, etc.

ST. MATT. XXIV.	ST. MARK XIII.	ST. LUKE XXI.
these things be fulfilled.	these things be done.	
35 Heaven and earth shall pass away: but my words shall not pass away.	31 Heaven and earth shall pass away: but my words shall not pass away.	33 fulfilled. Heaven and earth shall pass away: but my words shall not pass away.
36 But of that day and hour knoweth no *man*, no, not the angels of heaven, nor the Son[3] but the[4] Father only.	32 But of that day or[1] hour knoweth no man, no, not the angels[2] in heaven, neither the Son, but the Father.	
		34 And take heed to yourselves, lest at any time your hearts be overcharged with surfeiting, and drunkenness, and cares of this life, and *so* that day come upon you unawares as a snare. For 35 it[5] shall come on all them that dwell on the face of the whole earth.
42 Watch therefore: for ye know not what day[8] your Lord doth come.	33 Take ye heed, watch:[6] for ye know not when the time is.	36 But[7] watch ye and pray always, that ye may be able[9] to escape all these things that shall come to pass, and to stand before the Son of Man.
	34 *For the Son of Man is* as a man taking a far journey, who left his house, and gave authority to his servants,[10] to every man his work, and commanded the 35 porter to watch. Watch ye therefore: for ye know not when the	

[1] that day and *that* hour   [2] angels which are in heaven   [3] omit nor the Son
[4] my Father   [5] upon you unawares. For as a snare shall it come
[6] watch and pray: [7] Watch ye therefore   [8] what hour
[9] ye may be accounted worthy to escape   [10] and to every man

ST. MATT. XXIV.	ST. MARK XIII.	ST. LUKE XXI.
	master of the house cometh, whether[1] at even, or at midnight, or at the cockcrowing, or in the morning:	
	36 lest coming suddenly he find you sleeping.	
	37 And what I say unto you I say unto all, Watch.	

§ 127. The Parable of the Ten Virgins.

St. Matt. xxv. 1–13.

1 Then shall the kingdom of heaven be likened unto ten virgins, which took
2 their lamps, and went forth to meet the bridegroom. And five of them were
3 wise, and five *were* foolish. They that *were* foolish took the[2] lamps, and took
4 no oil with them: but the wise took oil in the[2] vessels with their lamps.
5 While the bridegroom tarried, they all slumbered and slept. And at midnight
6 there was a cry made, Behold! the bridegroom![3] go ye out to meet *him*.[4]
7 Then all those virgins arose, and trimmed their lamps. And the foolish said
9 unto the wise, Give us of your oil; for our lamps are gone out. But the wise answered, saying, *Not so;* lest there be not enough for us and you:
10 [5]go ye rather to them that sell, and buy for yourselves. And while they went to buy, the bridegroom came; and they that were ready went in with him to
11 the marriage: and the door was shut. Afterward came also the other virgins,
12 saying, Lord, Lord, open to us. But he answered and said, Verily I say unto
13 you, I know you not. Watch therefore, for ye know neither the day nor the hour.[6]

§ 128. The Judgment foretold.

St. Matt. xxv. 31–46.

31 When the Son of Man shall come in his glory, and all the[7] angels with
32 him, then shall he sit upon the throne of his glory: and before him shall be gathered all nations: and he shall separate them one from another, as a
33 shepherd divideth *his* sheep from the goats: and he shall set the sheep on his
34 right hand, but the goats on the left. Then shall the King say unto them on his right hand, Come, ye blessed of my Father, inherit the kingdom prepared
35 for you from the foundation of the world: for I was an hungered, and ye gave me meat: I was thirsty, and ye gave me drink: I was a stranger, and
36 ye took me in: naked, and ye clothed me: I was sick, and ye visited me: I

---

[1] omit whether   [2] *twice* their   [3] the bridegroom cometh   [4] him   [5] but go ye
[6] the hour wherein the Son of Man cometh   [7] the holy angels

ST. MATT. XXV.

37 was in prison, and ye came unto me. Then shall the righteous answer him, saying, Lord, when saw we thee an hungered, and fed *thee*? or thirsty, and 38 gave *thee* drink? [1]when saw we thee a stranger, and took *thee* in? or naked, 39 and clothed *thee*? or when saw we thee sick, or in prison, and came unto 40 thee? and the King shall answer and say unto them, Verily I say unto you, Inasmuch as ye have done *it* unto one of the least of these my brethren, ye 41 have done *it* unto me. Then shall he say also unto them on the left hand, Depart from me, ye cursed, into everlasting fire, prepared for the devil and 42 his angels: [1]for I was an hungered, and ye gave me no meat: I was thirsty, 43 and ye gave me no drink: [1]I was a stranger, and ye took me not in: naked, 44 and ye clothed me not: sick, and in prison, and ye visited me not. Then shall they also answer,[1] saying, Lord, when saw we thee an hungered, or athirst, or a stranger, or naked, or sick, or in prison, and did not minister 45 unto thee? Then shall he answer them, saying, Verily I say unto you, Inasmuch as ye did *it* not to one of the least of these, ye did *it* not to me. 46 And these shall go away into everlasting punishment: but the righteous into life eternal.

§ 129. The Rulers conspire to kill Jesus. Judas agrees to betray Him.

ST. MATT. XXVI. 1–5, 14–16. ST. MARK XIV. 1, 2, 10, 11. ST. LUKE XXII. 1–6.

1 And it came to pass, when Jesus had finished all these sayings, he said 2 unto his disciples, Ye know that after two days is *the feast of* the Passover, and the Son of Man is betrayed to be crucified. 3 Then assembled together the chief priests,[2] and the elders of the people, unto the palace of the high priest, who 4 was called Caiaphas, and consulted that they might take Jesus by subtlety,	1 After two days was *the feast of* the Passover, and of unleavened bread: and the chief priests and the scribes sought how they might take him by craft, and put *him*	1 Now the feast of unleavened bread drew nigh, which is called 2 the Passover. And the chief priests and scribes sought how they might kill him; .

[1] answer him, saying,   [2] priests, and the scribes, and the elders

---

§ 129. It has already been noticed (see § 112 note) that the verses of St. Matthew and St. Mark here omitted are of the nature of an episode to explain how Judas was led to his treachery just at this time, and are therefore properly transferred to the place they occupy in the order of St. John. The narrative of this section therefore remains strictly continuous.

ST. MATT. XXVI.	ST. MARK XIV.	ST. LUKE XXII.
5 and kill *him*. But they said, Not on the feast *day*, lest there be an uproar among the people. 14 Then one of the twelve, called Judas Iscariot, went unto the chief 15 priests, and said *unto them*, What will ye give me, and I will deliver him unto you? and they covenanted with him for thirty pieces of silver. 16 And from that time he sought opportunity to betray him.	2 to death. For[1] they said, Not on the feast *day*, lest there be an uproar of the people. 10 And Judas Iscariot, one of the twelve, went unto the chief priests, to betray him unto 11 them. And when they heard *it*, they were glad, and promised to give him money. And he sought how he might conveniently betray him.	for they feared the people. 3 Then entered Satan into Judas surnamed Iscariot, being of the number of the twelve. 4 And he went his way, and communed with the chief priests and captains, how he might betray him unto them. 5 And they were glad, and covenanted to give 6 him money. And he promised, and sought opportunity to betray him unto them in the absence of the multitude.

[1] But they said

FIFTH DAY OF THE WEEK.—THURSDAY (ENDING AT SUNSET.)

§ 130. The Preparation for the Passover.

ST. MATT. XXVI. 17–19.	ST. MARK XIV. 12–16.	ST. LUKE XXII. 7–13.
17 Now the first *day* of the *feast* of unleavened bread the disciples came to Jesus, saying,[2] Where wilt thou that we prepare for thee to eat the passover?	12 And the first day of unleavened bread, when they killed the passover, his disciples said unto him, Where wilt thou that we go and prepare that thou mayest eat 13 the passover? And he sendeth forth two of his disciples, and saith unto	7 Then came the day of unleavened bread, when the passover must be 8 killed. And he sent Peter and John, saying, Go and prepare us the passover, that we may 9 eat. And they said unto him, Where wilt thou 10 that we prepare? And

[2] saying unto him

---

§ 130. This section is postponed by Jarvis until after chap. xiii. and xiv. of St. John, on the supposition that St. John records in those chapters a supper which occurred on Wednesday evening, twenty-four hours before the Paschal supper. Lightfoot had previously distinguished two suppers, but had connected only Jno. xiii. with the earlier one, which he identifies with the supper in the house of Simon at Bethany. In the form in which the theory of two suppers is brought forward by Jarvis, there is so much to be said in its favor that it may be well to

ST. MATT. XXVI.	ST. MARK XIV.	ST. LUKE XXII.
18 And he said, Go into the city to such a man, and say unto him, The Master saith, My time is at hand; I will keep the passover at thy	them, Go ye into the city, and there shall meet you a man bearing a pitcher of water: follow him. 14 And wheresoever he shall go in, say ye to the goodman of the house, The Master saith, Where is my [2] guestchamber, where I shall eat the passover with my dis-	he said unto them, Behold! when ye are entered into the city, there shall a man meet you, bearing a pitcher of water: follow him into the house into which [1] he 11 entereth in. And ye shall say unto the goodman of the house, The Master saith unto thee, Where is the guestchamber, where I shall eat the passover with my

[1] house where he entereth   [2] the guestchamber

---

mention the arguments for it, and also the reasons why harmonists generally have felt constrained to adhere to the arrangement here given.

1. The expression in Jno. xiii. 1: *before the feast of the Passover,* thus receives its simplest and most natural explanation. The *feast* indeed, by common usage, refers rather to the seven days' feast as a whole, than specifically to the eating of the Paschal lamb; still, it must include the latter in its meaning, and if the assertion really is that the *washing of the disciples' feet* took place "before the feast of the Passover," then we must understand this of a previous supper. To this, however, it has been well replied that *before the Passover* refers to *know,* and the object of the expression will then be (quite in accordance with St. John's manner) to explain why our Lord did and said these things at the last supper — because he knew beforehand that his hour was come.

2. At the end of Jno. xiv. Jesus says "Arise, let us go hence." This shows a break between chapters xiv. and xv., and that the company must have left the place where the former was spoken, previously to the discourse of the latter. But we read in Jno. xviii. 1, that "when Jesus had spoken these words, he went forth with his disciples over the brook Cedron." The interval between leaving the room of the Paschal supper and the "going forth over the brook Cedron" seems too short for the long discourse of chaps. xv., xvi., and xvii. If, however, two suppers are supposed, the former ending with ch. xiv., all becomes clear. In answer to these things, it is easy to suppose that our Saviour, after saying "Arise, let us go hence," yet again resumed his discourse in the same place, and did not actually go forth until after the close of the latter discourse; and even if they did go out at the time supposed, we know too little of the localities to assert that there may not have been ample time for the subsequent discourse before they would have reached the gate of the city.

3. It is alleged that the lesson of humility in the washing of the disciples' feet is more appropriate to a previous supper, while the last supper itself is left to be occupied with still deeper spiritual teaching. Such arguments, however, resting upon our conceptions of what is fitting in the Scriptures are uncertain and hazardous. There is no *impropriety* in either supposition, and we must be guided simply by evidence.

4. The expressions in xiii. 33, "Yet a little while I am with you," and xiv. 19, "Yet a little while and the world seeth me no more," seem more agreeable to the supposition of a whole day intervening between their utterance and Christ's apprehension, than of only a few

ST. MATT. XXVI.	ST. MARK XIV.	ST. LUKE XXII.
house with my disciples.	15 ciples? And he will shew you a large upper room furnished *and* prepared: and[1] there make 16 ready for us. And the[2] disciples went forth, and came into the city, and found as he had said unto them: and they made ready the passover.	12 disciples? And he shall shew you a large upper room furnished: there 13 make ready. And they went, and found as he had said unto them: and they made ready the passover.
19 And the disciples did as Jesus had appointed them: and they made ready the passover.		

[1] *omit* and   [2] his disciples

hours of the night. To this it seems a sufficient answer that the point of these expressions is not the intervening time, but the nearness of the end.

5. The direction to Judas (xiii. 27), "that thou doest, do quickly," with the misunderstanding of the disciples that it related to the purchase of things needed for the feast, seems to imply that it was uttered before the feast. The word feast, however, as already noted, applies to the whole seven days; and more closely examined, this passage will be found to favor the opposite theory. If the supper was on Wednesday evening, there was no occasion for haste, nor would the disciples have supposed that Judas had gone out in the night to make his purchases, when he had the whole of the next day before him. If, on the other hand, this was at the Paschal supper, all this is explained, as the feast would be going on in the morning.

On the whole, therefore, there seems no very strong reason to suppose two suppers, and there are positive objections to this theory. All four Evangelists (Matt. xxvi. 1; Mar. xiv. 18; Lk. xxii. 21; Jno. xiii. 21) record our Saviour's pointing out Judas as the traitor, in answer to the inquiries of the disciples, by substantially the same sign. By emphasizing the slight differences in the narration, and understanding that St. John speaks of a private indication to himself, the others of a more open pointing out of Judas to all the disciples, it is indeed possible to suppose that the action was repeated, and actually took place at both suppers; but it is far more simple and natural to suppose all the narratives to relate to the same transaction. The other objection is insuperable and decisive. All the Evangelists (Matt. xxvi. 34, 35; Mar. xiv. 30, 31; Lk. xxii. 33, 34; Jno. xiii. 37, 38) record both St. Peter's expression of his devotion and our Saviour's prophecy of his threefold denial. It is in the highest degree improbable that this should have occurred twice on successive evenings without allusion in any of the four accounts to its repetition. But that what St. John relates did take place at the Paschal supper, as well as what the others relate, is conclusively shown by the limitation of time in vs. 38.: "The cock shall not crow till thou hast denied me thrice"; since no one supposes that Peter's threefold denial was repeated on successive nights. The attempt of Lightfoot (Har. of N. Test. § 80, Vol. iii. p. 144, ed. Pitman) to explain these words, "not as meaning that he should deny him three times over before any cock crew; but that he should deny him thrice in the time of cock's-crowing, which time was a fourth part of the night," can hardly be considered as admissible. It is very obvious that no one hearing the expression would have so understood it, and the language cannot without violence be taken to mean anything else than that Peter should be guilty of this threefold denial before morning.

INTRODUCTORY NOTE TO PART VIII.

To enter intelligently upon the consideration of the several narratives of our Lord's Passion, it is necessary to have distinctly in mind the customs and usages of the Passover as it was celebrated at the time among the Jews. A very clear and succinct account of these, so far as needed for the purpose in hand, will be found in Andrews' "Life of our Lord," 4th edition, pp. 432–438. The following are some of the more important points to be remembered:

1. There was a difference in several respects between the original Passover as observed on the night of the coming out from Egypt, and the festival as subsequently kept in commemoration of that event. The selection of the lamb on the tenth Nisan seems to have applied only to the original Passover, and to have been afterwards discontinued; and the command to put away all leaven from their houses on the fifteenth Nisan (Ex. xii. 15) was extended by the scrupulosity of the Jews to the fourteenth. Thus, Maimonides (as quoted by Lightfoot in Mar. xiv. 12, III.): "From the words of the scribes, they look for and rid away leaven in the beginning of the night of the fourteenth day, and that by the light of the candle. For in the night-time all are within their houses, and a candle is most proper for such a search." etc. They nevertheless allowed leavened bread to be eaten until near noon of that day (the day beginning of course at sunset), for the same author says, "It is lawful to eat leaven on the fourteenth day to the end of the fourth hour; but in the fifth hour it is not to be used." Hence it happened that the fourteenth Nisan, though not strictly a part of the feast, came to be commonly known as "the first day of unleavened bread."

Another important difference consisted in the killing of the Paschal lamb. Originally this was to be slain by each man at his own house, and the blood sprinkled upon his door-posts; but afterwards it was killed only by the Levites in the court of the temple. Thus again, Maimonides (in Corban Pesach, cap. 1. See Lightfoot, ub. sup.). "The Passover was not to be killed but in the court where the other sacrifices were killed, and it was to be killed on the fourteenth day in the afternoon, after the daily sacrifice."

2. This last quotation shows the time at which the lamb was slain. According to Ex. xii. 6; Lev. xxiii. 5; Num. ix. 3, it was to be "between the evenings," i.e. as generally understood by the Jews of the time (cf. Josephus, Bell. Jud. vi. 9, § 3; Antiq. xiv. 4, § 3), and, as expressed above by Maimonides, between the evening sacrifice, at 3 P.M., and the going down of the sun. The Karaites and

Samaritans are said to have understood the phrase of the time between the sunset and dark.

3. The Paschal lamb having thus been slain, was to be eaten on the following evening — according to our usage the same evening — the beginning of the fifteenth Nisan (See Ex. xii. 8). It must be wholly consumed before morning.

4. Other sacrifices were made on the fourteenth, and following days, called (Deut. xvi. 2) "the Passover of the flock and the herd," which were sometimes eaten with the true Passover, in case the company was too large for the lamb; but otherwise, belonged to the feast of the following days. These were called by the Jews *Chagigah*, or feast-offerings, and the especial time for them was on the following day. With these the rejoicings of the feast were more particularly connected.

5. On the "morrow after the Sabbath," the first-fruits of the harvest (barley) were offered, and waved by a priest before the Lord. Until this had been done no one might eat, ripened or green, any portion of the harvest (Lev. xxiii. 10–14).

6. The first and last days of the feast were marked by "an holy convocation," and in them "no servile work" could be done (Lev. xxiii. 7, 8). Precisely what was included in *servile work* cannot now be determined; but these days were very differently regarded from the ordinary weekly Sabbath. The Talmudists call them "good days." Maimonides says that everything connected with the preparation of food, as well as bathing and anointing were allowable, but not the ordinary labors of agriculture. Buying and selling do not appear to have been prohibited; in fact these were allowed upon the weekly Sabbath, provided no price was agreed upon, and no money paid. Probably these technical evasions were not required on the feast-sabbaths. Hence there does not appear to have been any "preparation-day" for these feast-sabbaths, as was rendered necessary before the weekly Sabbath by the greater strictness of the prohibition of labor.

7. Such of the people as were prevented, by reason of being "in a journey afar off," or by uncleanness on account of a dead body, from keeping the Passover at its appointed time, were allowed to celebrate it on the same day of the second month (Num. ix. 10–12). There is no evidence that there was any other variation in the time of the observance of the day.

It is unnecessary to enlarge upon these points or upon the ceremonies observed in the Paschal Supper itself, as all these will be found abundantly described in any of the numerous treatises on the Passover.

A serious question remains to be considered, on which there has been great difference of opinion among commentators: Did our Lord anticipate the Passover with his disciples, and thus himself give up his life upon the cross at the time of the killing of the Paschal lamb; or did they partake of it at the regularly appointed time, when it was eaten by the Jews generally? The presumption is, of course, strongly in favor of the latter; and, indeed, it is hardly possible to suppose that the Levites in the temple would have killed the Paschal lamb at any other than the regular time. The language of the first three Evangelists is clear and explicit (see especially Mar. xiv. 12; Lk. xxii. 7). A few expressions in St. John, however, have suggested difficulties of a character so serious as to induce some persons to adopt the other hypothesis. These must be examined in view of the conclusion already come to in the note to the last section, that the narratives of all four Evangelists relate to the same supper.

I. Jno. xiii. 1. The phrase "before the feast of the Passover" has already been considered in the note to the last section. To this may here be added the excellent remark of Andrews (p. 444), " From the preposition 'before,' we conclude that nothing definite in regard to the time of the supper can be determined. Supposing all between vs. 1 and vs. 4 to be stricken out, and the statement to read, 'Now before the feast of the Passover, etc., he riseth from supper and laid aside his garments,' it would still remain probable that the Paschal Supper was meant. The presumption is very strong, that this meal, thus incidentally mentioned, must have been that so prominently and inseparably associated with the feast."

II. Jno. xviii. 28. "And they themselves went not into the judgment-hall lest they should be defiled, but that they might eat the Passover." It is alleged that this expression shows that the Passover had not yet been eaten by the Jews, and must therefore have been anticipated by our Lord. Two points must first be determined in order to fix the bearing of this expression on the question at issue: (a) what is the meaning of "eat the Passover?" (b) what was the nature of the defilement here feared?

(a) The phrase "eat the Passover," occurs five times in the New Testament (Matt. xxvi. 17; Mar. xiv. 12, 14; Lk. xxii. 11, 15), and once in the Greek of the Old Testament (2 Chron. xxx. 18), and in all these places it means to eat the *Paschal Supper*, strictly. As all the instances in the New Testament, however, refer to one and the same occasion, this concurrence does not go very far to prove that the expression must be limited to this. Now the word *Passover* is used in the New Testament in a variety of significations: (1) For the Paschal lamb; Mar. xiv. 12; Lk. xxii. 7; (and metaph.) 1 Cor. v. 7. (2) For the Paschal Supper; Matt. xxvi. 18, 19; Lk. xxii. 8, 13; Heb. xi. 28, etc. (3) For the whole paschal festival of the seven days of unleavened bread; Lk. xxii. 1; ii. 41–43; Matt. xxvi. 2; Jno. ii. 23. (4) Indefinitely, in such a way that it may be understood either as in (2) or as in (3), and yet the latter meaning having once been established, more naturally in that; Jno. ii. 13; vi. 4; xi. 55; xii. 1; xiii. 1. In Jno. xviii. 28, 29; xix. 14, the meaning is in dispute. It will be observed that all the instances in (4) are from St. John, and that all the passages in St. John in which the word occurs fall under this head or under (3). It is apparent that he uses the word in its most general sense. The phrase therefore, "that they might eat the Passover," as used by him, would seem naturally to refer to the feasts during the seven days or any of them, and not specifically to the Paschal lamb. Thus this expression would have no bearing upon the question, since it may as well be understood of the subsequent feastings as of the Paschal lamb.

(b) But its meaning is more definitely fixed by the defilement which the Jews feared. Very definite information indeed is wanting as to the nature and effect of the defilements from various causes. Yet, in all probability, the defilement arising from entering the house of a heathen could only have belonged to that inferior class from which one might be cleansed by ablution at the going down of the sun. But, on the other hand, the eating of the Paschal lamb was a matter of such importance that only the most serious impediment was allowed to interfere, — in the Pentateuch the only defilement named is that from the dead body of a man (Num. ix. 6, 7), — a defilement which continued seven days (Num. xix. 11–13). It appears, therefore, that by entering the judgment-hall of Pilate the Jews would have contracted a defilement insufficient to prevent their eating of the Paschal lamb, but incapacitating them for eating of those subsequent feasts which were probably held at an earlier hour of the day. The inference from this passage, on the whole, is in favor of the Paschal Supper having taken place on the previous evening.

III. Jno. xix. 14. "It was the Preparation of the Passover." This has sometimes been understood as meaning the preparation *for* the Passover, and therefore as necessarily preceding it. As a matter of fact, however, there is no evidence that the day before the Passover (for which other phrases were in use, cf. Matt. xxvi. 17; Mar xiv. 12; Lk. xxii. 7), was ever called by this name, while there is evidence that this precise term was applied to the day before the weekly, or the festival, Sabbath (Matt. xxvii. 62; Mar. xv. 42; Lk. xxiii. 54; Jno. xix. 31, 42). In all these places it is used absolutely as the well-known designation of the day before the Sabbath. It would seem therefore, that "the Preparation of the Passover" as distinctly marks out the day before the Sabbath of the Passover week as we could do by saying "the Friday of the Passover."

Some other passages are brought forward which have either been sufficiently considered in the note to the previous section, or else do not seem to require consideration at all.

One other argument has been relied upon to show that the apprehension and trial of our Lord must have taken place before the Passover, which is quite without force, viz. that such a public judicial act was unlawful upon the Sabbath, and on all great festival days. The answer to this is patent in the Gospel narrative itself. Even the sanctity of the weekly Sabbath was not able to prevent the inhabitants of Nazareth from attempting to put Jesus to death on that day (Lk. iv. 16–30); and so at Jerusalem, at the Feast of Dedication, the Jews first attempted to stone, and then to arrest him (Jno. x. 22–39); on the last day of the Feast of Tabernacles, "the great day of the feast," the Sanhedrim was in session (Nicodemus being with them), and sent officers to take Jesus, and censured them for their failure to do so (Jno. vii. 37–52). Furthermore when the Sanhedrim at first determined not to put Jesus to death on the feast-day, it was not because of any illegality in the time, but only "lest there should be an uproar among the people." No scruples prevented the chief priests and Pharisees, on the weekly Sabbath, from going to Pilate for a guard, nor from taking measures to seal the sepulchre (Matt. xxvii. 62–66).

The objection that if our Lord was crucified on Friday and rose on Sunday He would not have been "three days" in the grave, can only be made by those not familiar with the Hebrew usage of numerals. Had He been crucified on Thursday, this usage would have required the expression "four days."

It seems quite unnecessary with this evidence to resort to the Rabbinical traditions, which, however, when fully examined, give testimony to the same effect.

In the early church, as is well known, the Eastern Christians kept their commemorative Passover on the evening following the fourteenth Nisan, at the same time with the Jews, and this they did on the authority, as they alleged, of St. John. Indeed, Polycarp testifies that he had once thus celebrated it with St. John himself. It can hardly, therefore, be supposed that St. John intended in his Gospel to teach that our Saviour himself kept the Passover on a different day.

PART VIII.

THE LAST PASSOVER; OUR LORD'S PASSION; THE SABBATH.

THE SIXTH DAY OF THE WEEK. — FRIDAY (BEGINNING AT SUNSET THURSDAY).

§ 131. At table with the Twelve, our Lord reproves their Ambition.

ST. MATT. XXVI. 20.   ST. MARK XIV. 17.   ST. LUKE XXII. 14–18, 24–30.

20 Now when the even was come, he sat down with the twelve apostles.[2]	17 And in the evening he cometh with the twelve.	14 And when the hour was come, he sat 15 down, and the[1] apostles with him. And he said unto them, With desire I have desired to eat this passover with you before I 16 suffer: for I say unto you, I will not any more eat it,[3] until it be fulfilled in the 17 kingdom of God. And he took the cup, and gave thanks, and said, Take this, and 18 divide *it* among yourselves: for I say unto you, I will not drink of the fruit of the vine, until the kingdom of God shall come. 24 And there was also a strife among them, which of them should be accounted the 25 greatest. And he said unto them, The kings of the Gentiles exercise lordship over them; and they that exercise authority upon 26 them are called benefactors. But ye *shall* not *be* so; but he that is greatest among you, let him be as the younger: and he that

[1] the twelve apostles   [2] *omit* apostles   [3] eat thereof

§ 131. It is plain from the concurrent order of the other three Evangelists that St Luke in his account of this supper, has not arranged the incidents chronologically. The verses omitted here will be found in §§ 133, 134.

The strife here mentioned by St. Luke alone was doubtless the immediate occasion for the washing of the disciples feet, as a basis for the lesson of humility recorded by St. John alone.

The preliminary cup taken before the Paschal meal in connection with the invocation of a blessing, and mentioned in Lk. xxii. 17, is not to be confounded with the cup given at the institution of the Lord's Supper at the close of the Paschal Supper.

ST. MATT. XXVI.	ST. MARK XIV.	ST. LUKE XXII.

27 is chief, as he that doth serve. For whether *is* greater, he that sitteth at meat, or he that serveth? *is* not he that sitteth at meat? but I am among you as he that serveth.
28 Ye are they which have continued with me
29 in my temptations. And I appoint unto you a kingdom, as my Father hath appointed
30 unto me; that ye may eat and drink at my table in my kingdom, and sit on thrones judging the twelve tribes of Israel.ᵃ

§ 132. He washes the Feet of the Disciples.
St. John xiii. 1–20.

1 Now before the feast of the passover, when Jesus knew that his hour was come that he should depart out of this world unto the Father, having loved
2 his own which were in the world, he loved them unto the end. And during¹ supper the devil having now put into the heart that Judas Iscariot, Simon's
3 *son*, should² betray him; ³knowing that the Father had given all things into
4 his hands, and that he was come from God, and went to God; he riseth from supper, and laid aside his garments; and took a towel, and girded himself.
5 After that he poureth water into a basin, and began to wash the disciples'
6 feet, and to wipe *them* with the towel wherewith he was girded. Then cometh he to Simon Peter: he⁴ saith unto him, Lord, dost thou wash my
7 feet? Jesus answered and said unto him, What I do thou knowest not now;
8 but thou shalt know hereafter. Peter saith unto him, Thou shalt never wash my feet. Jesus answered him, If I wash thee not, thou hast no part with
9 me. Simon Peter saith unto him, Lord, not my feet only, but also *my* hands
10 and *my* head. Jesus saith to him, He that is washed needeth not to wash⁵
11 but is clean every whit: and ye are clean, but not all. For he knew who
12 should betray him; therefore said he that⁶ Ye are not all clean. So after he had washed their feet, and had taken his garments, and was set down again,
13 he said unto them, Know ye what I have done to you? Ye call me Master,
14 and Lord: and ye say well; for *so* I am. If I then, *your* Lord and Master,
15 have washed your feet; ye also ought to wash one another's feet. For I
16 have given you an example, that ye should do as I have done to you. Verily, verily, I say unto you, The servant is not greater than his lord; neither he

---

¹ And supper being ended ² heart of Judas Iscariot, Simon's *son*, to betray
³ Jesus knowing ⁴ and Peter saith
⁵ needeth not save to wash *his* feet, but is ⁶ *omit* that

ᵃ See Matt. xix. 28.

---

§ 132. On the expression in vs. 1, "before the feast of the Passover," see note on § 130.

ST. JOHN XIII.

17 that is sent greater than he that sent him. If ye know these things, happy are ye if ye do them.
18 I speak not of you all: I know whom I have chosen: but that the scripture may be fulfilled, He that eateth bread with me hath lifted up his heel against
19 me.[a] Now I tell you before it come, that, when it is come to pass, ye may
20 believe that I am *he*. Verily, verily, I say unto you, He that receiveth whomsoever I send receiveth me; and he that receiveth me receiveth him that sent me.

§ 133. He points out the Traitor; Judas withdraws.

MATT. XXVI. 21-25.   MAR. XIV. 18-21.   LK. XXII. 21-23.   JNO. XIII. 21-35.

MATT.	MAR.	LK.	JNO.
21 And as they did eat, he said, Verily I say unto you, that one of you shall 22 betray me. And they were exceeding sorrowful, and began every one[2] to say unto him, Lord, is it I?	18 And as they sat and did eat, Jesus said, Verily I say unto you, One of you which eateth with me shall betray me. 19 [1]They began to be sorrowful, and to say unto him one by one, *Is* it I?[3]	21 But, behold! the hand of him that betrayeth me *is* with me on the table. 23 And they began to enquire among themselves, which of them it was that should do this thing.	21 When Jesus had thus said, he was troubled in spirit, and testified, and said, Verily, verily, I say unto you, that one of you shall betray 22 me. [4]The disciples looked one on another, doubting of whom he 23 spake. [5]There was leaning on Jesus' bosom one of his disciples, whom 24 Jesus loved. Simon Peter therefore beckoned to him, and saith to him, Say who it is of whom he 25 speaks.[6] He then lying thus[7] on Jesus' breast saith unto him, Lord, 26 who is it? Jesus

[1] And they began   [2] every one of them   [3] *add* another *said, Is* it I? and
[4] Then the disciples   [5] Now there was
[6] beckoned to him, that he should ask who it should be of whom he spake.   [7] *omit* thus
[a] Ps. xli. 9.

ST. MATT. XXVI.	ST. MARK XIV.	ST. LUKE XXII.	ST. JOHN. XIII.
			answered, He it is, to whom I shall give the[1] sop, when I have dipped *it*.
23 And he answered and said, He that dippeth *his* hand with me in the dish, the same shall 24 betray me. The Son of Man goeth as it is written of him: but woe unto that man by whom the Son of Man is betrayed! it had been good for that man if he had not been born.	20 And he[2] said unto them, *it is* one of the twelve, that dippeth with me in the dish. 21 For[3] the Son of Man indeed goeth, as it is written of him: but woe to that man by whom the Son of Man is betrayed! good *were it*[5] for that man if he had never been born.	22 For[4] truly the Son of Man goeth, as it was determined: but woe unto that man by whom he is betrayed!	
			And when he had

[1] a sop   [2] he answered and said   [3] *omit* For   [4] And truly   [5] were it

§ 133. Jno. xiii. 27–35 is inserted here on the supposition that Judas went out before the institution of the Lord's Supper. The want of connecting points between the narratives of St. John and of the other Evangelists prevents, perhaps, the absolute determination of this point, and there has consequently always been a diversity of opinion. The view here taken is that adopted, among the ancients, by Cyprian, Jerome, Augustine, Chrysostom, the two Cyrils, Theodoret, etc.; later, by Bellarmine, Baronius, Maldonatus, Gerhard, Beza, Bucer, Lightfoot, Bengel, etc.; and among recent commentators, McKnight, Krafft, Patritius, Stier, Olshausen, Ellicott, Alford, etc. The giving of the sop in the narrative of St John (after which Judas immediately went out) certainly seems to have been during the Paschal meal, and therefore before the institution; but as this does not admit of positive proof, the question must remain one in part of Christian sentiment and fitness.

The order of the incidents recorded in this section is thus happily expressed by Robinson (Harm. in loco p. 224); "Jesus first declares that one of the twelve shall betray him; they in amazement inquire, 'Lord, is it I? is it I?' and Peter makes a sign to John leaning on Jesus' bosom, that he should ask, who it was. John does so; and Jesus gives him privately a sign by which he may know the traitor; namely, the sop. The amazement and inquiry still continuing, Jesus gives the sop to Judas; who then, conscience-smitten, but desiring to conceal his confusion, asks, as the others had done, 'Lord, is it I?' Jesus answers him, and he immediately goes out, before the institution of the Eucharist."

ST. MATT. XXVI.	ST. MARK XIV.	ST. LUKE XXII.	ST. JOHN XIII.
			dipped the sop, he took it and[1] gave *it* to Judas *the son* of Simon Iscariot.[2]
25 Then Judas, which betrayed him, answered and said, Master, is it I? He said unto him, Thou hast said.			
			27 And after the sop Satan entered into him. Then said Jesus unto him, That thou doest, do quickly.
28 Now no man at the table knew for what intent he
29 spake this unto him. For some *of them* thought, because Judas had the bag, that Jesus had said unto him, Buy *those things* that we have need of against the feast; or, that he should give some-
30 thing to the poor. He then having received the sop went immediately out: and it was night.
31 Therefore, when he was gone out, Jesus said, Now is the Son of Man glorified, and God is glorified
32 in him. If God be glorified in him, God shall also glorify him in himself, and shall straight-
33 way glorify him. Little children, yet a little while I am with you. Ye shall seek me: and as I said unto the Jews,

[1] *omit* took it and

[2] Iscariot, *the son* of Simon

[Part VIII. § 134.]   OUR LORD'S PASSION; THE SABBATH.   227

ST. MATT. XXVI.	ST. MARK XIV.	ST. LUKE XXII.	ST. JOHN XIII.
			Whither I go, ye cannot come; so now I say to 34 you. A new commandment I give unto you, That ye love one another; as I have loved you, that ye also love one 35 another. By this shall all *men* know that ye are my disciples, if ye have love one to another.

§ 134. The Institution of the Lord's Supper.

MATT. XXVI. 26–29.   MAR. XIV. 22–25.   LK. XXII. 19, 20.   1 COR. XI. 23–25.

26 And as they were eating, Jesus took bread, and blessed *it*, and brake *it*, and giving *it* to the disciples, said,[2] Take, eat; this is my body.	22 And as they did eat, he[1] took bread, and blessed, and brake *it*, and gave to them, and said, Take,[3] this is my body.	19 And he took bread, and gave thanks, and brake *it*, and gave unto them, saying, This is my body which is given for you: this do in remembrance of me.	23 For I have received of the Lord, that which also I delivered unto you. That the Lord Jesus, the *same* night in which he was betrayed, took 24 bread: and when he had given thanks, he brake *it*, and said,[4] this is my body, which is[5] for you: this do in remembrance of me.
27 And he took a[6] cup, and gave thanks, and gave *it* to them, saying, Drink ye all 28 of it; For this is my blood of	23 And he took a[6] cup, and when he had given thanks, he gave *it* to them: and they all drank 24 of it. And he said unto them, This is my blood	20 Likewise also the cup after supper, saying, This cup *is* the	25 After the same manner also *he took* the cup, when he had supped, saying, This cup is the new tes-

---

[1] Jesus took   [2] gave *it* to the disciples, and said   [3] Take, eat; this is
[4] and said, Take, eat; this is   [5] is broken for you   [6] the cup

ST. MATT. XXIV.	ST. MARK XIV.	ST. LUKE XXII.	I COR. XI.
the¹ testament,ᵃ which is shed for many for the remission of sins.	of the¹ testament,ᵃ which is shed for many.	new testamentᵃ in my blood, which is shed for you.	tamentᵃ in my blood:
29 But I say unto you, I will not drink henceforth of this fruit of the vine, until that day when I drink it new with you in my Father's kingdom.	25 Verily I say unto you, I will drink no more of the fruit of the vine, until that day that I drink it new in the kingdom of God.		
			this do ye, as oft as ye drink *it*, in remembrance of me.

§ 135. The Dispersion of the Twelve, and the Denials of Peter foretold.

MATT. XXVI. 31–35.   MAR. XIV. 27–31.   LK. XXII. 31–38.   JNO. XIII. 36–38.

31 Then saith Jesus unto them, All ye shall be offended because of me this night: for it is written, I will smite the shepherd, and the sheep of the	27 And Jesus saith unto them, All ye shall be offended:² for it is written, I will smite the shepherd, and

¹ new testament   ² offended because of me this night: for
ᵃ Cf. Ex. xxiv. 8; Lev. xvii. 11; Heb. ix. 12, 14, 20; xiii. 20, etc. See also Jer. xxxi. 31.

§ 135. In St. Matthew and St. Luke, the incidents of this section follow the mention of their going out to the Mount of Olives, (Matt. xxvi. 30; Mar. xiv. 26); in St. Luke and St. John, they precede the corresponding statement (Lk. xxii. 39; Jno. xviii. 1). Hence it has sometimes been thought that the fall of Peter was foretold twice. It is better to suppose that the two former Evangelists mention the going out, and then pause to record this omitted incident, and then resume their narrative. In the verse immediately following this section (Matt. xxvi. 36; Mar. xiv. 32), both speak of their coming to Gethsemane.

It is, however, quite possible that this section should be placed after leaving the room in which they had partaken of the Supper, and before their arrival at the gate of the city. The objection to this arrangement is the great length of the following discourse in St. John.

ST. MATT. XXVI.	ST. MARK XIV.	ST. LUKE XXII.	ST. JOHN XIII.
flock shall be scattered abroad.ᵃ ³² But after I am risen again, I will go before you into Galilee.	the sheep shall be scattered.ᵃ ²⁸ But after that I am risen, I will go before you into Galilee.		
			³⁶ Simon Peter said unto him, Lord, whither goest thou? Jesus answered[1] Whither I go, thou canst not follow me now: but thou shalt follow[2] afterwards. Peter said unto him, Lord, why cannot I follow thee now?
³³ Peter answered and said unto him, If[3] all *men* shall be offended because of thee, *yet* will I never be offended.	²⁹ But Peter said unto him, Although all shall be offended, yet *will* not I.		³⁷
		³¹ ⁴'Simon, Simon, behold, Satan hath desired *to have* you, that he may sift ³² *you* as wheat: but I have prayed for thee, that thy faith fail not: and when thou art converted, strengthen thy ³³ brethren. And he said unto him, Lord, I am ready to go with thee, both into prison, and to death.	I will lay down my life for thy

[1] answered him [2] follow me afterwards [3] Though all *men*
⁴ And the Lord said, Simon
ᵃ Zech. xiii. 7.

ST. MATT. XXVI.	ST. MARK XIV.	ST. LUKE XXII.	ST. JOHN XIII.
34 Jesus said unto him, Verily I say unto thee, That this night, before the cock crow, thou shalt deny me thrice.	30 And Jesus saith unto him, Verily I say unto thee, That this day, *even* in this night, before the cock crow twice, thou shalt deny 31 me thrice. But	34 And he said, I tell thee, Peter, the cock shall not crow this day, until[2] thou shalt thrice deny that thou knowest me.	38 sake. Jesus answereth[1] him, Wilt thou lay down thy life for my sake? Verily, verily, I say unto thee, The cock shall not crow, till thou hast denied me thrice.
35 Peter said unto him, Though I should die with thee, yet will I not deny thee. Likewise also said all the disciples.	he spake the more vehemently, If I should die with thee, I will not deny thee in any wise. Likewise also said they all.		

35 And he said unto them, When I sent you without purse, and scrip, and shoes,[a] lacked ye anything? And they said, Nothing.
36 And he said[3] unto them, But now, he that hath a purse, let him take *it*, and likewise *his* script: and he that hath no sword, let him sell his garment,
37 and buy one. For I say unto you, that this that is written must[4] be accomplished in me, And he was reckoned among

---

[1] answered   [2] before that thou shalt   [3] Then said he unto them   [4] must yet be

[a] Matt. x. 5–15; Lk. ix. 1–5; comp. x. 1–11.

ST. MATT. XXVI.	ST. MARK XIV.	ST. LUKE XXII.	ST. JOHN XIII.
		the transgressors:[a] for that which[1] concerneth me hath[1] 38 an end. And they said, Lord, behold, here *are* two swords. And he said unto them, it is enough.	

§ 136. Our Lord's last Discourse with His Disciples before His Passion.

St. John xiv. 1.–xvi. 33.

1 Let not your heart be troubled: ye believe in God, believe also in me.
2 In my Father's house are many mansions: if *it were* not *so*, I would have
3 told you. For[2] I go to prepare a place for you. ¹And if I go and prepare a place for you, I will come again, and receive you unto myself; that where I
4 am, *there* ye may be also. And whither I go, ye know the way.[3] Thomas
5 saith unto him, Lord, we know not whither thou goest; and how know we[4]
6 the way? Jesus saith unto him, I am the way, the truth, and the life: no
7 man cometh unto the Father, but by me. If ye had known me, ye shall[5] know my Father also: and from henceforth ye know him, and have seen him.
8 Philip saith unto him, Lord, shew us the Father, and it sufficeth us.
9 Jesus saith unto him, Have I been so long time with you, and yet hast thou not known me, Philip? he that hath seen me hath seen the Father; [6]how
10 sayest thou *then*, Show us the Father? Believest thou not that I am in the Father, and the Father in me? the words that I speak unto you I speak not
11 of myself: but the Father dwelling[7] in me, doeth his works. Believe me that I *am* in the Father, and the Father in me: or else believe[8] for the very
12 works' sake. Verily, verily, I say unto you, He that believeth on me, the works that I do shall he do also; and greater *works* than these shall he do;
13 because I go unto the[9] Father. And whatsoever ye shall ask in my name,
14 that will I do, that the Father may be glorified in the Son. If ye shall ask me[10] any thing in my name, I will do *it*.
15, 16 If ye love me, keep my commandments. And I will pray the Father, and he shall give you another Comforter, that he may be[11] with you for ever;
17 *even* the Spirit of truth; whom the world cannot receive, because it seeth him not, neither knoweth him: [12]ye know him; for he dwelleth with you, and

---

[1] the things concerning me have   [2] *omit* For   [3] I go ye know, and the way ye know.
[4] how can we know   [5] ye should have known   [6] and how sayest
[7] the Father that dwelleth in me, he doeth the works.   [8] believe me
[9] my Father   [10] *omit* me   [11] abide with you   [12] but ye know

[a] Isa. liii. 12.

ST. JOHN XIV.

¹⁹ shall be in you. I will not leave you orphans:¹ I will come to you. Yet a little while, and the world seeth me no more; but ye see me: because I live, ²⁰ ye shall live also. At that day ye shall know that I *am* in my Father, and ²¹ ye in me, and I in you. He that hath my commandments, and keepeth them, he it is that loveth me: and he that loveth me shall be loved of my Father, and I will love him, and will manifest myself to him.

²² Judas saith unto him, not Iscariot, Lord, how is it that thou wilt manifest ²³ thyself unto us, and not unto the world? Jesus answered and said unto him, If a man love me, he will keep my words: and my Father will love him, and ²⁴ we will come unto him, and make our abode with him. He that loveth me not, keepeth not my sayings: and the word which ye hear is not mine, but the Father's which sent me.

²⁵ These things have I spoken unto you, being *yet* present with you. But ²⁶ the Comforter, *which is* the Holy Ghost, whom the Father will send in my name, he shall teach you all things, and bring all things to your remembrance, ²⁷ whatsoever I have said unto you. Peace I leave with you, my peace I give unto you: not as the world giveth, give I unto you. Let not your heart be ²⁸ troubled, neither let it be afraid. Ye have heard how I said unto you, I go away, and come *again* unto you. If ye loved me, ye would rejoice, because² ²⁹ I go unto the Father: for the³ Father is greater than I. And now I have told you before it come to pass, that when it is come to pass, ye might believe. ³⁰ Hereafter I will not talk much with you: for the prince of the⁴ world ³¹ cometh, and hath nothing in me. But that the world may know that I love the Father; and as the Father gave me commandment, even so I do. Arise, let us go hence.

ST. JOHN. XV.

¹₂ I am the true vine, and my Father is the husbandman. Every branch in me that beareth not fruit he taketh away: and every *branch* that beareth ³ fruit, he purgeth it, that it may bring forth more fruit. Now ye are clean ⁴ through the word which I have spoken unto you. Abide in me, and I in you. As the branch cannot bear fruit of itself, except it abide in the vine; ⁵ no more can ye, except ye abide in me. I am the vine, ye *are* the branches: he that abideth in me, and I in him, the same bringeth forth much fruit: ⁶ for without me ye can do nothing. If a man abide not in me, he is cast forth as a branch, and is withered; and men gather it and cast *it*⁵ into the fire, and ⁷ they are burned. If ye abide in me, and my words abide in you, ye shall ask ⁸ what ye will, and it shall be done unto you. Herein is my Father glorified, that ye bear much fruit; so shall ye be my disciples.

⁹ As the Father hath loved me, so have I loved you: continue ye in my love. ¹⁰ If ye keep my commandments, ye shall abide in my love; even as I also⁶ have kept my Father's commandments, and abide in his love.

---

¹ *translated* comfortless ² because I said, I go ³ my Father ⁴ this world
⁵ gather them and cast *them* ⁶ *omit* also

ST. JOHN XV.

11 These things have I spoken unto you, that my joy might be[1] in you, and
12 *that* your joy might be full. This is my commandment, That ye love one
13 another, as I have loved you. Greater love hath no man than this, that *a*
14 *man*[2] lay down his life for his friends. Ye are my friends, if ye do the things
15 which[3] I command you. Henceforth I call you not servants; for the servant knoweth not what his lord doeth: but I have called you friends; for all things
16 that I have heard of my Father I have made known unto you. Ye have not chosen me, but I have chosen you, and ordained you, that ye should go and bring forth fruit, and *that* your fruit should remain: that whatsoever ye shall
17 ask of the Father in my name, he may give it you. These things I command you, that ye love one another.

18,19 If the world hate you, ye know that it hated me before.[4] If ye were of the world, the world would love his own: but because ye are not of the world, but I have chosen you out of the world, therefore the world hateth you.
20 Remember the word that I said unto you, The servant is not greater than his lord. If they have persecuted me, they will also persecute you; if they have
21 kept my saying, they will keep your's also. But all these things will they do
22 unto you for my name's sake, because they know not him that sent me. If I had not come and spoken unto them, they had not had sin: but now they
23,24 have no cloke for their sin. He that hateth me hateth my Father also. If I had not done among them the works which none other man did, they had not had sin: but now have they both seen and hated both me and my Father.
25 But *this cometh to pass*, that the word might be fulfilled that is written in
26 their law, They hated me without a cause.[a] [5]When the Comforter is come, whom I will send unto you from the Father, *even* the Spirit of truth, which
27 proceedeth from the Father, he shall testify of me: and ye also shall bear witness, because ye have been with me from the beginning.

ST. JOHN XVI.

1,2 These things have I spoken unto you, that ye should not be offended. They shall put you out of the synagogues: yea, the time cometh, that whosoever
3 killeth you will think that he doeth God service. And these things will they
4 do,[6] because they have not known the Father, nor me. But these things have I told you, that when the time shall come, ye may remember that I told you of them. And these things I said not unto you at the beginning, because I
5 was with you. But now I go my way to him that sent me: and none of
6 you asketh me, Whither goest thou? But because I have said these things
7 unto you, sorrow hath filled your heart. Nevertheless I tell you the truth; it is expedient for you that I go away: for if I go not away, the Comforter
8 will not come unto you; but if I depart, I will send him unto you. And when he is come, he will convince[7] the world of sin, and of righteousness,

[1] might remain [2] a man [3] do whatsoever I [4] before *it hated* you
[5] But when [6] do unto you, because [7] *translated* reprove

[a] Ps. xxxv. 19; lxix. 5; see also xxxviii. 20; cix. 3.

ST. JOHN XVI.

10 ⁹and of judgment: of sin, because they believe not on me; of righteousness,
11 because I go to the¹ Father, and ye see me no more; of judgment, because the prince of this world is judged.
12 I have yet many things to say unto you, but ye cannot bear them now.
13 Howbeit when he, the Spirit of truth, is come he will guide you into all truth: for he shall not speak of himself; but whatsoever he shall hear, *that* shall he
14 speak: and he will shew you things to come. He shall glorify me: for he
15 shall receive of mine, and shall shew *it* unto you. All things that the Father hath are mine: therefore said I, that he taketh² of mine, and shall shew *it*
16 unto you. A little while, and ye shall no longer³ see me: and again, a little while, and ye shall see me.⁴

17 Then said *some* of his disciples among themselves, What is this that he saith unto us, A little while, and ye shall not see me: and again, a little while, and
18 ye shall see me: and, Because I go to' the Father? They said therefore,
19 What is this that he saith, A little while? we cannot tell what he saith. ⁵Jesus knew that they were desirous to ask him, and said unto them, Do ye enquire among yourselves of that I said, A little while, and ye shall not see me: and
20 again, a little while, and ye shall see me? Verily, verily, I say unto you, That ye shall weep and lament, but the world shall rejoice:⁶ ye shall be sor-
21 rowful, but your sorrow shall be turned into joy. A woman when she is in travail hath sorrow, because her hour is come: but as soon as she is delivered of the child, she remembereth no more the anguish, for joy that a man is born
22 into the world. And ye now therefore have sorrow: but I will see you again,
23 and your heart shall rejoice, and your joy no man taketh from you. And in that day ye shall ask me nothing. Verily, verily, I say unto you, Whatso-
24 ever ye shall ask the Father, he will give *it* you in my name.⁷ Hitherto have ye asked nothing in my name: ask, and ye shall receive, that your joy may be full.

25 These things have I spoken unto you in proverbs;⁸ the time cometh, when I shall no more speak unto you in proverbs, but I shall shew you plainly of
26 the Father. At that day ye shall ask in my name: and I say not unto you,
27 that I will pray the Father for you: for the Father himself loveth you, because ye have loved me, and have believed that I came out from God.
28 I came forth from the Father, and am come into the world: again, I leave the world, and go to the Father.

29 His disciples said,⁹ Lo, now speakest thou plainly, and speakest no proverb.
30 Now are we sure that thou knowest all things, and needest not that any man
31 should ask thee: by this we believe that thou camest forth from God. Jesus
32 answered them, Do ye now believe? Behold! the hour cometh, yea, is¹⁰ come,

---

¹ to my Father
² shall take
³ shall not see
⁴ *add* because I go to the Father
⁵ Now Jesus knew
⁶ and ye shall
⁷ ask the Father in my name, he will give *it* you.
⁸ but the time
⁹ said unto him
¹⁰ is now come

ST. JOHN XVI.

that ye shall be scattered, every man to his own, and shall leave me alone:
33 and yet I am not alone, because the Father is with me. These things I have spoken unto you, that in me ye might have peace. In the world ye[1] have tribulation: but be of good cheer; I have overcome the world.

§ 137. Our Lord's Sacerdotal Prayer.
St. John xvii. 1–26.

1 These words spake Jesus, and lifted up his eyes to heaven, and said, Father, the hour is come; glorify thy Son, that the[2] Son may glorify thee:
2 as thou hast given him power over all flesh, that he should give eternal life
3 to as many as thou hast given him. And this is life eternal, that they might
4 know thee the only true God, and Jesus Christ, whom thou hast sent. I have glorified thee on the earth, having[3] finished the work which thou gavest me
5 to do. And now, O Father, glorify thou me with thine own self with the glory which I had with thee before the world was.
6 I have manifested thy name unto the men which thou gavest me out of the world: thine they were, and thou gavest them me; and they have kept thy
7 word. Now they have known that all things whatsoever thou hast given me,
8 are of thee. For I have given unto them the words which thou gavest me; and they have received *them*, and have known surely that I came out from thee, and
9 they have believed that thou didst send me. I pray for them: I pray not for
10 the world, but for them which thou hast given me: for they are thine. And all
11 mine are thine, and thine are mine; and I am glorified in them. And now I am no more in the world, but they[4] are in the world, and I come to thee. Holy Father, keep them through thine own name wherein[5] thou hast given
12 *them* to me, that they may be one, as we *are*. While I was with them[6] I kept them in thy name wherein thou gavest *them* to me, and guarded *them*,[7] and none of them is lost, but the son of perdition; that the scripture might
13 be fulfilled. And now come I to thee: and these things I speak in the world, that they might have my joy fulfilled in themselves.
14 I have given them thy word; and the world hath hated them, because they
15 are not of the world, even as I am not of the world. I pray not that thou shouldest take them out of the world, but that thou shouldest keep them from
16,17 the evil. They are not of the world, even as I am not of the world. Sanctify
18 them through the[8] truth: thy word is truth. As thou hast sent me into the
19 world, even so have I also sent them into the world. And for their sakes I sanctify myself, that they also might be sanctified through the truth.
20 Neither pray I for these alone, but for them also which[9] believe on me

---

[1] ye shall have   [2] that thy Son also may   [3] on the earth: I have finished
[4] but these are   [5] keep through thine own name those whom thou hast given me
[6] with them in the world, I kept
[7] in thy name: those that thou gavest me I have kept, and none
[8] thy truth   [9] which shall believe

ST. JOHN XVII.

21 through their word; that they all may be one; as thou, Father, *art* in me, and I in thee, that they also may be[1] in us: that the world may believe that thou
22 hast sent me. And the glory which thou gavest me I have given them; that
23 they may be one, even as we *are*[2] one: I in them, and thou in me, that they may be made perfect in one; [3]that the world may know that thou hast sent me, and hast loved them as thou hast loved me.
24 Father, I will that they also, whom thou hast given me, be with me where I am; that they may behold my glory, which thou hast given me: for thou
25 lovedst me before the foundation of the world. O righteous Father, the world hath not known thee; but I have known thee, and these have known that thou
26 hast sent me. And I have declared unto them thy name, and will declare *it*: that the love wherewith thou hast loved me may be in them, and I in them.

§ 138. Our Lord goes out with the Disciples to the Mount of Olives.

MATT. XXVI. 30.	MARK XIV. 26.	LUKE XXII. 39.	JOHN XVIII. 1.
30 And when they had sung an hymn, they went out into the mount of Olives.	26 And when they had sung an hymn, they went out into the mount of Olives.	39 And he came out, and went, as he was wont, to the mount of Olives; and the[4] disciples also followed him.	1 When Jesus had spoken these words, he went forth with his disciples over the brook Cedron, where was a garden, into the which he entered, and his disciples.

§ 139. The Agony in Gethsemane.

ST. MATT. XXVI. 36–46.	ST. MARK XIV. 32–42.	ST. LUKE XXII. 40–46.
36 Then cometh Jesus with them unto a place called Gethsemane, and saith unto the disciples, Sit ye here, while I go and pray 37 yonder. And he took with him Peter and the two sons of Zebedee, and began to be sorrowful and very 38 heavy. Then saith he unto them, My soul is exceeding sorrowful,	32 And they came to a place which was named Gethsemane: and he saith to his disciples, Sit ye here, while I 33 shall pray. And he taketh with him Peter and James and John, and began to be sore amazed, and to be very 34 heavy; and saith unto them, My soul is exceeding sorrowful unto	40 And when he was at the place, he said unto them, Pray that ye enter not into temptation.

[1] may be one in us [2] are [3] in one; and that [4] his disciples

ST. MATT. XXVI.	ST. MARK XIV.	ST. LUKE XXII.
even unto death: tarry ye here, and watch 39 with me. And he went a little farther, and fell on his face, and prayed,	death: tarry ye here, 35 and watch. And he went forward a little, and fell on the ground, and prayed that, if it were possible, the hour might pass from him.	41 And he was withdrawn from them about a stone's cast, and kneeled down, and prayed.
saying,[1] Father, if it be possible, let this cup pass from me: nevertheless not as I will, but as thou *wilt*.	36 And he said, Abba, Father, all things *are* possible unto thee; take away this cup from me: nevertheless not what I will, but what thou wilt.	42 saying, Father, if thou be willing, remove this cup from me: nevertheless not my will, but 43 thine be done. [2]And there appeared an angel unto him from heaven, 44 strengthening him. And being in an agony he prayed more earnestly: and his sweat was as it were great drops of blood falling down to 45 the ground. And when he rose up from prayer, and was come to the[3] disciples, he found them 46 sleeping for sorrow, and said unto them.
40 And he cometh unto the disciples, and findeth them asleep, and saith unto Peter, What, could ye not watch with 41 me one hour? Watch and pray, that ye enter not into temptation: the spirit indeed *is* willing, but the flesh *is* 42 weak. He went away again the second time, and prayed, saying, O my Father, if this[4] may not pass away except I drink it, thy will be	37 And he cometh, and findeth them sleeping, and saith unto Peter, Simon, sleepest thou? couldest not thou 38 watch one hour. Watch ye and pray, lest ye enter into temptation. The spirit truly *is* ready, but the flesh 39 *is* weak. And again he went away, and prayed, and spake the same words.	Why sleep ye? rise and pray, lest ye enter into temptation.

[1] saying, O my Father,
[3] his disciples

[2] verses 43 and 44 are omitted in many of the early MSS.
[4] if this cup may not pass away from me except

ST. MATT. XXVI.	ST. MARK XIV.	ST. LUKE XXII.

43 done. And he came again[1] and found them asleep; for their eyes were heavy.

44 And he left them, and went away again, and prayed the third time, saying again[2] the same

45 words. Then cometh he to the[3] disciples, and saith unto them, Sleep on now, and take *your* rest: behold, the hour is at hand, and the Son of Man is betrayed into the hands

46 of sinners. Rise, let us be going: behold, he is at hand that doth betray me.

40 And when he returned, he found them asleep again, (for their eyes were heavy,) neither wist they what to answer him.

41 And he cometh the third time, and saith unto them, Sleep on now, and take *your* rest: it is enough, the hour is come; behold, the Son of Man is betrayed into the hands

42 of sinners. Rise up, let us go; lo, he that betrayeth me is at hand.

§ 140. Our Lord is made Prisoner.

MATT. XXVI. 47–56.   MAR. XIV. 43–52.   LK. XXII. 47–53.   JNO. XVIII. 2–12.

2 And Judas also, which betrayed him, knew the place: for Jesus ofttimes resorted thither with his 3 disciples. Judas then, having received a band *of men* and officers from the chief priests and from the[6] Pharisees, cometh thither with lanterns and

47 And while he yet spake, lo, Judas, one of the twelve, came, and with him a great multitude with swords and staves, from the chief priests and elders of the 48 people. Now he

43 And immediately, while he yet spake, cometh Judas Iscariot,[4] one of the twelve, and with him a[5] multitude with swords and staves, from the chief priests and the scribes and[7] 44 elders. And he

47 While ye yet spake, behold a multitude, and he that was called Judas, one of the twelve, went before them,

---

[1] came and found them asleep again   [2] *omit* again   [3] his disciples   [4] *omit* Iscariot
[5] a great multitude   [6] *omit* from the   [7] the elders

ST. MATT. XXVI.	ST. MARK XIV.	ST. LUKE XXII.	ST. JOHN XVIII.
that betrayed him gave them a sign, saying, Whomsoever I shall kiss, that same is he: hold 40 him fast. And forthwith he came to Jesus, and said, Hail, master; and 50 kissed him. And Jesus said unto him, Friend, wherefore art thou come?	that betrayed him had given them a token, saying, Whomsoever I shall kiss, that same is he; take him, and lead *him* away safely. 45 And as soon as he was come, he goeth straightway to him, and saith, Master;[1] and kissed him.	and drew near unto Jesus to 48 kiss him. But Jesus said unto him, Judas, betrayest thou the Son of Man with a kiss?	torches and weapons. 4 Jesus therefore, knowing all things that should come upon him, went forth, and said unto them, Whom 5 seek ye? They answered him, Jesus of Nazareth. Jesus saith unto them, I am *he*. And Judas also, which betrayed him, stood with 6 them. As soon then as he had said unto them, I am *he*, they went backward, and fell to the ground. 7 Then asked he them again,

[1] Master, master;

ST. MATT. XXVI.	ST. MARK XIV.	ST. LUKE XXII.	ST. JOHN XVIII.
			Whom seek ye? And they said, Jesus of Nazareth. Jesus answered, I have told you that I am *he:* if therefore ye seek me, let these go their way: that the saying might be fulfilled, which he spake, Of them which thou gavest me have I lost none.
Then came they, and laid hands on Jesus, and took him. And,	And they laid their hands on him, and took him. And one		
		When they which were about him saw what would follow, they said¹ Lord, shall we smite with the sword?	
behold! one of them which were with Jesus stretched out *his* hand, and drew his sword, and struck a servant of the high priest's, and smote off his ear.	of them that stood by drew a sword, and smote a servant of the high priest, and cut off his ear.	And one of them smote the servant of the high priest, and cut off his right ear. And Jesus answered and said, Suffer ye	Then Simon Peter having a sword drew it, and smote the high priest's servant, and cut off his right ear. The servant's name was Malchus.

¹ said unto him

ST. MATT. XXVI.	ST. MARK XIV.	ST. LUKE XXII.	ST. JOHN XVIII.
		thus far. And he touched the[1] ear, and healed him.	
52 Then said Jesus unto him, Put up again thy sword into his place: for all they that take the sword shall perish with the 53 sword. Thinkest thou that I cannot[3] pray to my Father, and he shall presently give me more than twelve legions 54 of angels? But how then shall the scriptures be fulfilled, that thus it must be?[a]			11 Then said Jesus unto Peter, Put up the[2] sword into the sheath: the cup which my Father hath given me, shall I not drink it?
			12 Then the band and the captain and officers of the Jews took Jesus, and bound him,—
55 In that same hour said Jesus to the multitudes, Are ye come out as against a thief with swords and	48 And Jesus answered and said unto them, Are ye come out, as against a thief, with swords and	52 Then Jesus said unto the chief priests, and captains of the temple, and the elders, which were come to him, Be ye come out, as against a thief, with swords and	

[1] his ear [2] thy sword [3] cannot now pray
[a] See Isa. lii. 13–liii. 12, etc.

ST. MATT. XXVI.	ST. MARK XIV.	ST. LUKE XXII.	ST. JOHN XVIII.
staves for to take me? I sat daily¹ teaching in the temple, and ye laid no 56 hold on me. But all this was done, that the scriptures of the prophets might be fulfilled.ᵃ Then all the disciples forsook him, and fled.	*with* staves to take me? I was daily with you in the temple teaching, and ye took me not: but the scriptures must be 50 fulfilled.ᵃ And they all forsook him, and fled. 51 And there followed him a certain young man, having a linen cloth cast about *his* naked *body;* and they² laid hold on 52 him: and he left the linen cloth, and fled³ naked.	53 staves? When I was daily with you in the temple, ye stretched forth no hands against me: but this is your hour, and the power of darkness.	

§ 141. He is taken before Annas and Caiaphas.

MATT. XXVI. 57, 58. MAR. XIV. 53, 54. LK. XXII. 54, 55. JNO. XVIII. 13–16, 18.

<blockquote>
13 —And led him⁴ to Annas first; for he was father in law to Caiaphas, which was the high priest that 14 same year. Now Caiaphas was he, which gave counsel to the Jews, that it was expedient that one man should die for the people.ᵇ
</blockquote>

¹ daily with you teaching ² and the young men laid hold ³ fled from them
³ led him away to Annas

ᵃ See Isa. lii. 13–liii. 12, etc. ᵇ Jno. xi. 49, 50.

ST. MATT. XXVI.	ST. MARK XIV.	ST. LUKE XXII.	ST. JOHN XVIII.
57 And they that had laid hold on Jesus led *him* away to Caiaphas the high priest, where the scribes and the elders were assembled. 58 But Peter followed him afar off unto the high priest's palace,	53 And they led Jesus away to the high priest: and there were assembled¹ all the chief priests and the elders and the scribes. 54 And Peter followed him afar off, even into the palace of the high priest:	54 Then took they him, and led *him*, and brought him into the high priest's house. And Peter followed afar off.	15 And Simon Peter followed Jesus, and *so did* another disciple: that disciple was known unto the high priest, and went in with Jesus into the palace of the high 16 priest. But Peter stood at the door without. Then went out that other disciple.

¹ and with him were assembled

§§ 141, 142. The Jews had now so far accomplished their horrid purpose that they held Jesus bound, a prisoner in their hands. What was to be done next? Very naturally they take him first to Annas, who had been formerly their high-priest, and was a man of great authority and of much esteem as a counsellor among them, and the father-in-law of Caiaphas, "the high-priest that same year." We have no certain indication of the time, but it must have been beyond midnight, perhaps an hour beyond. Annas, apparently without delay, sent him on to Caiaphas. This fact is distinctly mentioned by St. John in vs. 24. Arrived at the house of Caiaphas, a considerable time must have been consumed in notifying and assembling the members of the Sanhedrim. Some of them were doubtless already there, or came with Jesus. While they were assembling, Caiaphas appears to have made a preliminary examination in one of the rooms of his palace opening upon the large unroofed court around which oriental houses are built. It was here that the fire was built and that Peter uttered his first denial. Afterwards, he retired to the *porch* (Mar. vs. 68; Matt. vs. 71) or broad passageway leading from the gate of the house to the court. How long an interval elapsed between the first and second denials is not mentioned; probably not long. In that interval St. Mark mentions that the cock crew. This was the first cock-crowing, which occurred somewhat irregularly, not very long after midnight. St. Mark alone mentions it, as he alone had particularized the two cock-crowings in the prophecy of the Saviour. The second cock-crowing occurred with great regularity at day-break, or about three o'clock, A.M.

In the account of the second denial there are differences which have sometimes been imagined to be real discrepancies between the Evangelists. St. Matthew says the questioner was "another *maid*"; St. Mark "*the*" (i.e. probably, the same) "maid"; St. Luke, "another

ST. MATT. XXVI.	ST. MARK XIV.	ST. LUKE XXII.	ST. JOHN XVIII.
			which was known of¹ the high priest, and spake unto her that kept the door, and brought in Peter.
and went in,			
			18 —And the servants and officers stood there, who had made a fire of coals; for it was cold: and they warmed themselves: and Peter stood with them, and warmed himself.
and sat with the servants to see the end.	and he sat with the servants, and warmed himself at the fire.	55 And when they had kindled a fire in the midst of the hall, and were set down together, Peter sat down among them.	

§ 142. While the Sanhedrim assemble, He is examined by Caiaphas. Peter denies Him thrice.

MATT. XXVI. 69-75.   MAR. XIV. 66-72.   LK. XXII. 56-62.   JNO. XVIII. 17, 19-27.

69 Now Peter sat without in the palace: and a damsel came	66 And as Peter was beneath in the palace, there cometh one of the maids of the	56 But a certain maid beheld him as he sat by the	17 Then saith the damsel that kept the door unto Pe-

¹ known unto

man"; St. John, indefinitely, "they." In this last expression is the key to the whole. In such a crowd and under such a state of excitement, an accusation made by one would naturally be caught up and repeated by another and another. The first maid, we may suppose, points him out to her companion and others as a disciple (Mar.); her companion takes up and repeats the story, (Matt.), whereupon some man, hearing it, directly charges Peter himself with it (Lk.); all which St. John covers by the indefinite expression "they." After this followed an interval of about an hour (Lk. vs. 59) during which, it has been well suggested, he may have gained courage to join in conversation, and thus have betrayed his Galilean origin. In the third denial there is really no difference at all. The two first Evangelists speak only in general terms, using the plural, St. Luke also is indefinite — another; St. John alone describes the person particularly.

Meantime the Sanhedrim was assembling more and more fully. It was expressly illegal for them to pass a capital condemnation in the night. Their formal assembling for this purpose was therefore deferred until daybreak (Lk. xxii. 66; cf. Matt. xxvii. 1; Mar. xv. 1). In the interval, however, the Sanhedrim did its work, but whether in strictly formal session, or merely by common understanding, does not certainly appear. Such form of trial as was had

PART VIII. § 142.] OUR LORD'S PASSION; THE SABBATH. 245

ST. MATT. XXVI.	ST. MARK XIV.	ST. LUKE XXII.	ST. JOHN XVIII.
	67 high priest: and when she saw Peter warming himself, she looked upon		
unto him, saying, Thou also wast with Jesus of Galilee.	him, and said, And thou also wast with Jesus of Nazareth.	fire, and earnestly looked upon him, and said, This man was also with	ter, Art not thou also *one* of this man's disciples?
70 But he denied before *them* all, saying, I know not what thou sayest.	68 But he denied, saying, I know not, neither understand I what thou sayest. And he went out into the porch; and the cock crew.	57 him. And he denied him, saying, Woman, I know him not.	He saith, I am not.
			19 The high priest then asked Jesus of his disciples, and of his doctrine. Jesus answered him, I have spoken[1] openly to the world; I ever

[1] I spake

---

at all, however, was had during this time, and at the morning session nothing remained but to pronounce the legal condemnation.

In the account of this night, so full of events of deepest importance, some of which must have occurred nearly or quite simultaneously, it is difficult to determine the actual order of time of each incident. The first three Evangelists have recorded the denials of Peter consecutively, evidently because they formed one distinct subject in themselves, and not thereby forbidding the supposition that during their progress other incidents may have occurred. So too with other matters; so that it is not strange that some transpositions become necessary in order to place the parallel passages side by side. Thus, e.g. Jno. xviii. 18, quite as properly belongs in its place; but has been transposed to a previous section on account of the same thing being mentioned then by the other Evangelists, also quite as naturally and truly. Sections 142 and 143 may be considered as to some extent simultaneous. So also St. Luke (vs. 66) mentions the formal assembling of the Sanhedrim at daybreak, to avoid repetition, and then goes back to speak of their doings in the previous hours. These things create a difficulty in the arrangement of the parallel columns of a harmony, but constitute no real discrepancies.

ST. MATT. XXVI.	ST. MARK XIV.	ST. LUKE XXII.	ST. JOHN XVIII.
			taught in the synagogue, and in the temple, whither all[1] the Jews resort; and in secret have I said nothing. 21 Why askest thou me? ask them which heard me, what I have said unto them: behold! they know 22 what I said. And when he had thus spoken, one of the officers which stood by struck Jesus with the palm of his hand, saying, Answerest thou the high 23 priest so? Jesus answered him, If I have spoken evil, bear witness of the evil: but if well, why smitest 24 thou me? Now Annas had sent him bound unto Caiaphas the high 25 priest. And Simon Peter stood and warmed him-
71 And when he was gone out into the porch, another *maid* saw him, and said unto them that were there,	69 And a maid saw him and began again[2] to say to them that stood	58 And after a little while another saw him, and said, Thou art	self. They said therefore unto him, Art not thou also *one* of his

[1] whither the Jews always resort [2] saw him again, and began

ST. MATT. XXVI.	ST. MARK XIV.	ST. LUKE XXII.	ST. JOHN XVIII.
This *fellow* was also with Jesus of Nazareth. 72 And again he denied with an oath, I do not know the man. 73 And after a while came unto *him* they that stood by, and said to Peter, Surely thou also art *one* of them; for thy speech bewrayeth thee. 74 Then began he to curse and to swear, *saying*, I know not the man. And immediately the 75 cock crew. And Peter remembered the word of Jesus, which said,[4] Before the cock crow, thou shall deny me thrice. And he went out, and wept bitterly.	by. This is *one* of them. 70 And he denied it again. And a little after, they that stood by said again to Peter, Surely thou art *one* of them; for thou art a Galilæan.[1] 71 But he began to curse and to swear, *saying*, I know not this man of whom ye 72 speak. And immediately[2] the second time the cock crew. And Peter called to mind the word that Jesus said unto him, Before the cock crow twice, thou shalt deny me thrice. And when he thought thereon, he wept.	also of them. And Peter said, Man, I am not. 60 And about the space of one hour after another confidently affirmed, saying, Of a truth this *fellow* also was with him: for he is a Galilæan. And Pe- ter said, Man, I know not what thou sayest. And immediately, while he yet spake, a[3] cock 61 crew. And the Lord turned, and looked upon Peter. And Peter remembered the word of the Lord, how he had said unto him, Before the cock crow to-day,[5] thou shalt deny me thrice. 62 And he[6] went out, and wept bitterly.	disciples? He denied *it*, and said, 26 I am not. One of the servants of the high priest, being *his* kinsman whose ear Peter cut off, saith, Did not I see thee in the garden with 27 him? Peter then denied again: and immediately the cock crew.

[1] a Galilæan, and thy speech agreeth *thereto* [2] *omit* immediately [3] the cock
[4] said unto him, Before [5] *omit* to-day [6] And Peter went

§ 143. After further Examination, the Sanhedrim adjudge Jesus guilty of Blasphemy. He is mocked by the Servants.

Matt. xxvi. 59–68.	Mar. xiv. 55–65.	Lk. xxii. 67–71, 63–65.
59 Now the chief priests,[1] and all the council sought false witness against Jesus, to put him to death; 60 but found none, though many false witnesses came.[2] At the last came	55 And the chief priests and all the council sought for witness against Jesus to put him to death; and found none. For many bare false witness against him, but their witness agreed not 57 together. And there arose certain, and bare false witness against	
61 two[3] [1]and said, This *fellow* said, I am able to destroy the temple of God, and to build it in three days.[a]	58 him, saying, We heard him say, I will destroy this temple that is made with hands, and within three days I will build another made without hands.[a] 59 But neither so did their witness agree	
62 And the high priest arose, and said unto him, Answerest thou nothing? what *is it which* these witness against thee? 63 But Jesus held his peace. And the high priest answered and said unto him, I adjure thee by the living God, that thou tell us whether thou be the Christ, the Son of 64 God. Jesus saith unto him, Thou hast said: nevertheless I say unto	60 together. And the high priest stood up in the midst, and asked Jesus, saying, Answerest thou nothing? what *is it which* these wit- 61 ness against thee? But he held his peace, and answered nothing. Again the high priest asked him, and said unto him, Art thou the Christ, the Son of 62 the Blessed? And Jesus said, I am:	67 —Saying,[1]Art thou the Christ? tell us. And he said unto them, If I tell you, ye will not 68 believe: and if I[4] ask

[1] priests, and elders, and   [2] yea, though many false witnesses came, *yet* found they none
[3] two false witnesses   [4] if I also ask
[a] Jno. ii. 19; see Matt. xxvii. 40; Mar. xv. 29.

ST. MATT. XXVI.	ST. MARK XIV.	ST. JOHN XXII.
you, Hereafter shall ye see the Son of Man sitting on the right hand of power, and coming in the clouds of heaven.ᵃ	and ye shall see the Son of Man sitting on the right hand of power, and coming in the clouds of heaven.ᵃ	69 you, ye will not answer.¹ But² hereafter shall the Son of Man sit on the right hand of the power of God.ᵃ
65 Then the high priest rent his clothes, saying, He hath spoken blasphemy: what further need have we of witnesses? behold! now ye have heard the³ blasphemy: 66 what think ye? They answered and said, He 67 is guilty of death.ᵇ Then did they spit in his face, and buffeted him; and others smote *him* with the palms of their hands, 68 saying, Prophesy unto us, thou Christ, Who is he that smote thee?	63 Then the high priest rent his clothes, and saith, What need we any further witnesses? 64 Ye have heard the blasphemy: what think ye? And they all condemned him to be 65 guilty of death.ᵇ And some began to spit on him, and to cover his face, and to buffet him, and to say unto him, Prophesy: and the servants did strike him with the palms of their hands.	70 Then said they all, Art thou then the Son of God? And he said unto them, Ye say that 71 I am. And they said, What need we any further witness? for we ourselves have heard of his own mouth. 63 And the men that held him⁴ mocked him, 64 and smote *him*. And when they had blindfolded him, they⁵ asked him, saying, Prophesy, who is it that smote 65 thee? And many other things blasphemously spake they against him.

§ 144. They lead Him to Pilate.

MATT. XXVII. 1, 2.	MAR. XV. 1	LK. XXII. 66, XXIII. 1.	JNO. XVIII. 28.
1 When the morning was come, all the chief priests and elders of the people took counsel against Jesus to put him to death: 2 and when they had bound him, they led *him* away,	1 And straightway in the morning the chief priests held a consultation with the elders and scribes and the whole council, and bound Jesus,	66 And as soon as it was day, the elders of the people and the chief priests and the scribes came together, and led him away⁶ into their council.	28 Then led they

¹ answer me, nor let *me* go   ² *omit* But   ³ his blasphemy
⁴ held Jesus   ⁵ they struck him on the face, and asked   ⁶ *omit* away

ᵃ See Dan. vii. 13; Acts vii. 56.   ᵇ Lev. xxiv. 16.

ST. MATT. XXVII.	ST. MARK XV.	ST. LUKE XXIII.	ST. JOHN XVIII.
and delivered *him* to[1] Pilate the governor.	and carried *him* away, and delivered *him* to Pilate.	1 And the whole multitude of them arose, and led him unto Pilate.	Jesus from Caiaphas unto the hall of judgment: and it was early; and they themselves went not into the judgment hall, lest they should be defiled; but that they might eat the passover.

§ 145. Judas repents and hangs himself.

St. Matt. xxvii. 3–10.	(Acts i. 18, 19.)
3 Then Judas, which had betrayed him, when he saw that he was condemned, repented himself, and brought again the thirty pieces of silver to the chief 4 priests and elders, Saying, I have sinned in that I have betrayed[2] innocent blood. And they said, What *is that* to us? see 5 thou *to that*. And he cast down the pieces of silver in the temple, and departed, and went and hanged himself. 6 And the chief priests took the silver pieces, and said, It is not lawful for to put them into the treasury, because it 7 is the price of blood. And they took counsel, and bought with them the	18 Now this man purchased a field with the reward of iniquity; and falling headlong, he burst asunder in the midst, and all his bowels 19 gushed out. And it was known

[1] delivered him to Pontius Pilate   [2] the innocent

---

§ 145. There is no necessity for deferring the account of the remorse and suicide of Judas until after the final condemnation of Christ by Pilate. When the Sanhedrim had passed their judgment, and permitted our Lord to be treated by the attendants as a condemned malefactor, Judas must have seen that all was over. Doubtless St. Matthew has narrated this in its proper place.

The narrative of St. Luke in Acts i. 18, 19, is perfectly consistent with that of St. Matthew. If the traditional site of the suicide of Judas be correct — and there is no reason why it should not be — on a tree overhanging the precipices of the valley of Hinnom, the breaking of the rope, or of a branch of the tree, would have produced the effects described by St. Luke.

As to the purchase of the field: much needless ingenuity, as in the supposition of two fields, etc., has been expended on this point. The simple solution lies in the fact that Judas was the occasion of the purchase, since he gave the money by which it was effected; therefore he is said to have done it. For similar instances, see Matt. xxvii. 60; Jno. iii. 22; cf. iv. 2; 1 Cor. vii. 16; 1 Tim. iv. 16, etc.

ST. MATT. XXVII.

potter's field, to bury strangers in.
8 Wherefore that field was called, The
9 field of blood, unto this day. Then was fulfilled that which was spoken by Jeremy the prophet, saying, And they took the thirty pieces of silver, the price of him that was valued, whom they of the children of Israel did value;
10 and gave them for the potter's field, as the Lord appointed me.[a]

ACTS I.

unto all the dwellers at Jerusalem; insomuch as that field is called in their proper tongue, Aceldama, that is to say, The field of blood.

§ 146. Our Lord before Pilate. He seeks to release Him.

MATT. XXVII. 11–14.   MAR. XV. 2–5.   LK. XXIII. 2–5.   JNO. XVIII. 29–38.

29 Pilate then went out unto them, and saith,[1] What accusation bring ye against this man?
30 They answered and said unto him, If he were not a malefactor, we would not have delivered him up unto
31 thee. Then said Pilate unto them, Take ye him, and judge[2] according to your law. The Jews therefore said unto him, It is not lawful for us to put any man to death:
32 that the saying of Jesus might be fulfilled, which he spake, signifying what death he should die.[b]

[1] and said   [2] judge him

[a] Zech. xi. 12, 13. And I said unto them, If ye think good, give me my price; and if not, forbear. So they weighed for my price thirty pieces of silver. And the LORD said unto me, Cast it unto the potter: a goodly price that I was prized at of them. And I took the thirty pieces of silver, and cast them to the potter in the house of the LORD. See also Jer. xviii. 1, 2.

[b] Matt. xx. 19; Jno. xii. 32, 33.

ST. MATT. XXVII.	ST. MARK XV.	ST. LUKE XXIII.	ST. JOHN XVIII.
		2 And they began to accuse him, saying, We found this *fellow* perverting our[1] nation, and forbidding to give tribute to Cæsar,[a] and[2] saying, that he himself is Christ a King.	
11 And Jesus stood before the governor: and the governor asked him, saying, Art thou the King of the Jews?	2 And Pilate asked him, Art thou the King of the Jews?	3 And Pilate asked him, saying, Art thou the King of the Jews?	33 Then Pilate entered into the judgment hall again, and called Jesus, and said unto him, Art thou the King of the Jews? 34 Jesus answered,[3] Sayest thou this thing of thyself, or did others tell it thee of me? 35 Pilate answered, Am I a Jew? Thine own nation and the chief priests have delivered thee unto me: what hast thou done? 36 Jesus answered, My kingdom is not of this world: if my kingdom were of this world, then would my servants fight, that I should not be delivered to

[1] the nation [2] *omit* and [3] answered him
[a] See Matt. xvii. 24–27; xxii. 17–21; Mar. xii. 14–17.

ST. MATT. XXVII.	ST. MARK XV.	ST. LUKE XXIII.	ST. JOHN XVIII.
			the Jews: but now is my kingdom not from hence.
			37 Pilate therefore said unto him, Art thou a king then?
And Jesus said,[1] Thou sayest.	And he answering said unto him, Thou sayest *it*.	And he answered him and said, Thou sayest *it*.	Jesus answered, Thou sayest that I am a king. To this end was I born, and for this cause came I into the world, that I should bear witness unto the truth. Every one that is of the truth heareth my voice.
			38 Pilate saith unto him, What is truth?
			And when he had said this, he went out again unto the Jews,
12 And when he was accused of the chief priests and elders, he answered nothing. 13 Then said Pilate unto him, Hearest thou not how many things they witness against 14 thee? And he answered him to never a word; insomuch that the governor marvelled greatly.	3 And the chief priests accused him of many things: but he answered nothing. 4 And Pilate asked him again,[2] Answerest thou nothing? behold how many things they witness against 5 thee. But Jesus yet answered nothing; so that Pilate marvelled.		
		4 Then said Pilate to the chief	

[1] said unto him

[2] again, saying, Answerest

ST. MATT. XXVII.	ST. MARK XV.	ST. LUKE XXIII.	ST. JOHN XVIII.
		priests and *to* the people, I find no fault in 5 this man. And they were the more fierce, saying, He stirreth up the people, teaching throughout all Jewry, even¹ beginning from Galilee to this place.	and saith unto them, I find in him no fault *at all*.

§ 147. Our Lord before Herod. He is sent back to Pilate, who again seeks to release Him.

St. Luke xxiii. 6–16.

6,7 When Pilate heard,² he asked whether the man were a Galilæan. And as soon as he knew that he belonged unto Herod's jurisdiction, he sent him to Herod, who himself also was at Jerusalem at that time. 8 And when Herod saw Jesus, he was exceeding glad: for he was desirous to see him of a long season,³ because he had heard⁴ of him; and he hoped to 9 have seen some miracle done by him. Then he questioned with him in many 10 words; but he answered him nothing. And the chief priests and scribes 11 stood and vehemently accused him. And Herod with his men of war set him at nought, and mocked *him*, and arrayed *him*⁵ in a gorgeous robe, and 12 sent him again to Pilate. And the same day Herod and Pilate⁶ were made friends together: for before they were at enmity between themselves. 13 And Pilate, when he had called together the chief priests and the rulers 14 and the people, 'said unto them, Ye have brought this man unto me, as one that perverteth the people: and, behold! I, having examined *him* before you, have found no fault in this man touching those things whereof ye accuse him: 15 no, nor yet Herod: for he sent him to us;⁷ and, lo, nothing worthy of death 16 is done unto him. I will therefore chastise him, and release *him*.

§ 148. Pilate still further seeks to release Jesus; then, after scourging Him, delivers Him to be crucified.

MATT. XXVII. 15–26.	MAR. XV. 6–15.	LK. XXIII. 17–25.	JNO. XVIII. 39, 40, XIX. 1.
15 Now at *that* feast the governor was wont to release unto the people a prisoner, whom	6 Now at *that* feast he released unto them one prisoner, whomsoever they de-		39 But ye have a custom, that I should release unto you one at the passover:

¹ *omit* even   ² heard of Galilee, he asked   ³ *season*   ⁴ heard many things of him
⁵ him   ⁶ Pilate and Herod   ⁷ for I sent you to him; and, lo,

ST. MATT. XXVII.	ST. MARK XV.	ST. LUKE XXIII.	ST. JOHN XVIII.
16 they would. And they had then a notable prisoner, called Barabbas.	7 sired. And there was *one* named Barabbas, *which lay* bound with them that had made insurrection,[2] who had committed murder in the insurrection. And the multitude coming up[3] began to desire *him to do* as he was wont to do[4] unto them. But Pilate answered them, saying, Will ye that I release unto you the King of the Jews? For he knew that the chief priests had delivered him for envy.	19 [Barabbas][1] (who for a certain sedition made in the city, and for murder, was cast into prison.)	
17 Therefore when they were gathered together, Pilate said unto them, Whom will ye that I release unto you? Barabbas, or Jesus which is called Christ? 18 For he knew that for envy they had delivered him. 19 When he was set down on the judgment seat, his wife sent unto him, saying, Have thou nothing to do with that just man: for I have suffered many things this day in a dream because of him.			will ye therefore that I release unto you the King of the Jews?
20 But the chief priests and elders persuaded the multitude that they	11 But the chief priests moved the people, that he should rather	18 And they cried out all at once, saying, Away with this *man*,	40 Then cried they[5] again, saying, Not this man, but Ba-

[1] ver. 17. For of necessity he must release one unto them at the feast.
[2] made insurrection with him.   [3] the multitude crying aloud began
[4] as he had ever done unto them.   [5] cried they all again

ST. MATT. XXVII.	ST. MARK XV.	ST. LUKE XXIII.	ST. JOHN XVIII.
should ask Barabbas, and destroy Jesus. The governor answered and said unto them, Whether of the twain will ye that I release unto you? They said, Barabbas. Pilate saith unto them, What shall I do then with Jesus which is called Christ? *They* all say,[2] Let him be crucified. And he[3] said, Why, what evil hath he done?	release Barabbas unto them. And Pilate answered and said again unto them, What will ye then that I shall do *unto him* whom ye call the King of the Jews? And they cried out again, Crucify him! Then Pilate said unto them, Why, what evil hath he done?	and release unto us Barabbas: But Pilate,[1] willing to release Jesus, spake again to them. But they cried, saying, Crucify *him!* crucify him! And he said unto them the third time, Why, what evil hath he done? I have found no cause of death in him: I will therefore chastise him, and let *him* go.	rabbas. Now Barabbas was a robber.
21	12	20	
22	13, 14	21, 22	
23			
But they cried out the more, saying, Let him be crucified!	And they cried out the more exceedingly, Crucify him!	And they were instant with loud voices, requiring that he might be crucified. And their voices[4] prevailed.	
		23	
When Pilate saw that he could prevail nothing, but *that* rather a tumult was made, he took water, and washed *his* hands before the multi-			
24			

[1] Pilate therefore, willing   [2] all say unto him   [3] And the governor said
[4] And the voices of them and of the chief priests prevailed

ST. MATT. XXVII.	ST. MARK XV.	ST. LUKE XXIII.	ST. JOHN XIX.
tude,[a] saying, I am innocent of this blood:[1] see ye *to* 25 *it.* Then answered all the people, and said, His blood *be* on us, and on our children!			
	15 And *so* Pilate, willing to content the people,	24 And Pilate gave sentence that it should be as they required. 25 And he	
26 Then released he Barabbas unto them: and when he had scourged Jesus, he delivered *him* to be crucified.	released Barabbas unto them, and delivered Jesus, when he had scourged *him,* to be crucified.	released[2] him that for sedition and murder was cast into prison, whom they had desired; but he delivered Jesus to their will.	1 Then Pilate therefore took Jesus, and scourged *him.*

§ 149. The Soldiers mock Him.

ST. MATT. XXVII. 27–30.	ST. MARK XV. 16–19.	ST. JOHN XIX. 2, 3.
27 Then the soldiers of the governor took Jesus into the common hall, and gathered unto him the whole band *of sol-* 28 *diers.* And they stripped him, and put on him a scarlet robe. 29 And when they had	16 And the soldiers led him away into the hall, called Prætorium; and they call together the 17 whole band. And they clothed him with purple, and platted a	2 And the soldiers platted a crown of

[1] innocent of the blood of this just person
[2] released unto them him
[a] Comp. Deut. xxi. 6, 7.

---

§ 148. The words of St. Matthew, vs. 26, and St. Mark, vs. 15, " delivered him to be crucified," properly belong to § 151, but cannot well be separated from their context. They are introduced before § 149 because they really form part of the transaction now going on. Pilate reluctantly delivered our Lord to be crucified; after giving him up, he made still one effort more for his release, and then finally abandoned him.

§ 149. The robe of Matt. 28 was the military cloak of an officer. " Scarlet " of Matt. and " purple " of Mar. are frequently used in Greek of the same color — a purple-red.

ST. MATT. XXVII.	ST. MARK XV.	ST. JOHN XIX.
platted a crown of thorns, they put *it* upon his head, and a reed in his right hand: and they bowed the knee before him, and mocked him, saying, Hail, King of the ³⁰ Jews! And they spit upon him, and took the reed, and smote him on the head.	crown of thorns, and put it about his *head,* ¹⁸ and began to salute him, Hail, King of the ¹⁹ Jews! And they smote him on the head with a reed, and did spit upon him, and bowing *their* knees worshipped him.	thorns, and put *it* on his head, and they put on him a purple robe, ³ and they came to him[1] and said, Hail, King of the Jews! And they smote him with their hands.

§ 150. Pilate makes a final Effort for His release.
St. John xix. 4–16[a].

⁴ Pilate[2] went forth again, and saith unto them, Behold! I bring him forth
⁵ to you, that ye may know that I find no fault.[3] Then came Jesus forth, wearing the crown of thorns, and the purple robe. And *Pilate* saith unto
⁶ them, Behold the man! When the chief priests therefore and officers saw him, they cried out,[4] Crucify *him*, crucify *him!* Pilate saith unto them, Take
⁷ ye him, and crucify *him:* for I find no fault in him. The Jews answered,[5] We have a law, and by the[6] law he ought to die, because he made himself the Son of God.[a]

⁸₉ When Pilate therefore heard that saying, he was the more afraid; and went again into the judgment hall, and saith unto Jesus, Whence art thou?
¹⁰ But Jesus gave him no answer. Pilate saith[7] unto him, Speakest thou not unto me? knowest thou not that I have power to release thee, and have power
¹¹ to crucify thee?[8] Jesus answered, Thou hast[9] no power *at all* against me, except it were given thee from above: therefore he that delivered me unto thee hath the greater sin.

¹² And from thenceforth Pilate sought to release him: but the Jews cried out, saying, If thou let this man go, thou art not Cæsar's friend: whosoever maketh himself a king speaketh against Cæsar.

¹³ When Pilate therefore heard these sayings,[10] he brought Jesus forth, and sat down in the judgment seat in a place that is called the Pavement, but in

---

[1] *omit* they came to him and   [2] Pilate therefore went   [3] fault in him
[4] cried out, saying,   [5] answered him   [6] by our law
[7] Then saith Pilate   [8] I have power to crucify thee, and have power to release thee?
[9] Thou couldest have no   [10] that saying

[a] See Jno. v. 18; x. 33, etc.

PART VIII. § 151.]   OUR LORD'S PASSION; THE SABBATH.   259

ST. JOHN XIX.

14 the Hebrew, Gabbatha. And it was the preparation of the passover,[1] about
15 the sixth hour: and he saith unto the Jews, Behold your King! They
therefore[2] cried out, Away with *him*, away with *him*, crucify him! Pilate
saith unto them, Shall I crucify your King? The chief priests answered, We
16 have no king but Cæsar. Then delivered he him therefore unto them to be
crucified.

§ 151. Our Lord is led forth to be Crucified.

MATT. XXVII. 31–34.   MAR. XV. 20–23.   LK. XXIII. 26–33ᵃ.   JNO. XIX. 16ᵇ, 17.

MATT. XXVII. 31–34.	MAR. XV. 20–23.	LK. XXIII. 26–33ᵃ.	JNO. XIX. 16ᵇ, 17.
31 And after that they had mocked him, taking[3] the robe off from him, they put his own raiment on him, and led him away to crucify *him*. And 32 as they came out, they found a man of Cyrene, Simon by name:	20 And when they had mocked him, they took off the purple from him, and put his own clothes on him, and led him out to crucify *him*.[4] 21 And they compel one Simon a Cyrenian, who passed by, com-	26 And as they led him away, they laid hold upon one Simon, a Cyrenian, com-	16ᵇ And they took Jesus and led *him* away.

[1] and about the
[3] they took the robe off from him, and put
[2] But they cried
[4] him

---

§ 150. On the words "preparation of the passover" of vs. 14, see Introductory Note to Part viii. III. There has been much discussion in regard to the time mentioned in vs. 14. The apparent difference between it and the "third hour" of Mar. xv. 25 has led to a variation in the Greek text of St. John from the earliest times. The difference in the numerical notation by means of letters is indeed very slight (s' for $\digamma'$), yet there is no occasion for making any alteration in the text as it stands. The actual hour must have been not much later than 6 A.M. for our Lord was taken before Pilate early in the morning (Matt. xxvii. 1; Mar. xv. 1), as soon after daybreak as the Sanhedrim could assemble and formally deliver him up (Lk. xxii. 66) — and it was 9 A.M. when they crucified him (Mar. xv. 24). This time is exactly designated by St. John, if we understand him to use the Roman official computation of the hours from midnight.

§ 151. St. John says that our Lord bore his own cross, or rather, that he went forth bearing it; St. Matthew, that when they were come out of the city they met Simon, and compelled him to bear it. Both accounts are perfectly consistent. The other Evangelists mention only the part recorded by St. Matthew, perhaps because Simon was so well known in the Christian community as having borne the Lord's cross.

Simon was coming "out of the country;" but as it does not appear from what distance, nor for what purpose he had been there, no inference can be drawn from this fact as to the day of the week.

The drink offered (Matt. v. 34; Mar. v. 23) was the acid, drugged wine, ordinarily given to those about to be crucified, to dull the sense of pain.

ST. MATT. XXVII.	ST. MARK XV.	ST. LUKE XXIII.	ST. JOHN XIX.
him they compelled to bear his cross.	ing out of the country, the father of Alexander and Rufus, to bear his cross.	ing out of the country, and on him they laid the cross, that he might bear *it* after Jesus.	17 And he bearing the cross by himself[1]
		27 And there followed him a great company of people, and of women, which[2] bewailed and lamented	
		28 him. But Jesus turning unto them, said, Daughters of Jerusalem, weep not for me, but weep for yourselves, and for	
		29 your children. For, behold! the days are coming, in the which they shall say, Blessed *are* the barren, and the wombs that never bare, and the paps which never	
		30 gave suck. Then shall they begin to say to the mountains, Fall on us! and to the hills, Cover us![a]	
		31 For if they do these things in a green tree, what shall be done in the dry?	
		32 And there were also two other, malefactors, led with him to be put to death.	
33 And when they were come unto	22 And they bring him unto the	33 And when they were come to the	went forth into a place called

[1] bearing his cross (*omit* by himself)   [2] which also bewailed

[a] Hosea x. 8. And they shall say to the mountains, Cover us! and to the hills, Fall on us! Comp. Isa. ii. 19; Rev. vi. 16.

ST. MATT. XXVII.	ST. MARK XV.	ST. LUKE XXIII.	ST. JOHN XIX.
a place called Golgotha, that is to say, a place of a skull,	place Golgotha, which is, being interpreted, The place of a skull.	place, which is called a skull[1] —	*The place* of a skull, which is called in the Hebrew Golgotha: —
34 they gave him wine[2] to drink mingled with gall:[a] and when he had tasted *thereof,* he would not drink.	23 And they gave him[3] wine mingled with myrrh[a]: but he received *it* not.		

§ 152. The Crucifixion.

MATT. XXVII. 35–38. MAR. XV. 24–28. LK. XXIII. 33[b], 34, 38. JNO. XIX. 18–24.

	25 And it was the third hour, and they crucified him. And with him they crucify two thieves; the one on his right hand, and the other on his left.[4][b]	33[b] — There they crucified him, and the malefactors, one on the right hand, and the other on the left.[b]	18 — Where they crucified him, and two other with him, on either side one, and Jesus in the midst.[b]
38 Then were there two thieves crucified with him, one on the right hand, and another on the left.[b]			
		34 Then said Jesus, Father, forgive them; for they know not what they do. — And a superscription also was over him[5] THE KING OF THE JEWS IS THIS.	
37 —And set up over his head his accusation written, THIS IS JESUS THE KING OF THE JEWS.	26 And the superscription of his accusation was written over, THE KING OF THE JEWS.	38	19 And Pilate wrote a title, and put *it* on the cross. And the writing was, JESUS OF NAZARETH THE KING OF THE 20 JEWS. This title

---

[1] *translated* Calvary   [2] vinegar   [3] gave him to drink wine

[4] Ver. 28. And the scripture was fulfilled, which saith, And he was numbered with the transgressors.

[5] was written over him in letters of Greek, and Latin, and Hebrew, This is the King of the Jews.

[a] Comp. Matt. xxvii. 48; Ps. lxix. 21.   [b] See Isa. liii. 12.

ST. MATT. XXVII.	ST. MARK XV.	ST. LUKE XXIII.	ST. JOHN XIX.
			then read many of the Jews: for the place where Jesus was crucified was nigh to the city: and it was written in Hebrew, *and* Latin *and* Greek.[1]
			21 Then said the chief priests of the Jews to Pilate, Write not, The King of the Jews; but that he said, I am King of the Jews.
			22 Pilate answered, What I have written, I have written.
			23 Then the soldiers, when they had crucified Jesus, took his garments, and made four parts, to every soldier a part; and also *his* coat: now the coat was without seam, woven from the top throughout.
			24 They said therefore among themselves, Let us not rend it, but cast lots for it, whose it shall be: that the scripture might be fulfilled,[2] They

---

[1] Greek *and* Latin

[2] fulfilled, which saith, They

ST. MATT. XXVII.	ST. MARK XV.	ST. LUKE XXIII.	ST. JOHN XIX.
35 And they crucified him, and parted his garments, casting lots.ᵃ²	24 And they crucify him, and¹ part his garments, casting lots upon them, what every man should take.ᵃ	34ᵇ— And they parted his raiment, and cast lots.ᵃ	parted my raiment among them and for my vesture they did cast lots.ᵃ These things therefore the soldiers did.
36 And sitting down they watched him there;—			

§ 153. He is mocked upon the Cross. The penitent Thief.

MATT. XXVII. 39–44.	MAR. XV. 29–32.	LK. XXIII. 35–37, 39–43.
39 And they that passed by reviled him,ᵇ wagging their heads, and saying, Thou that destroyest the temple, and buildest *it* in three days,ᶜ save thyself,³ if thou be the Son of God, and come down from the cross! Likewise⁴ the chief priests mocking *him*, with the scribes and elders, said, He saved others; himself he cannot save.	29 And they that passed by railed on him,ᵇ wagging their heads, and saying, Ah, thou that destroyest the temple, and buildest *it* in three days,ᶜ save thyself, and come down from the cross! Likewise also the chief priests mocking said among themselves with the scribes, He saved others; himself he cannot save. Let Christ the	35 And the people stood beholding. And the rulers⁵ derided *him*, saying, He saved others; let him save himself, if he be Christ, the chosen of God. And the soldiers also mocked him, coming to him,⁶ offering him vinegar.

¹ And when they had crucified him, they parted his
² *add* that it might be fulfilled which was spoken by the prophet, They parted my garments among them, and upon my vesture did they cast lots.
³ save thyself. If thou be the Son of God, come down
⁴ Likewise also
⁵ the rulers also with them derided   ⁶ to him and offering
ᵃ Ps. xxii. 18.   ᵇ See Ps. xxii. 6, 7; cix. 25.   ᶜ Matt. xxvi. 61; Mar. xiv. 58; Jno. ii. 19.

§ 153. St. Matthew and St. Mark speak indefinitely of what was said by the thieves, using the plural. St. Luke alone is more particular, and gives the precious account of the penitence and forgiveness of one of them.

ST. MATT. XXVII.	ST. MARK XV.	ST. LUKE XXIII.
He is[1] the King of Israel, let him now come down from the cross, and we will believe ₄₁ on[2] him. He trusted in God; let him now, if he will,[a3] deliver him: for he said, I am the Son of ₄₄ God. The thieves also, which were crucified with him, cast the same in his teeth.	King of Israel descend now from the cross, that we may see and believe. And they that were crucified with him reviled him.	₃₇ and saying, If thou be the King of the Jews, save thyself. ₃₉ And one of the malefactors which were hanged railed on him, Art thou not the[4] Christ? Save ₄₀ thyself and us. But the other answering and rebuking him, said,[5] Dost not thou fear God, seeing thou art in the same con- ₄₁ demnation? And we indeed justly; for we receive the due reward of our deeds: but this man hath done nothing ₄₂ amiss. And he said,[6] Jesus, remember me when thou comest into thy ₄₃ kingdom. And he[7] said unto him, Verily I say unto thee, To day shalt thou be with me in paradise.

§ 154. He commends His Mother to St. John.

ST. JOHN XIX. 25–27.

₂₅ Now there stood by the cross of Jesus his mother, and his mother's sister,
₂₆ Mary the *wife* of Cleophas, and Mary Magdalene. When Jesus therefore saw his mother, and the disciple standing by, whom he loved, he saith unto
₂₇ his[8] mother, Woman, behold thy son! Then saith he to the disciple, Behold thy mother! And from that hour that disciple took her unto his own *home*.

---

[1] If he be the King [2] *omit* on [3] let him deliver him now, if he will have him; for
[4] railed on him, saying, If thou be Christ, save [5] answering rebuked him, saying, Dost not
[6] said unto Jesus, Lord, remember [7] And Jesus said [8] his
[a] Ps. xxii. 8.

§ 155. The noon-day Darkness. The Death.

MATT. XXVII. 45–50.   MAR. XV. 33–37.   LK. XXIII. 44–46.   JNO. XIX. 28–30.

Matt.	Mar.	Lk.	Jno.
45 Now from the sixth hour there was darkness over all the land unto the ninth 46 hour. And about the ninth hour Jesus cried with a loud voice, saying, Eli, Eli, lama sabachthani? that is to say, My God, my God, why hast thou forsaken me?ª 47 Some of them that stood there, when they heard *that*, said, This *man* calleth for Elias.	33 And when the sixth hour was come, there was darkness over the whole land until the ninth 34 hour. And at the ninth hour Jesus cried with a loud voice,³ Eloi, Eloi, lama sabachthani? which is, being interpreted, My God, my God, why hast thou forsaken me?ª 35 And some of them that stood by, when they heard *it*, said, Behold! he calleth Elias.	44 And it was now¹ about the sixth hour, and there was a darkness over all the earth until the ninth 45 hour, the sun being eclipsed²	
48 And straight-	36 And a certain⁴		28 After this, Jesus knowing that all things were now accomplished, that the scripture might be fulfilled, saith, I thirst. 29 ⁵There was set a

¹ *omit* now   ² And the sun was darkened   ³ loud voice, saying
⁴ *omit* a certain   ⁵ Now there was
ª Ps. xxii. 1.

---

§ 155. The *Eli* of Matt. 46, is the Hebrew form, which is also the form used in the Chaldee translation of Ps. xxii. 2; while the *Eloi* of Mar. 34, is the Aramaic form. They have the same meaning, '*My God.*'

The sponge is said by the two first Evangelists to be put "on a reed"; by St. John "on hyssop." This implies that a *stalk of hyssop* was used. The cross was probably of no great height, and yet just too high for reaching with the hand alone.

ST. MATT. XXVII.	ST. MARK XV.	ST. LUKE XXIII.	ST. JOHN XIX.
way one of them ran, and took a sponge, and filled *it* with vinegar, and put *it* on a reed, and gave him to 49 drink.ᵃ The rest said, Let be, let us see whether Elias will come to save him.	one ran and filled a sponge full of vinegar, putting¹ *it* on a reed, and gave him to drink,ᵃ saying, Let alone; let us see whether Elias will come to take him down.		vessel full of vinegar: they put therefore a sponge filled² with vinegar, upon hyssop, and put *it* to his mouth.ᵃ
		46 And when Jesus had cried with a loud voice, he said, Father, into thy hands I commend my spirit: and having said thus, he gave up the ghost.	30 When he³ therefore had received the vinegar, he said, It is finished: and he bowed his head, and gave up the ghost.
50 Jesus, when he had cried again with a loud voice, yielded up the ghost.	37 And Jesus cried with a loud voice, and gave up the ghost.		

§ 156. *Various Portents. The Centurion. The Women at the Cross.*

St. Matt. xxvii. 51–56.   St. Mark xv. 38–41.   St. Luke xxiii. 45ᵇ, 47–49.

51 And, behold! the veil of the temple was rent in twain from the top to the bottom; and the earth did quake, and the 52 rocks rent; and the graves were opened; and many bodies of the saints which 53 slept arose, and came out of the graves after	38 And the veil of the temple was rent in twain from the top to the bottom.	45ᵇ And the veil of the temple was rent in the midst.

¹ and put *it* on   ² and they filled a sponge with vinegar and put *it* upon hyssop
³ When Jesus therefore
ᵃ Ps. lxix. 21.

---

§ 156. St. Matthew speaks of the opening of the tombs, and then to complete the subject, adds what took place *after* our Lord's resurrection — "came out of the graves after his resurrection."

ST. MATT. XXVII.	ST. MARK XV.	ST. LUKE XXIII.
his resurrection, and went into the holy city, and appeared unto many. 54 Now when the centurion, and they that were with him, watching Jesus, saw the earthquake, and those things that were done, they feared greatly, saying, Truly this was the 55 Son of God. And many women were there beholding afar off, which followed Jesus from Galilee, ministering unto 56 him:ª among which was Mary Magdalene, and Mary the mother of James and Joseph,⁵ and the mother of Zebedee's children.	39 And when the centurion, which stood over against him, saw that he so¹ gave up the ghost, he said, Truly this man was the Son 40 of God. There were also women looking on afar off : among whom was²Mary Magdalene, and Mary the mother of James the less and of Joses, and 41 Salome; (who,⁴ when he was in Galilee, followed him, and ministered unto him;)ᵃ and many other women which came up with him unto Jerusalem.	47 Now when the centurion saw what was done, he glorified God, saying, Certainly this was a righteous man. 48 And all the people that came together to that sight, having beheld³ the things which were done, smote their breasts, and returned. 49 And all his acquaintance, and the women that followed him from Galilee,ª stood afar off, beholding these things.

§ 157. The piercing of our Lord's Side.
ST. JOHN XIX. 31–37.

31 The Jews therefore, because it was the preparation, that the bodies should not remain upon the cross ᵇ on the Sabbath day, (for that Sabbath day was an high day,) besought Pilate that their legs might be broken, and *that* they 32 might be taken away. Then came the soldiers, and brake the legs of the 33 first, and of the other which was crucified with him. But when they came to 34 Jesus, and saw that he was dead already, they brake not his legs: but one of the soldiers with a spear pierced his side, and forthwith came there out blood 35 and water.ᶜ And he that saw *it* bare record, and his record is true: and he 36 knoweth that he saith true, that ye also⁶ might believe. For these things were done, that the scripture should be fulfilled, A bone of him shall not be 37 broken.ᵈ And again another scripture saith, They shall look on him whom they pierced.ᵉ

¹ he so cried out, and gave up   ² was   ³ beholding
   ⁴ who also, when   ⁵ Joses   ⁶ omit also
ª See Lk. viii. 1–3.   ᵇ Deut. xxi. 22, 23.   ᶜ 1 Jno. v. 6.
ᵈ See Ex. xii. 46; Num. ix. 12; Ps. xxxiv. 20.   ᵉ Zech. xii. 10; comp. Ps. xxii. 17; Rev. i. 7.

§ 158. The Descent from the Cross and Burial.

MATT. XXVII. 57–61.	MAR. XV. 42–47.	LK. XXIII. 50–56.	JNO. XIX. 38–42.
57 When the even was come, there came a rich man[a] of Arimathæa, named Joseph, who also himself was Jesus' disciple:	42 And now when the even was come, because it was the preparation, that is, the day before the Sabbath, 43 Joseph of Arimathæa, an honorable counsellor,[a] which also	50 And that day was the preparation, and the Sabbath drew on. 50 And, behold! *there was* a man named Joseph, a counsellor;[a] and[1] *he was* a good man, and 51 a just; (the same had not consented to the counsel and deed of them;) *he was* of Arimathæa, a city of the Jews:	
58 he went to Pilate, and begged the body of Jesus.	waited for the kingdom of God, came, and went in boldly unto Pilate, and craved the body 44 of Jesus. And Pilate marvelled if he were already dead: and calling *unto him* the centurion, he asked him whether he had been any	who[2] waited for the kingdom of God. 52 This *man* went unto Pilate, and begged the body of Jesus.	38 And after this Joseph of Arimathæa, being a disciple of Jesus, but secretly for fear of the Jews, besought Pilate that he might take away the body of Jesus:
Then Pilate commanded *it*[3] to be delivered.	45 while dead. And when he knew *it* of the centu-		and Pilate gave *him* leave. They[4] came therefore,

[1] *and* [2] who also himself waited [3] commanded the body to be [4] He came

[a] Isa. liii. 9.

§ 158. On the meaning of the word "preparation," see Introductory Note to Part viii. III. p. 220.

ST. MATT. XXVII.	ST. MARK XV.	ST. LUKE XXIII.	ST. JOHN XIX.
	rion, he gave the body to		and took him.[1]
			39 And there came also Nicodemus, which at the first came to him[2] by night*, and brought a mixture of myrrh and aloes, about an hundred pound *weight*.
59 And when Joseph had taken the body, he wrapped it in a clean linen 60 cloth, and laid it in his own new tomb, which he had hewn out in the rock: and he rolled a great stone to the door of the sepulchre, and departed.	46 Joseph. And he bought fine linen,[3] took him down, and wrapped him in the linen, and laid him in a sepulchre which was hewn out of a rock, and rolled a stone unto the door of the sepulchre.	53 And he took it[4] down, and wrapped it in linen, and laid him[5] in a sepulchre that was hewn in stone, wherein never man before was laid.	40 Then took they the body of Jesus, and wound it in linen clothes with the spices, as the manner of the Jews is to bury. 41 Now in the place where he was crucified there was a garden; and in the garden a new sepulchre, wherein was never man yet laid. 42 There laid they Jesus therefore, because of the Jews' preparation *day*; for the sepulchre was nigh at hand.
61 And there was Mary Magdalene, and the other Mary, sitting over against the sepulchre.	47 And Mary Magdalene and Mary *the mother* of Joses beheld where he was **laid**.	55 And the women[6] which came with him from Galilee, followed after, and beheld the sepulchre, and how his body was laid. 56 And they returned, and prepared spices and ointments; and	

[1] took the body of Jesus. [2] came to Jesus by night [3] linen, and took
[4] it [5] laid it in a [6] the women also which
* Jno. iii. 1, 2; vii. 50.

ST. MATT. XXVII.	ST. MARK XV.	ST. LUKE XXIII.	ST. JOHN XIX.
		rested the Sabbath day according to the commandment.[a]	

THE SABBATH, THE SEVENTH DAY OF THE WEEK.

§ 159. The Watch at the Sepulchre.
St. Matt. xxvii. 62–66.

62 Now the next day, that followed the day of the preparation, the chief
63 priests and Pharisees came together unto Pilate, saying, Sir, we remember that that deceiver said, while he was yet alive, After three days I will rise
64 again.[b] Command therefore that the sepulchre be made sure until the third day, lest the[1] disciples come[2] and steal him away, and say unto the people, He is risen from the dead: so the last error shall be worse than the first.
65 Pilate said unto them, Ye have a watch: go your way, make *it* as sure as ye
66 can. So they went, and made the sepulchre sure, sealing the stone, and setting a watch.

[1] his disciples   [2] come by night and steal

[a] Ex. xx. 8–10, etc.

[b] Matt. xvi. 21; xvii. 23; xx. 19; xxvi. 61; Mar. viii. 31; ix. 31; x. 34; Lk. ix. 22; xviii. 33; xxiv. 7; Jno. ii. 19, etc.

INTRODUCTORY NOTE TO PART IX.

In the following narrative of the events connected with our Lord's resurrection, it is to be borne in mind that no one of the writers has undertaken to make a complete record of all that occurred. Each has mentioned those incidents which particularly concerned his own purpose or experience. In order to combine the four narratives into one consecutive story, it is necessary to make some conjectures in regard to intervening events which may probably have occurred. Such conjectures may not, perhaps, represent what actually took place, for in some instances several different conjectures may be formed; but so long as any of these are in themselves probable — likely to have occurred — and by means of them the statements of the several Evangelists are seen to be entirely consistent, it is impossible to allege contradictions between their narratives. Some study and careful attention is required thus to exhibit the four accounts harmoniously — perhaps more than is required in any other part of the Gospels, because here such a number of important events are crowded into so short a space of time; but beyond this, there is no other difficulty, nor is there any real discrepancy in the accounts.

For the convenience of the student, the following synopsis of the events is given, so far as the points of difficulty extend.

The resurrection itself occurred at or before the earliest dawn of the first day of the week (Matt. xxviii. 1; Mar. xvi. 2; Lk. xxiv. 1; Jno. xx. 1. On the "at the rising of the sun" of Mar. 2. see note in loco.) The women coming to the sepulchre, find the stone rolled away and the body gone. They are amazed and perplexed. Mary Magdalene alone runs to tell Peter and John (Jno. xx. 2.) The other women remain, enter the tomb, see the angels, are charged by them to announce the resurrection to the disciples, and depart on their errand. Meantime Peter and John run very rapidly (vs. 4) to the sepulchre. (A glance at the plan of Jerusalem shows that there were so many different gates by which persons might pass between the city and the sepulchre that they might easily have failed to meet the women on their way.) They enter the tomb, and are astonished at the orderly arrangement of the grave-clothes, and then return to the city. Mary follows to the tomb, unable quite to keep pace with them, and so falling behind. She remains standing at the entrance after they had gone; and looking in, sees the angels. Then turning about, she sees Jesus himself, and receives his charge for the disciples. This was our Lord's first appearance after his resurrection (Mar. xvi. 9).

To return to the women who were on their way from the sepulchre to the disciples. They went in haste, yet more slowly than Peter and John. There were many of them, and being in a state of great agitation and alarm (Mar. xvi. 8), they appear to have become separated and to have entered the city by different gates. One party of them, in their astonishment and fear, say nothing to any one (Matt. xxviii. 8); the others run to the disciples and announce all that they had seen, viz. the vision of the angels (Mar. xvi. 8; Lk. xxiv. 9–11).

At this time, before any report had come in of the appearance of our Lord himself, the two disciples set out for Emmaus (Lk. xxiv. 13). (In the Harmony Lk. xxiv. 13 is allowed to stand in connection with the whole account of the visit to Emmaus to avoid breaking too much the thread of the several narratives; but it is plain that these disciples started before Mary Magdalene had announced the appearance of the Lord).

Soon after, Mary Magdalene comes in, announcing that she had actually seen the risen Lord (Mar. xvi. 10, 11; Jno. xx. 18).

While these things are happening, the first-mentioned party of the women are stopped on the way by the appearance of the Lord himself, and they also receive a charge to his disciples (Matt. xxviii. 9, 10).

Beyond this point there is no difficulty in the narrative, and the course of events will, it is hoped, be sufficiently clear in the Harmony itself.

PART IX.

THE RESURRECTION, AND THE FORTY DAYS UNTIL THE ASCENSION.

THE FIRST DAY OF THE WEEK. — SUNDAY (BEGINNING AT SUNSET SATURDAY).

§ 160. The Resurrection. Visit of the Women to the Sepulchre.

MATT. XXVIII. 1–4.   MAR. XVI. 1–4.   LK. XXIV. 1, 2.   JNO. XX. 1.

1 In the end of the Sabbath, —

1 And when the Sabbath was past, Mary Magdalene, and Mary the *mother* of James, and Salome, had bought sweet spices, that they might come and anoint him.

2 And, behold! there was a great earthquake: for the angel of the Lord descended from heaven, and came and rolled back the stone[1] and sat upon it. 3 His countenance was like light-

---

[1] the stone from the door, and

§ 160. The buying of the spices in Mar. 1, properly belongs to the previous evening, i.e. it took place after sunset on Saturday, when therefore "the Sabbath was past." The clause cannot, however, be conveniently detached from the rest of the verse.

The expression of St. Mark at the close of vs. 2, "at the rising of the sun," must, of course, be understood consistently with the "very early" of the same verse, and therefore consistently with the similar expressions of the other Evangelists. The time designated in the original (see note in the Greek Harmony) is not so much the actual *rising* of the sun as the first appearance of its light at the dawn.

St. Matt. XXVIII.	St. Mark XVI.	St. Luke XXIV.	St. John XX.
ning, and his raiment white as snow: and for fear of him the keepers did shake, and became as dead *men*.			
4			
1ᵇ — as it began to dawn toward the first *day* of the week, came Mary Magdalene and the other Mary to see the sepulchre.	2 And very early in the morning the first *day* of the week, they came unto the sepulchre at the rising of the sun. 3 And they said among themselves, Who shall roll us away the stone from the door of the sepulchre?ᵃ And when they looked, they saw that the stone was rolled away: for it was very great.	1 Now upon the first *day* of the week, very early in the morning, they came unto the sepulchre, bringing the spices which they had prepared.¹ 2 And they found the stone rolled away from the sepulchre.	1 The first *day* of the week cometh Mary Magdalene early, when it was yet dark, unto the sepulchre, and seeth the stone taken away from the sepulchre.

§ 161. Mary Magdalene runs to tell Peter and John.

St. John xx. 2.

2 Then she runneth, and cometh to Simon Peter, and to the other disciple, whom Jesus loved, and saith unto them, They have taken away the Lord out of the sepulchre, and we know not where they have laid him.

§ 162. Two Angels appear to the Women; some of them are speechless with fear and amazement, others run to tell the Disciples.

St. Matt. XXVIII. 5–8.	St. Mark XVI. 5–8.	St. Luke XXIV. 3–8.
	5 And entering into the sepulchre,	3 And they entered in, and found not the body 4 of the Lord Jesus. And

---

¹ had prepared, and certain *others* with them
ᵃ See Mar. xv. 46.

---

§ 161. Mary Magdalene ran to tell Peter and John evidently before she had seen the angels.

ST. MATT. XXVIII.	ST. MARK XVI.	ST. LUKE XXIV.
		it came to pass, as they were[1] perplexed thereabout, behold! two men stood by them in shining
	they saw a young man sitting on the right side, clothed in a long white garment; and they were affrighted.	5 raiment:[2] and as they were afraid, and bowed down *their* faces to the earth, they said unto them, Why seek ye the living among the dead?
5 And the angel answered and said unto the woman, Fear not ye: for I know that ye seek Jesus, which 6 was crucified. He is not here: for he is risen, as he said.[a]	6 And he saith unto them, Be not affrighted: Ye seek Jesus of Nazareth, which was crucified: he is risen; he is not here;	6 He is not here, but is risen: remember how he spake unto you when he was yet in Galilee, 7 saying, The Son of Man must be delivered into the hands of sinful men, and be crucified, and the third day rise again.[a] 8 And they remembered his words,
Come, see the place 7 where he[3] lay. And go quickly, and tell his disciples that he is risen from the dead; and, behold! he goeth before you unto Galilee; there shall ye see him: lo, I have told	behold the place where 7 they laid him. But go your way, tell his disciples and Peter that he goeth before you unto Galilee: there shall ye see him, as he said unto you.	

[1] much perplexed   [2] shining garments   [3] where the Lord lay

[a] Matt. xii. 40; xvi. 21; xvii. 23; xx. 19; Mar. viii. 31; ix. 31; x. 34; Lk. ix. 22; xviii. 33; xxiv. 6, 7, etc.

§ 162. The angel, according to Matt. xxviii. 2, sat upon the stone. Either therefore, the stone rolled inward, or else he afterwards changed his position. He mentions only one angel: so also St. Mark, specifying that he was *on the right :* St. Luke mentions (vs. 4) two. This may be only greater minuteness, or the second one may have been on the other side of the sepulchre.

Matt. xxviii. 8 and Mar. xvi. 8 plainly refer to different parties of women: the former speaks of their returning with great joy to tell their tidings to the disciples; the latter, of their being in such a state of terror — "ecstasy" — that they said nothing to any one. The company of women was large (Lk. xxiv. 10, etc.) and on their return they doubtless became separated, as there were several different gates by which they could enter the city. Thus also Matt. xxviii. 9, 10, receives a simple and natural explanation; our Lord appeared to one of the parties of women, not to the other.

ST. MATT. XXVIII.	ST. MARK XVI.	ST. LUKE XXIV.
⁸ you. And they departed quickly from the sepulchre with fear and great joy; and did run to bring his disciples word.	⁸ And they went out,¹ and fled from the sepulchre; for they trembled and were amazed: neither said they anything to any *man;* for they were afraid.	

§ 163. Peter and John visit the Sepulchre and go away.

[ST. LUKE XXIV. 12.²]   ST. JOHN XX. 3–10.

[¹² Then arose Peter, and ran unto the sepulchre;

³ Peter therefore went forth, and that other disciple, ⁴ and came to the sepulchre. So they ran both together: and the other disciple did outrun Peter, ⁵ and came first to the sepulchre. And he, stooping down, *and looking in,* saw the linen clothes lying; ⁶ yet went he not in. Then cometh Simon Peter

and stooping down, he beheld the linen clothes laid by themselves,

following him, and went into the sepulchre, and ⁷ seeth the linen clothes lie, 'and the napkin, that was about his head, not lying with the linen clothes, ⁸ but wrapped together in a place by itself. Then went in also that other disciple, which came first to ⁹ the sepulchre, and he saw, and believed. For as

and departed, wondering in himself at that which was come to pass.]

yet they knew not the scripture, that he must rise again from the dead. Then the disciples went away again unto their own home.

§ 164. The Angels first, and then our Lord, appear to Mary Magdalene.

[ST. MARK XVI. 9–11.³]   ST. JOHN XX. 11–18.

¹¹ But Mary stood without at the sepulchre weeping: and as she wept, she stooped down, *and looked*

---

¹ went out quickly
² This verse is omitted by Tischendorf, and marked as doubtful by Lachmann and Tregelles.
³ The genuineness of Mark xvi. 9–20 has been much questioned. It is omitted from the two most important MSS., but contained in nearly all the others, although marked in some of them as doubtful. There is also much other authority against it, especially that it is not included in the canons of Eusebius. Griesbach marks the passage as probably to be omitted; Lachmann inserts it; Tregelles (on the printed text of the Greek Testament pp. 246–260) considers it a later addition, not written by St. Mark, but still to be received as a genuine part

---

§ 163. If vs. 12 of St. Luke be genuine, of which there is little doubt, it may have slipped from its proper place, and perhaps it was this which caused the ancient hesitation as to its genuineness.

ST. MARK XVI.	ST. JOHN XX.
	12 into the sepulchre, and seeth two angels in white sitting, the one at the head, and the other at the
13 feet, where the body of Jesus had lain. ¹They say unto her, Woman, why weepest thou? She saith unto them, Because they have taken away my Lord,
14 and I know not where they have laid him. ¹When
[9 Now when *Jesus* was risen early the first *day* of the week, he appeared first to Mary Magdalene, out of whom he had cast seven devils.	she had thus said, she turned herself back, and saw Jesus standing, and knew not that it was Jesus.
15 Jesus saith unto her, Woman, why weepest thou? whom seekest thou? She, supposing him to be the gardener, saith unto him, Sir, if thou have borne him hence, tell me where thou hast laid him,
16 and I will take him away. Jesus saith unto her, Mary! She turned herself, and said unto him in
17 Hebrew,² Rabboni! which is to say, Master! Jesus saith unto her, Touch me not; for I am not yet ascended to my Father: but go to my brethren, and say unto them, I ascend unto the³ Father, and
10 And⁴ she went and told them that had been with him, as they mourned and wept.
11 And they, when they had heard that he was alive, and had been seen of her, believed not.]	your Father; and *to* my God, and your God.
18 Mary Magdalene came and told the disciples that I have⁵ seen the Lord, and *that* he had spoken these things unto her.

§ 165. Some of the Women tell the Disciples of the Angels; to the others. Jesus Himself appears.

St. Matt. xxviii. 9, 10.	St. Luke xxiv. 9–11.
9 And⁶ behold! Jesus met them, saying, All hail. And they came and	9 —And returned from the sepulchre, and told all these things unto the

of the Gospel; Tischendorf rejects it. Possibly it may have been added by St. Mark himself at a later period than the first publication of his Gospel. This supposition would harmonize with all the facts.

¹ pref. And ² *omit* in Hebrew ³ my Father ⁴ And
⁵ that she had seen ⁶ And as they went to tell his disciples, behold!

---

§ 164. St. Mark says that our Lord appeared *first* to Mary Magdalene. The supposition that *first* is here used not absolutely but relatively, meaning only the first of the appearances recorded by St. Mark, is allowable indeed on the ground of usage, but is wholly uncalled for. It is better to consider this, as in the arrangement above, as absolutely the first appearance of our risen Lord. The second (Matt. xxviii. 9, 10) was to the party of women returning from the sepulchre.

ST. MATT. XXVIII.	ST. LUKE XXIV.
held him by the feet, and worshipped him. Then said Jesus unto them, Be not afraid: go tell my brethren that they go into Galilee, and there shall they see me. (10)	eleven, and to all the rest. It was Mary Magdalene, and Joanna, and Mary *the mother* of James, and other women *that were* with them, *which*[1] told these things unto the apostles. (10) And these[2] words seemed to them as idle tales, and they believed them not. (11)

§ 166. The Report of the Watch.
St. Matt. xxviii. 11–15.

11 Now when they were going, behold! some of the watch came into the city,
12 and shewed unto the chief priests all the things that were done. And when they were assembled with the elders, and had taken counsel, they gave large
13 money unto the soldiers, ¹saying, Say ye, His disciples came by night, and
14 stole him *away* while we slept. And if this come to the governor's ears, we
15 will persuade *him*,[3] and secure you. So they took the money, and did as they were taught: and this saying is commonly reported among the Jews until this day.

§ 167. Our Lord joins Himself to two Disciples going to Emmaus.

[St. Mark xvi. 12, 13.]   St. Luke xxiv. 13–35.

13 And, behold! two of them went that same day to a village called Emmaus, which was from Jerusalem *about*
14 threescore[4] furlongs. And they talked together of all
15 these things which had happened. And it came to pass, that, while they communed *together* and reasoned, Jesus
16 himself drew near, and went with them. But their
[12 After that he appeared in another form unto   17 eyes were holden that they should not know him.[a] And he said unto them, What manner of communications *are* these that ye have one to another, as ye walk? and

---

[1] which   [2] their words   [3] him
[4] some important MSS. read "one hundred and sixty."
[a] Comp. Jno. xx. 14; xxi. 4.

---

§ 165. The appearance of our Lord to one party of women, and the announcement of the angel's message to the disciples by the other party, appear to have taken place nearly or quite at the same time.

Our Lord forbad Mary Magdalene to touch him (Jno. xx. 7), but allowed the other women to seize his feet (Matt. xxviii. 9). For this there may have been personal reasons, growing out of the warmth and impetuosity of Mary's temperament, which made it fitting to impress upon her a sense of the sacredness of our Lord's person, and to hold her somewhat aloof; but which did not exist in the other case.

ST. MARK XVI.	ST. LUKE XXIV.
two of them, as they walked, and went into the country.	18 they stood sad.[1] And[2] one of them, whose name was Cleopas,[a] answering said unto him, Art thou only a stranger in Jerusalem, and hast not known the things 19 which are come to pass there in these days? And he said unto them, What things? And they said unto him, Concerning Jesus of Nazareth, which was a prophet mighty in deed and word before God and all the people: 20 and how the chief priests and our rulers delivered him 21 to be condemned to death, and have crucified him. But we trusted that it had been he which should have redeemed Israel: and beside all this, it[3] is the third day 22 since these things were done. Yea, and certain women also of our company made us astonished, which were 23 early at the sepulchre; and when they found not his body, they came, saying, that they had also seen a vision 24 of angels, which said that he was alive. And certain of them which were with us went to the sepulchre, and found it even so as the women had said: but him they 25 saw not. Then he said unto them, O fools, and slow of heart to believe all that the prophets have spoken! 26 ought not Christ to have suffered these things, and to 27 enter into his glory? And beginning at Moses[b] and all the prophets, he expounded unto them in all the scrip-28 tures the things concerning himself. And they drew nigh unto the village, whither they went: and he made 29 as though he would have gone further. But they constrained him, saying, Abide with us: for it is toward evening, and the day is now[4] far spent. And he went 30 in to tarry with them. And it came to pass, as he sat at meat with them, he took bread, and blessed it, and 31 brake, and gave to them. And their eyes were opened, and they knew him: and he vanished out of their sight. 32 And they said one to another, Did not our heart burn within us, while he talked with us by the way,[5] while

[1] us ye walk, and are sad?   [2] And the one of them   [3] to-day is the third
[4] omit now   [5] and while he

[a] Comp. Jno. xix. 25.
[b] Comp. e.g. Gen. iii. 15; xxii. 18; xxvi. 4; xlix. 10; Num. xxi. 9; Deut. xviii. 15, etc.

§ 167. The enumeration of our Lord's appearances after his resurrection in 1 Cor. xv. 4-8, being very brief, and only in part the same with the appearances recorded in the Gospels, cannot be conveniently arranged with them. The first of them, however, — "that he rose again the third day according to the scriptures: (5) and that he was seen of Cephas," — be-

ST. MARK XVI.

13 And they went and told

it unto the residue: neither believed they them.]

ST. LUKE XXIV.

he opened to us the scriptures? And they rose up the same hour, and returned to Jerusalem, and found the eleven gathered together, and them that were with them, 34 saying, The Lord is risen indeed, and hath appeared to 35 Simon. And they told what things *were done* in the way, and how he was known of them in breaking of bread.

§ 168. He appears in the midst of the Apostles, Thomas being absent.

[ST. MARK XVI. 14.]   ST. LUKE XXIV. 36–43.   ST. JOHN XX. 19–25.

[14 And[1] afterward he appeared unto the eleven as they sat at meat, and upbraided them with their unbelief and hardness of heart, because they believed not them which had seen him after he was risen.]

36 And as they thus spake, he[2] himself stood in 37 the midst of them.[4] But they were terrified and affrighted, and supposed that they had seen a 38 spirit. And he said unto them, Why are ye troubled? and why do thoughts arise in your 39 heart?[5] Behold my hands and my feet, that it is I myself: handle me, and see; for a spirit hath not flesh and bones, as

19 Then the same day at evening, being the first *day* of the week, when the doors were shut where the disciples were[3] for fear of the Jews, came Jesus and stood in the midst, and said unto them, Peace *be* unto you.

---

[1] *omit* And [2] Jesus himself [3] were assembled for fear
[4] midst of them, and saith unto them, Peace *be* unto you (Cf. Jno.) [5] your hearts

---

longs to this section, and is the same with that mentioned by several of the Apostles in Lk. xxiv. 34. It must have occurred after the two disciples had gone away to Emmaus, and before their return.

The appearance of discrepancy between the positive announcement of the resurrection by the assembled disciples in Lk. xxiv. 34, and their want of belief in the story of the two returned from Emmaus, mentioned in Mar. xvi. 13, is only on the surface. The disciples were in that state of mind so natural under the circumstances, when they both believed and refused to believe. They were ready to tell whatever was remarkable within their own knowledge, and to discredit whatever others told to them.

ST. MARK XVI.	ST. LUKE XXIV.	ST. JOHN XX.
	40 ye see me have. And when he had thus spoken, he shewed them *his* hands and *his* feet.[1] And 41 while they yet believed not for joy, and wondered, he said unto them, Have ye here any meat? 42 And they gave him a piece of a broiled fish,[3] 43 and he took *it*, and did eat before them.[a]	20 And when he had so said, he shewed unto them the hands and the side.[2] Then were the disciples glad, when they saw the Lord.

21 Then said he[4] to them again, Peace *be* unto you: as *my* Father hath sent me, even so send I you. 22 And when he had said this, he breathed on *them*, and said unto them, Receive ye the Holy Ghost: 23 whose soever sins ye remit, they are remitted unto them; *and* whose soever *sins* ye retain, they are retained. 24 But Thomas, one of the twelve, called Didymus, was not with them when 25 Jesus came. The other disciples therefore said unto him, We have seen the Lord. But he said unto them, Except I shall see in his hands the print of the nails, and put my finger into the place[5] of the nails, and thrust my hand into his side, I will not believe. |

[1] (Tischendorf omits vs. 40.) [2] *his* hands and his side [3] fish, and of an honeycomb
[4] said Jesus [5] the print of the
[a] Comp. Gen. xviii. 8.

§ 169. He again appears to them, Thomas being with them.

St. John xx. 26–29.

26 And after eight days again his disciples were within, and Thomas with them: *then* came Jesus, the doors being shut, and stood in the midst, and said, 27 Peace *be* unto you. Then saith he to Thomas, Reach hither thy finger, and behold my hands; and reach hither thy hand, and thrust *it* into my side: and 28 be not faithless, but believing. [1]Thomas answered and said unto him, My 29 Lord and my God. Jesus saith unto him,[2] because thou hast seen me, thou hast believed: blessed *are* they that have not seen, and *yet* have believed.

§ 170. He appears to seven of them as they fish in the Sea of Galilee.

St. Matt. xxviii. 16ᵃ.	St. John xxi. 1–24.
16ᵃ Then the eleven disciples went away into Galilee,—	1 After these things Jesus shewed himself again to the disciples at the sea of Tiberias; and on this wise shewed 2 he *himself*. There were together Simon Peter, and Thomas called Didymus, and Nathanael of Cana in Galilee, and the *sons* of Zebedee, and two other of his 3 disciples. Simon Peter saith unto them, I go a fishing. They say unto him, We also go with thee. They went forth, and entered into a ship;[3] and that night they caught nothing.

[1] And Thomas   [2] unto him, Thomas, because   [3] into a ship immediately

---

§ 169. To this section probably belongs the clause of 1 Cor. xv. 5 — "then of the twelve." If the question be asked "Why the Apostles remained so long in Jerusalem after Jesus had told them to go before him into Galilee?" it may be answered that they remained, of course, through the Passover, which extended to Thursday evening, and then they would have remained over the Sabbath for want of time to reach Galilee before it. Being thus in Jerusalem at the beginning of the "first day of the week," a recollection of the events of the previous "first day," must have suggested anticipations, justified by the event, which kept them still there through that day.

§ 170. Ver. 14. This was the third of the appearances to the assembled disciples mentioned by St. John. "The third time" is not meant to refer to all his appearances, for St. John himself has described particularly just before, his appearance to Mary Magdalene, then to the Apostles in the absence of Thomas, and again to them when he was present. This is the third manifestation only to the disciples.

Perhaps to this section, but in all probability to some part of the time while the Apostles remained in Galilee, belongs 1 Cor. xv. 6. "After that, he was seen of above five hundred brethren at once; of whom the greater part remain unto this present, but some are fallen asleep." The special appearance to St. James, 1 Cor. xv. 7, — "after that, he was seen of James," not being mentioned at all in the Gospels, cannot be definitely placed; neither can the following clause, "then of all the Apostles," unless it be supposed that this does not refer to any particular appearance, but rather to our Lord's frequent manifestation of himself to the Apostles during the forty days. Doubtless there were many such manifestations of which we have no other record than the brief allusion to them in Acts i. 3.

| ST. MATT. XXVIII. | ST. JOHN XXI. |

4 But when the morning was now come, Jesus stood on the shore: but the disciples knew not that it was Jesus. 5 Then Jesus saith unto them, Children, have ye any 6 meat? They answered him, No. He saith[1] unto them, Cast the net on the right side of the ship, and ye shall find. They cast therefore, and now they were not able 7 to draw it for the multitude of fishes. Therefore that disciple whom Jesus loved saith unto Peter, It is the Lord. Now when Simon Peter heard that it was the Lord, he girt *his* fisher's coat *unto him*, (for he was 8 naked,) and did cast himself into the sea. And the other disciples came in a little ship; (for they were not far from land, but as it were two hundred cubits,) 9 dragging the net with fishes. As soon then as they were come to land, they saw a fire of coals there, and 10 fish laid thereon, and bread. Jesus saith unto them, 11 Bring of the fish which ye have now caught. Simon Peter went up, and drew the net to land full of great fishes, an hundred and fifty and three: and for all there were so many, yet was not the net broken.

12 Jesus saith unto them, Come *and* dine. And none of the disciples durst ask him, Who art thou? knowing 13 that it was the Lord. Jesus[2] cometh, and taketh bread, 14 and giveth them, and fish likewise. This is now the third time that Jesus shewed himself to the[3] disciples, after that he was risen from the dead.

15 So when they had dined, Jesus saith to Simon Peter, Simon, *son* of John,[4] lovest thou me more than these? He saith unto him, Yea, Lord; thou knowest that I 16 love thee. He saith unto him, Feed my lambs. He saith to him again the second time, Simon, *son* of John,[4] lovest thou me? He saith unto him, Yea, Lord; thou knowest that I love thee. He saith unto him, Feed 17 my sheep. He saith unto him the third time, Simon, *son* of John,[4] lovest thou me? Peter was grieved because he said unto him the third time, Lovest thou me? And he saith[5] unto him, Lord, thou knowest all things; thou knowest that I love thee. He[6] saith unto him, 18 Feed my sheep. Verily, verily, I say unto thee, When thou wast young, thou girdedst thyself, and walkedst whither thou wouldest: but when thou shalt be old,

[1] And he said unto
[2] Jesus then cometh
[3] his disciples
[4] *thrice* Jonas
[5] he said
[6] Jesus saith

ST. MATT. XXVIII. ST. JOHN XXI.

thou shalt stretch forth thy hands, and another shall gird thee, and carry *thee* whither thou wouldest not.
19 This spake he, signifying by what death he should glorify God. And when he had spoken this, he saith unto him, Follow me.
20 [1]Peter, turning about, seeth the disciple whom Jesus loved, following, which also leaned on his breast at supper, and said, Lord, which is he that betrayeth thee?
21 Peter therefore[2] seeing him saith to Jesus, Lord, and
22 what *shall* this man *do*? Jesus saith unto him, If I will that he tarry till I come, what *is that* to thee? follow
23 thou me. Then went this saying abroad among the brethren, that that disciple should not die: yet Jesus said not unto him, He shall not die; but, If I will that he tarry till I come.[3]
24 This is the disciple which testifieth of these things, and wrote these things: and we know that his testimony is true.

§ 171. He appears to the Apostles on a Mountain of Galilee.

ST. MATT. XXVIII. 16b–20. [ST. MARK XVI. 15–18.]

16b — Into a mountain where Jesus had
17 appointed them. And when they saw him, they worshipped:[4] but
18 some doubted. And Jesus came and spake unto them, saying, All power is given unto me in heaven and in earth.
19 Go ye[5] and teach all nations, baptizing them in the name of the Father, and of the Son, and of the
20 Holy Ghost: teaching them to observe all things whatsoever I have commanded you: and, lo, I am with you alway, *even* unto the end of the world.[6]

[15 And he said unto them, Go ye into all the world, and preach the gospel
16 to every creature. He that believeth and is baptized shall be saved; but he that believeth not shall be damned.
17 And these signs shall follow them that believe; in my name shall they cast out devils; they shall speak with
18 new tongues; they shall take up serpents; and if they drink any deadly thing, it shall not hurt them; they shall lay hands on the sick, and they shall recover.]

[1] Then Peter
[2] *omit* therefore
[3] till I come, what *is that* to thee?
[4] worshipped him
[5] Go ye therefore, and
[6] *add* Amen.

§ 172. He gives His parting Instructions and ascends into Heaven.
[ST. MARK XVI. 19, 20.]   ST. LUKE XXIV. 44–53.   (ACTS I. 3–12.)

3 — The apostles — 'To whom also he shewed himself alive after his passion by many infallible proofs, being seen of them forty days, and speaking of the things pertaining to the kingdom of God.

44 And he said unto them, These *are* my[1] words which I spake unto you, while I was yet with you, that all things must be fulfilled, which were written in the law of Moses, and *in* the prophets, and *in* the psalms,
45 concerning me. Then opened he their understanding that they might understand the script-
46 ures, and said unto them, Thus it is written that Christ should[2] suffer, and rise from the dead
47 the third day: and that repentance for the[3] remission of sins should be preached in his name among all nations, beginning at Jerusalem.
48 [4]Ye are witnesses of these things.

4 And, being assembled together with *them*, commanded them that they should not depart from Jerusalem, but wait for the promise of the Father, which, *saith he*, ye have
5 heard of me. For John

---

[1] the words   [2] written, and thus it behoved Christ to suffer and to rise
[3] and remission   [4] And ye are

---

§ 172. After the close of this section must be placed 1 Cor. xv. 8, — " And last of all, he was seen of me also, as of one born out of due time."

To some undetermined place belongs the saying of our Lord recorded in Acts xx. 35, — " It is more blessed to give than to receive."

ST. MARK XVI.	ST. LUKE XXIV.	ACTS I.

<table>
<tr><td></td><td>49 And[1] I send the promise of my Father upon you: but tarry ye in the city,[2] until ye be endued with power from on high.</td><td>truly baptized with water; but ye shall be baptized with the Holy Ghost not many days hence.

6 When they therefore were come together, they asked of him, saying, Lord, wilt thou at this time restore again the
7 kingdom to Israel? He[3] said unto them, It is not for you to know the times or the seasons, which the Father hath put in his own power:
8 but ye shall receive power, after that the Holy Ghost is come upon you; and ye shall be my[4] witnesses both in Jerusalem, and in all Judæa, and in Samaria, and unto the uttermost part of the earth.</td></tr>
<tr><td>[19 So then after the Lord had spoken unto them, he was received up into heaven, and sat on the right hand of God.</td><td>50 And he led them out as far as to Bethany, and he lifted up his hands,
51 and blessed them. And it came to pass, while he blessed them, he was parted from them.[5]</td><td>9 And when he had spoken these things, while they beheld, he was taken up; and a cloud received him out of their
10 sight. And while they looked stedfastly toward heaven as he went up, behold, two men stood by them in white gar-
11 ments;[6] which also said, Ye men of Galilee, why stand ye gazing up into heaven? this same Jesus, which is taken up from</td></tr>
</table>

---

[1] And, behold, I send
[2] city of Jerusalem
[3] And he said
[4] be witnesses unto me
[5] from them, and carried up into heaven
[6] white apparel

ST. MARK XVI.	ST. LUKE XXIV.	ACTS I.
	52 And they¹ returned to Jerusalem with great joy: 53 And were continually in the temple, praising² God.³	you into heaven, shall so come in like manner as ye have seen him go into 12 heaven. Then returned they unto Jerusalem from the mount called Olivet, which is from Jerusalem a Sabbath day's journey.
20 And they went forth, and preached every where, the Lord working with *them*, and confirming the word with signs following.]³		

§ 173. The Conclusion of St. John's Gospel.
ST. JOHN XX. 30, 31. XXI. 25.

30 And many other signs truly did Jesus in the presence of his disciples, which
31 are not written in this book: but these are written, that ye might believe that Jesus is the Christ, the Son of God; and that believing ye might have life
25 through his name. [⁴And there are also many other things which Jesus did the which, if they should be written every one, I suppose that even the world itself could not contain the books that should be written.]³

¹ they worshipped him and returned ² praising and blessing God
³ *add* Amen. ⁴ (Tischendorf omits this verse).

www.ingramcontent.com/pod-product-compliance
Lightning Source LLC
Chambersburg PA
CBHW021213240426
43667CB00038B/560